Second Edition

W9-ABZ-112

IT STRATEGY

ISSUES AND PRACTICES

James D. McKeen
Queen's University

Heather A. Smith
Queen's University

Prentice Hall

Boston   Columbus   Indianapolis   New York   San Francisco   Upper Saddle River
Amsterdam   Cape Town   Dubai   London   Madrid   Milan   Munich   Paris   Montreal
Toronto   Delhi   Mexico City   Sao Paulo   Sydney   Hong Kong
Seoul   Singapore   Taipei   Tokyo

Editorial Director: Sally Yagan
Editor in Chief: Eric Svendsen
Executive Editor: Bob Horan
Director of Editorial Services: Ashley Santora
Senior Editorial Project Manager: Kelly Loftus
Director of Marketing: Patrice Lumumba Jones
Senior Marketing Manager: Anne Fahlgren
Editorial Assistant: Ashlee Bradbury
Senior Managing Editor: Judy Leale
Production Project Manager: Clara Bartunek
Creative Art Director: Jayne Conte
Cover Art Designer: Suzanne Duda
Cover Art: ©INFINITY-Fotolia.com
Lead Media Project Manager: Lisa Rinaldi
Full-Service Project Management: Munesh Kumar/Aptara®, Inc.
Printer/Binder: Edwards Brothers Incorporated
Cover Printer: Lehigh-Phoenix Color /Hagerstown
Text Font: Palatino

Credits and acknowledgments borrowed from other sources and reproduced, with permission, in this textbook appear on appropriate page within text.

Library of Congress Cataloging-in-Publication Data
McKeen, James D.
    IT strategy : issues and practices / James D. McKeen.—2nd ed.
    p.   cm.
Includes bibliographical references and index.
ISBN-13: 978-0-13-214566-4
ISBN-10: 0-13-214566-9
1. Information technology--Management.   I. Title.
HD30.2.M3987 2012
004.068—dc22   2011010798

10 9 8 7 6 5 4 3 2 1

ISBN 10:   0-13-214566-9
ISBN 13: 978-0-13-214566-4

BRIEF CONTENTS

CONTENTS

PREFACE

Today, with information technology (IT) driving constant business transformation, overwhelming organizations with information, enabling 24/7 global operations, and undermining traditional business models, the challenge for business leaders is not simply to *manage* IT, it is to *use* IT *to deliver business value.* Whereas until fairly recently, decisions about IT could be safely delegated to technology specialists *after* a business strategy had been developed, IT is now so closely integrated with business that, as one CIO explained to us, "We can no longer deliver business solutions in our company without using technology."

All too often, in our efforts to prepare future executives to deal effectively with the issues of IT strategy and management, we lead them into a foreign country where they encounter a different language, different culture, and different customs. Acronyms (e.g., SOA, FTP/IP, PKI, ITIL), buzzwords (e.g., asymmetric encryption, proxy servers, mailer-daemons), and the widely adopted practice of abstraction (e.g., Is a software monitor a person, place, or thing?) present formidable barriers to entry to the technologically uninitiated, but more important, they obscure the importance of teaching students how to make *business* decisions about a key organizational resource. By taking a critical issues perspective, *IT Strategy: Issues and Practices* treats IT as a tool to be leveraged to save and/or make money or transform an organization—not as a study by itself.

Key Features of This Book

- A focus on IT *management* issues as opposed to *technology* issues
- Critical IT issues explored within their organizational contexts
- Readily applicable models and frameworks for implementing IT strategies
- Mini cases to animate issues and focus classroom discussions on real-world decisions, enabling problem-based learning
- Proven strategies and best practices from leading-edge organizations
- Useful and practical advice and guidelines for delivering value with IT
- Extensive teaching notes for all mini cases

WHAT'S NEW IN THIS SECOND EDITION?

- Eight new chapters focusing on current critical issues in IT management, including identity management, collaboration, communicating with the business, improving relationships with the business, application portfolio management, managing IT-based risk, social computing, and master data management.
- Four new mini cases based on real companies and real IT management situations: Delivering Business Value at Hefty Hardware, Customer Service at Datatronics, Innovation at International Foods, and IT Investment at North American Financial.
- A revised structure based on reader feedback with six chapters and three mini cases from the first edition being moved to the Web site.

As in the first edition of this book, this second edition combines the experiences and insights of many senior IT managers from leading-edge organizations with thorough academic research to bring important issues in IT management to life and demonstrate how *IT strategy is put into action* in contemporary businesses. This new edition is designed around an enhanced set of critical real-world issues in IT management today, such as creating value with IT, building a strong relationship with the business, information and data management, using IT for innovation, enabling collaboration, and managing social computing, and it introduces students to the challenges of making IT decisions that will have significant impacts on how businesses function and deliver value to stakeholders.

IT Strategy, Issues and Practices focuses on how IT is changing and will continue to change organizations as we now know them. However, rather than learning concepts free of context, students are introduced to the complex decisions facing real organizations by means of a number of mini cases. These provide an opportunity to apply the models, theories, and frameworks presented and help students integrate and assimilate this material. By the end of this book, students will have the confidence and ability to tackle the tough issues regarding IT management and strategy and a clear understanding of their importance in delivering business value.

A DIFFERENT APPROACH TO TEACHING IT STRATEGY

The real world of IT is one of issues—critical issues—such as the following:

- How do we know if we are getting value from our IT investment?
- What specific IT functions should we seek from external providers?
- How do we build an IT leadership team that is a trusted partner with the business?
- How do we enhance IT capabilities?
- What is IT's role in delivering data and information to the business?
- How do we manage IT-based risk?

However, the majority of management information systems (MIS) textbooks are organized by system *category* (e.g., supply chain, customer relationship management [CRM], enterprise resource planning [ERP]), by system *component* (e.g., hardware, software, networks), by system *function* (e.g., marketing, financial, human resources), by system *type* (e.g., transactional, decisional, strategic), or by a combination of these. Unfortunately, such organization does not promote an understanding of IT management in practice.

IT Strategy: Issues and Practices tackles the real-world challenges of IT management. First it explores a set of the most important issues facing IT managers today, and second it provides a series of mini cases that present these critical IT issues within the context of real organizations. By focusing the text as well as the mini cases on today's critical issues, the book naturally reinforces problem-based learning.

IT Strategy, Issues and Practices includes twelve mini cases—each based on a real company presented anonymously.[1] Mini cases are *not* simply abbreviated versions of standard, full-length business cases. They differ in two significant ways:

---

[1]We are unable to identify these leading-edge companies by agreements established as part of our overall research program (described later).

1. *A horizontal perspective.*   Unlike standard cases that develop a single issue within an organizational setting (i.e., a "vertical" slice of organizational life), mini cases take a "horizontal" slice through a number of coexistent issues. Rather than looking for a *solution* to a specific problem, as in a standard case, students analyzing a mini case must first *identify and prioritize* the issues embedded within the case. This mimics real life in organizations where the challenge lies in knowing where to start as opposed to solving a predefined problem.

2. *Highly relevant information.*   Mini cases are densely written. Unlike standard cases, which intermix irrelevant information, in our mini cases each sentence exists for a reason and reflects relevant information. As a result, students must analyze each case very carefully so as not to miss critical aspects of the situation.

Teaching with mini cases is, thus, very different from teaching with standard cases. With mini cases, students must determine what is really going on within the organization. What first appears as a straightforward technology problem may in fact be a political problem or one of five other technology problems. Detective work is, therefore, required. The problem identification and prioritization skills needed are essential skills for future managers to learn for the simple reason that it is not possible for organizations to tackle all of their problems concurrently. Mini cases help teach these skills to students and can balance the problem-solving skills learned in other classes. Best of all, detective work is fun and promotes lively classroom discussion.

To assist instructors, extensive teaching notes are available for all mini cases. Developed by the authors and based on tried and true in-class experience, these notes include case summaries, identify the key issues within each case, present ancillary information about the company or industry represented in the case, and offer guidelines for organizing the classroom discussion. Because of the structure of these mini cases and their embedded issues, it is common for teaching notes to exceed the length of the actual mini case!

This book is most appropriate for MIS courses where the goal is to understand how IT delivers organizational value. These courses are frequently labeled "IT Strategy" or "IT Management" and are offered within undergraduate as well as MBA programs. For undergraduate juniors and seniors in business and commerce programs, this is usually the "capstone" MIS course. For MBA students, this course may be the compulsory core course in MIS, or it may be an elective course.

Each chapter and mini case in this book has been thoroughly tested in a variety of undergraduate, graduate, and executive programs at Queen's University School of Business.[2] These materials have proven highly successful within all programs because we adapt how the material is presented according to the level of the students. Whereas undergraduate students "learn" about critical business issues from the book and mini cases for the first time, graduate students are able to relate to these same critical issues based on their previous business experience. As a result, graduate students are able to introduce personal experiences into the discussion of these critical IT issues.

---

[2]Queen's School of Business (Kingston, Ontario) is consistently ranked among the best in the world for its full-time MBA, Executive MBA and Executive Education. From 2004 to 2010, the Queen's MBA program was ranked #1 in the world by *BusinessWeek* in its highly regarded ranking of non–U.S. business schools.

ORGANIZATION OF THIS BOOK

One of the advantages of an issues-focused structure is that chapters can be approached in any order because they do not build on one another. Chapter order is immaterial— that is, one does not need to read the first three chapters to understand the fourth. This provides an instructor with maximum flexibility to organize a course as he or she sees fit. Thus, within different courses and programs, the order of topics can be changed to focus on different IT concepts.

Furthermore, because each mini case includes multiple issues, they, too, can be used to serve different purposes. For example, the mini case "Information Management at Homestyle Hotels" can be used to focus on issues of governance, vendor selection, organizational structure, and/or change management just as easily as of information management. The result is a rich set of instructional materials that lends itself well to a variety of pedagogical applications, particularly problem-based learning, and that clearly illustrates the reality of IT strategy in action.

The book is organized into four sections, each emphasizing a key component of developing and delivering effective IT strategy:

- Section I: Delivering Value with IT is designed to examine the complex ways that IT and business value are related. Over the past twenty years, researchers and practitioners have come to understand that *business value* can mean many different things when applied to IT. Chapter 1 (Developing and Delivering on the IT Value Proposition) explores these concepts in depth. Unlike the simplistic value propositions often used when implementing IT in organizations, this chapter presents *value* as a multilayered business construct that must be effectively managed at several levels if technology is to achieve the benefits expected. Chapter 2 (Developing IT Strategy for Business Value) examines the dynamic interrelationship between business and IT strategy and looks at the processes and critical success factors used by organizations to ensure that both are well aligned. Chapter 3 (Communicating with Business Managers) explores the business and interpersonal competencies that IT staff will need in order to do their jobs effectively over the next five to seven years and what companies should be doing to help develop them. Chapter 4 (Building a Strong Relationship with the Business) examines the nature of the business–IT relationship and the characteristics of an effective relationship that deliver real value to the enterprise. Chapter 5 (Developing IT Professionalism) discusses the personal responsibilities of every IT staff member for the quality, effectiveness, and value of their work.

  In the mini cases associated with this section, the concepts of delivering value with IT are explored in a number of ways. We see business and IT executives at Hefty Hardware grappling with conflicting priorities and perspectives and how best to work together to achieve the company's strategy. In "Investing in TUFS," CIO Martin Drysdale watches as all the work his IT department has put into a major new system fails to deliver value. And the ModMeters mini case follows CIO Brian Smith's efforts to create a strategic IT plan that will align with business strategy, keep IT running, and *not* increase IT's budget.

- **Section II: IT Governance** explores key concepts in how the IT organization is structured and managed to effectively deliver IT products and services to the organization. Chapter 6 (Information Management: The Nexus of Business and IT) describes how new organizational needs for more useful and integrated information are driving the development of new business-oriented functions within IT that focus specifically on information and knowledge, as opposed to applications and data. Chapter 7 (The IT Budgeting Process) describes the "evil twin" of IT strategy, discussing how budgeting mechanisms can significantly undermine effective business strategies and suggesting practices for addressing this problem while maintaining traditional fiscal accountability. Chapter 8 (Creating and Evolving a Technology Roadmap) examines the challenges IT managers face in implementing new infrastructure, technology standards, and types of technology in their real-world business and technical environments, which are composed of a huge variety of hardware, software, applications, and other technologies, some of which date back more than thirty years. Chapter 9 (Delivering IT Functions: A Decision Framework) describes the variety of strategies, such as insourcing, outsourcing, and partnerships, that IT departments are using to deliver functionality to the organization and how they decide where and when to use these strategies. Chapter 10 (IT Sourcing) describes the challenges involved in managing IT when many functions are being performed by external service providers, some halfway around the globe. Chapter 11 (Application Portfolio Management) describes the ongoing management process of categorizing, assessing, and rationalizing the IT application portfolio.

    The mini cases in this section examine the difficulties of managing complex IT issues when they intersect substantially with important business issues. In "Building Shared Services at RR Communications," we see an IT organization in transition from a traditional divisional structure and governance model to a more centralized enterprise model, and the long-term challenges experienced by CIO Vince Patton in changing both business and IT practices, including information management and delivery, to support this new approach. "Creating a Process-Driven Organization at AgCredit" explores how this company is transforming itself from a function-based structure to a process-based one and explores the related business and IT challenges in establishing the appropriate governance and structure to manage them. In "IT Investment at North American Financial," we show the opportunities and challenges involved in prioritizing and resourcing enterprisewide IT projects and monitoring the achievement of anticipated benefits.

- **Section III: Information-Enabled Innovation** discusses some of the ways technology is being used to transform organizations. Chapter 12 (Strategic Experimentation with IT) looks at the processes and practices organizations are using to investigate new ways of using IT, particularly to change business models, value chains, and processes. Chapter 13 (Enabling Collaboration with IT) identifies the principal forms of collaboration used in organizations, the primary business drivers involved in them, how their business value is measured, and the roles of IT and the business in enabling collaboration. Chapter 14 (Social Computing: How Should It Be Managed?) explores how organizations are conceptualizing and managing the new phenomenon of social computing and how IT functions can prepare for a still nebulous future. Chapter 15 (Information Delivery: IT's Evolving Role) examines the fresh challenges IT faces in managing the exponential growth of data and digital assets, privacy and accountability concerns, and new demands for access to information on an anywhere/anytime basis. Chapter 16 (Master Data Management) explores the need for high-quality data in organizations and for developing a roadmap to create a single view of an enterprise's most important pieces of information.

The mini cases in this section focus on the key challenges companies face in innovating with IT. "Information Management at Homestyle Hotels" presents some of the obstacles IT managers must overcome to deliver an integrated information strategy to the business. "Innovation at International Foods" contrasts the need for process and control in corporate IT with the strong push to innovate with technology and the difficulties that ensue from the clash of style and culture. In "CRM at Minitrex," we see some of the internal technological and political conflicts that result from a strategic decision to become more customercentric. Finally, "Customer Service at Datatronics" explores the importance of presenting unified, customer-facing IT to customers.

- **Section IV: IT Capability Management** looks at how the IT function must transform itself to be able to deliver business value effectively. Chapter 17 (Developing IT Capabilities) provides an overview of the core IT capabilities needed in a modern organization and presents a framework for identifying, improving, managing, and maturing them. Chapter 18 (Building Better IT Leaders from the Bottom Up) tackles the increasing need for improved leadership skills for all IT staff and examines the expectations of the business for strategic and innovative guidance from IT. Chapter 19 (Managing IT-Based Risk) describes how many IT organizations have been given the responsibility of not only managing risk in their own activities (i.e., project development, operations, and delivering business strategy) but also of managing IT-based risk in *all* company activities (e.g., mobile computing, file sharing, and online access to information and software) and the need for a holistic framework to understand and deal with risk effectively. Chapter 20 (The Identity Management Challenge) looks into why identity management is increasingly a *business* concern, in addition to an IT concern, and describes the key challenges facing IT managers as they try to address the rapidly evolving needs for identity management in their organizations. And Chapter 21 (Linking IT to Business Metrics) discusses new ways of measuring IT's effectiveness that promote closer business–IT alignment and help drive greater business value.

The mini cases associated with this section describe many of these themes embedded within real organizational contexts. In the SleepSmart mini case, CIO Greg Danson works with multiple vendors to completely revamp his company's outdated technology to develop enhanced IT capabilities in a short time. "Project Management at MM" shows how a top-priority, strategic project can take a wrong turn when project management skills are ineffective. And in "Managing Technology at Genex Fuels," we follow CIO Nick Devlin trying to implement enterprisewide technology for competitive advantage in an organization that has been limping along with obscure and outdated systems.

SUPPLEMENTARY MATERIALS

Online Instructor Resource Center

The following supplements are available online to adopting instructors:

- PowerPoint Lecture Notes
- Image Library (text art)
- Mini Cases Teaching Notes
- Test Item File
- TestGen test-generating software with WebCT- and Blackboard-ready conversions.
- Additional chapters addressing managing perceptions of IT; IT in the new world of corporate governance reforms, enhancing customer experiences with technology, creating digital dashboards, and managing electronic communications.
- Additional cases include IT Leadership at MaxTrade, Knowledge Management at Acme Consulting, and Desktop Provisioning at CanCredit.

To access the supplements listed above, please visit: www.pearsonhighered .com/irc.

CourseSmart eTextbooks

CourseSmart eTextbooks were developed for students looking to save on required or recommended textbooks. Students simply select their eText by title or author and purchase immediate access to the content for the duration of the course using any major credit card. With a CourseSmart eText, students can search for specific keywords or page numbers, take notes online, print out reading assignments that incorporate lecture notes, and bookmark important passages for later review. For more information or to purchase a CourseSmart eTextbook, visit www.coursesmart.com.

THE GENESIS OF THIS BOOK

Since 1990 we have been meeting quarterly with a group of senior IT managers from a number of leading-edge organizations (Eli Lilly, Honda, HP, IBM, Sears, Bell Canada, and Sun Life, among others) to identify and discuss critical IT management issues. This focus group represents a wide variety of industry sectors, including retail, manufacturing, pharmaceutical, banking, telecommunications, insurance, media, food processing, government, and automotive. Originally, the group was established to meet the companies' needs for well-balanced, thoughtful, yet practical information on emerging IT management topics, about which little or no research was available. However, we soon recognized the value of this premise for our own research in the rapidly evolving field of IT management. As a result, it quickly became a full-scale research program in which we were able to use the focus group as an "early warning system" to document new IT management issues, develop case studies around them, and explore more collaborative approaches to identifying trends, challenges, and effective practices in each topic area.[3]

---

[3]This now includes best-practice case studies, field research in organizations, multidisciplinary qualitative and quantitative research projects, and participation in numerous CIO research consortia.

As we shared our materials with our business students, we realized that this issues-based approach resonated strongly with them, and we began to incorporate more of our research into the classroom.[4] This book is the result of our many years' work with senior IT managers, in organizations, and with students in the classroom.

Each issue in this book has been selected collaboratively by the focus group after debate and discussion. As facilitators, our job has been to keep the group's focus on IT management issues, not technology per se. In preparation for each meeting, focus group members researched the topic within their own organization, often involving a number of members of their senior IT management team as well as subject matter experts in the process. To guide them, we provided a series of questions about the issue, although members are always free to explore it as they see fit. This approach provided both structure for the ensuing discussion and flexibility for those members whose organizations are approaching the issue in a different fashion.

The focus group then met in a full-day session, where all aspects of the issue at hand were discussed by the members. Many also shared corporate documents with the group. We facilitated the discussion, in particular pushing the group to achieve a common understanding of the dimensions of the issue and seeking examples, best practices, and guidelines for dealing with the challenges involved. Following each session, we wrote a report based on the discussion, incorporating relevant academic and practitioner materials where these were available. (Because topics are "bleeding edge," there is often little traditional IT research available on them.)

Each report has three parts:

1. A description of the issue and the challenges it presents for both business and IT managers
2. Models and concepts derived from the literature to position the issue within a contextual framework
3. Near-term strategies (i.e., those that can be implemented immediately) that have proven successful within organizations for dealing with the specific issue

Each chapter in this book focuses on one of these critical IT issues. We have learned over the years that the issues themselves vary little across industries and organizations, even in enterprises with unique IT strategies. However, each organization tackles the same issue somewhat differently. It is this diversity that provides the richness of insight in these chapters. Our collaborative research approach is based on our belief that when dealing with complex and leading-edge issues, "Everyone has part of the solution." Every focus group, therefore, provides us an opportunity to explore a topic from a variety of perspectives and to integrate different experiences (both successful and otherwise) so that, collectively, a thorough understanding of each issue can be developed and strategies for how it can be managed most successfully can be identified.

---

[4]See our three previous books for practitioners: IT Strategy in Action (Pearson Prentice Hall, 2009), *Management Challenges in IS: Successful Strategies and Appropriate Action* (Wiley, 1996) and *Making IT Happen: Critical Issues in IT Management* (Wiley, 2003).

ABOUT THE AUTHORS

James D. McKeen is a professor of IT Strategy and Distinguished Research Fellow in MIS at the School of Business, Queen's University at Kingston, Canada. Jim received his Ph.D. in Business Administration from the University of Minnesota. He has been working in the IT field for many years as a practitioner, researcher, and consultant and is a frequent speaker at business and academic conferences. Dr. McKeen co-facilitates the networking of senior executives in the IT sector through two well-known industry forums: the IT Management Forum and the CIO Brief. He also has extensive international experience, having taught at universities in the United Kingdom, France, Germany, and the United States. His research has been widely published in various journals, including *MIS Quarterly, Knowledge Management Research and Practice, ournal of Information Technology Management*, the *Communications of the Association for Information Systems, MIS Quarterly Executive, Journal of Systems and Software, International Journal of Management Reviews, Information and Management, Communications of the ACM, Computers and Education, OMEGA, Canadian Journal of Administrative Sciences, Journal of MIS, KM Review, Journal of Information Science and Technology*, and *Database*. Jim is a co-author of three books on IT management with Heather Smith, the most recent being *IT Strategy in Action* (Pearson Prentice Hall, 2009). He currently serves on a number of editorial boards.

Heather A. Smith has been named the most-published researcher on IT management issues in two successive studies (2006, 2009). A Senior Research Associate with Queen's University School of Business, she is the author of five books, the most recent being *IT Strategy in Action* (Pearson Prentice Hall, 2009). A former senior IT manager, she is currently co-director of the IT Management Forum and the CIO Brief, which facilitate interorganizational learning among senior IT executives. She is also a Senior Research Associate with the American Society for Information Management's Advanced Practices Council and a Research Associate with the Lac Carling Congress on E-Government. In addition, she consults, presents, and collaborates with organizations worldwide, including the Information and Communications Technology Council, the Institute for Citizen-Centred Service, British Petroleum, TD Bank, Canada Post, École des Hautes Études Commerciales, Ontario Provincial Police (OPP), Boston University, Bank of Montreal, and Farm Credit Canada. Her research is published in a variety of journals and books including *MIT Sloan Management Review, MIS Quarterly-Executive, Communications of the Association for Information Systems, Knowledge Management Research and Practice, Journal of Information Systems and Technology, Journal of Information Technology Management, Information and Management, Database, CIO Canada*, and the *CIO Governments Review*, and she is on the editorial board of *MIS Quarterly Executive*.

ACKNOWLEDGMENTS

The work contained in this book is based on numerous meetings with many senior IT managers. We would like to acknowledge our indebtedness to the following individuals who willingly shared their insights based on their experiences "earned the hard way":

Sergei Beliaev, Matthias Benfey, Eduardo Cadena, Dale Castle, Marc Collins, Diane Cope, Dan Di Salvo, Ken Dschankilic, Michael East, Nada Farah, Mark Gillard, Gary Goldsmith, Ian Graham, Keiko Gutierrez, Maureen Hall, Bruce Harding, Theresa Harrington, Tom Hopson, Heather Hutchison, Zeeshan Khan, Konstantine Liris, Lisa MacKay, Mark O'Gorman, Amin Panjwani, Troy Pariag, Brian Patton, Marius Podaru, Helen Restivo, Pat Sadler, Joanne Scher, Stewart Scott, Andy Secord, Helen Shih, Trudy Sykes, Bruce Thompson, Len Van Greuning, and Ted Vincent.

We would also like to recognize the contribution of Queen's University School of Business to this work. The school has facilitated and supported our vision of better integrating academic research and practice and has helped make our collaborative approach to the study of IT management and strategy an effective model for interorganizational learning.

James D. McKeen
Heather A. Smith
Queen's University School of Business
Kingston, Ontario
March 2011

Chapter 1

Developing and Delivering on the IT Value Proposition[1]

It's déjà vu all over again. For at least twenty years, business leaders have been trying to figure out exactly how and where IT can be of value in their organizations. And IT managers have been trying to learn how to deliver this value. When IT was used mainly as a productivity improvement tool in small areas of a business, this was a relatively straightforward process. Value was measured by reduced head counts—usually in clerical areas—and/or the ability to process more transactions per person. However, as systems grew in scope and complexity, unfortunately so did the risks. Very few companies escaped this period without making at least a few disastrous investments in systems that didn't work or didn't deliver the bottom-line benefits executives thought they would. Naturally, fingers were pointed at IT.

With the advent of the strategic use of IT in business, it became even more difficult to isolate and deliver on the IT value proposition. It was often hard to tell if an investment had paid off. Who could say how many competitors had been deterred or how many customers had been attracted by a particular IT initiative? More recently, many companies have been left with a substantial investment in e-business and little to show for it. Although over the years there have been many improvements in where and how IT investments are made and good controls have been established to limit time and cost overruns, we are still not able to accurately articulate and deliver on a value proposition for IT when it comes to anything other than simple productivity improvements or cost savings.

Problems in delivering IT value can lie with how a value proposition is conceived or in what is done to actually implement an idea—that is, selecting the right project and doing the project right (Cooper et al. 2000; McKeen and Smith 2003). In addition, although most firms attempt to calculate the expected payback of an IT investment before making it, few actually follow up to ensure that value has been achieved or to question what needs to be done to make sure that value will be delivered.

This chapter first looks at the nature of IT value and "peels the onion" into its different layers. Then it examines the three components of delivering IT value: value identification, conversion, and value realization. Finally, it identifies five general principles for ensuring IT value will be achieved.

---

[1]Smith, H. A., and J. D. McKeen, "Developing and Delivering on the IT Value Proposition," *Communications of the Association for Information Systems* 11 (April 2003): 438–50. Reproduced by permission of the Association for Information Systems.

PEELING THE ONION: UNDERSTANDING IT VALUE

Thirty years ago the IT value proposition was seen as a simple equation: deliver the right technology to the organization, and financial benefits will follow (Cronk and Fitzgerald 1999; Marchand et al. 2000). In the early days of IT, when computers were most often used as direct substitutes for people, this equation was understandable, even if it rarely worked this simply. It was easy to compute a bottom-line benefit where "technology" dollars replaced "salary" dollars.

Problems with this simplistic view quickly arose when technology came to be used as a productivity support tool and as a strategic tool. Under these conditions, managers had to decide if an IT investment was worth making if it saved people time, helped them make better decisions, or improved service. Thus, other factors, such as how well technology was used by people or how IT and business processes worked together, became important considerations in how much value was realized from an IT investment. These issues have long confounded our understanding of the IT value proposition, leading to a plethora of opinions (many negative) about how and where technology has actually contributed to business value over the past fifteen years. Stephen Roach (1989) made headlines with his macroeconomic analysis showing that IT had had absolutely no impact on productivity in the services sector. More recently, many companies feel they have been sold a bill of goods by the promise of e-business and have been lured into spending millions on Web sites and online shopping with very little payback (Earle and Keen 2000).

These perceptions, plus ever-increasing IT expenditures, have meant business managers are taking a closer look at how and where IT delivers value to an organization (Ginzberg 2001). As they do this, they are beginning to change their understanding of the IT value proposition. Although, unfortunately, "silver bullet thinking" (i.e., plug in technology and deliver bottom-line impact) still predominates, IT value is increasingly seen as a multilayered concept, far more complex than it first appeared. This suggests that before an IT value proposition can be identified and delivered, it is essential that managers first "peel the onion" and understand more about the nature of IT value itself (see Figure 1.1).

What Is IT Value?

Value is defined as the worth or desirability of a thing (Cronk and Fitzgerald 1999). It is a subjective assessment. Although many believe this is not so, the value of IT depends very much on how a business and its individual managers choose to view it. Different companies and even different executives will define it quite differently. Strategic positioning, increased productivity, improved decision making, cost savings, or improved service are all ways *value* could be defined. Today most businesses define *value* broadly and loosely, not simply as a financial concept (Ginzberg 2001). Ideally, it is tied to the organization's business model because adding value with IT should enable a firm to do its business better. In the focus group (see the Preface), one company sees value resulting from all parts of the organization having the same processes; another defines value by return on investment (ROI); still another measures it by a composite of key performance indicators. In short, there is no single agreed-on measure of IT value. As a result, misunderstandings about the definition of *value* either between IT and the business or

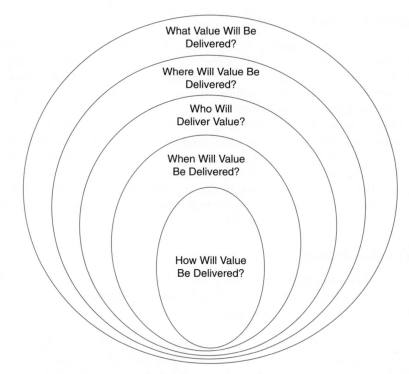

FIGURE 1.1   IT Value Is a Many-Layered Concept

among business managers themselves can lead to feelings that value has not been delivered. Therefore, a prerequisite of any IT value proposition is that everyone involved in an IT initiative agree on what value they are trying to deliver and how they will recognize it.

Where Is IT Value?

Value may also vary according to where one looks for it (Davern and Kauffman 2000). For example, value to an enterprise may not be perceived as value in a work group or by an individual. In fact, delivering value at one level in an organization may actually conflict with optimizing value at another level. Decisions about IT value are often made to optimize firm or business process value, even if they cause difficulties for business units or individuals. As one manager explained, "At the senior levels, our bottom-line drivers of value are cost savings, cash flow, customer satisfaction, and revenue. These are not always visible at the lower levels of the organization." Failure to consider value implications at all levels can lead to a value proposition that is counterproductive and may not deliver the value that is anticipated. Many executives take a hard line with these value conflicts. However, it is far more desirable to aim for value that is not a win–lose proposition but is a win–win at all levels. This can leverage overall value many times over (Chan 2000).

Who Delivers IT Value?

Increasingly, managers are realizing that it is the *interaction* of people, information, and technology that delivers value, not IT alone.[2] Studies have confirmed that strong IT practices *alone* do not deliver superior performance. It is only the combination of these IT practices with an organization's skills at managing information and people's behaviors and beliefs that leads to real value (Ginzberg 2001; Marchand et al. 2000). In the past, IT has borne most of the responsibility for delivering IT value. Today, however, business managers exhibit a growing willingness to share responsibility with IT to ensure value is realized from the organization's investments in technology. Most companies now expect to have an executive sponsor for any IT initiative and some business participation in the development team. However, many IT projects still do not have the degree of support or commitment from the business that IT managers feel is necessary to deliver fully on a value proposition (Thorp 1999).

When Is IT Value Realized?

Value also has a time dimension. It has long been known that the benefits of technology take time to be realized (Chan 2000). People must be trained, organizations and processes must adapt to new ways of working, information must be compiled, and customers must realize what new products and services are being offered. Companies are often unprepared for the time it takes an investment to pay off. Typically, full payback can take between three and five years and can have at least two spikes as a business adapts to the deployment of technology. Figure 1.2 shows this "W" effect, named for the way the chart looks, for a single IT project.

Initially, companies spend a considerable amount in deploying a new technology. During this twelve-to-sixteen-month period, no benefits occur. Following implementation, some value is realized as companies achieve initial efficiencies. This period lasts for about six months. However, as use increases, complexities also grow. Information overload can occur and costs increase. At this stage, many can lose faith in the initiative. This is a dangerous period. The final set of benefits can occur only by making the business simpler and applying technology, information, and people more effectively. If a business can manage to do this, it can achieve sustainable, long-term value from its IT investment (Seagars and Chatterjee 2010). If it can't, value from technology can be offset by increased complexity.

Time also changes perceptions of value. Many IT managers can tell stories of how an initiative is vilified as having little or no value when first implemented, only to have people say they couldn't imagine running the business without it a few years later. Similarly, most managers can identify projects where time has led to a clearer understanding of the potential value of a project. Unfortunately, in cases where anticipated value declines or disappears, projects don't always get killed (Cooper et al. 2000).

---

[2]These interactions in a structured form are known as *processes*. Processes are often the focus of much organizational effort in the belief that streamlining and reengineering them will deliver value. In fact, new research shows that without attention to information and people, very little value is delivered (Seagars and Chatterjee 2010). In addition, attention to processes in organizations often ignores the informal processes that contribute to value.

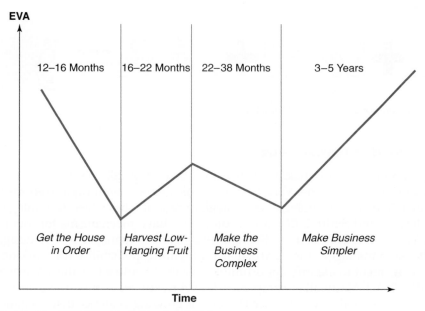

FIGURE 1.2 The "W" Effect in Delivering IT Value

Source: Seagars and Chatterjee 2010. Reproduced by permission of the authors.

Clarifying and agreeing on these different layers of IT value is the first step involved in developing and delivering on the IT value proposition. All too often, this work is forgotten or given short shrift in the organization's haste to answer this question: How will IT value be delivered? (See next section.) As a result, misunderstandings arise and technology projects do not fulfill their expected promises. It will be next to impossible to do a good job developing and delivering IT value unless and until the concepts involved in IT value are clearly understood and agreed on by both business and IT managers.

> ## Best Practices in Understanding IT Value
>
> - Link IT value directly to your business model.
> - Recognize value is subjective, and manage perceptions accordingly.
> - Aim for a value "win–win" across processes, work units, and individuals.
> - Seek business commitment to all IT projects.
> - Manage value over time.

THE THREE COMPONENTS OF THE IT VALUE PROPOSITION

Developing and delivering an IT value proposition involves addressing three components. First, potential opportunities for adding value must be identified. Next, these opportunities must be converted into effective applications of technology. Finally, value must be realized by the organization. Together, these components comprise the fundamentals of any value proposition (see Figure 1.3).

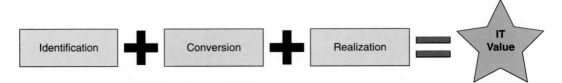

FIGURE 1.3   The Three Components of the IT Value Proposition

Identification of Potential Value

Identifying opportunities for making IT investments has typically been a fairly informal activity in most organizations. Very few companies have a well-organized means of doing research into new technologies or strategizing about where these technologies can be used (McKeen and Smith 2010). More companies have mechanisms for identifying opportunities within business units. Sometimes a senior IT manager will be designated as a "relationship manager" for a particular unit with responsibility for working with business management to identify opportunities where IT could add value (Agarwal and Sambamurthy 2002). Many other companies, however, still leave it up to business managers to identify where they want to use IT. There is growing evidence that relegating the IT organization to a passive role in developing systems according to business instructions is unlikely to lead to high IT value. Research is beginning to show that involving IT in business planning can have a direct and positive influence on the development of successful business strategies using IT (Ginzberg 2001; Marchand et al. 2000). This suggests that organizations should establish joint business–IT mechanisms to identify and evaluate both business and technical opportunities where IT can add value.

Once opportunities have been identified, companies must then make decisions about where they want to focus their dollars to achieve optimal value. Selecting the right projects for an organization always involves balancing three fundamental factors: cash, timing, and risk (Luehrman 1997). In principle, every company wants to undertake only high-return projects. In reality, project selection is based on many different factors. For example, pet or political projects or those mandated by the government or competitors are often part of a company's IT portfolio (Carte et al. 2001). Disagreement at senior levels about which projects to undertake can arise because of a lack of a coherent and consistent mechanism for assessing project value. All organizations need some formal mechanism for prioritizing projects. Without one, it is very likely that project selection will become highly politicized and, hence, ineffective at delivering value. There are a variety of means to do this, ranging from using strictly bottom-line metrics, to comparing balanced scorecards, to adopting a formal value-assessment methodology. However, although these methods help to weed out higher cost–lower return projects, they do not constitute a foolproof means of selecting the right projects for an organization. Using strict financial selection criteria, for example, can exclude potentially high-value strategic projects that have less well-defined returns, longer payback periods, and more risk (Cooper et al. 2000). Similarly, it can be difficult getting important infrastructure initiatives funded even though these may be fundamental to improving organizational capabilities (Byrd 2001).

Therefore, organizations are increasingly taking a portfolio approach to project selection. This approach allocates resources and funding to different types of projects, enabling each type of opportunity to be evaluated according to different criteria (McKeen and Smith 2003). One company has identified three different classes of IT—infrastructure, common systems, and business unit applications—and funds them in different proportions. In other companies, funding for strategic initiatives is allocated in stages so their potential value can be reassessed as more information about them becomes known (Luehrman 1997). Almost all companies have found it necessary to justify infrastructure initiatives differently than more business-oriented projects. In fact, some remove these types of projects from the selection process altogether and fund them with a "tax" on all other development (McKeen and Smith 2003). Other companies allocate a fixed percentage of their IT budgets to a technology renewal fund.

Organizations have come a long way in formalizing where and how they choose to invest their IT dollars. Nevertheless, there is still considerable room for judgment based on solid business and technical knowledge. It is, therefore, essential that all executives involved have the ability to think strategically and systematically as well as financially about project identification and selection.

Best Practices in Identifying Potential Value

- Joint business–IT structures to recognize and evaluate opportunities
- A means of comparing value across projects
- A portfolio approach to project selection
- A funding mechanism for infrastructure

Effective Conversion

"Conversion" from idea/opportunity to reality has been what IT organizations have been all about since their inception. A huge amount of effort has gone into this central component of the IT value proposition. As a result, many IT organizations have become very good at developing and delivering projects on time and on budget. Excellent project management, effective execution, and reliable operations are a critical part of IT value. However, they are not, in and of themselves, sufficient to convert a good idea into value or to deliver value to an organization.

Today managers and researchers are both recognizing that more is involved in effective conversion than good IT practices. Organizations can set themselves up for failure by not providing adequate and qualified resources. Many companies start more projects than they can effectively deliver with the resources they have available. Not having enough time or resources to do the job means that people are spread too thin and end up taking shortcuts that are potentially damaging to value (Cooper et al. 2000). Resource limitations on the business side of a project team can be as damaging to conversion as a lack of technical resources. "[Value is about] far more than just sophisticated managerial visions. . . . Training and other efforts . . . to obtain value from IT investments are often hamstrung by insufficient resources" (Chircu and Kauffman 2000). Inadequate business resources can lead to poor communication and ineffective problem solving on a project (Ginzberg 2001). Companies are beginning to recognize that the number and quality of the staff assigned to an IT project can make a difference to its eventual outcome. They are insisting that the organization's best IT and business-people be assigned to critical projects.

Other significant barriers to conversion that are becoming more apparent now that IT has improved its own internal practices include the following:

- *Organizational barriers.*   The effective implementation of IT frequently requires the extensive redesign of current business processes (Chircu and Kauffman 2000). However, organizations are often reluctant to make the difficult complementary business changes and investments that are required (Carte et al. 2001). "When new IT is implemented, everyone expects to see costs come down," explained one manager. "However, most projects involve both business and IT deliverables. We, therefore, need to take a multifunctional approach to driving business value." In recognition of this fact, some companies are beginning to put formal change management programs in place to help businesses prepare for the changes involved with IT projects and to adapt and simplify as they learn how to take advantage of new technology.
- *Knowledge barriers.*   Most often new technology and processes require employees to work differently, learn new skills, and have new understanding of how and where information, people, and technologies fit together (Chircu and Kauffman 2000). Although training has long been part of new IT implementations, more recently businesses are recognizing that delivering value from technology requires a broader and more coordinated learning effort (Smith and McKeen 2002). Lasting value comes from people and technology working *together* as a system rather than as discrete entities. Recent research confirms that high-performing organizations not only have strong IT practices but also have people who have good information management practices and who are able to effectively use the information they receive (Marchand et al. 2000).

Best Practices in Conversion

- Availability of adequate and qualified IT and business resources
- Training in business goals and processes
- Multifunctional change management
- Emphasis on higher-level learning and knowledge management

Realizing Value

The final component of the IT value proposition has been the most frequently ignored. This is the work involved in actually realizing value *after* technology has been implemented. Value realization is a proactive and long-term process for any major initiative (Thorp 1999). All too often, after an intense implementation period, a development team is disbanded to work on other projects, and the business areas affected by new technology are left to sink or swim. As a result, a project's benefits can be imperfectly realized. Technology must be used extensively if it is to deliver value. Poorly designed technology can lead to high levels of frustration, resistance to change, and low levels of use (Chircu and Kauffman 2000).

Resistance to change can have its root cause in an assumption or an action that doesn't make sense in the everyday work people do. Sometimes this means challenging workers' understanding of work expectations or information flows. At other times it means doing better analysis of where and how a new process is causing bottlenecks, overwork, or overload. As one manager put it, "If value is not being delivered, we need to understand the root causes and do something about it." His company takes the unusual position that it is important to keep a team working on a project until the expected benefits have been realized. This approach is ideal but can also be very costly and, therefore, must be carefully managed. Some companies try to short-circuit the value management process by simply taking anticipated cost savings out of a business unit's budget once technology has been implemented, thereby forcing it to do more with less whether or not the technology has been as beneficial as anticipated. However, most often organizations do little or no follow-up to determine whether or not benefits have been achieved.

Measurement is a key component of value realization (Thorp 1999). After implementation, it is essential that all stakeholders systematically compare outcomes against expected value and take appropriate actions to achieve benefits. In addition to monitoring metrics, a thorough and ongoing assessment of value and information flows must also be undertaken at all levels of analysis: individual, team, work unit, and enterprise. Efforts must be taken to understand and improve aspects of process, information, and technology that are acting as barriers to achieving value.

A significant problem with not paying attention to value recognition is that areas of unexpected value or opportunity are also ignored. This is unfortunate because it is only after technology has been installed that many businesspeople can see how it could be leveraged in other parts of their work. Realizing value should, therefore, also include provisions to evaluate new opportunities arising through serendipity.

Best Practices in Realizing Value

- Plan a value-realization phase for all IT projects.
- Measure outcomes against expected results.
- Look for and eliminate root causes of problems.
- Assess value realization at all levels in the organization.
- Have provisions for acting on new opportunities to leverage value.

FIVE PRINCIPLES FOR DELIVERING VALUE

In addition to clearly understanding what value means in a particular organization and ensuring that the three components of the IT value proposition are addressed by every project, five principles have been identified that are central to developing and delivering value in every organization.

Principle 1. Have a Clearly Defined Portfolio Value Management Process

Every organization should have a common process for managing the overall value being delivered to the organization from its IT portfolio. This would begin as a means of identifying and prioritizing IT opportunities by potential value relative to each other. It would also include mechanisms to optimize *enterprise* value (e.g., through tactical, strategic, and infrastructure projects) according to a rubric of how the organization wants to allocate its resources.

A portfolio value management process should continue to track projects as they are being developed. It should ensure not only that projects are meeting schedule and budget milestones but also that other elements of conversion effectiveness are being addressed (e.g., business process redesign, training, change management, information management, and usability). A key barrier to achieving value can be an organization's unwillingness to revisit the decisions made about its portfolio (Carte et al. 2001). Yet this is critically important for strategic and infrastructure initiatives in particular. Companies may have to approve investments in these types of projects based on imperfect information in an uncertain environment. As they develop, improved information can lead to better decision making about an investment. In some cases this might lead to a decision to kill a project; in others, to speed it up or to reshape it as a value proposition becomes clearer.

Finally, a portfolio value management process should include an ongoing means of ensuring that value is realized from an investment. Management must monitor expected outcomes at appropriate times following implementation and hold someone in the organization accountable for delivering benefits (Thorp 1999).

Principle 2. Aim for Chunks of Value

Much value can be frittered away by dissipating IT investments on too many projects (Marchand et al. 2000). Focusing on a few key areas and designing a set of complementary projects that will really make a difference is one way companies are trying to address this concern. Many companies are undertaking larger and larger technology initiatives that will have a significant transformational and/or strategic impact on the organization. However, unlike earlier efforts, which often took years to complete and ended up having questionable value, these initiatives are aiming to deliver major value through a series of small, focused projects that, linked together, will result in both immediate short-term impact and long-term strategic value. For example, one company has about three hundred to four hundred projects underway linked to one of a dozen major initiatives.

Principle 3. Adopt a Holistic Orientation to Technology Value

Because value comes from the effective interaction of people, information, and technology, it is critical that organizations aim to optimize their ability to manage and use them together (Marchand et al. 2000). Adopting a systemic approach to value, where technology is not viewed in isolation and interactions and impacts are anticipated and planned, has been demonstrated to contribute to perceived business value (Ginzberg 2001). Managers should aim to incorporate technology as an integral part of an overall program of business change rather than dealing with people and information management as afterthoughts to technology (Thorp 1999). One company has done this by taking a single business objective (e.g., "increase market penetration by 15 percent over five years") and designing a program around it that includes a number of bundled technology projects.

Principle 4. Aim for Joint Ownership of Technology Initiatives

This principle covers a lot of territory. It includes the necessity for strong executive sponsorship of all IT projects. "Without an executive sponsor for a project, we simply won't start it," explained one manager. It also emphasizes that all people involved in a project must feel they are responsible for the results. Said another manager, "These days it is very hard to isolate the impact of technology, therefore there must be a 'we' mentality." This perspective is reinforced by research that has found that the quality of the IT-business relationship is central to the delivery of IT value. Mutual trust, visible business support for IT and its staff, and IT staff who consider themselves to be part of a business problem-solving team all make a significant difference in how much value technology is perceived to deliver (Ginzberg 2001).

Principle 5. Experiment More Often

The growing complexity of technology, the range of options available, and the uncertainty of the business environment have each made it considerably more difficult to determine where and how technology investments can most effectively be made. Executives naturally object to the risks involved in investing heavily in possible business scenarios or technical gambles that may or may not realize value. As a result, many companies are looking for ways to firm up their understanding of the value proposition for a particular opportunity without incurring too much risk. Undertaking pilot studies is one way of doing this (Thomke 2001). Such experiments can prove the value of an idea, uncover new opportunities, and identify more about what will be needed to make an idea successful. They provide senior managers with a greater number of options in managing a project and an overall technology portfolio. They also enable potential value to be reassessed and investments in a particular project to be reevaluated and rebalanced against other opportunities more frequently. In short, experimentation enables technology investments to be made in chunks and makes "go/no go" decisions at key milestones much easier to make.

Conclusion

This chapter has explored the concepts and activities involved in developing and delivering IT value to an organization. In their efforts to use technology to deliver business value, IT managers should keep clearly in mind the maxim "Value is in the eye of the beholder." Because there is no single agreed-on notion of business value, it is important to make sure that both business and IT managers are working to a common goal. This could be traditional cost reduction, process efficiencies, new business capabilities, improved communication, or a host of other objectives. Although each organization or business unit approaches value differently, increasingly this goal includes much more than the simple delivery of technology to a business unit. Today technology is being used as a catalyst to drive many different types of organizational transformation and strategy. Therefore, IT value can no longer be viewed in isolation from other parts of the business, namely people and information. Thus, it is no longer adequate to focus simply on the development and delivery of IT projects in order to deliver value. Today delivering IT value means managing the entire process from conception to cash.

References

Agarwal, R., and V. Sambamurthy. "Organizing the IT Function for Business Innovation Leadership." Society for Information Management Advanced Practices Council Report, Chicago, September 2002.

Byrd, T. A. "Information Technology, Core Competencies, and Sustained Competitive Advantage." *Information Resources Management Journal* 14, no. 2 (April–June 2001): 27–36.

Carte, T., D. Ghosh, and R. Zmud. "The Influence of IT Budgeting Practices on the Return Derived from IT Investments." CMISS White Paper, November 2001.

Chan, Y. "IT Value: The Great Divide Between Qualitative and Quantitative and Individual and Organizational Measures." *Journal of Management Information Systems* 16, no. 4 (Spring 2000): 225–61.

Chircu, A., and R. J. Kauffman. "Limits to Value in Electronic Commerce-Related IT Investments." *Journal of Management Information Systems* 17, no. 2 (Fall 2000): 59–80.

Cooper, R., S. Edgett, and E. Kleinschmidt. "New Problems, New Solutions: Making Portfolio Management More Effective." *Research Technology Management* 43, no. 2 (March/April 2000): 18–33.

Cronk, M., and E. Fitzgerald. "Understanding 'IS Business Value': Derivation of Dimensions." *Logistics Information Management* 12, no. 1–2 (1999): 40–49.

Davern, M., and R. Kauffman. "Discovering Potential and Realizing Value from Information Technology Investments." *Journal of Management Information Systems* 16, no. 4 (Spring 2000): 121–43.

Earle, N., and P. Keen. *From .com to .profit: Inventing Business Models That Deliver Value and Profit.* San Francisco: Jossey-Bass, 2000.

Ginzberg, M. "Achieving Business Value Through Information Technology: The Nature of High Business Value IT Organizations." Society for Information Management Advanced Practices Council Report, Chicago, November 2001.

Luehrman, T. A. "What's It Worth? A General Manager's Guide to Valuation." *Harvard Business Review* May–June (1997): 131–41.

Marchand, D., W. Kettinger, and J. Rollins. "Information Orientation: People, Technology and the Bottom Line." *Sloan Management Review* Summer (2000): 69–80.

McKeen, J., and H. Smith. *Making IT Happen.* Chichester, England: John Wiley & Sons, 2003.

McKeen, J. D., and Smith, H. A., "Application Portfolio Management," *Communications for the Association of Information Systems* 26, Article 9 (March 2010), 157–70.

Roach, S. "The Case of the Missing Technology Payback." Presentation at the Tenth International Conference on Information Systems, Boston, December 1989.

Segars, A. H., and Chatterjee, D. (2010). Diets That Don't Work: Where Enterprise Resource Planning Goes Wrong. *Wall Street Journal,* August 23, 2010. online.wsj.com/article/SB1000142405274870351440457488060852535906.html.

Smith, H., and J. McKeen. "Instilling a Knowledge Sharing Culture." Presentation at the KM Forum, Queen's School of Business, Kingston, Ontario, Canada, 2002.

Thomke, S. "Enlightened Experimentation: The New Imperative for Innovation." *Harvard Business Review* February (2001): 67–75.

Thorp, J. "Computing the Payoff from IT." *Journal of Business Strategy* 20, no. 3 (May/June 1999): 35–39.

Chapter 2

Developing IT Strategy for Business Value[1]

Suddenly, it seems, executives are "getting" the strategic potential of IT. Instead of being relegated to the back rooms of the enterprise, IT is now being invited to the boardrooms and is being expected to play a leading role in delivering top-line value and business transformation (Venkatramen and Henderson 1998). Thus, it can no longer be assumed that business strategy will naturally drive IT strategy, as has traditionally been the case. Instead, different approaches to strategy development are now possible and sometimes desirable. For example, the capabilities of new technologies could shape the strategic direction of a firm (e.g., e-business, wireless). IT could enable new competencies that would then make new business strategies possible (e.g., just-in-time inventory). New options for governance using IT could also change how a company works with other firms (think Wal-Mart or Dell Computer). Today new technologies coevolve with new business strategies and new behaviors and structures (see Figure 2.1). However, whichever way it is developed, if IT is to deliver business value, IT strategy must always be closely linked with sound business strategy.

Ideally, therefore, business and IT strategies should complement and support each other relative to the business environment. Strategy development should be a two-way process between the business and IT. Yet unfortunately, poor alignment between them remains a perennial problem (Frohman 1982; McKeen and Smith 1996; Rivard et al. 2004). Research has already identified many organizational challenges to effective strategic alignment. For example, if their strategy-development processes are not compatible (e.g., if they take place at different times or involve different levels of the business), it is unlikely that the business and IT will be working toward the same goals at the same time (Frohman 1982). Aligning with individual business units can lead to initiatives that suboptimize the effectiveness of corporate strategies (McKeen and Smith 1996). Strategy implementation must also be carefully aligned to ensure the integration of business and IT efforts. Finally, companies often try to address too many priorities, leading to an inadequate focus on key strategic goals.

However, strategic *alignment* is only one problem facing IT managers when they develop IT strategy. With IT becoming so much more central to the development and delivery of business strategy, much more attention is now being paid to strategy *development* than in the past.

---

[1]Smith, H. A., J. D. McKeen, and S. Singh, "Developing IT Strategy for Business Value," *Journal of Information Technology Management* XVIII, no. 1 (June 2007): 49–58. Reproduced by permission of the Association of Management.

FIGURE 2.1   Business and IT Strategies Co-evolve to Create New Capabilities

What businesses want to accomplish with their IT and how IT shapes its own delivery strategy are increasingly vital to the success of an enterprise. This chapter explores how organizations are working to improve IT strategy development and its relationship with business strategy. It looks first at how our understanding of business and IT strategies has changed over time and at the forces that will drive even further changes in the future. Then it discusses some critical success factors for IT strategy development about which there is general consensus. Next it looks at the different dimensions of the strategic use of IT that IT management must address. Finally, it examines how some organizations are beginning to evolve a more formal IT strategy-development process and some of the challenges they are facing in doing so.

BUSINESS AND IT STRATEGIES: PAST, PRESENT, AND FUTURE

At the highest level, a strategy is an approach to doing business (Gebauer 1997). Traditionally, a competitive business strategy has involved performing different activities from competitors or performing similar activities in different ways (Porter 1996). Ideally, these activities were difficult or expensive for others to copy and, therefore, resulted in a long-term competitive advantage (Gebauer 1997). They enabled firms to charge a premium for their products and services.

Until recently, the job of an IT function was to understand the business's strategy and figure out a plan to support it. However, all too often IT's strategic contribution was inhibited by IT managers' limited understanding of business strategy and by business managers' poor understanding of IT's potential. Therefore, most *formal* IT plans were focused on the more tactical and tangible line of business needs or opportunities for operational integration rather than on supporting enterprise strategy (Burgelman and Doz 2001). And projects were selected largely on their abilities to affect the short-term bottom line rather than on delivering top-line business value. "In the past IT had to be a strategic incubator because businesspeople simply didn't recognize the potential of technology," said a member of the focus group.

As a result, instead of looking for ways to be different, in the past much business strategy became a relentless race to compete on efficiencies with IT as the primary means of doing so (Hitt et al. 1998; Porter 1996). In many industries, companies' improved information-processing capabilities have been used to drive down transaction costs to near zero, threatening traditional value propositions and shaving profit margins. This is leading to considerable disruption as business models (i.e., the way companies add value) are under attack by new, technology-enabled approaches to delivering products and services (e.g., the music industry, bookselling). Therefore:

> Strategists [have to] honestly face the many weaknesses inherent in [the] industrial-age ways of doing things. They [must] redesign, build upon and reconfigure their components to radically transform the value proposition. (Tapscott 1996)

Such new business strategies are inconceivable without the use of IT. Other factors, also facilitated by IT, are further influencing the relationship between the business and IT strategy. Increasingly, globalization is altering the economic playing field. As countries and companies become more deeply interrelated, instability is amplified. Instead of being generals plotting out a structured campaign, business leaders are now more likely to be participating in guerilla warfare (Eisenhardt 2002). Flexibility, speed, and innovation are, therefore, becoming the watchwords of competition and must be incorporated into any business or IT strategy–development process (Hitt et al. 1998).

These conditions have dramatically elevated the business's attention to the value of IT strategy (Ross and Beath 2002). As a result, business executives recognize that it was a mistake to consider technology projects to be solely the responsibility of IT. There is, thus, a much greater understanding that business executives have to take leadership in making technology investments in ways that will shape and/or complement business strategy. There is also recognition at the top of most organizations that problems with IT strategy implementation are largely the fault of leaders who "failed to realize that adopting . . . systems posed a business—not just a technological—challenge" and didn't take responsibility for the organizational and process changes that would deliver business value.

Changing value models and the development of integrated, cross-functional systems have elevated the importance of both a *corporate* strategy and a technology strategy that crosses traditional lines of business. Many participants remarked that their executive teams at last understand the potential of IT to affect the top line. "IT recently added some new distribution channels, and our business has just exploded," stated one manager. Others are finding that there is a much greater emphasis on IT's ability to grow revenues, and this is being reflected in how IT budgets are allocated and projects prioritized. "Our executives have finally recognized that business strategy is not only enabled by IT, but that it can provide new business opportunities as well," said another manager. This is reflected in the changing position of the CIO in many organizations over the past decade. "Today our CIO sits on the executive team and takes part in all business strategy discussions because IT has credibility," said a group member. "Our executives now want to work closely with IT and understand the implications of technology decisions," said another. "It's not the same as it was even five years ago." Today CIOs are valued for their insight into business opportunities, their perspective across the entire organization, and their ability to take the long view.

However, this does not mean that organizations have become good at developing strategy or at effectively integrating business and IT strategies. "There are many inconsistencies and problems with strategy development," said a participant. Organizations have to develop new strategy-making capabilities to cope in the future competitive environment. This will mean changing their current top–down method of developing and implementing strategy. If there's one thing leading academics agree on, it's that future strategy development will have to become a more dynamic and continuous process (Eisenhardt 2002; Kanter 2002; Prahalad and Krishnan 2002; Quinn 2002; Weill et al. 2002). Instead of business strategy being a well-crafted plan of action for the next three to five years, from which IT can devise an appropriate and supportive technology strategy, business strategy must become more and more evolutionary and interactive with IT. IT strategy development must, therefore, become more dynamic itself and focused on developing strategic *capabilities* that will support a variety of changing business objectives. In the future, managers will not align business strategy and IT at particular points in time but will participate in an organic process that will address the need to continually evolve IT and business plans in concert with each other (Prahalad and Krishnan 2002).

FOUR CRITICAL SUCCESS FACTORS

Each focus group member had a different approach to developing IT strategy, but there was general agreement that four factors had to be in place for strategy development to be effective.

1. *Revisit your business model.*   The worlds of business and IT have traditionally been isolated from each other, leading to misaligned and sometimes conflicting strategies. Although there is now a greater willingness among business managers to understand the implications of technology in their world, it is still IT that must translate their ideas and concepts into business language. "IT must absolutely understand and focus on the business," said a participant.

    Similarly, it is essential that all managers thoroughly understand how their business as a whole works. Although this sounds like a truism, almost any IT manager can tell "war stories" of business managers who have very different visions of what they think their enterprise should look like. Business models and strategies are often confused with each other (Ross and Beath 2002). A business model explains how the different pieces of a business fit together. It ensures that everyone in an organization is focused on the kind of value a company wants to create. Only when the business model is clear can strategies be developed to articulate how a company will deliver that value in a *unique* way that others cannot easily duplicate (Ross and Beath 2002).

2. *Have strategic themes.*   IT strategy used to be about individual projects. Now it is about carefully crafted *programs* that focus on developing specific business capabilities. Each program consists of many smaller, interrelated business and IT initiatives cutting across several functional areas. These are designed to be adapted, reconfigured, accelerated, or canceled as the strategic program evolves. Themes give both business and IT leaders a broad yet focused topic of interest that challenges them to move beyond current operations (Kanter 2002). For example, one retail company decided it wanted to be "a great place to work." A bank selected e-banking as a critical differentiator. Both firms used a theme to engage the imaginations of their employees and mobilize a variety of ideas and actions

around a broad strategic direction. By grouping IT and business programs around a few key themes, managers find it easier to track and direct important strategic threads in an organization's development and to visualize the synergies and interdependencies involved across a variety of projects spread out across the organization and over time.

3. *Get the right people involved.*   One of the most important distinguishing factors between companies that get high business value from their IT investment and those that don't is that senior managers in high-performing companies take a leadership role in IT decision making. Abdication of this responsibility is a recipe for disaster (Ross and Weill 2002). "In the past it was very hard to get the right people involved," said a focus group member. "Now it's easier." Another noted, "You don't send a minion to an IT strategy meeting anymore; it's just not done." In this type of organization, the CIO typically meets regularly with the president and senior business leaders to discuss both business and IT strategies.

   Getting the right people involved also means getting business managers and other key stakeholders involved in strategy as well. To do this, many companies have established "account manager" positions in IT to work with and learn about the business and bring opportunities for using technology to the table. Research shows that the best strategies often stem from grassroots innovations, and it is, therefore, critical that organizations take steps to ensure that good ideas are nurtured and not filtered out by different layers of management (Kanter 2002). "We have two levels of strategy development in our organization," said a focus group participant. "Our account managers work with functional managers and our CIO with our business unit presidents on the IT steering committee." This company also looks for cross-functional synergies and strategic dependencies by holding regular meetings of IT account managers and between account managers and infrastructure managers.

4. *Work in partnership with the business.*   Successful strategy demands a true *partnership* between IT and the business, not just use of the term. Strategy decisions are best made with input from both business and IT executives (Ross and Weill 2002). The focus group agreed. "Our partnerships are key to our success," stated a manager. "It's not the same as it was a few years ago. People now work very closely together." Partnership is not just a matter of "involving" business leaders in IT strategy or vice versa or "aligning" business and IT strategies. Effective strategizing is about continuous and dynamic synchronization of capabilities (Prahalad and Krishnan 2002). "Our IT programs need synchronizing with business strategy—not only at a high level, but right down to the individual projects and the business changes that are necessary to implement them properly," explained another participant.

THE MANY DIMENSIONS OF IT STRATEGY

One of the many challenges of developing effective IT strategy is the fact that technology can be used in so many different ways. The opportunities are practically limitless. Unfortunately, the available resources are not. Thus, a key element of IT strategy is determining how best to allocate the IT budget. This issue is complicated by the fact that most businesses today require significant IT services just to operate. Utility and basic support costs eat up between 30 and 70 percent of the focus group members' budgets. That's just the cost of "keeping the lights on"—running existing applications, fixing problems, and dealing with mandatory changes (e.g., new legislation). IT strategy, therefore, has two components: how to do more with less (i.e., driving down fixed costs) and how to allocate the remaining budget toward those projects that will support and further the organization's business strategy.

With occasional exceptions, CIOs and their teams are mostly left alone to determine the most cost-effective way of providing the IT utility. This has led to a variety of IT-led initiatives to save money, including outsourcing, shared services, use of software-as-a-service (SaaS), global sourcing, and partnerships. However, it is the way that IT spends the rest of its budget that has captured the attention of business strategists. "It used to be that every line of business had an IT budget and that we would work with each one to determine the most effective way to spend it," said a manager. "Now there is much more recognition that the big opportunities are at the enterprise level and cut across lines of business."

Focus group members explained that implementing a strategic program in IT will usually involve five types of initiatives. Determining what the balance among them will be is a significant component of how IT strategy delivers business value. Too much or too little emphasis on one type of project can mean a failure to derive maximum value from a particular strategic business theme:

1. *Business improvement.* These projects are probably the easiest to agree on because they stress relatively low-risk investments with a tangible short-to-medium-term payback. These are often reengineering initiatives to help organizations streamline their processes and save substantial amounts of money by eliminating unnecessary or duplicate activities or empowering customers/suppliers to self-manage transactions with a company. Easy to justify with a business case, these types of projects have traditionally formed the bulk of IT's discretionary spending. "Cost-reduction projects have and always will be important to our company," stated one member. "However, it is important to balance what we do in this area with other types of equally important projects that have often been given short shrift."

2. *Business enabling.* These projects extend or transform how a company does business. As a result, they are more focused on the top-line or revenue-growing aspects of an enterprise. For example, a data warehouse could enable different parts of a company to "mine" transaction information to improve customer service, assist target marketing, better understand buying patterns, or identify new business opportunities. Adding a new Web-based channel could make it easier for customers to buy more or attract new customers. A customer information file could make it more enjoyable for a customer to do business with a company (e.g., only one address change) and also facilitate new ways of doing business. Often the return on these types of projects is less clear, and as a result it has been harder to get them on the IT priority list. Yet many of these initiatives represent the foundations on which future business strategy will be built. For example, one CIO described the creation of a customer information file as "a key enabler for many different business units. . . . It has helped us build bench strength and move to a new level of service that other companies cannot match" (Smith 2003).

3. *Business opportunities.*   These are small-scale, experimental initiatives designed to test the viability of new concepts or technologies. In the past these types of projects have not received funding by traditional methods because of their high-risk nature. Often it has been left up to the CIO to scrounge money for such "skunkworks." There is a growing recognition of the potential value of strategic experiments in helping companies to learn about and prepare for the future. In some companies the CEO and CFO have freed up seed money to finance a number of these initiatives. However, although there is considerably more acceptance for such projects, there is still significant organizational resistance to financing projects for which the end results are unpredictable (Quinn 2002). In fact, it typically requires discipline to support and encourage experiments, which, by definition, will have a high number of false starts and wrong moves (Kanter 2002). The group agreed that the key to benefiting from experiments is to design them for learning, incorporate feedback from a variety of sources, and make quick corrections of direction.

4. *Opportunity leverage.*   A neglected but important type of IT project is one that operationalizes, scales up, or leverages successful strategic experiments or prototypes. "We are having a great deal of success taking advantage of what we have learned earlier," said one manager. Coming up with a new strategic or technological idea needs a different set of skills than is required to take full advantage of it in the marketplace (Charitou and Markides 2003). Some companies actually use their ability to leverage others' ideas to their strategic advantage. "We can't compete in coming up with new ideas," said the manager of a medium-sized company, "but we can copy other peoples' ideas and do them better."

5. *Infrastructure.*   This final type of IT initiative is one that often falls between the cracks when business and IT strategies are developed. However, it is clear that the hardware, software, middleware, communications, and data available will affect an organization's capacity to build new capabilities and respond to change. One study found that most companies feel their legacy infrastructure can be an impediment to what they want to do (Prahalad and Krishnan 2002). Research also shows that leading companies have a framework for making targeted investments in their IT infrastructure that will further their overall strategic direction (Weill et al. 2002). Unfortunately, investing in infrastructure is rarely seen as strategic. As a result, many companies struggle with how to justify and appropriately fund it.

Although each type of project delivers a different type of business value, typically IT strategy has stressed only those initiatives with strong business cases. Others are shelved or must struggle for a very small piece of the pie. However, there was a general recognition in the group that this approach to investment leads to an IT strategy with a heavy emphasis on the bottom line. As a result, all participating companies were looking at new ways to build a strategy-development process that reflects a more appropriate balance of all dimensions of IT strategy.

TOWARD AN IT STRATEGY-DEVELOPMENT PROCESS

Strategy is still very much an art, not a science, explained the focus group. And it is likely to remain so, according to strategy experts. Strategy will never again be a coherent, long-term plan with predictable outcomes—if it ever was. "Leaders can't predict which combinations [of strategic elements] will succeed [and] they can't drive their organizations towards predetermined positions" (Quinn 2002, 96). This situation only exacerbates the problem that has long faced IT strategists—that is, it is difficult to build systems, information, and infrastructure when a business's direction is continually changing. Yet this degree of flexibility is exactly what businesses are demanding (Prahalad and Krishnan 2002). Traditional IT planning and budgeting mechanisms done once a year simply don't work in today's fast-paced business environment. "We always seem to lag behind the business, no matter how hard we try," said a manager.

Clearly, organizations need to be developing strategy differently. How to do this is not always apparent, but several companies are trying ways to more dynamically link IT strategy with that of the business. Although no one company in the focus group claimed to have *the* answer, they did identify several practices that are moving them closer to this goal:

- *"Rolling" planning and budget cycles.*   All participants agreed that IT plans and budgets need attention more frequently than once a year. One company has created an eighteen-month rolling plan that is reviewed and updated quarterly with the business to maintain currency.
- *An enterprise architecture.*   This is an integrated blueprint for the development of the enterprise—both the business and IT. "Our enterprise architecture includes business processes, applications, infrastructure, and data," said a member. "Our EA function has to approve all business and IT projects and is helpful in identifying duplicate solutions." In some companies this architecture is IT initiated and business validated; in others it is a joint initiative. However, participants warned that an architecture has the potential to be a corporate bottleneck if it becomes too bureaucratic.
- *Different funding "buckets."*   Balancing short-term returns with the company's longer-term interests is a continual challenge. As noted earlier, all five types of IT projects are necessary for an effective IT strategy (i.e., business improvement, business enabling, business opportunities, opportunity leverage, and infrastructure). In order to ensure that each different type of IT is appropriately funded, many companies are allocating predetermined percentages of their IT budget to different types of projects (Ross and Beath 2002). This helps keep continual pressure on IT to reduce its "utility costs" to free up more resources for other types of projects. "Since we implemented this method of budgeting, we've gone from spending 70 percent of our revenues on mandatory and support projects to spending 70 percent on discretionary and strategic ones," said a manager. This is also an effective way to ensure that IT infrastructure is continually enhanced. Leading companies build their infrastructures not through a few large investments but gradually through incremental, modular investments that build IT capabilities (Weill et al. 2002).
- *Account or relationship managers.*   There is no substitute for a deep and rich understanding of the business. This is why many companies have appointed IT account managers to work closely with key lines of business. These managers help business leaders to observe their environments systematically and identify new opportunities for which IT could be effective. Furthermore, together account managers can identify synergies and interdependencies among lines of business.

One organization holds both intra- and interfunctional strategy sessions on a regular basis with business managers to understand future needs, develop programs, and design specific roadmaps for reaching business goals. "Our account managers have been a significant factor in synchronizing IT and business strategies," said its manager.

- *A prioritization rubric.*   "We don't do prioritization well," said one participant. IT managers have long complained that it is extremely difficult to justify certain types of initiatives using the traditional business case method of prioritization. This has led to an overrepresentation of business improvement projects in the IT portfolio and has inhibited more strategic investments in general capabilities and business opportunities. This problem is leading some companies to adopt multiple approaches to justifying IT projects (Ross and Beath 2002). For example, business-enabling projects must be sponsored at a cross-functional level on the basis of the capabilities they will provide the enterprise as a whole. Senior management must then take responsibility to ensure that these capabilities are fully leveraged over time. Infrastructure priorities are often left up to IT to determine once a budget is set. One IT department does this by holding strategy sessions with its account and utility managers to align infrastructure spending with the organization's strategic needs. Unfortunately, no one has yet figured out a way to prioritize business opportunity experiments. At present this is typically left to the "enthusiasms and intuitions" of the sponsoring managers, either in IT or in the business (Ross and Beath 2002). "Overall," said a manager, "we need to do a better job of thinking through the key performance indicators we'd like to use for each type of project."

Although it is unlikely that strategy development will ever become a completely formalized process, there is a clear need to add more structure to how it is done. A greater understanding of how strategy is developed will ensure that all stakeholders are involved and a broader range of IT investments are considered. The outcomes of strategy will always be uncertain, but the process of identifying new opportunities and how they should be funded must become more systematic if a business is going to realize optimum value from its IT resources.

CHALLENGES FOR CIOs

As often happens in organizations, recognition of a need precedes the ability to put it into place. IT leaders are now making significant strides in articulating IT strategy and linking it more effectively with business strategy. Business leaders are also more open to a more integrated process. Nevertheless, some important organizational barriers that inhibit strategy development remain.

A supportive governance structure is frequently lacking. "Now that so many strategies are enterprisewide, we need a better way to manage them," explained one manager. Often there are no formal structures to identify and manage interdependencies between business functions and processes. "It used to be that everything was aligned around organizational boundaries, but strategy is now more complex since we're working on programs with broader organizational scope," said another. Similarly, current managerial control systems and incentives are often designed to reward thinking that is aligned to a line of business, not to the greater organizational good. Enterprisewide funding models are also lacking. "Everything we do now requires negotiation for funding between the lines of business who control the resources," a third stated. Even within IT, the group suggested it is not always clear who in the organization is responsible for taking IT strategies and turning them into detailed IT plans.

Traditional planning and budgetary practices are a further challenge. This is an often-neglected element of IT strategy. "Our business and IT strategies are not always done in parallel or even around the same time," said a participant. As a result, it is not easy to stay aligned or to integrate the two sets of plans. Another commented, "Our business plans change constantly. It is, therefore, common for IT strategies to grow farther and farther apart over time." Similarly, an annual budgeting process tends to lock an organization into fixed expenditures that may not be practical in a rapidly changing environment. IT organizations, therefore, need both a longer-term view of their resourcing practices and the opportunity to make changes to it more frequently. Even though rolling budgets are becoming more acceptable, they are by no means common in either IT or the business world today.

Both business and IT leaders need to develop better skills in strategizing. "We've gotten really good at implementing projects," said an IT manager. "Strategy and innovation are our least developed capabilities." IT is pushing the business toward better articulation of its goals. "Right now, in many areas of our business, strategy is not well thought through," said another manager. "IT is having to play the devil's advocate and get them to think beyond generalities such as 'We are going to grow the business by 20 percent this year.'" With more attention to the process, it is almost certain to get better, but managers' rudimentary skills in this area limit the quality of strategy development.

Over and over, the group stressed that IT strategy is mainly about getting the balance right between conflicting strategic imperatives. "It's always a balancing act between our tactical and operational commitments and the work that builds our long-term capabilities," said a participant. Deciding how to make the trade-offs between the different types of IT work is the essence of effective strategy. Unfortunately, few businesses do this very well (Burgelman and Doz 2001). According to the focus group, traditional business thinking tends to favor short-term profitability, while IT leaders tend to take a longer-term view. Making sure some types of IT work (e.g., infrastructure, new business opportunities) are not underfunded while others (e.g., utility, business improvement) are not overfunded is a continual challenge for all IT and business leaders.

Barriers to Effective IT Strategy Development

- Lack of a governance structure for enterprisewide projects
- Inadequate enterprisewide funding models
- Poorly integrated processes for developing IT and business strategies
- Traditional budget cycles
- Unbalanced strategic and tactical initiatives
- Weak strategizing skills

Conclusion

Effective strategy development is becoming vital for organizations. As the impact of IT has grown in companies, IT strategy is finally getting the attention it deserves in business. Nevertheless, most organizations are still at the earliest stages of learning how to develop an effective IT strategy and synchronize it with an overall business strategy. Getting the balance right between the many different ways IT can be used to affect a business is a constant challenge for leaders and one on which they do not always agree. Although there is, as yet, no well-developed IT strategy–development process, there appears to be general agreement on certain critical success factors and the key elements involved. Over time, these will likely be refined and better integrated with overall business strategy development. Those who learn to do this well without locking the enterprise into inflexible technical solutions are likely to win big in our rapidly evolving business environment.

References

Burgelman, R., and Y. Doz. "The Power of Strategic Integration." *MIT Sloan Management Review* 42, no. 3 (Spring 2001): 28–38.

Charitou, C., and C. Markides. "Responses to Disruptive Strategic Innovation." *MIT Sloan Management Review* (Winter 2003): 55–63.

Eisenhardt, K. "Has Strategy Changed?" *MIT Sloan Management Review* 43, no. 2 (Winter 2002): 88–91.

Frohman, A. "Technology as a Competitive Weapon." *Harvard Business Review* January–February (1982): 80–94.

Gebauer, J. "Virtual Organizations from an Economic Perspective." *Communications of the ACM* 40 (September 1997): 91–103.

Hitt, M., B. Keats, and S. DeMarire. "Navigating in the New Competitive Landscape: Building Strategic Flexibility." *Academy of Management Executive* 12, no. 4 (1998): 22–42.

Kanter, R. "Strategy as Improvisational Theater." *MIT Sloan Management Review* (Winter 2002): 76–81.

McKeen, J., and H. Smith. *Management Challenges in IS: Successful Strategies and Appropriate Action.* Chichester, England: John Wiley & Sons, 1996.

Porter, M. "What Is Strategy?" *Harvard Business Review* November–December (1996): 61–78.

Prahalad, C., and M. Krishnan, "The Dynamic Synchronization of Strategy and Information Technology." *MIT Sloan Management Review* (Summer 2002): 24–33.

Quinn, J. "Strategy, Science, and Management." *MIT Sloan Management Review* (Summer 2002): 96.

Rivard, S., B. Aubert, M. Patry, G. Pare, and H. Smith. *Information Technology and Organizational Transformation: Solving the Management Puzzle.* New York: Butterworth Heinemann, 2004.

Ross, J., and C. Beath. "Beyond the Business Case: New Approaches to IT Investment." *MIT Sloan Management Review* (Winter 2002): 51–59.

Smith, H. A. "The Best of the Best: Part II." *CIO Canada,* October 1 (2003).

Tapscott, D. *The Digital Economy: Promise and Peril in the Age of Networked Intelligence.* New York: McGraw-Hill, 1996.

Weill, P., M. Subramani, and M. Broadbent. "Building IT Infrastructure for Strategic Agility." *MIT Sloan Management Review* (Fall 2002): 57–65.

Venkatramen, N., and J. Henderson. "Real Strategies for Virtual Organizing." *Sloan Management Review* 40, no. 33 (Fall 1998).

Chapter 3

Communicating with Business Managers[1]

At an IT governance meeting, attended by all our business executives, our IT architect was asked to discuss IT security and what steps needed to be taken to improve it. The architect proceeded to bombard the executives with extremely low-level details—an oversaturation of information, which they did not understand—and he lost their attention in very short order. What he did not do was deliver information in a positive manner geared to his audience. As a result, there was diminished business interest and understanding about this topic and a slowed-down budget for needed upgrades, which also affected other projects.

—(Senior IT manager in a global retail organization)

A s this true story illustrates, the ability to communicate with the business in business terms does not appear to be a current IT strength. This is a serious problem for IT managers because as IT and business grow more entwined, IT staff are going to need to be increasingly organization savvy and possess greater business and interpersonal competencies (Bassellier and Benbasat 2004; Karlsen et al.; 2008; Mingay 2005). Yet, despite consistent complaints business and IT leaders alike make about how IT staff lack business and communication skills, it seems that many IT departments still hire largely for technical competencies and have little budget available for "soft skills" development (Cukier 2007). Problems communicating with business continue to play a significant part in today's poor perceptions of IT in organizations and inhibit what IT is able to do *for* the organization (McKeen and Smith 2009). IT managers often bemoan the fact that IT-based initiatives—for example, to implement new technologies or establish a standard infrastructure—which they believe could have significant benefits for their organizations are not funded. Many of the reasons for this lie in IT's inability to explain the value of such investments in terms the business will understand.

In short, one of the most important skills all IT staff need to develop today is how to communicate effectively with business. "Effective communication between IT . . . and its stakeholders has never been so important . . . so complex or so difficult to get right." (Mingay 2005). Over and over, research has shown that if IT and business cannot speak the same language, focus on the same issues, and communicate constructively, they cannot build a trusting relationship (Karlsen et al. 2008). And business is consistently more negative than IT about IT's

---

[1]Smith, H. A., and McKeen, J. D., "How to Talk so Business Will Listen . . . and Listen so Business Can Talk," *Communications of the Association for Information Systems* 27, Article 13 (August 2010): 207–216. Reproduced by permission of the Association for Information Systems.

abilities in communicating effectively. In fact, even while IT collaboration is improving, business's assessment of IT's communication skills is declining (Willcoxson and Chatham 2004).

Much attention has been paid to organizational alignment between IT and business (e.g., governance, structure) while very little has been paid to the nature and impact of the social dimension of alignment, a big element of which involves communication (Reich and Benbasat 2000). This chapter explores the business and interpersonal competencies that IT staff will need in order to do their jobs effectively over the next five to seven years and what companies should be doing to help develop them. It begins by characterizing the state of communication in the business–IT relationship and why "good communication" is becoming increasingly important. Then, it explores what is meant by "good communication" in this relationship and looks at some of the inhibitors of effective communication between these groups. Finally, it discusses the key communication skills that need to be developed by IT staff and makes recommendations for how organizations can improve or develop communication in the business–IT relationship.

COMMUNICATION IN THE BUSINESS–IT RELATIONSHIP

"Poor communication is a constant source of irritation, confusion, and animosity," said one focus group manager. Another agreed: "So many of our IT staff don't understand organizational dynamics. They say and do things that would be completely inappropriate anywhere else in our company." There is general agreement between practitioners and researchers that poor business–IT communication is the source of poor relationships and alignment between these groups (Bittler 2008; Reich and Benbasat 2000). One study noted:

> Many IT people have "turned off" their business peers with too much technical jargon. This is one reason why the number of IT people that are "allowed" to speak with business people has been deliberately limited in many organizations. (Bittler 2008)

Communication is both an enabler and an inhibitor of a good business–IT relationship. One study found that it consistently made both "top ten" lists of managers over a number of years (Luftman and Brier 1999). On one hand, poor communication tends to be persistent and of lasting concern to practitioners (Coughlan et al. 2005). Often, IT personnel are perceived to live in an "ivory tower," disengaged from the needs of the business (Burton et al. 2008). Typically, these problems are described as a communication or a cultural "gap" between the two groups (Coughlan et al. 2005; Reich and Benbasat 2000) and are considered a major cause of systems development failures (Taylor-Cummings 1998). "We struggle with communication gaps and challenges," said a manager. "There's a lot of IT arrogance we need to deal with." Another commented, "IT doesn't listen and doesn't talk the talk."

On the other hand, there is broad recognition that good communication is essential for many reasons. First, it is fundamental to building a strong, positive business–IT relationship. "When business people believe IT people 'get it,' the relationships are always improved" (Bittler 2008). Second, it helps set sensible expectations of IT and helps IT to manage how it is perceived in business (Day 2007). Third, it is an essential element of building trust and partnership, which in turn help drive the delivery of business value (McKeen and Smith 2009). Fourth, it is essential to conveying the business value of IT (Hunter 2007). And finally, it is critical to understanding the priorities and pressures of the business. Focus group managers spoke of the need for staff who would listen and look for new opportunities to deliver business value. In short, good communication is widely seen as being critical for IT to deliver successful projects, effective performance, and value (Benbasat and Reich 2000; Karlsen et al. 2008; Willcoxson and Chatham 2004).

As a result, improving communication is increasingly recommended as a top priority for IT managers (Burton et al. 2005; Mingay 2005). Several managers stated that they are working on building communication into their annual goals and into their expectations of staff. What is missing, however, is a better understanding of the nature of good business–IT communication and some of the obstacles IT managers face in improving it (Coughlan et al. 2005). Thus, poor communication continues to be the norm in most organizations (Pawlowski and Robey 2004).

WHAT IS "GOOD" COMMUNICATION?

Unfortunately, there is no magic formula for defining and teaching "good" communication since it is a complex concept that has many dimensions. There are, however, some principles that are recognized as important elements of effective communication which can be used as guidelines for those who wish to assess their communication performance.

- *Principle 1: The effectiveness of communication is measured by its outcomes.* Communication is successful when it achieves the outcomes we desire (Gilberg 2006). However, all too often we measure communication by our intentions rather than its outcomes. The problem with that is this: "Communication is in the ear of the beholder," and even the most direct, clear, understandable, and consistent message can therefore get distorted through such filters as politics, culture, and personal points of view. As messages get passed along to others, they get further distorted, much like in the children's game of "Telephone." One study showed that although 97 percent of managers believed their own communication was clear, only 25 percent of the same people believed that the communication they received from their direct superior was clear and effective (Martin 2006). Another study showed that IT managers feel their communication is more effective than business managers feel it is (Willcoxson and Chatham 2004).
- *Principle 2: Communication is social behavior.*   Communication not only transmits ideas; it also negotiates relationships. Thus, *how* you say what you mean is just as important as *what* you say (Tannen 1995). This is an especially important principle for IT staff to learn because, as teams become increasingly diverse and virtual, many of the traditional nonverbal signals that we instinctively rely on to provide meaning are lost. A host of factors act as a social subtext to our communication: tone of voice, rate of speed, degree of loudness, and pacing and pausing. These are all culturally learned signals that affect how we evaluate each other as people (Tannen 1995). Gender and culture are key social filters that all of us use. For example, the degree of directness and indirectness in communication has often been a source of significant misunderstandings. Women learn to be more indirect when telling others what to do so as not to be perceived as "bossy"; men are indirect when admitting to

fault or weakness. In short, there is no one "right" way to speak, but speakers and listeners need to become more aware of the power of different linguistic styles, and managers must learn to use and take advantage of these styles in different communication situations (Tannen 1995).

- *Principle 3: Shared knowledge improves communication.*   It is all too well known that many IT people don't "speak the language of the business." As one manager stated, "Many IT staff think they've 'communicated' by explaining a technology need or a technology decision, instead of ensuring that everyone understands the business implications of what's involved." Studies show that the more IT staff learns about the business, the better communication becomes (Reich and Benbasat 2000). This is true not only because IT people understand business better but also because shared knowledge leads to increased *frequency* of communication and greater *mutual understanding*, both of which lead to more success in implementation, which in turn leads to more communication and improved relationships (Reich and Benbasat 2000). Thus, the creation of shared knowledge can be the beginning of a "virtuous circle" of continuously improving communication (see Figure 3.1).

- *Principle 4: Mature organizations have better communication.*   Although communication is a social process, it is also embedded within and fundamental to organizational processes (Coughlan et al. 2005). Organizational maturity plays a significant part in the effectiveness of business–IT communication because strong practices support and reinforce good interpersonal communication. "You can't be a partner unless you're a mature IT organization," explained one manager. The

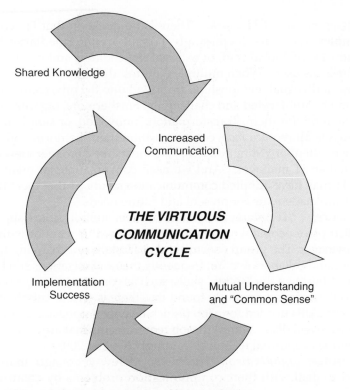

Shared Knowledge

Increased
Communication

**THE VIRTUOUS
COMMUNICATION
CYCLE**

Implementation
Success

Mutual Understanding
and "Common Sense"

FIGURE 3.1 • Shared Knowledge Leads to Improved Communication

research supports this contention, showing that high-performing IT functions have a strong foundation of communication (Peppard and Ward 1999; Reich and Benbasat 2000). Thus, successful IT organizations embed appropriate communication in their processes and consider this to be a significant component of IT's work (Mingay 2005). This work is even more important in times of organization transformation. "We are quite good about communicating operationally," said a manager, "but we need to improve when talking with our business executives about strategy." Another commented, "we need better skills to move up the 'run, change, innovate' curve, and we need the organizational maturity to do this." The focus group identified some of the areas where improved maturity could help communication: developing business cases; risk assessments; integrating with the 'big picture'; and communicating across business silos. In short, although communication is often seen as an individual competency, it should also be viewed and managed as an IT functional competency at all levels.

OBSTACLES TO EFFECTIVE COMMUNICATION

Why is it so difficult to achieve effective business–IT communication? The principles haven't changed much over time, but they have often not been applied, or they have been forgotten or ignored as busy IT managers focus on tight timelines and major deliverables (Mingay 2005). However, in addition to these considerations, some other obstacles to effective communication can hinder or prevent communication from occurring. These include the following:

- *The changing nature of IT work.* There is no question that IT work has become more complex over time. Increasingly, IT staff are intermediaries between third-party contract staff, global staff, or external stakeholders and vendors as well as traditional business users. When multiple cultures, different political contexts, diverse time zones, and virtual relationships are added into the mix, communication simply becomes more multifaceted and challenging. Furthermore, organizations are expecting IT to do more for them. Transformation, innovation, or simply bigger and more visible projects all require *more* communication than the norm and therefore more management attention (Mingay 2005). "We must take a broader view of communication," stated an IT manager. "And we need conversations at many levels." Thus, although IT may have adopted communication solutions that meet the needs of the past, these are inadequate for present and future needs.
- *Hiring practices.* "IT organizations can no longer support smart, super-talented, but socially disruptive people who cannot work well with a team or with the business," said one manager. The group concurred that IT skills are changing to become more consultative and collaborative. Yet frequently their organizations still hire for technology skills, rather than the "softer" skills, such as communication, which are essential for success these days. One study found that there is serious misalignment in hiring between "the skills needed for a job (which heavily emphasize communication and general business skills . . .) [and] the job requirements that are . . . advertised (which tend to emphasize formal technical training)" (Cukier 2007).
- *IT and business organization structures.* A few years ago, many IT functions attempted to deal with their communication problems by creating relationship

managers. These were skilled IT individuals whose job was to bridge the business and IT organizations and thus act as a communication conduit between the two groups. Unfortunately, relationship managers have become a mixed blessing at best and an obstacle at worst, restricting contact between the two groups and thereby limiting the development of shared knowledge and mutual understanding. "Relationship managers appear to do more to exacerbate rather than ameliorate" found one study (Coughlan et al. 2005). A focus group manager agreed, "You can't partner if your only contact is through a relationship manager." Furthermore, business silos can make communication about enterprise issues extremely challenging for IT staff, who can be expected to play a "knowledge broker" role, not only between IT and business but also between business units (Pawlowski and Robey 2004).

- *Nature and frequency of communication.*   It's a bit of a chicken-and-egg situation: More frequent contact with business leads to improved communication, but IT's communication is often so full of jargon, technocentric, and inappropriate that many organizations have sought ways to limit the amount and nature of communication between the two groups. One study found that about one-third of IT staff simply did not speak to the business at all (Basselier and Benbasat 2004). However, some of the focus group stated that, even when they are not restricted, IT staff often have trouble getting business to take the time to sit with them. Researchers have pointed out that it is the sharing of tacit and unstructured knowledge, which takes place in low-risk and informal settings, that contributes most to effective communication and mutual understanding (Basillier and Benbasat 2004; Dunne 2002; Kitzis and Gomolski 2006). Limiting one's focus to formal interactions (e.g., through IT governance processes) has been shown to be the *least* effective way of communicating successfully (Dunne 2002).

- *Attitude.*   Finally, IT's attitude can be a huge obstacle to good communication. It was surprising to hear this complaint from so many in the focus group. "Our IT staff think their work is about IT. They don't understand that we're here to deliver business value with technology," one manager stated. One manager described IT staff as "crotchety"; another as "obtuse"; several stated IT staff are "defensive." It is not surprising that if this is the case, a negative attitude on the part of an IT worker toward his or her work, business, or employer ends up being reflected in communication and how it is perceived (McKeen and Smith 2009). In turn, this can color how the communication is received (Anonymous 2005; Martin 2006). Unfortunately as well, many IT staff are motivated by the desire to be right rather than the desire to communicate effectively (Gilberg 2006). "We definitely need a 'we' attitude in IT," said a manager, "not an 'us–them' attitude."

Overcoming these obstacles will require a combination of management attention to all dimensions of business–IT communication and the development of critical communication skills in IT staff. The next two sections of this chapter address these issues.

"T-LEVEL" COMMUNICATION SKILLS FOR IT STAFF

Although IT workers' communication skills need upgrading, there is no one-size-fits-all strategy for doing this (Kalin 2006). Nor do lists of communication competencies move us much further forward in clarifying exactly what IT workers are doing wrong and what needs to change in their communication style (see Appendix A for a sample list). It has been suggested that as business becomes more complex, it really needs more T-shaped professionals who are deep problem solvers in their home discipline but also capable of interacting with and understanding others from a wide range of disciplines and functional areas (Ding 2008). People possessing these skills are able to shape their knowledge to fit problems and apply synergistic thinking (Leonard-Barton 1995). Unfortunately, most IT organizations encourage I-shaped skills—that is, deep functional expertise. As a result, the individual is driven ever deeper into his or her specialized set of skills (Leonard-Barton 1995).

Developing T-shaped IT staff addresses the concern some in the focus group expressed that emphasizing the development of "soft skills" could come at the expense of the excellent technology skills still needed by the organization. "You don't want your staff becoming disconnected from their technological capabilities," said one. "Connecting the dots" between the group's comments and the research on communication shows that four communication skills form the horizontal bar of the "T" for IT professionals (the vertical one being the professionals' technology skills and knowledge):

1. *Translation.*   IT staff typically fail miserably at translating IT issues and concerns into business impacts—as illustrated by the story at the beginning of this paper. Eliminating jargon is the first step. "Too often our IT population speaks in nano-words and gigabits, instead of using the English language," said a manager. However, translation requires more than this because it requires the ability to understand *how* IT initiatives will affect the business or deliver value to it. To communicate effectively about IT's value, IT managers "must translate IT's operational performance into business performance . . . and drive home the message that all IT initiatives are business initiatives" (Hunter 2007). It is not often recognized that IT staff are effectively knowledge brokers and that translation is a critical part of their work (Pawlowski and Robey 2004). As a result, bridging and translation skills are still rare in IT, agreed the focus group.

The work involved in translation can be characterized as a four-step process where IT staff move from the world of technology into the world of business to discuss problems in terms of business impact and possible business solutions and then *back* into IT to translate these solutions into technological reality (see Figure 3.2). "In

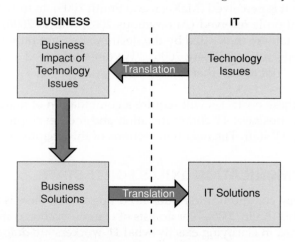

FIGURE 3.2   Communicating with Business Involves Translation

the end," said a manager, "we must be able to translate what the business knows and wants into actionable IT proposals."

2. *Tailoring.*   IT staff also need to adapt their communication to the needs of their audience. This involves two skills. First, IT workers need to know their audience— understanding *their* needs, *their* agendas, and *their* politics—so that they communicate in ways the business needs and wants to hear (Burton et al. 2008). Second, all IT personnel need to know how to choose communication methods appropriately. For example, bad news is best delivered in face-to-face meetings, not in reports or e-mails (as some in the focus group reported); and presentations to executives are not the place to expound on one's technology expertise (Martin 2006).

3. *Transparency.*   Transparency is a cornerstone of trust in the business–IT relationship (Smith and McKeen 2007), and IT managers should not assume that success speaks for itself. The business needs to see what is being done in IT and what it costs. In fact, it has been suggested that transparency is the key to changing the business's perception of IT's value (Levinson and Pastore 2005). At an individual level, one member of the focus group defined transparency as communication that is "honest, accurate, ethical, and respectful." "We need honesty and openness," stated another. Transparency also means involving the right people in making decisions and recognizing that the goal is to get the communication process flowing both ways (Burton et al. 2008; Dunne 2002). Other ways to promote transparent communication include checking assumptions, clarifying goals, stating intentions up front, and asking for feedback on understanding (Dunne 2002; Gilberg 2006).

4. *Thinking, talking, and listening.*   An important communication skill that is increasingly valued by business is the ability to "think outside the box" and to challenge the status quo, albeit diplomatically and responsibly. Focus group managers suggested that IT staff need to think "horizontally" across the enterprise in order to do what is best for the business. Communicating innovative ideas effectively involves "getting inside the head of the business," they explained. In the future, the ideal IT manager will "think and talk like a business person with a strong background in technology" (Kitzis and Gomolski 2006). Thinking, however, does not mean simply blurting out ideas; it means understanding how and where to speak and how to listen to others. Learning to listen can be a challenge for IT staff who tend to be impatient with politics and the process of coming to a solution that everyone can live with (Dunne 2002). Similarly, IT staff can underestimate the importance of listening to nonverbal communication or the "noise" of the context in which communication takes place (Anonymous 2005; Coughlin et al. 2005). In short, this skill involves more than simply "talking and waiting to talk" but also incorporates a more sophisticated and nuanced awareness of the *process* of communication, recognizing that *how* one reaches a decision is as important to the success of communication as the actual decision itself.

IMPROVING BUSINESS–IT COMMUNICATION

The focus group managers were the first to admit that much more needs to be done in their own organizations to improve communication between IT and the business at all levels. However, they were also implementing a number of practices that they believed would promote the development of good communication skills among their staff and also as an IT function. Their recommendations included the following:

- *Make the importance of effective communication visible.*   It is well accepted that if you want people to pay attention to something, you need to measure and incentivize for it. Several managers felt that good communication skills should be expected of every IT staff member. "These are now baseline expectations for us," said one. A key way to get staff to pay attention is to incorporate communication skills into performance appraisals. One company makes it clear that specialized "niche" skills are more likely to be outsourced and that those who understand and can work with the business are more likely to have a long-term career in its organization.

- *Work with HR to develop new skills expectations and roles.*   Several firms are incorporating specific communication competencies into staff role descriptions. One is even trying to create jobs that have titles which reflect the types of competencies needed, such as "senior business consultant," "technology relationship manager," and "business technology specialist." Another is trying to make it easier for IT staff to transfer laterally into the business for a period of time.

- *Develop communication skills both formally and informally.*   To support these new expectations, some firms offer formal training in communication skills in areas such as making presentations, communication styles, and negotiations. Incorporating communication skills into personal development plans is one way some managers tailor formal skills development for personal needs. However, the effectiveness of formal training is "mixed," said many managers, and some firms don't offer it at all, or only as part of management development. More informal approaches include mentoring, lunch-and-learn sessions, and self-assessment tools.

- *Increase the nature and frequency of communication.*   Although not an initiative of any of the focus groups, the research is clear that creating a "virtuous communication cycle" starts with creating shared knowledge between the two groups all levels. There are few "quick fixes" to the communication problem, but the importance of regular communication between IT and business at all levels cannot be overemphasized (Reich and Benbasat 2000). Wherever possible, priority should be given to informal communication and social interaction as these are the best ways to build up shared language and understanding (Burton et al.; 2008; Dunne 2002). These types of interactions are particularly important when face-to-face communication is irregular or impossible (Greenberg et al. 2007). Recognizing this, one company that makes extensive use of global, virtual teams encourages socialization, and even virtual parties, through its social networking technologies.

- *Spend more time on communication.*   Most important, IT leaders at all levels need to spend more time on communication—not only in what and how they communicate personally but, rather, in learning how their staff and organizations communicate. They need to seek out and remove obstacles to communication, coach their staff, become sensitized to their organization's communication processes (both formal and informal), and do whatever it takes to develop a shared understanding and language with the business. Although the initial investment of time may be high, it is certain to pay off in terms of an improved relationship with business and greater perceptions of IT value.

Conclusion

"What we have here is a failure to communicate" is a famous (and sarcastic) movie quote that is nevertheless an extraordinarily accurate description of the business–IT relationship. Although many words and documents may flow between the two groups, it is fair to say that often little true communication is occurring. This has resulted in misunderstandings, dysfunctional behavior, and, above all, a failure to deliver value to the organization. This chapter has examined the difficult and complex challenges facing IT leaders as they attempt to improve their function's communication with the business. It demonstrated that good communication has both social and organizational dimensions, both of which need to be appropriately managed. It also showed that there is a "virtuous circle" of communication, which is associated with improved IT performance

and perceptions of IT value. In short, good communication *is* important to the successful implementation of IT in business, and developing it is therefore worth more time and attention than most managers currently pay to it. This chapter has focused on the IT side of the communication equation—since it is usually held to be the culprit in the sometimes nasty war of words that ranges back and forth between the two groups. There is much that can be done within IT to improve communication skills—without losing technology capabilities—but it nevertheless behooves business managers to explore ways in which they can assist IT in doing this. Most important, they can make the time and effort to ensure that IT staff are well educated in how their business works. If they do, business leaders just might find that many of IT's "communication problems" disappear.

References

Anonymous. "The Tone of Communication." *CIO Magazine,* July 8, 2005.

Basselier, G., and I. Benbasat. "Business Competence of Information Technology Professionals: Conceptual Development and Influence on IT-Business Partnerships." *MIS Quarterly* 28, no. 4 (December 2004).

Bittler, R. "Align Enterprise Architecture to the Top 2008 CIO Priorities." Gartner Inc., ID Number: G00159369, September 2, 2008.

Burton, B., D. Weiss, and P. Allega. "Q&A: Architects Must Advocate, Evangelize and Educate" Gartner Inc., ID Number: G00155902, March 11, 2008.

Coughlan, J., M. Lycett, and R. Macredie. "Understanding the Business-IT Relationship." *International Journal of Information Management* 24, no. 4 (2005).

Cukier, W. "Diversity—The Competitive Edge: Implications for the ICT Labour Market." Information and Communications Technology Council, Ottawa, Canada, March 2007.

Day, J. "Strangers on the Train: The Relationship of the IT Department with the Rest of the Business." *Information Technology & People* 20, no. 1 (2007).

Ding, David. "T-Shaped Professionals, T-Shaped Skills, Hybrid Managers." *Coevolving Innovations in Business Organizations and Information Technologies,* September 6, 2008. coevolving.com/blogs/index.php/archive/t-shaped-professionals-t-shaped-skills-hybrid-managers.

Dunne, D. "Q&A with the Wharton School's Richard Shell: Communication." *CIO Magazine,* March 1, 2002.

Gilberg, D. "A CIO's Guide to Communication Basics." *CIO Magazine,* June 14, 2006.

Greenberg, P., R. Greenberg, and Y. Antonucci. "Creating and Sustaining Trust in Virtual Teams." *Business Horizons* 50 (2007).

Hunter, R. "Executive Summary: Business Performance Is the Value of IT." Gartner Inc., ID Number: G00148820, April 1, 2007.

Information and Communications Technology Council (ICTC). *ICT Competency Profiles: A Framework for Developing Tomorrow's ICT Workforce.* Ottawa, Canada: ICTC. www.ictc-ctic.ca, 2009.

Leonard-Barton, D. *Wellsprings of Knowledge: Building and Sustaining the Sources of Innovation.* Boston: Harvard Business School Press, 1995.

Luftman, J., and T. Brier. "Achieving and Sustaining Business-IT Alignment." *California Management Review* 42, no. 1 (Fall 1999).

Kalin, S. "Tools and Tactics for Communicating IT's Value to the Business." *CIO Magazine,* August 1, 2006.

Karlsen, J., K. Graee, and M. Massaoud. "Building Trust in Project-Stakeholder Relationships." *Baltic Journal of Management* 3, no. 1 (2008).

Kitzis, E., and B. Gomolski. "IT Leaders Must Think Like Business Leaders." Gartner Inc., ID Number: G00143430, October 26, 2006.

Levinson, M., and R. Pastore. "Transparency Helps Align IT with the Business." *CIO Magazine,* June 1, 2005.

Martin, C. "Check What Was Heard, Not What Was Said." *CIO Magazine,* December 28, 2006.

McKeen, J., and H. Smith. *IT Strategy in Action.* Upper Saddle River, NJ: Pearson-Prentice Hall, 2009.

Mingay, S. "Effective Communication Between IT Leaders and Stakeholders Must Be Structured and Contextual." Gartner Inc., ID Number: G00130023, 2005.

Pawlowski, S., and D. Robey. "Bridging User Organizations: Knowledge Brokering and the Work of Information Technology Professionals." *MIS Quarterly* 28, no. 4 (December 2004).

Peppard, J., and J. Ward. "Mind the Gap: Diagnosing the Relationship Between the IT Organization and the Rest of the Business." *Journal of Strategic Information Systems* 8, no. 2 (1999).

Reich, B., and I. Benbasat. "Factors That Influence the Social Dimension of Alignment Between Business and Information Technology Objectives." *MIS Quarterly* 24, no. 1 (March 2000).

Smith, H., and McKeen, J. "Managing Perceptions of IS." *Communications of the Association for Information Systems* 20, Article 47 (November 2007): 760–73.

Tannen, D. "The Power of Talk: Who Gets Heard and Why." *Harvard Business Review,* September–October 1995.

Taylor-Cummings, A. "Bridging the User-IS Gap: A Study of Major Information Systems Projects." *Journal of Information Technology* 13 (1998).

Willcoxson, L., and R. Chatham. "Progress in the IT/Business Relationship: A Longitudinal Assessment." *Journal of Information Technology* 19, no. 1 (March 2004).

APPENDIX A

IT Communication Competencies

Level 1
Listens and clearly presents information

- Listens/pays attention actively and objectively (Persons with hearing impairments may lip-read.)
- Presents information and facts in a logical manner, using appropriate phrasing and vocabulary
- Shares information willingly and on a timely basis
- Communicates with others honestly, respectfully, and sensitively
- Recognizes and uses nonverbal communications

Level 2
Fosters two-way communication

- Recalls others' main points and takes them into account in own communication
- Checks own understanding of others' communication (e.g., paraphrases, asks questions)
- Elicits comments or feedback on what has been said
- Maintains continuous, open, and consistent communication with others, considering nonverbal messaging as required

Level 3
Adapts communication

- Tailors communication (e.g., content, style, and medium) to diverse audiences
- Reads cues from diverse listeners to assess when and how to change planned communication approach to effectively deliver message
- Communicates equally effectively with all organizational levels and sells ideas and concepts
- Understands others' complex or underlying needs, motivations, emotions, or concerns and communicates effectively despite the sensitivity of the situation

Level 4
Communicates complex messages

- Communicates complex issues clearly and credibly with widely varied audiences
- Handles difficult on-the-spot questions (e.g., from senior executives, public officials, interest groups, or the media)
- Reads nonverbal communications signs and adapts materials and approach as required
- Overcomes resistance and secures support for ideas or initiatives through high-impact communication

Level 5
Communicates strategically

- Scans the environment for key information and messages to form the development of communication strategies
- Communicates strategically to achieve specific objectives (e.g., considers optimal "messaging" and timing of communication)
- Uses varied communication vehicles and opportunities to promote dialogue and develop shared understanding and consensus

Chapter 4

Building a Strong Relationship with the Business[1]

There is no doubt that a strong business–IT relationship is now critical to the success of an organization's successful and effective use of IT (Bassellier and Benbasat 2004; Kitzis and Gomolski 2006). With the rapid evolution of IT in business, simply "keeping the lights on" and delivering systems on time and on budget are not enough. Today, IT's ability to deliver value is closely linked with the nature of its relationship with a large number of business stakeholders. Recognizing this, many IT functions have tried to become "partners" with the business at the most senior strategic levels, but with limited success (Gordon and Gordon 2002). It has become clear from these initiatives that business–IT interactions are more complex and highly resistant to change than first assumed and that building a strong relationship with business is a major challenge for most IT leaders.

We know that the nature and quality of the business–IT relationship are affected by many factors such as the subfunction of IT involved (e.g., operations, application development), the business unit involved, the management levels involved, changing expectations, and general perceptions of IT (McKeen and Smith 2008). However, research suggests that IT managers are still somewhat naïve about how relationships work in business and that interpersonal interaction and clear communication are often missing between the groups. We have also learned that perceptions of the value IT delivers are correlated with how well IT is perceived to understand and identify with the business (Anonymous 2002; Gold 2006; Tallon et al. 2000).

Nevertheless, we still know very little about the elements that contribute to a "strong relationship" between IT and business, nor even about how to characterize such a relationship (Day 2007). This chapter first looks at the nature of the business–IT relationship and how an effective relationship could be characterized. Then it examines in turn each of the four foundational elements of a strong, positive relationship, making suggestions for how IT managers could strengthen them.

---

[1]Smith, H. A., and J. D. McKeen. "Building a Strong Relationship with the Business," *Communications of the Association for Information Systems,* Volume 26, Article 19, April 2010, pp. 429–440. Reproduced by permission of the Association for Information Systems.

THE NATURE OF THE BUSINESS–IT RELATIONSHIP

"The IT-business relationship is a set of beliefs that one party holds about the other and how these beliefs are formed from the interactions of . . . individuals as they engage in tasks associated with an IT service" (Day 2007). The business–IT relationship in organizations tends to span the full range of relationship possibilities. Some members of the focus group felt they had generally healthy and positive relationships, and others labeled them negative or ineffective. Overall, "there's still a general perception that IT is slow, expensive, and gets in the way," said one manager. Even the focus group member with the most positive business–IT relationship admitted it was "not easy," and one set of researchers has described it as typically "arduous" (Pawlowski and Robey 2004).

Although "you can't have a one-sided relationship," as one focus group manager remarked, agreement is almost universal that IT needs to change if it is to improve. Literally dozens of articles have been written about what IT *should* be doing to make it better. For example, IT should better understand the fundamentals of business and aim to satisfy the "right" customers (Kitzis and Gomolski 2006); act as a knowledge broker (Pawlowski and Robey 2004); get involved in the business and be skilled marketers (Schindler 2007); manage expectations (Ross 2006); convince the business that it understands its goals and concerns and communicate in business language (Bassellier and Benbasat 2004); and demonstrate its competencies (Day 2007). In short, "IT has to keep proving itself" to the business to demonstrate its value (Kaarst-Brown 2005). Thus, practitioners and researchers both stress that cultivating a strong business–IT relationship is "a continuous effort" (a focus group member); "ongoing" (Luftman and Brier 1999); a "core IT skill" (Feeny and Willcocks 1998); and "emergent" (Day 2007).

On the business side of the relationship, two features stand out. First, business managers are often disengaged from IT work, according to both the focus group and researchers (Ross and Weill 2002). For example, in some cases in the focus group, IT staff have taken on business roles in projects in order to get them done. Second, it is clear that what business wants from this relationship is continually changing. "The business–IT relationship is cyclical," explained one manager. "The business goes back and forth about whether it wants IT to be an order taker or an innovator. Every time the business changes what it wants, the relationship goes sour."

So what *do* we know about the business–IT relationship in organizations? First, we know it is a multifaceted interaction of people and processes. It is unfortunately true that the existence of positive relationships between individual business and IT professionals does not necessarily mean that interactions will be positive on a particular development project, with the IT help desk, with an individual business unit, or between IT and the business as a whole (McKeen and Smith 2008). Because relationships manifest themselves in so many ways—formal and informal, tacit and explicit, procedural and cultural—we must recognize that their complexity means that they don't lend themselves to simplistic solutions (Day 2007; Guillemette et al. 2008; Ross 2006).

Second, we know difficult, complex relationships often exhibit lack of clarity around expectations and accountabilities and difficulty communicating (Galford and Drapeau 2003; Pawlowski and Robey 2004). This, in turn, leads to lack of trust. In the business–IT relationship, "complexity often arises when expectations differ in various parts of an organization, leaving a CIO with the difficult task of reconciling them and elucidating exactly what the IT function's mission and strategic role should be"

(Guillemette et al. 2008). Several focus group members complained that different parts of their business expected different things from IT. "In some parts of our business, they want IT to be an order-taker; in others, they want us to be thought leaders and innovators," stated one manager. Another noted, "We live in an age of unmet expectations. There's never enough resources to do everything the business wants us to do."

Third, assumptions by the business about IT tend to cluster into patterns. One researcher has identified five sets of assumptions: (1) IT is a necessary evil, (2) IT is a support, not a partner, (3) IT rules, (4) business can do IT better, and (5) business and IT are equal partners. Business leaders who espouse one of these sets will tend to have similar ideas about who should control IT's direction, how central IT is to business strategy, the value of IT skills and knowledge, how to justify IT investments, and who benefits from IT (Kaarst-Brown 2005). Building on this idea, another study has also shown that business–IT relationships tend to vary along similar patterns. Different organizations tend to adopt one of five IT value profiles and expect IT to behave in accordance with the profile selected (see Appendix A). Problems arise when the assumptions and value profiles espoused by IT conflict with those of the organization or a specific part of the organization. As a result, many "disconnects" are often present in the relationship. For example, although IT organizations often seek to be a business partner, their participation in this way is not always welcomed by the business (Pawlowski and Robey 2004).

Focus group members defined a strong business–IT relationship in ways that recognize each of these factors. To them, it should include the following:

- Clearly defined expectations, governance models and accountabilities
- Trust between the two groups.
- Articulation and incorporation of corporate and client values and priorities in all IT work
- A blurred line between business and IT (i.e., no "us vs. them")
- IT dedicated to business success
- IT serving as a trusted advisor to the business
- Mutual recognition of IT value

In short, a strong business–IT relationship is one where realistic, mutual expectations are clearly articulated and communicated through individual and procedural interactions and where both groups recognize that all facets of this relationship are important to the successful delivery of IT value.

Characteristics of the Business–IT Relationship

- IT has to keep proving itself.
- The business is often disengaged from IT work.
- Business expectations of IT change continually.
- The relationship is affected by the interaction of many people and processes at multiple levels.

- Clarity is often lacking around expectations and accountabilities.
- Business assumptions of IT tend to cluster.
- There are many "disconnects" between the two groups.

THE FOUNDATION OF A STRONG BUSINESS–IT RELATIONSHIP

Strong relationships do not simply happen. They are built over time and, if they are to deliver value for the organization, they must be built to endure (Day 2007). The focus group told several stories of how the business–IT relationship in their organization had deteriorated when a business or IT leader changed or when a project wasn't delivered on time. Because it can so easily become dysfunctional, constant attention and nurturing are needed at all levels, said the focus group. However, building a strong relationship is not easy to do. Although there is no shortage of prescriptions, the sustained nature of problems in this relationship suggests that some underlying root causes need to be addressed (Appendix B provides one organization's view of what is needed in this relationship).

We have suggested previously that four components must be in place in order to deliver real business value with IT: competence, credibility, interpersonal interaction, and trust. The focus group reviewed these components and agreed that they also form the foundation of a successful and effective business–IT relationship. The focus group saw that developing, sustaining, and growing a strong business–IT relationship in each of these areas is closely intertwined with IT's ability to deliver value with technology. Therefore, a consistent and structured initiative to strengthen the business–IT relationship in these dimensions will also lead to an improved ability to deliver value successfully (see Figure 4.1). In the remainder of this chapter, we look at these four components in turn, discussing in detail how each acts as an important building block of a strong business–IT relationship and suggesting how each could be strengthened.

Building Block #1: Competence

Although a competent IT organization that consistently delivers cost-efficient and reliable services is the bare minimum for an IT function, businesses today expect a great deal more of both their IT organizations and their IT professionals. Although many IT organizations have adopted an internal service model in order to "operate IT like a business" and have demonstrated that they can provide services as effectively as external service providers, these competencies fall short of what business now expects of IT (Kitzis and Gomolski 2006). Over the last decade, researchers and practitioners have identified a number of new competencies that are now required—to a greater or lesser extent—from all IT professionals.

First and foremost, IT staff need *business knowledge*. This goes beyond basic knowledge of a single business unit to include the "big picture" of the whole organization. IT personnel need to understand the business context in which their technologies are deployed, including organizational goals and objectives, capabilities, critical success factors, environment, and constraints. At all levels, they need to be able to "think about and understand the development of the business as [any other business] member would and participate in making [it] successful in the same way" (Bassellier and Benbasat 2004). Furthermore, they need to be able to apply their business understanding to help the organization visualize the ways in which "IT can contribute to organizational performance and look for synergies between IT and

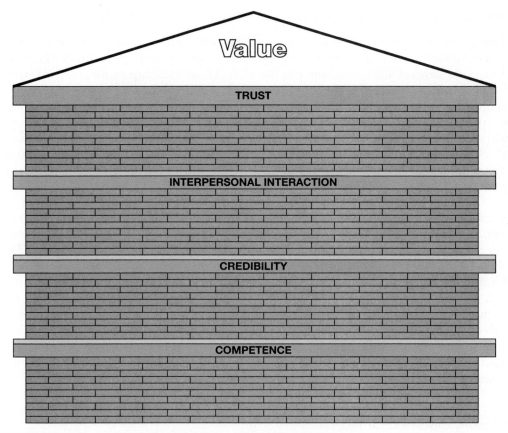

FIGURE 4.1 Strong Relationships Are Built on a Strong Foundation

business activities" (Bassellier and Benbasat 2004). In this regard, an important competence an IT department and its staff can bring to an organization is cross-domain and cross-functional business knowledge (Kitzis and Gomolski 2006; Wailgum 2008a).

Developing business knowledge does not mean that IT staff should become businesspeople but that they should be able to demonstrate they understand the business's goals, concerns, language, and processes and are working to help achieve them (Feeny and Willcocks 1998). One focus group organization surveyed its senior managers about IT and found that these managers felt IT staff had a poor understanding of the business; as a result, they didn't trust IT's ideas.

Other key competencies which IT must cultivate include the following:

- *Expertise.* This includes having up-to-date knowledge, being able to support a technical recommendation, applying expertise to a particular business situation, and offering wise advice on risks, options, and trade-offs, as well as the ability to bring useful new ideas and external information (e.g., about new technologies or what the competition is doing with technology) to the business (Joni 2004; Pawlowski and Robey 2004).

- *Financial Awareness.* Awareness of how IT delivers value and the ability to act in accordance with this value is a rare and prized skill (Mahoney and Gerrard 2007). All the focus group members felt pressure to continually demonstrate the business value of IT and recognized a strong need to make all IT staff more aware of such concepts as ROI, total cost of ownership, and how IT affects the bottom line and/or business strategy.
- *Execution.* It is not enough to understand the business and develop a vision; IT must also operationalize them. Since much of the business–IT relationship is dynamic—that is, continually being re-created—every IT action speaks about its competence. It is well known that the inability to deliver an individual project on time and within budget will undermine the business's view of IT's overall competence. However, it is also the case that the actions of IT operations, the help desk, and other IT subfunctions will also be held up to similar scrutiny. As one focus group manager stated, "Poor delivery of *any* type can break a relationship."

In short, if the IT function is not seen to be competent at executing basic IT services or able to communicate in business terms, it will simply not be given an opportunity to participate in higher-order business activities, such as planning and strategy development (Gerrard 2006).

STRENGTHENING COMPETENCE

- *Find ways to develop business knowledge in all IT staff.* Focus group members use "lunch and learn" sessions, job shadowing, and short-term assignments in the business to accomplish this, but they recognize that more needs to be done to develop this competence.
- *Link IT's success criteria to business metrics.* This not only lifts IT's perspective to larger business concerns, but it also introduces all IT staff to the key financial and other measures that drive the rest of the organization.
- *Make business value an explicit criteria in all IT decisions.* Asking why the business should care about a particular IT decision, and how it will affect the business in both the long and short term, changes the focus of IT professionals in a subtle but very effective way, enabling them to communicate even technical decisions in business terms.
- *Ensure effective execution in all IT activities.* This ensures that IT sends a consistent message of competence to all parts and levels of the organization.

Building Block #2: Credibility

Credibility is the belief that others can be counted on to do what they say they will do. It is built in many ways. Keeping agreements and acting with integrity, honesty, and openness are essential behaviors, whereas lack of timely and substantive responses and failure to observe deadlines can undermine it (Greenberg et al. 2007; Feeny et al. 1992). Focus group managers concurred that credibility is very important to the business–IT relationship. Although in earlier days, credibility was largely about the ability to deliver systems on time and budget, now earning and maintaining credibility with the business has become more complex. Today's IT projects often involve many more elements (e.g., multiple platforms, risk management, adherence to laws and standards) and stakeholders than in the past, and the methods and tools of delivery are constantly changing. Furthermore, new research shows that it is often the "little things" that can be most significant in undermining credibility and that people often make decisions based on IT's attention or inattention to such details (Buchanan 2005). One study concluded that "each and every IT service incident and event must be considered for its long-term influence" (Day 2007).

IT staff often assume that because they are *competent* they will be *credible*, but this is an invalid assumption. Thus, for example, a recent survey of CIOs found that they wished their developers "didn't appear so clueless to the rest of the organization" (Wailgum 2008b). It is essential, therefore, that competence be *demonstrated* for others to feel someone is credible (Ross 2006). This is especially important in relationships where there is little face-to-face interaction. In these cases in particular, work must be visible and communication constant in order to demonstrate credibility (Hurley 2006).

STRENGTHENING CREDIBILITY

- *Communicate frequently and explicitly.*   Make progress and accomplishments visible in clear and nontechnical ways. Focus group members found that when difficult decisions are planned together and clearly articulated in advance, much less tension develops in the relationship.
- *Pay attention to the "little things."*   Wherever possible, take steps to provide prompt feedback and responses to queries and to ensure consistently high-quality service encounters.
- *Utilize external cues to credibility.*   Examples include awards, endorsements from third parties, and the experience and background of IT staff. These specifics can be very useful when starting a new relationship with the business.
- *Assess all business touch points.*   All focus group members stressed the need to really listen to what the business says about its expectations and the problems it feels exist in the relationship. Just the effort alone sends a strong and positive message about the importance of this relationship, said a manager. However, he also stressed that undertaking such a review creates expectations that changes will be made, so regular reports back to the business about what is being done to improve things are especially important.

Building Block #3: Interpersonal Interaction

The business–IT relationship is shaped by the development of mutual understanding, interests, and expectations, which are formed and shaped during a wide variety of interpersonal interactions (Gold 2006). Business–IT interactions must be developed and nurtured at many different levels in the business–IT relationship, said focus group managers, and although CEO–CIO interactions can set the tone for the relationship, the connections at multiple touch points contribute to its overall quality (Flint 2004; Prewitt 2005). The following are the four significant dimensions of interpersonal interaction:

- *Professionalism.* This is the unarticulated set of working behaviors, attitudes, and expectations that serves as the glue which keeps teams of diverse individuals working together toward the same goal. These behaviors are not only carefully watched by the business; they are also just as important *within* IT, said the focus group. Members noted that difficult internal IT relationships can lead to problems delivering effective IT services. Five sets of attitudes and behaviors contribute to developing IT professionalism: (1) comportment (i.e., appearance and manners on the job), (2) preparation (i.e., displaying competence and good organization), (3) communication skill (i.e., both clarity and etiquette), (4) judgment (i.e., the ability to make right choices for the organization), and (5) attitude (i.e., caring about doing a job well and about doing the right thing for the company) (McKeen and Smith 2008).

- *Nontechnical communication.* Over and over, research has found that the inability to communicate clearly with the business in its own terms can undermine the business–IT relationship (Bassellier and Benbasat 2004; Kitzis and Gomolski 2006). Today, because IT staff work across many organizational boundaries, they must also be effective at translating and interpreting needs, not only from business to technology and vice versa, but also between business units, in order to enable members of different communities to understand each other (Wailgum 2008a). Increasingly, as IT programs and services are delivered collaboratively *by* external partners and *to* external partners, clarity in communication is becoming mission critical.

- *Social skills.* The social dimension of the business–IT relationship is often ignored by both sides, leading to misunderstandings and lack of trust (Day 2007). Social bonds help diverse groups build trust and develop a common language, both of which are essential to a strong relationship. Socialization also helps build mutual understanding, enabling all parties to get comfortable with one another and uncovering hidden assumptions, which may become obstacles to success (Kaarst-Brown 2005). Socialization also develops empathy and facilitates problem solving (Feeny and Willcocks 1998).

  Unfortunately, many IT organizations are structured in ways that create barriers between business and IT. For example, the use of "relationship managers" to act as interfaces between IT and the business is a mixed blessing. Although individually, these managers may be skilled and viewed positively by the business, focus group members noted that their position often leads them to act as gatekeepers to the business. One manager told of being hauled on the carpet to explain his lunch with a business manager (a personal friend), which hadn't been approved by the relationship manager! "We need a broad range of social interactions with the business," said another manager. "We use account managers, but we also encourage interactions through such things as lunches and social events." Ongoing, face-to-face interaction is the ideal, but with today's virtual teams and global organizations, other forms of social interaction, such as networking and collaboration tools, are being introduced to help bridge gaps in this area. Social bonds can be created in a virtual environment, but these take longer and are harder to develop although they are, if anything, more important than in a more traditional workplace (Greenberg et al. 2007).

- *Management of politics and conflict.* The business–IT relationship can be turbulent, and IT personnel are not noted for their skills in dealing with the conflicts and challenges involved. Furthermore, conflict and politics tend to be exacerbated by the types of projects most commonly undertaken by IT—that is, those that cross internal and external organizational boundaries (Weiss and Hughes 2005). As a result, IT functions and personnel need ways to effectively address conflict and use it to deliver creative solutions. All too often, conflict is avoided or treated as a "hot potato" to be tossed up the management hierarchy (Weiss and Hughes 2005). Straight talk and the development of a healthy give-and-take attitude are fundamental to dealing with conflict at its source. Experts also recommend the development of transparent processes for managing disagreements and frank discussions of the trade-offs involved in dealing with problems (Pascale et al. 1997). These not only help stop damaging escalation and growing uncertainty but also help to model conflict-resolution skills for the staff involved.

As well, failure to understand the role of politics in a particular organization makes IT personnel less effective in their business interactions because they cannot craft "win–win" solutions. Thus, all IT staff need to understand something about politics and how they can affect their work. At more senior levels, it is imperative that IT professionals learn how to act "wisely and shrewdly in a political environment" (Kitzis and Gomolski 2006). Since politics are part of every business relationship and cannot be avoided, IT personnel must learn how to work with them, said focus group members, even if they are trying to avoid them as much as possible.

STRENGTHENING INTERPERSONAL INTERACTIONS

- *Expect professionalism.*   IT managers must not only articulate professional values and behaviors; they must *live* them and measure and reward them in their staff.
- *Promote a wide variety of social interactions at all levels.*   Whether face-to-face or virtual, sharing information about each other's background and interests is an important way to bolster working relationships at all levels. Therefore, even where formal relationship managers are in place, IT leaders should encourage all IT staff to connect informally with their business colleagues. "Social interaction facilitates quick problem ownership and resolution and helps to develop a common language," said a focus group participant. Although the need for socialization increases as one moves up the organizational hierarchy, even at the lowest levels staff should be expected to spend about 10 percent of their time in this type of interaction (Kitzis and Gomolski 2006).
- *Develop "soft skills" in IT staff.*   Although the need for interpersonal skills in IT has never been greater, many companies still give their development short shrift, preferring instead to stress technical competencies. In developing interpersonal skills, formal training should be only one component. It is even more important that IT managers take time to develop such skills in their staff through mentoring and coaching. Many focus group members have implemented "soft" skills development initiatives informally, but they also have admitted that the pressure to be instantly productive often detracts from both business and IT participation in them.

Building Block #4: Trust

Effective interpersonal interactions, a belief that the job at hand will get done and get done right, and demonstrated business and technical competence are all required to facilitate trust that IT can be a successful partner with the business. But *even if* these are in place, proactive measures are still needed to actually *build* trust between the two groups. In many firms, an underlying sense of distrust of IT *as a whole* remains:

> IT's processes are notoriously convoluted and bureaucratic, leaving the business unsure of how to accomplish their business strategies with IT. From strategy alignment to prioritization to budgeting and resourcing to delivering value to managing costs, it must be clear that what IT is doing is for the benefit of the enterprise, not itself. (McKeen and Smith 2008)

The most important way to build trust at this level is through effective governance. The story of how one CIO managed to transform the business–IT relationship at Farm Credit Canada illustrates its importance:

> [At FCC, when Paul MacDonald became CIO], IT was considered a necessary evil. Business people were afraid of it and wished it would just go away. . . . [Transforming this relationship] was a very difficult and complex job—especially for cross-functional processes. Clear responsibilities and accountabilities had to be defined. . . . "It's all about clarity of roles and responsibilities," MacDonald said. The new IT governance model was validated and refined through sessions with key business stakeholders. "These sessions were important to demonstrate that we weren't just shuffling the boxes around in IT," [MacDonald] said. . . . MacDonald also made sure that the new model actually worked the way it was supposed to. "There were cases where it didn't . . . and with these, we made changes in our processes." He attributes his willingness to make changes where needed to his ability to make the new model actually function the way it was supposed to. . . .
>
> "Today, at FCC user satisfaction is very high and IT is seen as being indispensable. . . . [MacDonald] stressed that it is important to review and refine the new governance model continually. "There were some things that just didn't work," he said. "We are still constantly learning." (Smith and McKeen 2008)

Effective governance should be designed to build common business goals and establish a good decision-making process (Gerrard 2006). Mature processes in IT and transparency about costs develop trust (Levinson and Pastore 2005; Overby 2005). A focus group manager stated succinctly, "[M]ore transparency equals fewer surprises and you get transparency through governance." Aspects of governance that have enhanced trust in focus group organizations include integrated planning, defined accountabilities, a clear picture of mandates and authorities, and clarity around how work gets done.

Another focus group manager explained the importance of governance in this way:

> *In the past, we couldn't break the trust barrier. Now, [with an effective governance structure] we are more proactive and are fighting fewer fires. Our processes ensure proper escalation and a new focus on value. In short, governance captures the value of a good relationship and good fences make good neighbours.*

Trust is essential for both superior performance and for developing the collaborative relationships that lead to success (Greenberg et al. 2007). It is developed through consistency, clear communication, willingness to tackle challenges, and owning up to and learning from mistakes (Upton and Staats 2008). Both inconsistent messages to stakeholders and inconsistent processes and standards can seriously undermine trust (Galford and Drapeau 2003).

Nevertheless, it must be stressed that there is no optimal form of governance (Gordon and Gordon 2002). The key is to develop a model of IT governance that addresses the business's *expectations* of its IT function. Thus, an IT organization can best build trust if it clearly understands the organization's priorities for IT and designs its governance model to match (Guillemette et al. 2008).

STRENGTHENING TRUST

- *Design governance for clarity and transparency.*   IT leaders should assess how the business views IT processes—from the help desk on up. It is important to recognize that all processes play a very visible role in how IT is viewed in the organization and that clear, effective, and fair processes are needed to break the "trust barrier" between business and IT at all levels.
- *Mandate the relationship.*   Although it may seem counterintuitive, companies have had success from strictly enforcing relationship basics such as formal roles and responsibilities, joint scorecards, and the use of common metrics. Such structural measures can ensure that common expectations, language, and goals are developed and met.
- *Design IT for business expectations.*   Clearly understanding the *primary* value the business wants IT to deliver can help IT understand how to focus its process and governance models (see Appendix A).

Conclusion

There is clearly no panacea for a strong business–IT relationship. Yet, the corelation between a good relationship and the ability to deliver value with IT makes it imperative that leaders do all they can to develop effective interpersonal and interfunctional business–IT relations. It is unfortunately still incumbent on IT leadership to take on the bulk of this task, if only because it will make IT organizations more effective. Business–IT relationships are complex, with interactions of many types, at many levels, and between both individuals and across functional and organizational entities. This chapter has not only identified and explored what a strong business–IT relationship should look like in its many dimensions but also has described the four major components needed to build it: competence, credibility, interpersonal skills, and trust. Unfortunately, business–IT relationships still leave a lot to be desired in most organizations. Recognizing what it takes to build a strong business–IT partnership is so closely related to what is needed to deliver IT value may help to focus more attention on these mission-critical activities.

References

Anonymous. "Senior IT People Excluded from IT Decision-Making." *Career Development International* 7, no. 6/7 (2002).

Bassellier, G., and I. Benbasat. "Business Competence of Information Technology Professionals: Conceptual Development and Influence on IT-Business Partnerships." *MIS Quarterly* 28, no. 4 (December 2004).

Buchanan, L. "Sweat the Small Stuff." *Harvard Business Review* (April 2005). hbr.org/2005/04/sweat-the-small-stuff/ar/1 (accessed March 10, 2011).

Day, J. "Strangers on the Train: The Relationship of the IT Department with the Rest of the Business." *Information Technology and People* 20, no. 1. (2007).

Feeny, D., B. Edwards, and K. Simpson. "Understanding the CEO/CIO Relationship." *MIS Quarterly* 16, no. 4 (1992).

Feeny, D., and L. Willcocks. "Core IS Capabilities for Exploiting Information Technology." *Sloan Management Review* 39, no. 3 (Spring 1998).

Flint, D. "Senior Executives Don't Always Realize the True Value of IT." Gartner Inc., ID Number: COM-22-5499, June 21, 2004.

Galford, R., and A. Drapeau. "The Enemies of Trust." *Harvard Business Review* #R0302G, February 2003.

Gerrard, M. "Three Critical Success Factors in the Business/IT Relationship." Gartner Inc., ID Number: G00143352, October 18, 2006.

Gold, R. "Perception *Is* Reality: Why Subjective Measures Matter and How to Maximize Their Impact." *Harvard Business School Publishing Balanced Scorecard Report*, July–August, 2006.

Gordon, S., and J. Gordon. "Organizational Options for Resolving the Tension Between IT Departments and Business Units in the Delivery of IT services." *Information Technology and People* 15, no. 4 (2002).

Greenberg, P., R. Greenberg, and Y. Antonucci. "Creating and Sustaining Trust in Virtual Teams." *Business Horizons* 50 (2007).

Guillemette, M., G. Paré, and H. Smith. "What's Your IT Value Profile?" *Cahier du GReSI #08-04.* Montréal, Canada: HEC Montréal, November 2008.

Hurley, R. "The Decision to Trust." *Harvard Business Review* #R0609B, September 2006.

Joni, S. "The Geography of trust." *Harvard Business Review* #R0403F, March 2004.

Kaarst-Brown, M. "Understanding an Organization's View of the CIO: The Role of Assumptions About IT." *MIS Quarterly Executive* 4, no. 2 (June 2005).

Kitzis, E., and B. Gomolski. "IT Leaders Must Think Like Business Leaders." Gartner Inc., ID Number: G00143430, October 26, 2006.

Levinson, M., and R. Pastore. "Transparency Helps Align IT with Business." *CIO Magazine,* June 1, 2005.

Luftman, J., and T. Brier. "Achieving and Sustaining Business-IT Alignment." *California Management Review* 41, no. 1 (Fall 1999).

Mahoney, J., and M. Gerrard. "IT Value Performance Tools Link to Business-IT Alignment." Gartner Inc., ID Number: G00152551, November 2, 2007.

McKeen, J., and H. Smith. *IT Strategy in Action.* Upper Saddle River, NJ: Pearson-Prentice Hall, 2008.

Overby, S. "Turning IT Doubters into True Believers: Executive Summary." *CIO Research Reports,* June 1, 2005.

Pascale, R., M. Millemann, and L. Gioja. "Changing the Way We Change." *Harvard Business Review,* November–December 2007.

Pawlowski, S., and D. Robey. "Bridging User Organizations: Knowledge Brokering and the Work of Information Technology Professionals." *MIS Quarterly* 28, no. 4 (2004).

Prewitt, E. "The Communication Gap." *CIO Magazine,* June 1, 2005.

Ross, J. "Trust Makes the Team Go 'Round." *Harvard Management Update* 11, no. 6 (June 2006): 3–6.

Ross, J., and P. Weill. "Six IT Decisions Your IT People Shouldn't Make." *Harvard Business Review* #R0211F, November 2002.

Schindler, E. "What IT Can Learn from the Marketing Department." CIO Web 2.0 Advisor, September 21, 2007. advice.cio.com/esther_schindler/what_it_can_learn_from_the_marketing_department (accessed March 10, 2011).

Smith, H., and J. McKeen. "Creating a Process-Centric Organization at FCC: SOA from the Top Down." *MIS Quarterly Executive* 7, no. 2 (June 2008): 71–84.

Tallon, P., K. Kramer, and V. Gurbaxani. "Executives' Perceptions of the Business Value of Information Technology: A Process-Oriented Approach." *Journal of Management Information Systems* 16, no. 4 (Spring 2000).

Upton, D., and B. Staats. "Radically Simple IT." *Harvard Business Review* R0803, March 2008.

Wailgum, T. "Why Business Analysts Are So Important for IT and CIOs." *CIO Magazine,* April 16, 2008a.

Wailgum, T. "Eight Reasons Why CIOs Think Their Application Developers Are Clueless." *CIO Magazine,* September 3, 2008b.

Weiss, J., and J. Hughes. "Want collaboration? Accept—and Actively Manage—Conflict." *Harvard Business Review* #R0503F, March 2005.

The Five IT Value Profiles

Each of the following profiles is a unique way for IT to contribute to an organization. One is not "better" than the other, nor is one profile more or less mature than any other. Each represents a different, consistent way of organizing IT to deliver value. Each is different in five ways: main activities, dominant skills and knowledge, the business–IT relationship, governance and decision-making, and accountabilities.

PROFILE A: PROJECT COORDINATOR. This type of IT function coordinates IT activities between the business and outsourcers. Therefore, the primary value it delivers is organizational flexibility through the IT outsourcing strategy it establishes and through promoting informed IT decision making in the business units. The Project Coordinator function works with the business units, helping them formalize their requirements, and then finds an outsourcer to develop and implement what is needed. The Project Coordinator also manages the relationships between vendors and business units, not only with the organization's current activities but also in planning for the future by developing strategic partnerships.

PROFILE B: SYSTEMS PROVIDER. The primary mission of the Systems Provider is to provide the organization with quality information systems at the lowest possible cost. Strategically, the Systems Provider uses the organization's business plans to set IT's goals, prepare budgets, and determine the resources needed to implement the organization's strategy for the required systems development projects.

PROFILE C: ARCHITECTURE BUILDER. The primary mission of this type of IT function is to link the firm's various business units by integrating computerized systems, data, and technological platforms. The Architecture Builder seeks to design a flexible architecture and infrastructure that will meet the company's needs. The architecture builder typically receives broad strategic direction from the organization and designs an architecture and infrastructure with which the organization can implement its strategy.

PROFILE D: PARTNER. The main objective of the Partner IT function is to create IT-enabled business capabilities to support current business strategies. IT and the business collaborate to achieve a two-way strategic alignment that is developed iteratively and reciprocally over time. The Partner is a catalyst for change in business processes and seeks to improve organizational efficiency. As guardian of the organization's business processes, the Partner's mission therefore extends far beyond its technological tools.

PROFILE E: TECHNOLOGICAL LEADER. The Technological Leader tries above all to use innovation to transform the organization's strategy. IT's main objective is therefore to identify opportunities, find innovative organizational applications for technology that will enable the organization to secure a significant competitive advantage, and then implement such applications.

Source: Guillemette et al. 2008.

APPENDIX B

Guidelines for Building a Strong Business–IT Relationship

The following was provided by a focus group member and is an excerpt from a company memo on improving the business–IT relationship:

Now more than ever, we must truly understand the business transformation agenda. This will require us to potentially interact differently than in the past or in a mode beyond what our executives may be looking for. We must:

- Stop acting as and being viewed as order takers once IT projects have been identified.
- Develop an understanding of business improvement ideas before they become initiatives or projects.
- Be prepared to offer alternative perspectives on business solutions.
- Be part of the strategic equation and have "feet on the street."
- Engage early before ideas and issues turn into projects.
- Continue to shape the solution during pre-concept and concept phases.

To develop a relationship with the business units where we are viewed as a trusted advisor and as adding value, we need to truly be part of their decision-making process and team. We must ask ourselves:

- Are we considered a member of the business's senior leadership team?
- Are we consulted before decisions are made or just asked to execute what has already been decided?
- Are we involved in shaping the content of the strategic agenda not just its schedule?

Creating a consistent forum for one-on-one strategic interaction should allow us to rise above the normal churn of issues, projects, or other regularly scheduled meetings and be positioned to truly start understanding where our help is needed. Potential short-term next steps include the following:

- Get invited to each business unit's leadership team meetings.
- Schedule a monthly 1-1 strategy meeting with no set agenda.

Chapter 5

Developing IT Professionalism[1]

"We had visitors from overseas meeting with us. At four o'clock p.m., Jack, our senior technician, just got up and left and didn't come back. We were all left floundering. The next day, when I asked him where he'd gone, he said he'd had to catch his regular train home!"

"So many of our people are in a 'what can you do for me?' mode. They don't want to wear a pager. They are arrogant. They don't take the time to understand the impact of their work on the business. They don't seem to care."

"Some IT people simply don't understand organizational dynamics. I've seen them send blistering e-mails to people with cc's to the whole world. How can they do that?"

These anecdotes from recent conversations with IT managers suggest that IT professionalism is a growing problem for them and for their organizations. Managers are frustrated that many of their newer employees simply don't understand what it means to "be professional" in their jobs. And older staff are sometimes stuck in a comfort zone, doing a job that was acceptable fifteen years ago and not recognizing that standards of working behavior have been ratcheted up since then.

"Our colleges and universities don't teach professionalism," remarked one IT manager. Neither do companies, other managers pointed out. Instead, professionalism remains an unarticulated set of working behaviors, attitudes, and expectations. Yet IT professionalism has never been more important. The days when eccentric IT workers were hidden away in a "glass house" or ivory tower somewhere are long gone. Teamwork—with users, vendors, consultants, and business partners—is the name of the game today, and with it comes an increased dependency on and interaction with others. And professionalism is the glue that keeps teams of diverse individuals working together toward the same goal. Today IT workers are being held accountable to this new, unwritten set of standards that governs not only their work and how they, themselves, are perceived, but also how the whole of IT is perceived by the rest of the organization and others outside it. No wonder IT managers want to polish up their people a little!

---

[1]Smith, H. A., and J. D. McKeen, "Developing IT Professionalism," *Communications of the Association for Information Systems* 12, article 20 (October 2003): 312–325. Reproduced by permission of the Association for Information Systems.

This chapter provides a composite picture of IT professionalism and how to develop it and is derived from personal interviews with IT managers and research about professionalism in several occupational groups. It first defines what is meant by *professionalism* and distinguishes it from the traditional meaning of *professional*. Next it explores the role of management in creating an environment where professionalism is either encouraged or discouraged. Then it looks at the specific ways an IT worker is expected to demonstrate professionalism and contrasts these with behaviors that are deemed to be unprofessional. Finally, it identifies several actions that managers can take to develop professionalism in their IT staff.

PROFESSIONAL VERSUS PROFESSIONALISM

Although IT specialists have called themselves "professionals" for a long time, it is clear that IT work does not meet most of the traditional standards for this classification. A classic profession is characterized by a systematic body of theory; recognized professional authority; community sanctions; a regulative code of ethics; and a culture of norms, values, and symbols (Caplow 1966; Greenwood 1965). These characteristics are clearly met by the well-established professional groups in U.S. society (e.g., accountants, doctors, engineers). In fact, IT workers have a systematic body of theory, but they meet none of the other criteria for an established professional group.

> Professionalism is a description you hope others will apply to you, not a set of degrees of job qualifications (Maister 1993).

In contrast, *professionalism* refers to a person's attitude to, behavior on, and capabilities in the job. Many occupational groups and businesses use the term *professional* to refer to this aspect of their work, rather than to its more traditional meaning. The terminology is further confused by the fact that no generally accepted norm constitutes *professionalism*. Specific behavior or attitudes may be professional in one occupation or organization and not in another. A recent Internet search yielded literally thousands of relevant sites containing professional behavior standards for such widely diverse groups as real estate salespeople, audiologists, librarians, and party planners, as well as lawyers, doctors, and other traditional professionals. Clearly, professionalism is on people's minds.

A general list of professional behaviors in many occupational groups can read like an endorsement of motherhood. And yet these various groups have felt it is necessary to write down such expectations as the following:

- *"Treat your peers with respect and consideration"* (Belilos 1998).
- *"Behave with integrity at all times"* (Belilos 1998).
- *"A professional does not make hateful or threatening statements about others"* (Boushka 1998).
- *"A professional does not behave in a bizarre manner"* (Boushka 1998).
- *"A professional shows up on time and is prepared"* (Chial 1998).

On further analysis, it is clear that professionalism actually involves several different *sets* of behaviors, such as those oriented toward an employer (e.g., loyalty, identification with company values), those oriented toward clients (e.g., commitment and enthusiasm, capacity to solve problems), and those oriented toward a peer group (e.g., maintaining skills) (Scott 1967; Texas State Library 2002). In addition, professionalism also involves adherence to certain ethical standards—of an employer, the state, and one's occupational group. More recently, the term *professionalism* is also being widely used in business to refer to a broad set of job capabilities such as ability to manage commitments, ability to deal with cultural diversity, and ability to cope with change.

Several different approaches have been taken toward delineating what is meant by IT professionalism in recent years. For example, the Association for Computing Machinery (ACM) established a Code of Ethics and Professional Conduct in 1992, which outlines three main sets of imperatives (for the complete list, see Appendix A):

- *General moral imperatives* (e.g., I will give proper credit for intellectual property and honor confidentiality.)
- *Specific professional responsibilities* (e.g., I will acquire and maintain professional competence; I will accept and provide appropriate professional review.)
- *Organizational leadership imperatives* (e.g., I will manage personnel and resources to design and build information systems that enhance the quality of working life; I will ensure that users and those who will be affected by a system have their needs clearly articulated during the assessment and design of requirements.).

The University of Virginia's Department of Computer Sciences has also identified a number of areas in which IT professionalism could/should be exercised, such as censorship, hacking, fraud and dishonesty in business, netiquette, privacy, and computer viruses. (For a complete list, see Appendix B.) Tom DeMarco describes four key characteristics of IT professionalism in *The Responsible Software Engineer* (Myers et al. 1997):

1. *Proficient.* IT work is done with deftness, agility, and skill.
2. *Permanent.* IT professionals are permanently dedicated to IT work.
3. *Professing.* IT workers declare themselves to be part of the IT profession.
4. *Promise keeping.* IT workers make and keep promises to themselves about what they will and won't do.

Although it is clearly desirable for IT workers to ascribe to all these standards, they do not fully address the areas of attitude and behavior that most IT managers want to see from their IT workers. Therefore, other writers have documented some very specific tactical behaviors that they feel constitute IT professionalism:

- A professional makes a reasonable investment in the tools of the trade, such as a PC or laptop with current technology.
- A professional makes himself available to support his work in an on-call situation with reasonable reliability and frequency.
- A professional does not overcommit his personal time in a manner that conflicts with his responsibilities.
- A professional should not criticize his employer or his employer's industry (Boushka 1998).

The problem with these types of statements is that they are too specific and fail to apply in many situations. The solution is, therefore, to identify a set of principles of professionalism that IT workers and managers can use to identify specific appropriate behaviors for their jobs and against which they can evaluate their own and others' behaviors in a wide variety of circumstances (Maister 1993).

PRINCIPLES OF PROFESSIONALISM FOR IT MANAGEMENT

Principles of Managing for Professionalism

- Corporate values and behavior can promote or discourage professionalism.
- Much professional behavior is "caught," not taught.

- Expectations of professionalism should be consistent from the top down and through all parts of the organization.
- Companies get the behavior they actually expect, not the behavior they say they want.

Professionalism in the workplace per se has not been studied by researchers, although a great deal of work has been done on organizational citizenship behavior (OCB), which is a surrogate for some forms of professionalism. OCB is defined as an employee's willingness to go above and beyond the roles that he or she has been assigned (Organ 1990) and includes such behaviors as helping others, enhancing the social and psychological context that supports task performance, peacemaking, courtesy, and taking steps to avoid problems for others (Organ 1990; Podsakoff et al. 2000). Two meta-analysis studies have shown that such behaviors will occur if and only if employees are emotionally attached to the organization (Organ and Ryan 1995; Podsakoff et al. 2000). These findings underline the importance of an organization's leadership in establishing an environment in which people *want* to behave professionally. Thus, IT professionalism will flourish in some environments and be stifled in others.

It is important that a positive environment for IT professionalism be created and nurtured within the organization because professionalism is not usually taught but is, rather, picked up by osmosis through observation and interaction with others, particularly with leaders and managers. Anecdotal evidence suggests that management is responsible for much unprofessional behavior at work. "We've turfed people out and brought in outside contractors. How can we blame them for disloyalty?" asked one manager. Another noted, "We've slashed funding for all the training in 'soft skills.' It's easy to get money for Java training but not for anything to do with emotional intelligence." One company was trying to do something about management's influence in this area. "We are working with HR to develop our senior management, from the CIO down, to change their behaviors, which will, in turn, send a message through our teams that we are changing," stated the manager.

Other parts of an organization can also drive out professionalism in IT workers. "Human resources can often create programs that discourage professionalism," stated one manager. "If you're treated as a nine-to-fiver and not given the benefits of a professional, why should you act like one?" "If people see their leaders acting without integrity, how can we expect to see it in lower-level workers?" said another. Similarly, too many managers send mixed messages about the behaviors they value. For example, they may *say* they want innovation and "out-of-the-box thinking," but they make it clear that mistakes and risks will not be tolerated. Tom Siebel of Siebel Systems believes that professionalism should be one of a company's core values. "Too many companies . . . have an arrogant self-image. . . . I want to be absolutely certain that our values drive our behavior and not vice versa" (Fryer 2001). In other words, companies get the behavior that they model themselves.

The daily working environment can also stifle professionalism. Outside consultants are frequently perceived to be more professional than internal staff. This is often because of the "baggage" with which most IT workers have to deal. Outsiders have fewer distractions, are given better instructions about their work, have fewer demands on their time (e.g., meetings, politics), get more support, and receive less e-mail. "What has happened to our own people that we can't see professionalism in them?" asked one manager. Another answered, "They've had to endure bad management."

Tips for IT Managers

- Identify your corporate values and *live them.*
- Measure and reward what you value.
- Model professionalism for your staff.

- Seek out and eliminate inconsistencies between espoused company values and actual HR and management practices.
- Provide mentoring and training (if possible) in professional attitudes and behavior.

PRINCIPLES OF PROFESSIONALISM FOR IT WORKERS

As noted above, professionalism is actually several different sets of attitudes and behaviors that an IT worker is expected to display at all times. Five sets of behaviors can be considered indicative of IT professionalism:

1. *Comportment.*   This old-fashioned word covers one's appearance and manners on the job. Although *technically* neither attribute should make a difference to one's job performance, *practically* they do. It is unfortunate but true that it is much easier to acquire the label "unprofessional" than to reverse it. IT workers would be wise to be aware that perceptions of professionalism are sometimes equally as important as actual behavior on the job. Thus, if an IT worker does not appear to fit the image of a professional, particularly if his or her appearance is at odds with that of the rest of the organization, what he or she has to say may be immediately discounted by others. A good example of this is casual dress, which is often misinterpreted by those outside IT. As Tom Siebel explains it, "Dressing in jeans and a T-shirt to greet the CEO of a major financial institution, who just got off the plane from Munich, is not acceptable" (Fryer 2001). Furthermore, "Everyone's definition of casual is different," stated one participant, "and it's easy to go from casual dress to casual approaches to work."

   Similarly, manners and bearing are often perceived to be surrogates for professionalism. This explains the emphasis on treating one's colleagues and customers with courtesy and respect in many of the codes of professionalism described above. Siebel notes, "Our comportment is always professional, whether we are interacting with each other or with customers, partners, suppliers, or others" (Fryer 2001). In addition, it is not professional to take disagreements personally. "We should be able to disagree without rancor," said one manager. "IT people are particularly bad at finger-pointing when a problem arises. Defensiveness is unprofessional. It's better to just help solve the problem and get on with the job."

Principle 1: *An IT worker's professionalism is often judged by his or her dress and manner toward others.*	**Tip:** When in doubt, an IT worker should model the comportment of the *best* exemplar in the office and dress as well as one's immediate supervisor.

2. *Preparation.*   No one appears more unprofessional than someone who doesn't know what he or she is doing. For an IT worker, this means having not only the technical skills to do a job but also a good understanding of the business context in which the work is taking place. "The biggest complaint we get is that our people don't understand the business," remarked one manager. "Far too many people see technology itself as the end product, instead of as a business enabler." "Businesspeople are always asking, 'How much credence should I place in this IT person?'" explained another. Understanding the big picture is essential to doing a good job both because it helps IT people make better decisions about their work for the organization *and* because it gives users confidence that the person working on their problem will do a good job.

   Preparation is important in an IT worker's daily interactions with others as well. People are perceived as more professional if they are well organized and proactive. Good organization skills involve anticipating problems and dealing with them before they become bigger, careful planning of meetings and schedules (e.g., using an agenda), and a disciplined approach to work (e.g., a methodology, root-cause analysis). Preparation *for* work accomplishes two very important goals. First, it means that an IT professional's promises can be relied on to be met because enough homework has been done to make educated commitments. Second, it is respectful of the other people whose efforts must be integrated with those of the IT worker. The achievement of both goals helps others to have confidence in what the IT worker says and does, and this is the very essence of professionalism.

Principle 2: *Professionalism means that others can trust what an IT worker says and does. This comes from being prepared and organized.* **Tips:** Take time to interact informally with users and "pick their brains" about how the business operates.	When starting a new job or project, take time to get to know the business. Seek out and make use of any resources that will help better organize your work (e.g., project offices, methodologies, online training, or others who have organizational skills).

3. *Communication.*   Although "a failure to communicate" can be a catch-all category when things go wrong, it remains true that good communication skills are a fundamental aspect of all professional relationships and, therefore, contribute strongly to the effectiveness of IT work. Good communication is actually made up of a number of subskills. First, IT workers need to know how to write. Misspellings, grammatical errors, and poorly organized documents are all too common in the IT field. Such sloppiness not only makes the author look unprofessional but can also fail to get the

message across because it is difficult to read. Another common mistake is to dash off e-mails as if they were not "real" documents. However, as e-mail is increasingly taking the place of traditional office correspondence, the same care must be taken with it as with a business letter.

Beyond writing, a whole host of skills must be mastered surrounding e-mail and voice communication. All IT professionals should have a routine for managing such media (e.g., updating voice-mail messages daily, returning messages within twenty-four hours, even if it's just to respond that you'll reply shortly). Responsiveness is a much-desired trait in an IT professional, and living up to a reasonable standard in this area ensures that the IT worker is perceived as being in control of his or her work and able to manage commitments.

Communication concerning commitments is especially important. IT workers should document important commitments in writing and include any caveats that might change what they have promised (e.g., a schedule or a budget). Paperwork should not languish on a desk week after week. And when situations change or problems arise, IT professionals must be willing to communicate the bad news and deal with the consequences. The following true story illustrates how an IT professional should do this:

> [When] Richard realized that the extra work was going to cost considerably more than had been planned, [he] decided . . . it was best to bring the extra costs forward to the Project Committee. "It was a brutal meeting," he remembered. "The senior guys beat us up. We had to sell like crazy." But eventually the committee agreed it was the best direction to go and gave them the money they needed to hire consultants . . . to help them do the job. (Smith 1999)

In addition, IT workers must understand how and when to communicate appropriately. Many people receive hundreds of unnecessary e-mails daily because someone hits the "Reply All" button for no good reason. Others copy large numbers of people when only one or two need to know the information. Still others, as the story at the beginning of this chapter illustrates, try to handle sensitive issues in an e-mail, rather than in person or by phone. Finally, it is unfortunate but true that most people's listening skills need improvement. IT workers need to cultivate the ability to ask questions, take checkpoints in meetings, and confirm that they have indeed understood what is being said.

Principle 3: *Good communication skills are essential to building professional relationships.*

Tips: Seek advice from others who are viewed as being highly professional about how they communicate (e.g., standards of responsiveness, addressing a problem on the job).

Find out about and use resources that are available to assist with written communication (e.g., spell-checkers, editors, etc.).

Adopt communication routines and standards even if none are expected.

Document any commitments and promises, and make sure they are met.

4. *Judgment.*   IT workers often have difficult decisions to make, and it is very easy to get caught in a professionalism paradox. That is, people who are agreeable and who don't make waves are often *perceived* as being more professional than those who speak out

and say "no" when they are asked to do something unreasonable. As a result, it is not uncommon to see IT people and others give a lip-service commitment to a decision when they don't agree with it and don't plan to make it work. This may buy an individual IT worker a short period of grace, but it is not professional and doesn't work in the longer term. "We often wimp out, bow to pressure, and undertake something that is highly unlikely to be realized. We do this again and again" (Gack 2002). As a result, IT workers are often perceived as making bad decisions.

IT workers need to know how to make the right choices for the organization as a whole, which means being able to take a strategic view of what they are being asked to do. For example, they must know when they *must* do something, such as fixing a serious problem for the business, even if it means taking time away from another job. In short, they must know where they can add true business value. In making such difficult judgment calls, it is important for an IT worker to maintain a service orientation while not being servile. "Inflexibility is seen as being unprofessional," one manager noted. Thus, good judgment involves being honest about the full implications of a decision, stating concerns and objections, listening to the other points of view, negotiating a direction forward that everyone can live with, and documenting what was agreed.

Good judgment also includes making sure that decisions are in keeping with the organization's ethical guidelines (e.g., privacy) and that they follow all legal and moral standards. Although it is hoped that no IT worker or organization would deliberately contravene these, it is often the case that poor decisions occur simply because of ignorance. A recent furor over a company database that was outsourced to a third-party service provider, thus contravening privacy laws, is a good example. Laws and standards in computing are changing rapidly. Therefore, it is essential that IT workers maintain currency on those rules that affect their work and their business so they may advise others appropriately.

Principle 4: *Professionalism means making the right choices for the organization as a whole, not just a specific area.* **Tips:** Be sure of all the facts before making a decision. Don't get pressured into it.	Always maintain a service orientation. Become familiar with corporate standards and changing laws regarding computing. Don't be inflexible; try to find a negotiated way forward that everyone can accept.

5. *Attitude.*   Attitude is such an important part of professionalism that some feel that "firms should hire for attitude and train for skill" (Maister 1993). People often believe that their skills qualify them as professionals when it is actually attitude that most believe is the distinguishing feature of a true professional. Basically, professionalism is about *caring*—about doing a job to the best of one's ability and about doing the right thing for the company. People who care have a "can do" approach to their work, seek to constantly improve their skills, take reasonable risks, and are responsible and accountable for their work. They are willing to invest their time and energy in helping others and "go the extra mile." "We are looking for passion without arrogance or cockiness," said one IT manager. Stated another, "The best people are those who have an 'I can do it' attitude and

who are looking for challenges, rather than those who just have particular skills. These can always be developed or supplemented." A professional is also willing to accept criticism and coaching for personal growth and works well in a team, sharing the credit and not blaming others when problems arise.

Other characteristics of a positive attitude include calmness, stability, and self-control. Professionals do not lose their temper easily, display an erratic temperament, or make highly critical remarks, especially of others or of their companies. This attitude should extend beyond daily work into the public arena as well. "People often forget that they represent our company even when they aren't at work," stated one participant. One manager from a well-known manufacturer explained how his company had set up a hotline for employees who heard about problems with the company's products while socializing outside work. The phone number enabled them to learn and do something about the problem, and this reinforced the company's image of professionalism. In smaller communities IT workers and managers may be expected to represent their companies at charitable events. Their attitude may be important in building respect for the company in their communities.

It should be pointed out that these characteristics are ideals, and it is unrealistic to expect everyone to exhibit all of them in practice. "People are built in many ways and have different styles," said one manager. "We must be able to understand and accommodate them and make the blend work."

There is often a great deal of interaction between an organization's culture and individual attitudes. A stifling or highly politicized work environment, lack of appreciation and support, and poor communication about organization or team goals can destroy or dampen an IT worker's positive attitude. One manager noted that many "underperforming" staff simply need better support and education to work more effectively, and providing these can lead to dramatic differences in both attitude and productivity.

Principle 5: *Professionalism means a positive attitude toward work, other people, and one's employer.*

Tips: Seek opportunities for personal growth—courses, coaching, or new experiences.

Save highly critical remarks for private communication.

Recognize that you, your department and your employer will be judged by your attitude and demeanor.

DEVELOPING PROFESSIONALISM: ADVICE TO IT MANAGERS

Some people appear to have been born with professional skills, although it is widely agreed that professionalism can be developed in all IT workers. The following list provides a good start to the promotion of professionalism:

- *Get consensus on the meaning of professionalism.* Because it is a "soft" skill, *professionalism* means different things in different organizations. A team meeting to identify the key elements of professionalism in a particular company can help clarify expectations and develop group values around these behaviors.

- *Articulate values.*   It is pointless to preach one set of values and reward others. Ideally, corporate values should be consistently upheld throughout the company. However, where they are not, try to articulate where they differ and then help IT workers to make effective judgments (e.g., How much will risk taking actually be valued?)
- *Provide resources to support professionalism.*   Ideally, these should include training, but where this is not possible, provide books or speakers who will address this topic to your staff. Similarly, making some administrative support available can be very useful in helping people to appear professional to those outside IT. At a minimum, ensure that resources such as document templates, editors, and guidelines for e-mail are made available for staff to use.
- *Grow professionalism in small steps.*   People will not develop these skills overnight. Managers should work with individuals in their groups on specific areas of professionalism, then provide them with the coaching and support they need.
- *Offer intensive mentoring for staff who are willing to change.*   Employees who appear to be more malleable and willing to listen should be given attention from a manager. This can help them develop professional skills more rapidly.
- *Help people find their niche.*   No employee (even those who appear to be unwilling to change) should be sidelined; doing so will only leave the employee increasingly further behind in a rapidly evolving workplace. A better strategy is to help employees identify where they feel they can best make a contribution and to help them develop the particular professional skills they will need.
- *Weed out people whose attitudes are destructive.*   If people are consistently negative about change, managers must try to get rid of them or at least contain them in the short term. A longer-term plan must be put in place for dealing with such individuals because they could risk poisoning their whole team's effectiveness.

Conclusion

Professional is a label that many in IT seek but few earn. Unlike the traditional definition of the term, today's professional is a member of any occupational group who behaves in a professional manner. Professionalism can mean different things to different groups and organizations, but there is general agreement that it constitutes a set of behaviors that are expected over and above the technical skills of the job. This chapter has explored what professionalism means for IT workers. By delineating five principles of behavior, it has presented some of the areas in which IT managers should expect to see professionalism displayed. Comportment, preparation, communication, judgment, and attitude are "soft" skills but are often as important as technical ability for getting a job done. Professionalism is difficult to teach but easy to *catch* through exposure to exemplars, corporate and team culture, values and standards, and an environment that appreciates and rewards this behavior. As IT work becomes increasingly interconnected with that of the rest of the organization, the professionalism of IT staff will make a big difference in the effectiveness of the IT department as a whole. IT managers would, therefore, be well advised to make professionalism an important value for all IT staff and to recognize and reward it when it is displayed.

References

Belilos, C. "Networking on the Net: Professionalism, Ethics and Courtesy on the Net." Vancouver, BC: CHIC Hospitality Consulting Services, 1998.

Boushka, B. "Business Ethics, Professionalism and the Workplace: Information Systems." High ProductivityPublishing.com, 1998. www.doaskdotell.com/hppub/3rdparty/isethics.htm (accessed March 9, 2011).

Caplow, T. "The Sequence of Professionalization." In H. Vollmer and D. Mills (Eds.), *Professionalization*. Englewood Cliffs, NJ: Prentice-Hall, 1966.

Chial, M. "Conveying Expectations About Professional Behavior." *Audiology Today* 10, no. 4 (July 1998).

Fryer, B. "Tom Siebel of Siebel Systems: High Tech the Old-fashioned Way." *Harvard Business Review* March (2001).

Gack, G. "Professionalism." Information Technology Effectiveness Inc., 2002. www.iteffectiveness.com/professionalism.htm (accessed January 20, 2003).

Greenwood, W. *Management and Organizational Behavior Theory: An Interdisciplinary Approach*. Cincinnati, OH: Southwestern Publishing, 1965.

Maister, D. *True Professionalism*. New York: The Free Press, 1993.

Myers, C., T. Hall, and D. Pitt. *The Responsible Software Engineer*. Heidelberg, Germany: Springer-Verlag, 1997.

Organ, D. "The Motivational Basis of Organizational Citizenship Behavior." In B. M. Staw and L. L. Cummings (Eds.), *Research in Organizational Behavior* 12 (pp. 43–72). Greenwich, CT: JAI Press, 1990.

Organ, D., and K. Ryan. "A Meta-analytic Review of Attitudinal and Dispositional Predictors of Organizational Citizenship Behavior." *Personnel Psychology* 48 (1995): 775–802.

Podsakoff, P., S. MacKenzie, J. Paine, and D. Bachrach. "Organizational Citizenship Behaviors: A Critical Review of the Theoretical and Empirical Literature and Suggestions for Future Research." *Journal of Management* 26, no. 3 (2000): 513–63.

Scott, W. *Organizational Theory and Behavior Analysis for Management*. Homewood, IL: Irwin, 1967.

Smith, H. "Leading Change at Investco." 1999. www.itworldcanada.com (accessed January 20, 2003).

Texas State Library and Archives Commission. "Small Library Management Training Program." www.tsl.state.tx.us/ld/tutorials/professionalism/IB.html (accessed January 20, 2003).

APPENDIX A

ACM Code of Ethics and Professional Conduct 1992

1. General Moral Imperatives
I will . . .
  1.1. Contribute to society and human well-being.
  1.2. Avoid harm to others.
  1.3. Be honest and trustworthy.
  1.4. Be fair and take action not to discriminate.
  1.5. Honor property rights including copyrights and patents.
  1.6. Give proper credit for intellectual property.
  1.7. Respect the privacy of others.
  1.8. Honor confidentiality.

2. Personal Responsibilities
I will . . .
  2.1. Strive to achieve the highest quality, effectiveness, and dignity in both the process and products of professional work.
  2.2. Acquire and maintain professional competence.
  2.3. Know and respect existing laws pertaining to professional work.
  2.4. Accept and provide appropriate professional review.
  2.5. Give comprehensive and thorough evaluations of computer systems and their impacts, including analysis of possible risks.
  2.6. Honor contracts, agreements, and assigned responsibilities.
  2.7. Improve public understanding of computing and its consequences.

  2.8. Access computing and communication resources only when authorized to do so.

3. Organizational Leadership Imperatives
I will . . .
  3.1. Articulate social responsibilities of members of an organizational unit and encourage full acceptance of those responsibilities.
  3.2. Manage personnel and resources to design and build information systems that enhance the quality of working life.
  3.3. Acknowledge and support proper and authorized uses of an organization's computing and communications resources.
  3.4. Ensure that users and those who will be affected by a system have their needs clearly articulated during the assessment and design of requirements; later the system must be validated to meet requirements.
  3.5. Articulate and support policies that protect the dignity of users and others affected by a computing system.
  3.6. Create opportunities for members of the organization to learn the principles and limitations of computer systems.

Source: Excerpted from ACM Code of Ethics and Professional Conduct, adopted October 16, 1992, Association for Computing Machinery. www.acm.org/constitution/code.html (accessed March 4, 2011).

APPENDIX B

IT Professional Standards and Professionalism

Professionalism and standards should be exercised in the following areas:

- Censorship
- Community values
- Computer ethics and social impact in schools
- Copyrights, patents, trademarks, intellectual property
- Crime
- Disabilities
- Discrimination and harassment
- Ethics
- Fraud and dishonesty in business
- Freedom of speech
- "Green" machines
- Hacking
- History of computing
- Impact
- Liabilities
- Netiquette
- Privacy
- Relationships
- Responsibilities
- Safety critical systems
- Viruses
- World codes

Source: Department of Computer Science, University of Virginia.

MINI CASE

Delivering Business Value with IT at Hefty Hardware[2]

"IT is a pain in the neck," groused Cheryl O'Shea, VP of retail marketing, as she slipped into a seat at the table in the Hefty Hardware executive dining room, next to her colleagues. "It's all technical mumbo-jumbo when they talk to you and I still don't know if they have any idea about what we're trying to accomplish with our Savvy Store program. I keep explaining that we have to improve the customer experience and that we need IT's help to do this, but they keep talking about infrastructure and bandwidth and technical architecture, which is all their internal stuff and doesn't relate to what we're trying to do at all! They have so many processes and reviews that I'm not sure we'll ever get this project off the ground unless we go outside the company."

"You've got that right," agreed Glen Vogel, the COO. "I really like my IT account manager, Jenny Henderson. She sits in on all our strategy meetings and seems to really understand our business, but that's about as far as it goes. By the time we get a project going, my staff are all complaining that the IT people don't even know some of our basic business functions, like how our warehouses operate. It takes so long to deliver any sort of technology to the field, and when it doesn't work the way we want it to, they just shrug and tell us to add it to the list for the next release! Are we really getting value for all of the millions that we pour into IT?"

"Well, I don't think it's as bad as you both seem to believe," added Michelle Wright, the CFO. "My EA sings the praises of the help desk and the new ERP system we put in last year. We can now close the books at month-end in 24 hours. Before that, it took days. And I've seen the benchmarking reports on our computer operations. We

are in the top quartile for reliability and cost-effectiveness for all our hardware and systems. I don't think we could get IT any cheaper outside the company."

"You are talking 'apples and oranges' here," said Glen. "On one hand, you're saying that we're getting good, cheap, reliable computer operations and value for the money we're spending here. On the other hand, we don't feel IT is contributing to creating new business value for Hefty. They're really two different things."

"Yes, they are," agreed Cheryl. "I'd even agree with you that they do a pretty good job of keeping our systems functioning and preventing viruses and things. At least we've never lost any data like some of our competitors. But I don't see how they're contributing to executing our business strategy. And surely in this day and age with increased competition, new technologies coming out all over the place, and so many changes in our economy, we should be able to get them to help us be more flexible, not less, and deliver new products and services to our customers quickly!"

The conversation moved on then, but Glen was thoughtful as he walked back to his office after lunch. Truthfully, he only ever thought about IT when it affected him and his area. Like his other colleagues, he found most of his communication with the department, Jenny excepted, to be unintelligible, so he delegated it to his subordinates, unless it absolutely couldn't be avoided. But Cheryl was right. IT was becoming increasingly important to how the company did its business. Although Hefty's success was built on its excellent supply chain logistics and the assortment of products in its stores, IT played a huge role in this. And to implement Hefty's new Savvy Store strategy, IT

[2]Smith, H. A., and J. D. McKeen. "Delivering Business Value with IT at Hefty Hardware," #1-L10-1-001, Queen's School of Business, May 2010. Reproduced by permission of Queen's University, School of Business, Kingston, Ontario, Canada.

would be critical for ensuring that the products were there when a customer wanted them and that every store associate had the proper information to answer customers' questions.

In Europe, he knew from his travels, IT was front and center in most cutting-edge retail stores. It provided extensive self-service to improve checkout; multichannel access to information inside stores to enable customers to browse an extended product base and better support sales associates assisting customers; and multimedia to engage customers with extended product knowledge. Part of Hefty's new Savvy Store business strategy was to copy some of these initiatives, hoping to become the first retailer in North America to completely integrate multimedia and digital information into each of its 1,000 stores. They'd spent months at the executive committee meetings working out this new strategic thrust—using information and multimedia to improve the customer experience in a variety of ways and to make it consistent in each of their stores. Now, they had to figure out exactly how to execute it, and IT was a key player. The question in Glen's mind now was how could the business and IT work together to deliver on this vision, when IT was essentially operating in its own technical world, which bore very little relationship to the world of business?

Entering his office, with its panoramic view of the downtown core, Glen had an idea. "Hefty's stores operate in a different world than we do at our head office. Wouldn't it be great to take some of our best IT folks out on the road so they could see what it's really like in the field? What seems like a good idea here at corporate doesn't always work out there, and we need to balance our corporate needs with those of our store operations." He remembered going to one of Hefty's smaller stores in Moose River and seeing how its managers had circumvented the company's stringent security protocols by writing their passwords on Post-it notes stuck to the store's only computer terminal.

So, on his next trip to the field he decided he would take Jenny, along with Cheryl and the Marketing IT Relationship Manager, Paul Gutierez, and maybe even invite the CIO, Farzad Mohammed, and a couple of the IT architects. "It would be good for them to see what's actually happening in the stores," he reasoned. "Maybe once they do, it will help them understand what we're trying to accomplish."

A few days later, Glen's e-mailed invitation had Farzad in a quandary. "He wants to take me and some of my top people—including you—on the road two weeks from now," he complained to his chief architect, Sergei Grozny. "Maybe I could spare Jenny to go, since she's Glen's main contact, but we're up to our wazoos in alligators trying to put together our strategic IT architecture so we can support their Savvy Stores initiative and half a dozen more 'top priority' projects. We're supposed to present our IT strategy to the steering committee in three weeks!"

"And I need Paul to work with the architecture team over the next couple of weeks to review our plans and then to work with the master data team to help them outline their information strategy," said Sergei. "If we don't have the infrastructure and integrated information in place there aren't going to be any 'Savvy Stores'! You can't send Paul and my core architects off on some boondoggle for a whole week! They've all seen a Hefty store. It's not like they're going to see anything different."

"You're right," agreed Farzad. "Glen's just going to have to understand that I can't send five of our top people into the field right now. Maybe in six months after we've finished this planning and budget cycle. We've got too much work to do now. I'll send Jenny and maybe that new intern, Joyce Li, who we're thinking of hiring. She could use some exposure to the business, and she's not working on anything critical. I'll e-mail Jenny and get her to set it up with Glen. She's so great with these business guys. I don't know how she does it, but she seems to really get them onside."

Three hours later, Jenny Henderson arrived back from a refreshing noontime workout to find Farzad's request in her priority in-box. "Oh #*!#*@!" she swore. She had a more finely nuanced understanding of the politics involved in this situation, and she was standing on a land mine for sure. Her business contacts had all known about the invitation, and she knew it was more than a simple request. However, Farzad, having been with the company for only eighteen months, might not recognize the olive branch that it represented, nor the problems that it would cause if he turned down the trip or if he sent a very junior staff member in his place. "I have to speak with him about this before I do anything," she concluded, reaching for her jacket.

But just as she swiveled around to go see Farzad, Paul Gutierez appeared in her doorway, looking furious. "Got a moment?" he asked and, not waiting for her answer, plunked himself down in her visitor's chair. Jenny could almost see the steam coming out of his ears, and his face was beet red. Paul was a great colleague, so mentally putting the "pause" button on her own problems, Jenny replied, "Sure, what's up?"

"Well, I just got back from the new technology meeting between marketing and our R&D guys, and it was just terrible!" he moaned. I've been trying to get Cheryl and her group to consider doing some experimentation with cell phone promotions—you know, using that new Japanese bar coding system. There are a million things you can do with mobile these days. So, she asked me to set up a demonstration of the technology and to have the R&D guys explain what it might do. At first, everyone was really excited. They'd read about these things in magazines and wanted to know more. But our guys kept droning on about 3G and 4G technology and different types of connectivity and security and how the data move around and how we have to model and architect everything so it all fits together. They had the business guys so confused we never actually got talking about how the technology might be used for marketing and whether it was a good business idea. After about half an hour, everyone just tuned out. I tried to bring it back to the applications we could develop if we just invested a little in the mobile connectivity infrastructure, but by then we were dead in the water. They wouldn't fund the project because they couldn't see why customers would want to use mobile in our stores when we had perfectly good cash registers and in-store kiosks!"

"I despair!" he said dramatically. "And you know what's going to happen don't you? In a year or so, when everyone else has got mobile apps, they're going to want us to do something for them yesterday, and we're going to have to throw some sort of stopgap technology in place to deal with it, and everyone's going to be complaining that IT isn't helping the business with what it needs!"

Jenny was sympathetic. "Been there, done that, and got the T-shirt," she laughed wryly. "These tech guys are so brilliant, but they can't ever seem to connect what they know to what the business thinks it needs. Sometimes, they're too

farsighted and need to just paint the next couple of steps of what could be done, not the 'flying around in jetpacks vision.' And sometimes I think they truly don't understand why the business can't see how these bits and bytes they're talking about translate into something that it can use to make money." She looked at her watch, and Paul got the hint. He stood up. "Thanks for letting me vent," he said. "You're a good listener."

"I hope Farzad is," she thought grimly as she headed down the hall. "Or he's going to be out of here by Thanksgiving." It was a sad truth that CIOs seemed to turn over every two years or so at Hefty. It was almost predictable. A new CEO would come in, and the next thing you knew the CIO would be history. Or the user satisfaction rate would plummet, or there would be a major application crash, or the executives would complain about how much IT cost, or there would be an expensive new system failure. Whatever it was, IT would always get blamed, and the CIO would be gone. "We have some world-class people in IT," she thought, "but everywhere we go in the business, we get a bad rap. And it's not always our fault."

She remembered the recent CIM project to produce a single customer database for all of Hefty's divisions: hardware, clothing, sporting goods, and credit. It had seemed to be a straightforward project with lots of ROI, but the infighting between the client divisions had dragged the project (and the costs) out. No one could agree about whose version of the truth they should use, and the divisions had assigned their most junior people to it and insisted on numerous exceptions, workarounds, and enhancements, all of which had rendered the original business case useless. On top of that, the company had undergone a major restructuring in the middle of it, and a lot of the major players had changed. "It would be a lot easier for us in IT if the business would get its act together about what it wants from IT," she thought. But just as quickly, she recognized that this was probably an unrealistic goal. A more practical one would be to find ways for business and IT to work collaboratively at all levels. "We each hold pieces of the future picture of the business," she mused. "We need to figure out a better way to put them together than simply trying to force them to fit."

Knocking on Farzad's door, she peeked into the window beside it. He seemed lost in thought but smiled when he saw her. "Jenny!" he exclaimed. "I was just thinking about you and the e-mail I sent you. Have you done anything about it yet?" When she shook her head, he gave a sigh of relief. "I was just rethinking my decision about this trip, and I'd like your advice." Jenny gave her own mental sigh and stepped into the office. "I think we have a problem with the business and we need to fix it—fast," she said. "I've got some ideas, and what to do about the trip is just part of them. Can we talk?" Farzad nodded encouragingly and invited her to sit down. "I agree with you, and I'd like to hear what you have to say. We need to do things differently around here, and I think with your help we can. What did you have in mind?"

Discussion Questions

1. Overall, how effective is the partnership between IT and the business at Hefty Hardware? Identify the shortcomings of both IT and the business.
2. Create a plan for how IT and the business can work collaboratively to deliver the Savvy Store program successfully.

MINI CASE
Investing in TUFS[3]

"Why do I keep this around?" Martin Drysdale wondered. "It infuriates me every time I see all that satisfaction over something that is now the bane of my existence."

He looked gloomily at the offending photo, which showed the project team happily "clinking" pop cans and coffee cups in a toast: "Here's to TUFS!" The Technical Underwriting Financial System (TUFS) was the largest single investment in IT ever made by Northern Insurance, and it was going to transform Northern by streamlining the underwriting processes and providing strategic e-business capabilities. The TUFS team had brought the project in on time and on budget, so the party was a thank-you for all of the team's dedicated, hard work. But it was two years ago when the camera captured the happy moment for posterity, and Martin, CIO for Northern, had celebrated with the rest.

"Yeah, right," Martin grimaced as he turned from the photo to the e-mail message on his computer screen, summoning him to a meeting with his boss that morning to discuss TUFS. The system had turned into a nightmare in its first few months of operation. Now his job was on the line. What was supposed to have brought efficiency to the underwriting process and new opportunities for top-line growth had become a major corporate money pit. TUFS was still eating up the vast majority of Northern's IT budget and resources to fix the underwriting errors that kept appearing, and resistance to the system had grown from sniping and grumbling into calls for Martin's head. "No wonder we're not saving any money, though, with senior underwriting managers still insisting on receiving some of their old reports, even though TUFS lets them look up the same information online anytime they want," Martin fumed. The meeting with the CFO was to discuss TUFS and the company's "very significant investment in this system." Feeling like a condemned prisoner on his way to the gallows, Martin grabbed his suit jacket, straightened his tie, and headed up to the seventh-floor executive suite.

An hour later Martin was feeling very well grilled as he was confronted with a long list of the problems with TUFS. The CFO, Melissa Freeman, had done her homework. Before her was a binder full of TUFS documentation, stretching back almost three years from when the project had been first identified. "According to my calculations, Northern has spent almost $4 million on this system, if you include all of the resources dedicated to fixing the problems identified *after* implementation," she noted. "And I have yet to see any cost savings in the underwriting department. Why?"

"It's true that there have been some unanticipated changes to the system that have cost us, but the underwriters have never bought into the system," Martin conceded. "They insist on following their old procedures and then using the system at the last possible moment as a double-check. What can we do if they won't use the system the way it was designed?"

"Could there *possibly* be a reason why they don't like the system?" Freeman asked. "It seems to me from looking at these change reports that the system hasn't been meeting our basic underwriting needs."

Martin acknowledged that there had been some problems. "But my guys are technicians, not underwriters. They didn't get much participation from the underwriters in the first place. The underwriting department wouldn't take the time to bring my people up to speed on what they needed and why. As well, we were facing a very tight deadline, which meant that we had to defer some of the functionality we had originally intended to include. That was senior management's decision, and everyone was informed about it when it was

[3]Smith, H. A., and J. D. McKeen. "Investing in TUFS," #9-L05-1-003, Queen's School of Business, February 2005. Reproduced by permission of Queen's University, School of Business, Kingston, Ontario, Canada.

made." He added that they were now asking for a TUFS training program and a help desk to handle questions that underwriters might face while using the system!

"A help desk and training program weren't in our original plan," Martin reminded Freeman. "These extras are eating away at the system's benefits." According to the business case prepared by the users, TUFS was supposed to pay for itself over its first two years of operations from savings realized from the underwriting process. The system's problems certainly accounted for some of the extra costs, but the users hadn't made any of the process changes that would help those savings be realized. "They think we can just plug in the system and cost savings will appear like magic. And other parts of the system are going to take time to deliver benefits."

The "other parts" he was referring to were the e-business capabilities that TUFS provided. "If you will recall, this system was approved in the days when we *had* to have e-business or we were going to be dinosaurs. In retrospect, we could have cut back on this functionality more easily and left some of the underwriting functionality in, but who knew?"

"Well, as you know, our financial resources are very limited at present." Freeman leaned forward.

"I've been asked to make some recommendations to the executive committee about whether or not we should put more money into this system. TUFS has been our number-one priority for two years now, and quite a few people are saying that enough is enough—that we need to make some major changes around here."

Martin took a deep breath, waiting for the ax to fall. Freeman continued, "What I need to know now from you is this: What went wrong with our TUFS investment, and what can we do to prevent these problems in the future? What do we need to do to realize the benefits that were projected for TUFS? How can we measure these benefits? And how can we best decide how to apportion our IT budget between TUFS and these other projects?"

As he slowly exhaled and felt his pulse resume, Martin nodded. "I've got some ideas. Can I get them to you in writing by the end of the week?"

Discussion Questions

1. What went wrong with the TUFS investment, and what can be done to prevent these problems in the future?
2. What does Northern need to do to realize the benefits that were projected for TUFS?
3. How can Northern measure these benefits?

MINI CASE
IT Planning at ModMeters[4]

Brian Smith, CIO of ModMeters, groaned inwardly as he listened to CEO John Johnson wrapping up his remarks. "So our executive team thinks there are real business opportunities for us in developing these two new strategic thrusts. But before I go to the board for final approval next month, I need to know that our IT, marketing, and sales plans will support us all the way," Johnson concluded.

Brian mentally calculated the impact these new initiatives would have on his organization. He had heard rumors from his boss, the COO, that something big was coming down. He had even been asked his opinion about whether these strategies were technically doable, *theoretically*. But *both* at once? Resources—people, time, and money—were tight, as usual. ModMeters was making a reasonable profit, but the CFO, Stan Abrams, had always kept the lid screwed down tightly on IT spending. Brian had to fight for every dime. How he was going to find the wherewithal to support not one but *two* new strategic initiatives, he didn't know.

The other VPs at this strategy presentation were smiling. Taking ModMeters global from a North American operation seemed to be a logical next step for the company. Its products, metering components of all types, were highly specialized and in great demand from such diverse customers as utility companies, manufacturers, and a host of other industries. Originally founded as Modern Meters, the firm had grown steadily as demand for its metering expertise and components had grown over the past century or so. Today ModMeters was the largest producer of metering components in the world with a full range of both mechanical and, now, digital products. Expanding into meter assembly with plants in Asia and Eastern Europe was a good plan, thought Brian, but he wasn't exactly sure how he was going to get the infrastructure in place to support it. "Many of these countries simply don't have the telecommunica-

tions and equipment we are going to need, and the training and new systems we have to put in place are going to be substantial," he said.

But it was the second strategic thrust that was going to give him nightmares, he predicted. How on earth did they expect him to put direct-to-customer sales in place so they could sell "green" electric meters to individual users? His attention was jerked back to the present by a flashy new logo on an easel that the CEO had just unveiled.

"In keeping with our updated strategy, may I present our new name—MM!" Johnson announced portentously.

"Oh, this is just great," thought Brian. "Now I have to go into every single application and every single document this company produces and change our name!"

Because of its age and scientific orientation, ModMeters (as he still preferred to call it) had been in the IT business a long time. Starting back in the early 1960s, the company had gradually automated almost every aspect of its business from finance and accounting to supply- chain management. About the only thing it didn't have was a fancy Web site for consumers, although even *that* was about to change. ModMeters currently had systems reflecting just about every era of computers from punch cards to PCs. Unfortunately, the company never seemed to have the resources to invest in reengineering its existing systems. It just layered more systems on top of the others. A diagram of all the interactions among systems looked like a plate of spaghetti. There was *no way* they were going to be able to support two new strategic thrusts with their current budget levels, he thought as he applauded the new design along with the others. "Next week's IT budget meeting is going to be a doozy!"

Sure enough, the following week found them all, except for the CEO, back in the same meeting

[4]Smith, H. A., and McKeen, J. D. "IT Planning at ModMeters," #1-L05-1-008, Queen's School of Business, September 2005. Reproduced by permission of Queen's University, School of Business, Kingston, Ontario, Canada.

room, ready to do battle. Holding his fire, Brian waited until all the VPs had presented their essential IT initiatives. In addition to what needed to be done to support the new business strategies, each division had a full laundry list of essentials for maintaining the *current* business of the firm. Even Abrams had gotten into the act this year because of new legislation that gave the firm's outside auditors immense scope to peer into the inner workings of every financial and governance process the organization had.

After listening carefully to each speaker in turn, Brian stood up. "As many of you know, we have always been cautious about how we spend our IT budget. We have been given a budget that is equal to 2 percent of revenues, which seriously limits what we in IT have been able to do for the company. Every year we spend a lot of time paring our project list down to bare bones, and every year we make do with a patchwork of infrastructure investments. We are now at the point where 80 percent of our budget in IT is fixed. Here's how we spend our money." Brian clicked on a PowerPoint presentation showing a multicolored pie chart.

"This large chunk in blue is just about half our budget," he stated. "This is simply the cost of keeping the lights on—running our systems and replacing a bare minimum of equipment. The red chunk is about 30 percent of the pie. This is the stuff we *have* to do—fixing errors, dealing with changes mandated by government and our own industry, and providing essential services like the help desk. How we divide up the remainder of the pie is what this meeting is all about."

Brian clicked to a second slide showing a second pie chart. "As you know, we have typically divided up the remaining IT budget proportionately, according to who has the biggest overall operating budget. This large pink chunk is you, Fred." Brian gestured at Fred Tompkins, head of manufacturing and the most powerful executive in the room. It was his division that made the firm's profit. The pink chunk easily took up more than half of the pie. Tompkins smiled. Brian went on, pointing out the slice that each part of the firm had been allotted in the previous year. "Finally, we come to Harriet and Brenda," he said with a smile. Harriet Simpson and Brenda Barnes were the VPs of human resources and marketing, respectively. Their tiny slivers were barely visible—just a few percent of the total budget.

"This approach to divvying up our IT budget may have served us well over the years"—Brian didn't think it had, but he wasn't going to fight past battles—"however, we all heard what John said last week, and this approach to budgeting doesn't give us *any* room to develop our new strategies *or* cover our new infrastructure or staffing needs. Although we might get a little more money to obtain some new applications and buy some more computers"—Abrams nodded slightly—"it won't get us where we need to go in the future."

A third graph went up on the screen, showing the next five years. "If we don't do something *now* to address our IT challenges, within five years our entire IT budget will be eaten up by just operations and maintenance. In the past we have paid minimal attention to our infrastructure or our information and technology architecture or to reengineering our existing systems and processes." A diagram of the "spaghetti" flashed on. "This is what you're asking me to manage in a cost-effective manner. It isn't pretty. We need a better plan for making our systems more robust and flexible. If we are going to be moving in new directions with this firm, the foundation just isn't there. Stan, you *should* be worried that we won't be able to give our auditors what they ask for. But you should also be worried about our risk exposure if one of these systems fails and about how we are going to integrate two new business ventures into this mess."

Tompkins looked up from his papers. It was clear he wasn't pleased with where this presentation was headed. "Well, I, for one, *need* everything I've asked for on my list," he stated flatly. "You can't expect me to be the cash cow of the organization and not enable me to make the money we need to invest elsewhere."

Brian was conciliatory. "I'm not saying that you don't, Fred. I'm just saying that we've been given a new strategic direction from the top and that some things are going to have to change to enable IT to support the whole enterprise better. For example, until now, we have always prioritized divisional IT projects on the basis of ROI. How should we prioritize these new strategic initiatives? Furthermore, these new ventures will require a *lot* of additional infrastructure, so we need to figure out a way to afford this. And right now our systems don't 'talk' to the ones running in other divisions because they don't use the same terminology. But in the future, if we're going to have systems that won't cost increasing amounts of our budget, we are going to have to simplify and integrate them better.

Tompkins clearly hadn't considered the enterprise's needs at all. He scowled but said nothing. Brian continued, "We are being asked to do some new things in the company. Obviously, John hopes there's going to be a payback, but it may take a while. New strategies don't always bear fruit right away." Now looking at Abrams, he said pointedly, "There's more to IT value than short-term profit. Part of our business strategy is to *make* new markets for our company. That requires investment, not only in equipment and product but also in the underlying processes and information we need to manage and monitor that investment."

Harriet Simpson spoke for the first time. "It's like when we hire someone new in R&D. We hire for quality because we want their ideas and innovation, not just a warm body. I think we need to better understand how we are going to translate our five key corporate objectives into IT projects. Yes, we need to make a profit, but Stan needs to satisfy regulators and Brenda's going to be on the hot seat when we start marketing to individuals. And we haven't even spoken about Ted's needs." As the VP of R&D, Ted Kwok was tasked with keeping one or more steps ahead of the competition. New types of products and customer needs would mean expansion in his area as well.

Abrams cleared his throat. "*All* of you are right. As I see it, we are going to have to keep the cash flowing from Fred's area while we expand. But Brian's got a point. We may be being penny wise and pound foolish if we don't think things through more carefully. We've put a lot of effort into developing this new strategy, and there *will* be some extra money for IT but not enough to do that plus everything all of you want. We need to retrench and regroup *and* move forward at the same time."

There was silence in the room. Abrams had an annoying way of stating the obvious without really helping to move the ball forward. Brian spoke again. "The way I see it, we have to understand two things before we can really make a new budget. First, we need to figure out how each of the IT projects we've got on the table contributes to one of our key corporate objectives. Second, we need to figure out a way to determine the *value* of each to ModMeters so that we can prioritize it. Then I need to incorporate a reasonable amount of IT regeneration so that we can continue to do new projects at all."

Everyone was nodding now. Brian breathed a small sigh of relief. That was step one accomplished. But step two was going to be harder. "We have a month to get back to the board with our assurances that the IT plan can incorporate the new strategies and what we're going to need in terms of extra funds to do this. As I said earlier, this is *not* just a matter of throwing money at the problem. What we need is a *process* for IT planning and budgeting that will serve us well over the next few years. This process will need to accomplish a number of things: It will need to take an *enterprise* perspective on IT. We're all in these new strategies together. It will have to incorporate all types of IT initiatives—our new strategies, the needs of Fred and others for the new IT to operate and improve our existing business, Stan's new auditing needs, and our operations and maintenance needs. In addition, we *must* find some way of allocating some of the budget to fixing the mess we have in IT right now. It must provide a better way to connect new IT work with our corporate objectives. It must help us prioritize projects with different types of value. Finally, it must ensure we have the business *and* IT resources in place to deliver that value."

Looking at each of his colleagues in turn, he asked, "Now how are we going to do this?"

Discussion Question

Develop an IT planning process for ModMeters to accomplish the demands as set out above.

Chapter 6

Information Management: The Nexus of Business and IT[1]

More than ever before, we are living in an information age. Yet until very recently, information and its sibling, knowledge, were given very little attention in IT organizations. Data ruled. And information proliferated quietly in various corners of the business—file cabinets, PCs, databases, microfiche, e-mail, and libraries. Then along came the Internet, and the business began to understand the power and the potential of information. For the past few years, businesses have been clamoring for IT to deliver more and better information to them (Smith and McKeen 2005c). As a result, information delivery has become an important part of IT's job.

Now that businesses recognize the value of improved information, IT is facing huge challenges in delivering it:

> Not only does effective information delivery require IT to implement new technologies, it also means that IT must develop new internal nontechnical and analytic capabilities. Information delivery makes IT work much more visible in the organization. Developing standard data models, integrating information into work processes, and forcing (encouraging) business managers to put the customer/ employee/supplier first in their decision making involves IT practitioners in organizational and political conflicts that most would likely prefer to avoid. Unfortunately, the days of hiding in the "glass house" are now completely over and IT managers are front and center of an information revolution that will completely transform how organizations operate. (Smith and McKeen 2005A)

This points out a truth that is only just beginning to sink into the organization's collective consciousness. That is, although information *delivery* may be the responsibility of IT, information *management* (IM) requires a true partnership between IT and the business. IT is *involved* with almost every aspect of IM, but information is the heart and soul of the business, and its management cannot be delegated or abdicated to IT. Thus, IM represents the true nexus of the business and IT. Because of this, IM has all the hallmarks of an emerging discipline—the offspring of a committed, long-term relationship between the business and

---

[1]Smith, H. A., and J. D. McKeen. "Information Management: The Nexus of Business and IT." *Communications of the Association for Information Systems* 19, article 3 (January 2007): 34–46. Reproduced by permission of the Association for Information Systems.

IT. It requires new skills and competencies, new frames of reference, and new processes. As is often the case, IT workers are further advanced in their understanding of this new discipline, but many business leaders are also recognizing their responsibilities in this field. In some organizations, notably government, IM is now a separate organizational entity, distinct from IT.

This chapter explores the nature and dimensions of IM and its implications for IT, looking at IM from the enterprise point of view. Information delivery can be viewed from a purely IT perspective, whereas information management addresses the business *and* IT issues and challenges in managing information effectively. The first section examines the scope and nature of IM and how it is being conceptualized in organizations. The next presents a framework for the comprehensive management of information. Then the key issues currently facing organizations in implementing an effective IM program are addressed. Finally, the chapter presents some recommendations for getting started in IM.

INFORMATION MANAGEMENT: HOW DOES IT FIT?

Information management is an idea whose time has come for a number of reasons. One focus group member explained it in this way:

> In today's business environment, it is a given that we must know who our customer is and ensure our organization's information enables us to make the right business decisions. As well, emerging regulations are starting to shape the IM requirements of all companies. These include privacy and security safeguards on customer information, long-term storage of historical records, and stronger auditability. We are now being held legally accountable for our information.

Thus, IM has three distinct but related drivers: (1) compliance, (2) operational effectiveness and efficiency, and (3) strategy.

Information, as we are now recognizing, is a key organizational resource, along with human and financial capital. Captured and used in the right way, many believe information is a different form of capital, known as *structural capital* (Stewart 1999). However, unlike human and financial capital, information is not finite. It cannot be used up, nor can it walk out the door. Furthermore, information capabilities—that is, the ability to capture, organize, use, and maintain information—have been shown to contribute to IT effectiveness, individual effectiveness, and overall business performance (Kettinger and Marchand 2005; Marchand et al. 2000). Therefore, many companies now believe that creating useful structural capital is a strategic priority (Davenport and Prusak 1998; Kettinger and Marchand 2005).

Unlike information technology, which provides the technology, tools, and processes with which to *manipulate data,* or knowledge management (KM), which focuses on how best to leverage the know-how and *intangible experience* of the organization's human capital, IM provides the mechanisms for managing enterprise information itself. IM represents the "meat" in the data–information–knowledge continuum and provides a foundation that can be used by both IT and KM to create business value (see Figure 6.1).

As noted earlier, organizations today are beset with demands for more and better information and more controls over it. IM is the means to get above the fray and clarify how the enterprise will manage information as an integrated resource. In theory, it

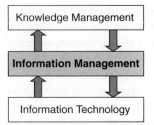

FIGURE 6.1   IM Is Fundamental to Organizational Success—Both IT Effectiveness and Individual Performance

covers all forms of information needed and produced by the business, both structured and unstructured, including the following:

- Customer information
- Financial information
- Operational information
- Product information
- HR information
- Performance information
- Documents
- E-mail and instant messages
- Images and multimedia materials
- Business intelligence
- Relationship information (e.g., suppliers, partners)

In practice, some of these forms will be more thoroughly managed than others, depending on the organization involved.

The "IM function" is also responsible for the complete information life cycle: acquisition or creation, organization, navigation, access, security, administration, storage, and retention. Because IM falls into the gray area between the business and IT and is not yet a separate organizational entity, many organizations are finding it is essential to develop an enterprisewide framework that clarifies the policies, principles, roles, responsibilities and accountabilities, and practices for IM in both groups.

A FRAMEWORK FOR IM

Because much information use crosses traditional functional boundaries, organizations must take an enterprise perspective on IM for it to be effective. A framework for implementing IM involves several stages that move from general principles to specific applications. Although these are presented as distinct activities, in practice they will likely evolve iteratively as the organization and its management learn by doing. For example, one company developed and implemented its privacy policy first then recognized the need for an information security policy. As this was being implemented, it created a more generic IM policy that incorporated the other two in its principles.

Stage One: Develop an IM Policy

A policy outlines the terms of reference for making decisions about information. It provides the basis for corporate directives and for developing the processes, standards, and guidelines needed to manage information assets well throughout the enterprise. Because information is a corporate asset, an IM policy needs to be established at a very senior management level and approved by the board of directors. This policy should provide guidance for more detailed directives on accountabilities, quality, security, privacy, risk tolerances, and prioritization of effort.

Because of the number of business functions affected by information, a draft policy should be developed by a multidisciplinary team. At minimum, IT, the privacy office, legal, HR, corporate audit, and key lines of business should be involved. "We had lots of support for this from our audit people," said one manager. "They recognize that an IM policy will help improve the traceability of information and its transformations, and this makes their jobs easier." Another recommended reviewing the draft policy with many executives and ensuring that all business partners are identified. "Ideally, the policy should also link to existing IM processes such as security classifications," stated another. "It's less threatening if people are familiar with what it implies, and this also helps to identify gaps in practices that need to be addressed."

Stage Two: Articulate the Operational Components

The operational components describe what needs to be in place in order to put the corporate IM policy into practice across the organization (see Figure 6.2). In turn, each component will have several "elements." These could vary according to what different organizations deem important. For example, the strategy component at one company has six elements: (1) interacting with the external environment, (2) strategic planning, (3) information life cycle, (4) general planning, (5) program integration, and (6) performance monitoring (for a description of the elements identified by this firm, see Appendix A). Together, the operational components act as a context to describe current IM practices in the organization and reference existing best practices in each area. "This is a living document, and you should expect it to be continually refined," noted a focus group member.

The IM framework's operational components and individual elements act as a discussion document to position IM in the business and to illustrate its breadth and scope. "There's a danger of IM being perceived as a 'technology thing,'" stated a manager. At present, it is mostly IT groups that are spearheading the IM effort, but they recognize

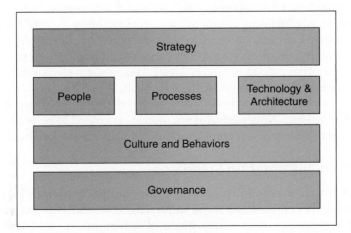

FIGURE 6.2 Operational Components of an IM Framework

that it shouldn't necessarily be located in IT permanently. "Ideally, we need a corporate information office that cuts across lines of business and corporate groups, just like IT," said another manager.

Stage Three: Establish Information Stewardship

Many roles and responsibilities associated with IM need to be clearly articulated. These are especially important to clarify because of the boundary-spanning nature of information. Both political and practical issues arise when certain questions are asked: Who is responsible for the quality of our customer data? Whose version of name and address do we use? Who must sign off on the accuracy of our financial information? Ideally, most organizations would like to have a single version of each of their key information subjects (e.g., customer, product, employees) that all lines of business and systems would use. This would enable proper protections and controls to be put in place. And this is clearly a long-term IM goal for most. However, legacy environments, political realities, and tight budgets mean that the reality is somewhat less perfect with duplicate versions of the same information and several variants being used by parts of the business.

Information stewards are businesspeople. They should be responsible for determining the meaning of information "chunks" (e.g., customer name and address) and their business rules and contextual use. They should be responsible for the accuracy, timeliness, consistency, validity, completeness, and redundancy of information. Stewards also determine who may access information according to privacy and security policies and provide guidance for the retention and deletion of information in accordance with regulatory and legal requirements. In addition, stewards make the information's characteristics available to a broad audience through the organization's metadata.

Stewardship, like IM, is an evolving role that few understand fully. Ideally, there should be one steward for each information subject, but this is nowhere near the reality in most organizations. One organization has established a working group for each of its major subjects, with representatives from all affected stakeholder groups as well as IT. The working groups' goals are to reduce duplicate records, correct information, simplify processes, and close "back doors." In the longer term, these groups hope to develop standard definitions and a formal stewardship process and ultimately use these to retool IT's data infrastructure.

"We are struggling with this concept," admitted a manager. "This is not a simple task, and no one in our business wants to take accountability as yet." Stewardship also takes time, and many business units are not yet prepared to allocate resources to it. "At present, we are hitching our wagons to other projects and hoping to make some progress in this way," said another manager. "Every area is taking some steps, but they're all at different levels of maturity. This can be frustrating because progress is so slow." All agreed that the role of information steward needs to be better defined and incorporated into organizational and HR models. New performance metrics also need to be established to monitor progress against these goals in ways that link IM activities to key business objectives.

Stage Four: Build Information Standards

Standards help ensure that quality, accuracy, and control goals can be met. When all parts of an organization follow the same standards, it is relatively easy to simplify the processes and technology that use a piece of information, said the focus group. Conversely, different information standards used by different business groups will inhibit effective IM. *Setting* information standards can be challenging, and it's even harder to actually *implement* them, participants noted. The latter is partly due to the large number of legacy applications in most organizations and also because it is difficult to get funding for this work.

Not all information needs to be standardized, however—only that which is used by more than one business unit. When information *is* used more broadly, a standard needs to be established. A metadata repository is useful for this. This repository stores information definitions; standards for use and change; and provides cross-references for all models, processes, and programs using a particular piece of information. A metadata repository can be jointly used by the business, when beginning a new project, and IT, when developing or modifying applications. It can be invaluable to both groups (and to the enterprise) in helping them to understand how their work will affect others, thus preventing potential problems.

Typically, cross-functional working groups composed of business and IT staff establish standards. "Metadata is really where the rubber meets the road," said one manager. "It can be a very powerful tool to prevent the duplication of data in the organization." However, it is a huge undertaking and takes time to show value. "You need strong IT executive support for this," he said. "It is not something that those outside of IT initially understand." The focus group recommended starting with what exists currently (e.g., a data warehouse), then growing from there. One firm initially established a procedure that any changes to production systems had to update the metadata repository first. "We weren't prepared for the demand this created," stated the manager involved. "It's much better to incorporate this step in front-end analysis than at the end of development."

Finally, education and awareness play an essential role at this stage. "We always underestimate the importance of awareness," said a participant. "We must make sure that no project starts in the organization that doesn't use standards. The only way to do this is to keep this issue continually in front of our business executives." The other group members agreed. "Standards are the cornerstone of IM," said one. "If they are followed, they will ensure we don't add further layers of complexity and new steps."

Standards require . . .

- a unique name and definition
- data elements, examples, and character length (e.g., name prefix)
- relationship rules
- implementation requirements
- spacing and order

ISSUES IN IM

As with anything new, those involved with IM in their organizations face a host of challenges and opportunities as they try to implement more effective processes and practices around information. Some of these can be mixed blessings in that they are both drivers of IM and complications (e.g., legislation). Others are simply new ways of looking at information and new perspectives on the way organizations work. Still others are genuinely new problems that must be addressed. When combined with the fact that IM "belongs" exclusively to neither IT nor the business, these add up to a huge organizational headache, especially for IT. "Sometimes the businesspeople are not ready for the disciplines associated with IM," said one manager. "If they're not ready, we move on to an area that is." Another said, "Sometimes it's more trouble than it's worth to involve the business, and we just do the work ourselves."

Culture and Behavior

In the longer term, however, the focus group agreed that IM is something that all parts of the organization will have to better understand and participate in. One of the most comprehensive challenges is changing the culture and behavior surrounding information. Marchand et al. (2000) suggest that six interdependent beliefs and behaviors are needed by all staff to support a positive "information orientation." These have been strongly correlated to organizational performance when they are present with strong IT and IM practices:

1. *Integrity.*   Integrity "defines both the boundaries beyond which people in an organization should not go in using information and the 'space' in which people can trust their colleagues to do with information what they would do themselves" (Marchand et al. 2000). Where integrity exists, people will have confidence that information will not be used inappropriately.
2. *Formality.*   Formality is the ability to trust formal sources of information (as opposed to informal ones). Formality enables an organization to provide accurate and consistent information about the business and establish formal processes and information flows that can be used to improve performance and provide services to customers.
3. *Control.*   Once formal information is trusted, it can be used to develop integrated performance criteria and measures for all levels of the company. In time, these will enable monitoring and performance improvement at the individual and work unit levels and can be linked to compensation and rewards.
4. *Transparency.*   Transparency describes a level of trust among members of an organization that enables them to speak about errors or failures "in an open and constructive manner without fear of unfair repercussions" (Marchand et al. 2000). Transparency is necessary to identify and respond effectively to problems and for learning to take place.
5. *Sharing.*   At this level, both sensitive and nonsensitive information is freely shared among individuals and across functional boundaries. Information exchanges are both initiated by employees and formally promoted through programs and forums.[2]
6. *Proactiveness.*   Ultimately, every member of an organization should be proactive about picking up new information about business conditions and testing new concepts.

Information Risk Management

The increasing breadth and scope of IT, combined with greater use of outsourcing, has made information more vulnerable to both internal and external fraud and has raised the level of risk associated with it. Management must, therefore, take proactive measures to

---

[2]New privacy laws in many countries inhibit the sharing of personal information for any purpose other than that for which it was collected. Customer information can, therefore, be shared only with consent.

determine an appropriate risk/return trade-off for information security. Costs are associated with information security mechanisms, and the business must be educated about them. In some cases these mechanisms are "table stakes"—that is, they must be taken if the company wants to "be in the game." Other risks in information security include internal and external interdependencies, implications for corporate governance, and impact on the value proposition. Risk exposures can also change over time and with outsourcing.

The focus group agreed that security is essential in the new world of IM. Today most organizations have basic information protection, such as virus scanners, firewalls, and virtual private networks. Many are also working on the next level of security, which includes real-time response, intrusion detection and monitoring, and vulnerability analysis. Soon, however, information security will need to include role-based identity and access management. An effective information-security strategy includes several components:

- An information protection center, which classifies data, analyzes vulnerabilities, and issues alerts
- Risk management
- Identity management, including access management, digital rights management, and encryption technology
- Education and awareness
- Establishment of priorities, standards, and resource requirements
- Compliance reviews and audits

Many of the decisions involved must be made by the lines of business, not IT, as only the business can determine access rules for content and the other controls that will facilitate identity and access management.

Information Value

At present, the economics of information have not yet been established in most organizations. It is, therefore, often hard to make the case for IM investments not only because the benefits are difficult to quantify but also because of the large number of variables involved. A value proposition for IM should address its strategic, tactical, and operational value and how it will lower risk and develop new capabilities. Furthermore, an effort should be made to quantify the value of the organization's existing information assets and to recognize their importance to its products and services.

Determining "value" is a highly subjective assessment. Thus, different companies and even different executives will define it differently. Today businesses define *value* broadly and loosely, not simply as a financial concept (Ginzberg 2001). However, because there is no single, agreed-on measure of information value, misunderstandings about its definition can easily arise. Therefore, it is essential that everyone involved in IM activities agree on what value they are trying to deliver and how they will recognize it. Furthermore, value has a time dimension. It takes time for an IM investment to pay off and become apparent. This also must be recognized by all concerned.

Privacy

Concern for the privacy of personal information has been raised to new levels, thanks to legislation being enacted around the world. All companies need enterprisewide privacy policies that address the highest privacy standards required in their working environments. For example, if they operate globally, policies and practices should satisfy all legislation worldwide. Privacy clearly should be part of any long-term IM initiatives, but it also affects what an organization is doing *currently*. As such, it is both an IM issue and an initiative in its own right. Both existing processes and staff behavior will be affected by privacy considerations. "Privacy is about respect for personal information and fair and ethical information practices. Training should start with all new employees and then be extended to all employees," said a manager. Many countries now require organizations to have a chief privacy officer. If so, this person should be a key stakeholder in ensuring that the organization's IM practices around data quality and accuracy, retention, information stewardship, and security are also in keeping with all privacy standards and legislation.

As with other IM initiatives, it is important that senior management understand and support the changes needed to improve privacy practices over time. "Good practices take time to surface," said a manager. "It takes time and resources to ensure all our frontline staff and our information collection and management processes are compliant." Accountabilities should be clearly defined as well. Ideally, IM policy and stewards set the standards in this area with privacy specialists and operational staff (in both IT and the business) responsible for implementing them. With the increase in outsourcing, particularly to offshore companies, all contracts and subcontracting arrangements must be reviewed for compliance in this area. "Our company is still liable for privacy breaches if they occur in one of our vendor firms," noted a group member.

Knowledge Management

Although many organizations have been soured on knowledge management (KM) because of its "soft and fuzzy" nature (Smith and McKeen 2004), the fact remains that IM provides a solid foundation that will enable the organization to do more with what it knows (see Figure 6.1). Even firms that do not have a separate KM function recognize that better IM will help them build valuable structural capital. There are many levels at which IM can be improved. At the most elementary, data warehouses can be built and the information in them can be analyzed for trends and patterns. One company is working on identifying its "single points of knowledge" (i.e., those staff members who have specialized knowledge in an important area) and capturing this knowledge in a formal way (e.g., in business processes or metadata). Many firms are making customer information management a priority so they can use this information to both serve their customers better and to learn more about them.[3] This clearly cannot be done unless information is integrated across processes and accessible in a usable format (Davenport and Prusak 1998; Smith and McKeen 2005b). Finally, information can be aggregated and synthesized to create new and useful knowledge. For example, Wal-Mart takes transaction-level information from its sales process and aggregates and analyzes it to make it useful both to the sales process and to other areas of the business. It identifies trends and opportunities based on this analysis and enables information to be viewed in different ways, leading to new insights.

---

[3]Customer information is particularly sensitive and may be analyzed only with a customer's consent in many countries. The need to monitor consents adds a further layer of complexity to this already challenging activity.

The Knowing–Doing Gap

Most organizations assume that better information will lead to better decisions and actions, but research shows that this is not always (or even often) the case. All too often companies do not utilize the information they have. One problem is that we really understand very little about how organizations and groups actually use information in their work (Pfeffer and Sutton 2000). Some organizations do not make clear links between desired actions and the acquisition and packaging of specific information. Although this may seem like common sense, the focus group agreed that the complex connections between decisions and actions are not always well understood. Effective technology, strong IM practices, and appropriate behaviors and values are *all* necessary to ensure the information–action connection is made (Smith et al. 2006).

GETTING STARTED IN IM

Although IM is not IT, the fact remains that IT is largely driving IM in organizations today. Whether this will be the case in the longer term remains to be seen. Most members would like to see the situation reversed, with the business driving the effort to establish appropriate IM policies, procedures, stewardship, and standards and IT supporting IM with software, data custodianship, security and access controls, information applications and administration, and integrated systems. In the shorter term, however, IT is working hard to get IM the attention it deserves in the business.

Focus group participants had several recommendations for others wishing to get started in IM:

- *Start with what you have.* "Doing IM is like trying to solve world hunger," said one manager. "It just gets bigger and bigger the longer you look at it." Even just listing all of the information types and locations in the organization can be a daunting task, and the job will probably never be fully complete. The group, therefore, recommended doing an inventory of what practices, processes, standards, groups, and repositories already exist in the organization and trying to grow IM from there. It is most important to get the key information needed to achieve business objectives under control first. For many companies, this may be customer information; for others, it may be product or financial information. "It's really important to prioritize in IM," said a manager. "We need to focus on the right information that's going to have the biggest return." It may help to try to quantify the value of company information in some way. Despite the fact that there is no accepted accounting method for doing so as yet, some firms are adapting the value assessment methodologies used for other assets. "When you really look at the value of information, it's worth a staggering amount of money. This really gets senior management attention and support," noted a focus group member.

  A top–down approach is ideal, yet it may not always be practical. "It took us over a year to get an information policy in place," said a participant. "In the meantime, there are significant savings that can be realized by taking a bottom-up approach and cleaning up some of the worst problems." Harnessing existing compliance efforts around privacy, security, and the Sarbanes–Oxley Act is also effective. At minimum, these will affect information architecture, access to data, document retention, and data administration for financial and personal information (Smith and McKeen 2006). "We can take either an opportunity or a fear mindset toward regulation," said a manager. Companies that see compliance from a purely tactical perspective will likely not see the value of increased controls. If, however, they see regulation as a chance to streamline and revamp business processes and the information they use, their compliance investments will likely pay off. Those interested in IM can also take advantage of the dramatically elevated attention levels of the board and executives to compliance matters.

- *Ensure cross-functional coordination among all stakeholders.*   Business involvement in IT initiatives is always desirable, and it is impossible to do IM without it. "No IM effort should go ahead without fully identifying all areas that are affected," stated one manager. Typically, legal, audit, and the privacy office will have a keen interest in this area. Equally typical, many of the business units affected will not be interested in it. For operational groups, IM is often seen as bureaucratic overhead and extra cost, which is why education and communication about IM are essential. "You have to allow time for these groups to get on board with this concept and come around to the necessity of taking the time to do IM right," said a participant. He noted that this effort has to be repeated at each level of the organization. "Senior management may be supportive, but members of the working groups may not really understand what we're trying to accomplish."

- *Get the incentives right.*   Even with IM "socialization" (i.e., education and communication), politics is likely to become a major hurdle to the success of any IM efforts. Both giving up control and taking accountability for key pieces of information can be hard for many business managers. Therefore, it is important to ensure incentives are in place that will motivate collaboration. Metrics are an important way to make progress (or the lack of it) highly visible in the organization. One firm developed a team scorecard for its customer information working group that reported two key measures to executives: the percentage of remaining duplicate records and the percentage of "perfect" customer records. Each of these was broken down into a number of leading indicators that helped focus the group's behavior on the overall effort rather than on individual territories. Another firm linked its process and information simplification efforts to budgets. The savings generated from eliminating duplicate or redundant information (and its associated storage and processing) were returned to the business units involved to be reinvested as they saw fit. This proved to be a huge motivator of enterprise-oriented behavior.

- *Establish and model sound information values.*   Because frontline workers, who make many decisions about information and procedures, ultimately cannot cover all eventualities, all staff need to understand the fundamental reasons for key company information policies and directives. Corporate values around information guide how staff should behave even when their managers aren't around. And they provide a basis for sound decision making about information (Stewart 2004). Others have noted that senior IT leadership should primarily be about forming and modeling values, not managing tasks, and this is especially true for IM, said the focus group. Values are particularly important, they noted, now that staff are more mobile and virtual and, thus, more empowered. If such values are effectively articulated and modeled by leaders, they will drive the development of the appropriate culture and behaviors around information.

Conclusion

Information management is gaining increasing attention in both IT and the business. Driven by new compliance and privacy legislation, the increasing vulnerability of corporate information, and the desire for greater integration of systems, IM is beginning to look like an emerging discipline in its own right. However, the challenges facing organizations in implementing effective IM practices are many and daunting. Not least is the need to try to conceptualize the scope and complexity of work to be done. Tackling IM is likely to be a long-term task. IT managers have a huge communications job ahead in trying to educate business leaders about their responsibilities in information stewardship, developing sound IM practices, and inculcating the culture and behaviors needed to achieve the desired results. Developing a plan for tackling the large and ever-increasing amount of information involved is only the first step. The more difficult effort will be involving every member of the organization—from the board to frontline workers—in seeing that it is carried out effectively. Although IT can lead this effort initially and provide substantial support for IM, ultimately its success or failure will be due to how well the business does its part.

References

Davenport, T., and L. Prusak. *Working Knowledge: How Organizations Manage What They Know.* Boston: Harvard Business School Press, 1998.

Ginzberg, M. "Achieving Business Value Through Information Technology: The Nature of High Business Value IT Organizations." Report commissioned by the Society for Information Management Advanced Practices Council, November 2001.

Kettinger, W., and D. Marchand. "Driving Value from IT: Investigating Senior Executives' Perspectives." Report commissioned by the Society for Information Management, Advanced Practices Council, May 2005.

Marchand, D., W. Kettinger, and J. Rollins. "Information Orientation: People, Technology and the Bottom Line." *MIT Sloan Management Review* Summer (2000).

Pfeffer, J., and R. Sutton. *The Knowing-Doing Gap.* Boston: Harvard Business School Press, 2000.

Smith, H. A., and J. D. McKeen. "Marketing KM to the Business." *Communications of the Association for Information Systems* 14, article 23 (November 2004): 513–25.

———. "Information Delivery: IT's Evolving Role." *Communications of the Association for Information Systems* 15, article 11 (February 2005a): 197–210.

———. "A Framework for KM Evaluation." *Communications of the Association for Information Systems* 16, article 9 (May 2005b): 233–46.

———. "Customer Knowledge Management: Adding Value for Our Customers." *Communications of the Association for Information Systems* 16, article 36 (November 2005c): 744–55.

———. "IT in the New World of Corporate Governance Reforms." *Communications of the Association for Information Systems* 17, article 32 (May 2006): 714–27.

Smith, H. A., J. D. McKeen, and S. Singh. "Making Knowledge Work: Five Principles for Action-Oriented Knowledge Management." *Knowledge Management Research and Practice* 4, no. 2 (2006): 116–24.

Stewart, T. *Intellectual Capital: The New Wealth of Organizations.* New York: Doubleday, 1999.

———. "Leading Change When Business Is Good: An Interview with Samuel J. Palmisano." *Harvard Business Review* 82, no. 12 (December 2004).

APPENDIX A

Elements of IM Operations

A. Strategy

- External environment
- Strategic planning
- Information life cycle
- Planning
- Program integration
- Performance monitoring

B. People

- Roles and responsibilities
- Training and support
- Subject-matter experts
- Relationship management

C. Processes

- Project management
- Change management
- Risk management
- Business continuity
- Information life cycle:
  - Collect, create, and capture
  - Use and dissemination
  - Maintenance, protection, and preservation
  - Retention and disposition

D. Technology and Architecture

- IM tools
- Technology integration
- Information life cycle: organization
- Data standards

E. Culture and Behaviors

- Leadership
- IM awareness
- Incentives
- IM competencies
- Communities of interest

F. Governance

- Principles, policies, and standards
- Compliance
- IM program evaluation
- Quality of information
- Security of information
- Privacy of information

Chapter 7

The IT Budgeting Process

Don't ever try to contact an IT manager in September because you won't get very far. September is budget month for most companies, and *that* means that most managers are hunkered down over a spreadsheet or in all-day meetings trying to "make the numbers work." "Budgeting is a very negative process at our firm," one IT manager told us. "And it takes way too long." Asking many IT managers about budgeting elicits much caustic comment. Apparently, significant difficulties with IT budgeting lead to widespread disenchantment among IT leaders who feel much of the work involved is both artificial and overly time consuming.

Others agree. While there has been little research done on IT budgeting per se (Hu and Quan 2006; Kobelsky et al. 2006), there appears to be broad, general consensus that the budgeting processes of many corporations are broken and need to be fixed (Buytendijk 2004; Hope and Fraser 2003; Jensen 2001). There are many problems. First, budgeting takes too long and consumes too much managerial time. One study found that budgeting is a protracted process taking at least four months and consuming about 30 percent of management's time (Hope and Fraser 2003). Second, most budgeting processes are no longer effective or efficient. They have become disconnected from business objectives, slow, and expensive (Buytendijk 2004). Third, rigid adherence to these annual plans has been found to stifle innovation and discourage frontline staff from taking responsibility for performance (Hope and Fraser 2003; Norton 2006). And fourth, although many researchers have studied how organizations choose among strategic investment opportunities, studies show that the budgeting process frequently undercuts management's strategic intentions, causing significant frustration among managers at all levels (Norton 2006; Steele and Albright 2004).

Finally, the annual planning cycle can cast spending plans "in concrete" at a time when the business needs to be flexible and agile. This is particularly true in IT. "Over time . . . IT budgeting processes become institutionalized. As a result, IT investments become less about creating competitive advantages for firms [and] more about following organizational routine and creating legitimacy for management as well as organizations" (Hu and Quan 2006). Now that senior business leaders have at last recognized the strategic importance of IT (Smith et al. 2007) and IT has become many firms' largest capital expenditure (Koch 2006), a hard look at how IT budgets are created and spent is clearly merited.

This chapter first looks at key concepts in IT budgeting to establish what they mean for IT managers and how they can differ among IT organizations. Then it explores why budgets are an important part of the management process. Next the chapter examines the elements of the IT budget cycle. Finally, it identifies some recommended practices for improving IT budgeting.

KEY CONCEPTS IN IT BUDGETING

Before looking at how budgeting is actually practiced in IT organizations, it is important to understand what a budget *is* and *why* an effective IT budgeting process is so important, both within IT and for the enterprise as a whole. Current organizational budgeting practices emerged in the 1920s as a tool for managing costs and cash flows. Present-day annual fixed plans and budgets were established in the 1970s to drive performance improvements (Hope and Fraser 2003). Since then most organizations have adhered rigidly to the ideals of this process, in spite of much evidence of their negative influence on innovation and flexibility (Hope and Fraser 2003). These problems are clearly illustrated by the impact this larger corporate fiscal management process has on IT budgeting and the problems IT managers experience in trying to make their budget processes work effectively. The concepts and practices of the corporate fiscal world bear little similarity to how IT actually works. As a result, there are clear discontinuities between these two worlds.

These gaps are especially apparent in the differences between the fiscal view of IT and the functional one. *Fiscal IT budgets* (i.e., those prepared for the CFO) are broken down into two major categories: *capital expenditures* and *operating expenses,* although what expenditures go into each is highly variable across firms. In accounting, capital budgets are utilized to spread large expenses (e.g., buying a building) over several years, and operating expenses cover the annual cost of running the business. The distinction between these two concepts gets very fuzzy, however, when it comes to IT.

Generally speaking, all IT organizations want to capitalize as much of their spending as possible because it makes their annual costs look smaller. However, CIOs are limited by both organizational and tax policies as to the types of IT expenditures they can capitalize. It is the CFO who, through corporate financial strategy, establishes what may be capitalized, and this, in turn, determines what IT can capitalize in its fiscal budget and what it must consider as an operating expense. As a result, some firms capitalize project development, infrastructure, consulting fees, and full-time staff, whereas others capitalize only major technology purchases.

How capital budgets are determined and the degree to which they are scrutinized also vary widely. Some firms allocate and prioritize IT capital expenses out of a corporate "pot"; others manage IT capital separately. Typically, capital expenses appear to be more carefully scrutinized than operating expenses, but not always. It is surprising to learn how different types of expenses are handled by different firms and the wide degree of latitude allowed for IT costs under generally accepted accounting principles. In fact, there are few generally accepted accounting principles when it comes to IT spending (Koch 2006). As a result, researchers should use caution in relying on measures of the amount of capital spent on IT in firms or industries.

It is within this rather fuzzy fiscal context that the structure and purpose of *functional IT budgets* (i.e., those used by IT managers as spending plans) must be understood because these accounting concepts do not usually correspond exactly with how IT managers and researchers view IT work and how they plan and budget for it. In contrast to how fiscal IT budgets are designed, IT managers plan their spending using two some-what different categories: *operations costs* and *strategic investments:*

- *Operations costs.* This category consists of what it costs to "keep the lights on" in IT. These are the expenses involved in running IT like a utility. Operations involves the cost of maintenance, computing and peripheral functions (e.g., stor-age, network), and support, regardless of how it is delivered (i.e., in-house or out-sourced). This category can, therefore, include both operating and capital costs. Between 50 and 90 percent of a firm's IT budget (average 76 percent) is spent in this area, so the spending involved is significant (Gruman 2006). In most firms there is continual pressure on the CIO to reduce operations costs year after year (Smith and McKeen 2006).
- *Strategic investment.* The balance of the IT budget consists of the "new" spend-ing—that is, spending on initiatives and technology designed to deliver new busi-ness value and achieve the enterprise's strategic objectives. Because of the interactive nature of IT and business strategy these days, this part of the IT budget can include a number of different types of spending, such as business improvement initiatives to streamline processes and cut costs, business-enabling initiatives to extend or transform how a company does business, business opportunity projects to test the viability of new concepts or technologies and scale them up, and some-times infrastructure (Smith et al. 2007). Because spending in this area can include many different kinds of expense (e.g., full-time and contract staff, software and hardware), some parts of the strategic investment budget may be considered capi-tal expenses whereas others are classified as operating expenses.

Another fuzzy fiscal budgeting concept is *cost allocation*—the process of allocating the cost of the services IT provides to others' budgets. The cost of IT can be viewed as a corporate expense, a business unit expense, or a combination of both, and the way in which IT costs are allocated can have a significant impact on what is spent for IT. For example, a majority of companies allocate their operating expenses to their business units' operating budgets—usually using a formula based on factors such as the size and previous year's spending of the business unit. Similarly, strategic expenses are typically allocated on the basis of which business unit will benefit from the investment. In today's IT environment, these approaches are not always effective for a number of reasons.

Many strategic IT investments involve the participation of more than one business unit, but budgeting systems still tend to be designed around the structure of the organiza-tion (Norton 2006). This leads to considerable artificiality in allocating development resources to projects, which in turn can lead to dysfunctional behavior, such as lobbying, games, nonsupportive cross-functional work, and the inability to successfully implement strategy (Buytendijk 2004; Norton 2006). "We don't fund corporate projects very well," admitted one manager whose company allocates all costs to individual business units.

Allocations can also lead to operational inefficiencies. "The different allocation models tend to lead to 'gaming' between our business units," said another participant. "Our business unit managers have no control over their percentage of operating costs," explained a third. "This is very frustrating for them and tends to be a real problem for some of our smaller units." Because of these allocations, some business units may not be willing to share in the cost of new hardware, software, or processes that would lead to reduced enterprise costs in the longer term. This is one of the primary reasons so many IT organizations end up supporting several different applications all doing the same thing. Furthermore, sometimes, when senior managers get disgruntled with their IT expenses, this method of allocating operations costs can lead to their cutting their IT operational spending in ways that have little to do with running a cost-effective IT organization. For example, one company cut back on its budget for hardware and software upgrades, which meant that a significant percentage of IT staff then had to be redeployed to testing, modifying, and maintaining new systems so they would run on the old machines. Although IT managers have done some work educating their CEOs and CFOs about what constitutes effective cost cutting (e.g., appropriate outsourcing, adjusting service levels), the fact remains that most business executives still do not understand or appreciate the factors that contribute to the overall cost of IT. As a result, allocations can lead to a great deal of angst for IT managers at budget time as they try to justify each expense while business managers try to "nickel and dime" each expense category (Koch 2006).

As a result of all this fuzziness, modern IT budgeting practices do little to give business leaders confidence that IT spending is both effective and efficient (Gruman 2006). And the challenges IT managers face in making IT spending fit into contemporary corporate budgeting practices are significant.

THE IMPORTANCE OF BUDGETS

Ideally, budgets are a key component of corporate performance management. "If done well, a budget is the operational translation of an enterprise's strategy into costs and planned revenue" (Buytendijk 2004). Budgets are also a subset of good governance processes in that they enable management to understand and communicate what is being spent and where. Ideally, therefore, a budget is more than a math exercise; it is "a blueprint for fiscally sound IT and business success" (Overby 2004). Effective IT budgeting is important for many reasons, but two of the most important are as follows:

1. *Fiscal discipline.*   As overall IT spending has been rising, senior business leaders have been paying much closer attention to what IT costs and how its budgets are spent. In many organizations a great deal of skepticism remains that IT budgets are used wisely, so reducing spending, or at least the operations portion of the budget, is now considered a key way for a CIO to build trust with the executive team (Gruman 2006). Demonstrating an understanding and appreciation of the realities of business finance has become a significant part of IT leadership (Goldberg 2004), and the ability to create and monitor a budget is, therefore, "table stakes" for a CIO (Overby 2004).

   It is clear that senior executives are using the budgeting process to enforce tougher rules on how IT dollars are spent. Some organizations have centralized IT budgeting in an effort to better understand what is being spent; others are making the link between reducing operations spending and increasing investment in IT a reason for introducing new operations disciplines (e.g., limiting maintenance, establishing appropriate support levels). Still others have established tighter requirements for business cases and monitoring returns on investment. Organizations also use their IT budgets to manage and limit demand. "Our IT budget is capped by our CEO," stated one manager. "And it's always less than the demand." Using budgets in this way, although likely effective for the enterprise, can cause problems for CIOs in that they must in turn enforce spending disciplines on business unit leaders.

Finally, budgets and performance against budgets are a key way of holding IT management accountable for what it spends, both internally to the leadership of the organization and externally to shareholders and regulatory bodies. Improperly used, budgets can distort reality and encourage inappropriate behavior (Hope and Fraser 2003; Jensen 2001). However, when used responsibly they can be "a basis for clear understanding between organizational levels and can help executives maintain control over divisions and the business" (Hope and Fraser 2003). Research is beginning to show a positive relationship between good IT budgeting practices (i.e., using IT budgets to manage demand, make investment decisions, and govern IT) and overall company performance (Kobelsky et al. 2006; Overby 2004).

2. *Strategy implementation.*   Budgets are also the means to implement IT strategy, linking the long-term goals of the organization and short-term goal execution through the allocation of resources to activities. Unfortunately, research shows that the majority of organizations do not link their strategies to their budgets, which is why so many have difficulty making strategic changes (Norton 2006). This is particularly true in IT. As one manager complained, "No one knows what we're doing in the future. Therefore, our goals change regularly and at random." Another noted, "The lines of business pay little attention to IT resources when they're establishing their strategic plans. They just expect IT to make it happen."

Budgets can affect IT strategy implementation in a number of ways. First, *where* IT dollars are spent determines the impact IT can have on corporate performance. Clearly, if 80 percent of IT expenditures are going to operations and maintenance, IT can have less strategic impact than if this percentage is lower. Second, *how* discretionary IT dollars are spent is important. For example, some companies decide to invest in infrastructure, and others do not; some will choose to "bet the company" on a single large IT initiative, and others will choose more focused projects. In short, the outcome of how a company chooses among investment opportunities is reflected in its budgets (Steele and Albright 2004).

Third, the budgeting process itself reflects and reinforces the ability of strategic decision making to have an impact. Norton (2006) states that because budget processes are inherently biased toward the short term, operational needs will systematically preempt strategic ones. In IT the common practice of routinely allocating a fixed percentage of the IT strategic budget to individual business units makes it almost impossible to easily reallocate resources to higher-priority projects at the enterprise level or in other business units. In addition, siloed budgeting processes make it difficult to manage the cross-business costs of strategic IT decisions.

Overall, budgets are a critical element of most managerial decisions and processes and are used to accomplish a number of different purposes in IT: compliance, fiscal accountability, cost reduction, business unit and enterprise strategy implementation, internal customer service, delivering business value, and operational excellence, to name just a few. This, in a nutshell, is the reason IT budgeting is such a complex and challenging process.

THE IT PLANNING AND BUDGET PROCESS

Given that IT budgets are used in so many different ways and serve so many stakeholders, it is no wonder that the whole process of IT budgeting is "painful," "artificial," and in need of some serious improvement. Figure 7.1 illustrates a generic and simplified IT

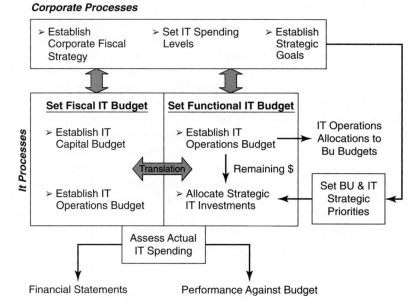

FIGURE 7.1 A Generic IT Planning and Budgeting Process

planning and budgeting process. This section outlines the steps involved in putting together an IT budget utilizing some of the key concepts presented earlier.

Corporate Processes

The following three activities set the corporate context within which IT plans and budgets are created.

1. *Establish corporate fiscal policy.*   This process is usually so far removed from the annual budget cycle that IT leaders may not even be aware of its influence or the wide number of options in the choices that are made (particularly around capitalization). Corporate fiscal policies are not created with IT spending in mind but, as noted above, can significantly impact how a fiscal IT budget is created and the levels of scrutiny under which certain kinds of expenses are placed. A more direct way that corporate fiscal policies affect IT is in company expectations around the return on investment for IT projects. Most companies now have an explicit expected return rate for all new projects that is closely monitored.

2. *Establish strategic goals.*   Conversely, IT budgeting *is* directly and continuously affected by many corporate strategic goals. The process of establishing IT and business unit strategies occurs within the context of these overall goals. In some organizations there is tight integration between enterprise, business unit, and IT strategic planning; in others these elements are more loosely coupled, informal, and iterative. However, what is truly rare is a provision for enterprise funding for enterprise IT initiatives. Thus, corporate strategic goals are typically broken down into business unit budgets. As one manager explained, "First our executives decide our profits and then the business units decide how to achieve them and then IT develops a plan with the business unit. . . . We still don't do many corporate projects."

3. *Set IT spending levels.*   Establishing how much to spend on IT is the area that has been most closely studied by researchers. This is a complex process, influenced by many external and internal factors. *Externally*, firms look to others in their industry to determine the level of their spending (Hu and Quan 2006). In particular, companies frequently use benchmarks with similar firms to identify a percentage of revenue to spend on IT (Koch 2006). Unfortunately, this approach can be dangerous for a number of reasons. First, it can be a strong driver in inhibiting competitive advantage and leading to greater similarities among firms in an industry (Hu and Quan 2006). Second, this metric tells management nothing about how well its money is being spent (Koch 2006). Third, it does not address IT's ability to use IT strategically (Kobelsky et al. 2006).

A second and increasingly strong external driver of IT spending is the regulatory environment within which a firm operates. Legislation, standards, and professional practices all affect what IT can and cannot do and how its work is done (Smith and McKeen 2006). These, in turn, affect how much is spent on IT and where it is spent (Hu and Quan 2006). Other external factors that have been shown to affect how much money is spent on IT include the following:

- *Number of competitors.*   More concentration in an industry reduces the amount spent.
- *Uncertainty.*   More uncertainty in a business's external environment leads to larger IT budgets.
- *Diversification of products and services.*   Firms competing in more markets will tend to spend more on IT (Kobelsky et al. 2006).

Internal factors affecting the size of the IT budget include the following:

- *Affordability.*   A firm's overall performance and cash flow will influence how much discretion it has to spend on IT.
- *Growth.*   Growing firms tend to invest more in IT than mature firms.
- *Previous year's spending.*   Firm spending on IT is unlikely to deviate significantly year to year (Hu and Quan 2006; Kobelsky et al. 2006).

IT Processes

These are multilevel and complex and frequently occur in parallel with each other.

- *Set functional IT budget.*   This budget documents spending as it relates to how IT organizations *work*—that is, what is to be spent on IT operations and how much is available to be spent on strategic investments. As noted above, the operations budget is relatively fixed and contains the lion's share of the dollars. In spite of this, IT managers must go through a number of machinations annually to justify this expenditure. Most IT organizations are still seen as cost centers, so obtaining budget approvals is often a delicate, ongoing exercise of relationship building and education to prevent inappropriate cost cutting (Koch 2006). Once the overall IT operations budget has been established, the challenge of allocating it to the individual business units remains, which, given the complexity of today's shared technical environment, is often a fixed or negotiated percentage of the total. Business units can resent these allocations over which they have no control, and at best, they are viewed as a "necessary evil." In organizations where the IT operations budget is centralized, IT managers have a better opportunity to reduce expenses year by year by introducing standards, streamlining hardware and software, and sharing services. However, in many companies, operations budgets are decentralized into the business units and aggregated up into the overall IT budget. This approach makes it considerably more difficult for IT managers to implement effective cost-reduction measures. However, even in those firms that are highly effective and efficient, the relentless pressure from executives to do more with less makes this part of the annual budgeting process a highly stressful activity.

Allocating the funds remaining to strategic investments is a completely separate process in which potential new IT projects are prioritized and their costs justified. Companies have many different ways of doing this, and most appear to be in a transition phase between methods of prioritization. Traditionally, IT organizations have been designed to parallel the organization structure, and new development funds have been allocated to business units on the basis of some rule of thumb. For example, each business unit might be allotted a certain number of IT staff and dollars to spend on new development (based on percentage of overall revenue) that would remain relatively stable over time. More recently, however, with greater integration of technology, systems, and data, there has been recognition of the cross-business costs of new development and of the need for more enterprise spending to address these. Increasingly, therefore, organizations are moving to prioritize some or all new development at the enterprise level, thereby removing fixed allocations of new development resources from the business units.

However it is determined, the strategic portion of the functional IT budget also involves staffing the initiatives. This introduces yet another level of complexity in that, even if the dollars are available, appropriate IT resources must also be available to be assigned to particular projects to address the organization's cost-cutting requirements. Thus, undertaking a new project involves not only cost justification and prioritization but also requires the availability of the right mix of skills and types of staff. Although some firms use fixed percentages of full-time, contract, and offshore staff in their projects, most use a mix of employees and contract staff in their development projects in order to keep overhead costs low. As a result, creating new IT development budgets often involves a complementary exercise in staff planning.

* *Set the fiscal IT budget.*   A second, parallel stream of IT budgeting involves establishing the *fiscal* IT budget, which the CFO uses to implement the company's fiscal strategy and provide financial reports to shareholders and regulatory and tax authorities. This is seen largely by IT managers as a "translation" exercise where the functional IT budget is reconstituted into the operating and capital spending buckets. Nevertheless, it represents an additional "hoop" through which IT managers must jump before their budgets can be approved. In some companies capital funding is difficult to obtain and must be justified against an additional set of financial criteria. Some organizations require IT capital expenditures be prioritized against all other corporate capital expenses (e.g., buildings, trucks), which can be a very challenging exercise. In other firms CFOs are more concerned about increasing operating expenses. In either case this is an area where many IT managers set themselves up for failure by failing to "speak the language of finance" (Girard 2004). Because most IT managers think of their work in terms of operations and strategic investments, they fail to understand some of the larger drivers of fiscal strategy such as investor value and earnings per share. To get more "traction" for their budgets, it is, therefore, important for IT leaders to better translate what IT can do for the company into monetary terms (Girard

2004). To this end, many companies have begun working more closely with their internal finance staff and are seeing greater acceptance of their budgets as a result.

Assess Actual IT Spending

At the other end of the budgeting process is the need to assess actual IT spending and performance. A new focus on financial accountability has meant that results are more rigorously tracked than in the past. In many companies finance staff now monitor business cases for all new IT projects, thus relieving IT of having to prove the business returns on what is delivered. Often the challenge of finding the right resources for a project or unexpected delays means that the entire available development budget may not be spent within a given fiscal year. "We typically tend to spend about 85 percent of our available development budget because of delays or resourcing problems," said one manager. Hitting budget targets *exactly* in the strategic investment budget is, therefore, a challenge, and current IT budgeting practices typically do not allow for much flexibility. On the one hand, such practices can create a "use it or lose it" mentality; if money is not spent in the fiscal year, it will disappear. "This leads to some creative accruals and aggressive forecasting," said the focus group. On the other hand, IT managers who want to ensure there is *enough* money for key expenditures create "placeholders" (i.e., approximations of what they think a project will cost) and "coffee cans" (i.e., unofficial slush funds) in their budgets. The artificial timing of the budget process, combined with the difficulties of planning and estimation and reporting complexity, all mean that accurate reporting of what is spent can get distorted.

IT BUDGETING PRACTICES THAT DELIVER VALUE

Although there is general agreement that current budgeting practices are flawed, there are still no widely accepted alternatives. Within IT itself, companies seem to be experimenting with ways to tweak budgeting to make it both easier and more effective. The following five practices have proven to be useful in this regard:

1. *Appoint an IT finance specialist.*   Many companies now have a finance expert working in IT or on staff with the CFO working *with* IT. "Getting help with finance has really made the job of budgeting easier," said one manager. "Having a good partnership with finance helps us to leverage their expertise," said another. Financial specialists can help IT managers to understand their costs and drivers in new ways. Within operations, they can assist with cost and value analysis of services and infrastructure (Gruman 2006) and also manage the "translation" process between the functional IT budget and the fiscal IT budget. "Finance helps us to understand depreciation and gives us a deeper understanding of our cost components," a focus group member noted. Finance specialists are also being used to build and monitor business cases for new projects, often acting as brokers between IT and the business units. "They've really helped us to better articulate business value. Now they're in charge of ensuring that the business gets the benefits they say they will, not IT." The improving relationship between finance and IT is making it easier to gain acceptance of IT budgets. "Having dedicated IT finance people is great since this is not what IT managers want to do," said a participant.

2. *Use budgeting tools and methodologies.*   About one-half of the members of the focus group felt they had effective budgeting tools for such things as asset tracking,

rolling up and breaking down budgets into different levels of granularity, and reporting. "We have a good, integrated suite of tools," said a manager, "and they really help." Because budgets serve so many different stakeholders, tools and methodologies can help "slice and dice" the numbers many ways, dynamically enabling changes in one area to be reflected in all other areas. Those who did not have good or well-integrated tools found that there were gaps in their budgeting processes that were hard to fill. "Our poor tools lead to disconnects all over the place," claimed an IT manager. Good links to the IT planning process are also needed. Ideally, tools should tie budgets directly to corporate strategic planning, resource strategies, and performance metrics, enabling a further translation among the company's accounting categories and hierarchy and its strategic themes and targets (Norton 2006).

3. *Separate operations from innovation.*   Most IT managers mentally separate operations from innovation, but in practical terms maintenance and support are often mixed up with new project development. This happens especially when IT organizations are aligned with and funded by the business units. Once IT funds and resources are allotted to a particular business unit, rather than to a strategic deliverable, it is very difficult to reduce these allocations. Agreement appears to be growing that operations (including maintenance) must be fully financially separated from new development in order to ensure that the costs of the first are fully scrutinized and kept under control while focus is kept on increasing the proportion of resources devoted to new project development (Dragoon 2005; Girard 2004; Gruman 2006; Norton 2006). Repeatedly, focus group managers told stories of how their current budget processes discourage accuracy. "There are many disincentives built into our budgeting processes to keep operational costs down," said one manager. Separating operations from innovation in budgets provides a level of visibility in IT spending that has traditionally been absent and that helps business unit leaders better understand the true costs of delivering both new systems and ongoing services.

4. *Adopt enterprise funding models.*   It is still rare to find organizations that provide corporate funding for enterprisewide strategic IT initiatives, yet there is broad recognition that this is needed (Norton 2006). The conflict between the need for truly integrated initiatives and traditional siloed budgets frequently stymies innovation, frustrates behavior designed for the common good, and discourages accountability for results (Hope and Fraser 2003; Norton 2006; Steele and Albright 2004). It is, therefore, expected that more organizations will adopt enterprise funding models for at least some IT initiatives over the next few years. Similarly, decentralized budgeting for core IT services is declining due to the cost-saving opportunities available from sharing these. Since costs will likely continue to be charged back to the differing business units, the current best practice is for IT operation budgets to be developed at an enterprise level.

5. *Adopt rolling budget cycles.*   IT plans and budgets need attention more frequently than once a year. Although not used by many companies, an eighteen-month rolling plan that is reviewed and updated quarterly appears to be a more effective way of budgeting, especially for new project development (Hope and Fraser 2003; Smith et al. 2007). "It is very difficult to plan new projects a year in advance," said one manager. "Often we are asked for our 'best estimates' in our budgets. The problem is that, once they're in the budget, they are then viewed as reality." The artificial timing of budgets and the difficulty of estimating the costs of new projects are key

sources of frustration for IT managers. Rolling budget cycles, when combined with integrated budgeting tools, should better address this problem while still providing the financial snapshots needed by the enterprise on an annual basis.

Conclusion

Although IT budget processes have been largely ignored by researchers, they are a critical linchpin between many different organizational stakeholders: finance and IT, business units and IT, corporate strategy and IT, and different internal IT groups. Not surprisingly, therefore, IT budgeting is much more complex and difficult to navigate than it appears. This chapter has outlined some of the challenges faced by IT managers trying to juggle the realities of dealing with both IT operations and strategic investments while meeting the differing needs of their budget stakeholders. Surprisingly, very few guidelines are available for IT managers in this area. Each organization appears to have quite different corporate financial policies, which, in turn, drive different IT budgeting practices. Nevertheless, IT managers do face many common challenges in budgeting. Although other IT practices have benefited from focused management attention in recent years (e.g., prioritization, operations rationalization), budgeting has not as yet been targeted in this way. However, as business and IT leaders begin to recognize the key role that budgets play in implementing strategy and controlling costs, it is hoped they will make a serious effort to address the budgeting issues faced by IT.

References

Buytendijk, F. "New Way to Budget Enhances Corporate Performance Measurement." Gartner Inc., ID Number: 423484, January 28, 2004.

Dragoon, A. "Journey to the IT Promised Land." *CIO Magazine*, April 1, 2005.

Girard, K. "What CIOs Need to Know about Money." *CIO Magazine* Special Money Issue, September 22, 2004.

Goldberg, M. "The Final Frontier for CIOs." *CIO Magazine* Special Money Issue, September 22, 2004.

Gruman, G. "Trimming for Dollars." *CIO Magazine*, July 1, 2006.

Hope, J., and R. Fraser. "Who Needs Budgets?" *Harvard Business Review* 81, no. 2 (February 2003): 2–8.

Hu, Q., and J. Quan. "The Institutionalization of IT Budgeting: Empirical Evidence from the Financial Sector." *Information Resources Management Journal* 19, no. 1 (January–March 2006): 84–97.

Jensen, M. "Corporate Budgeting Is Broken— Let's Fix It." *Harvard Business Review* 79, no. 11 (November 2001): 95–101.

Kobelsky, K., V. Richardson, R. Smith, and R. Zmud. "Determinants and Consequences of Firm Information Technology Budgets." Draft paper provided by the authors, May 2006.

Koch, C. "The Metrics Trap . . . and How to Avoid It." *CIO Magazine* (April 1, 2006).

Norton, D. "Linking Strategy and Planning to Budgets." *Balanced Scorecard Report*. Cambridge, MA: Harvard Business School Publishing, May–June 2006.

Overby, S. "Tips from the Budget Masters." *CIO Magazine* Special Money Issue, September 22, 2004.

Smith, H. A., and J. D. McKeen. "IT in 2010." *MIS Quarterly Executive* 5, no. 3 (September 2006): 125–36.

Smith, H. A., J. D. McKeen, and S. Singh. "Developing IT Strategy for Business Value." *Journal of Information Technology Management* XVIII, no. 1 (June 2007): 49–58.

Steele, R., and C. Albright. "Games Managers Play at Budget Time." *MIT Sloan Management Review* 45, no. 3 (Spring 2004): 81–84.

Chapter 8

Creating and Evolving a Technology Roadmap[1]

If you don't know where you are going, any road will get you there. Lewis Carroll (1865)

The preceding quote applies rather well to technology roadmaps. In the past, companies have followed a number of different technology paths that have not always led to the "promised land" despite conscientious effort. There are many reasons for this. First, the target evolves, which means that development of a technology roadmap should be an ongoing process. To continue the analogy, we are forever "traveling" but never "arriving." Second, technology has many different masters. Vendors, trade associations, standards-setting boards, alliance and/or trade partners, merger/acquisition initiatives, growth, strategic directional change, new technological development, and economic shifts (e.g., price performance, adoption patterns, and obsolescence) are all continuously influencing where companies want to go with technology. Third, unexpected roadblocks occur—for example, the company that produces the application platform that runs your business just declared bankruptcy. If building and evolving a technology roadmap were easy, it would always be done well.

Why do we need a technology roadmap? IT managers believe that without the guidance of a roadmap, their companies run the risk of making suboptimal decisions—technology choices that make sense today but position the company poorly for the future. There is also a strong sense that the exercise of developing a technology roadmap is valuable even if the actual roadmap that is developed is subject to change. Another adage applies: "Plans are nothing; planning is everything." It is through the articulation of a technology roadmap that you learn what you did well, where you failed, and how to improve the process. Finally, a technology roadmap limits the range of technology options and reduces the decision-making effort compared to facing one-off decisions repeatedly over time. Because a roadmap has cast the evolution of technology on a certain path, it means that an organization can simply accept this decision and not revisit it repeatedly. Thus, a technology roadmap reduces the organization's cognitive workload.

This chapter begins with a general discussion of technology roadmaps and presents a model to explain various input factors. It then describes each of the components of a technology roadmap and offers advice derived from the shared experiences of the focus group's managers.

---

[1]McKeen, J. D., and H. A. Smith, "Creating and Evolving a Technology Roadmap." *Communication of the Association for Information Systems* 20, article 21 (September 2006): 451–63. Reproduced by permission of the Association for Information Systems.

WHAT IS A TECHNOLOGY ROADMAP?

It is important to develop an understanding of what a technology roadmap actually is. To do so, we can build on the analogy of a travel map. A travel map is a guide that tells you where you are now by positioning you within the greater environs and highlights existing options to get you where you want to go. In offering directions, it can suggest travel times, routes, and scenic alternatives, but that's about as far as it goes. A technology roadmap differs. Unlike a travel map, it is difficult to purchase a technology "map" for the simple reason that organizations all have uniquely different starting points, different goals, and, therefore, different destinations. Travel maps accommodate travel regardless of destination or purpose. Technology roadmaps must also entertain external factors such as industry trends, the competitive landscape, and vendor strategies and offerings. Finally, alternative technology options are not self-evident and must be identified through research and exploration (and sometimes experimentation). Thus, each option bears a different cost and time structure. As an analogy, the travel map provides an excellent starting point, but when creating a technology roadmap, more is needed. The first step is to develop a common understanding of what exactly is meant by the term *technology roadmap.*

In the group, every participant used a different definition of the term. On analysis, we reached consensus on aspects of the definition. It was clear that the main purpose of a technology roadmap is to establish the technology direction for the organization. It has two objectives. The first is to articulate how technology will support the enterprise's overall vision, strategy, and objectives. This was evident in the definition used at one company:

> *Our technology roadmap is the collective vision of the opportunities for technology to serve the business.*

The second goal is to frame and constrain technology solutions to provide coherence and integration among those solutions across the enterprise and to define target architectures to implementers. These dual objectives simply recognize the need for IT to forge a relationship between IT and the business while, at the same time, serving the unique internal needs of IT. After some discussion, the group agreed on the following definition:

> *A technology roadmap is a mechanism for the identification, justification, planned evolution, and orchestration of technologies to enhance business performance.*

THE BENEFITS OF A TECHNOLOGY ROADMAP

That every participating organization had a technology roadmap suggests that there are perceived benefits in building and evolving one. These benefits fit into two categories—external and internal—reflecting the dual purpose of the technology roadmap as described previously.

External Benefits (Effectiveness)

External benefits relate to aligning IT with the business, result in IT *effectiveness,* and include the following:

- *Achieving business goals.* A technology roadmap compares the business plan with the current technological environment to identify gaps. To the extent that the technology roadmap effectively addresses these gaps, business goals should be supported by technology.

- *Reducing complexity.*   The technology environment is highly complex due to the degree of interaction among systems. The adoption of a technology roadmap typically reduces the number and variety of technological choices, thereby simplifying things. Just getting to single versions of applications, such as one e-mail program, greatly reduces complexity.

- *Enhancing interoperability of business functionality across lines of business (LOBs).*   Identifying the technology that supports different LOBs is the first step toward integration. The degree of integration and interoperability is first and foremost a business decision. The technology should be designed to support this vision.

- *Increasing flexibility.*   This begs the question of whether differentiation or integration enables flexibility. With respect to technology, the argument is usually won by commonalities.

- *Increasing speed of implementation.*   Common standards, methodologies, and technology platforms relieve the learning burden and, thereby, increase the time to market with new systems.

- *Preserving investments in new and existing systems.*   Mapping technologies on an evolutionary trajectory means that IT investments are based on long-term considerations.

- *Responding to market changes.*   Having an up-to-date technology roadmap means that IT can respond accurately and appropriately to market changes. Organizations without the benefit of a technology roadmap are forced to build decisions "from the ground up" as opposed to building from an established framework.

- *Focusing investment dollars.*   Having a technology roadmap means that investments in IT can be much more focused. Fewer dollars, better targeted, produce enhanced results.

- *Responding to new legislation.*   Compliance with new legislation (e.g., the Sarbanes–Oxley Act, privacy, environmental programs) is greatly simplified with a rationalized technology roadmap.

- *Reducing difficulties associated with deployment of new technologies.*   New technologies require learning and change. Therefore, fewer technologies, common platforms, and similar approaches effectively relieve this burden.

Internal Benefits (Efficiency)

Internal benefits attribute to IT directly and result in IT *efficiency*, including the following:

- *Providing a common design point.*   This facilitates the end-to-end integration of reusable components and applications.

- *Building a consistent and cohesive technology base.*   Without the proliferation of haphazard technology, one can create a critical mass of skills dedicated to select technologies.

- *Ability to move forward in planned phases.*   With technologies mapped onto a life cycle, there is an orderly evolution for each technology, which creates synergies.

- *Consolidating global solutions.*   For global companies, the local in-country technologies are synched to the global technology roadmap, which introduces even greater consistency across business processes, reducing overall IT expenditure.

- *Lowering the cost of development and maintenance.* Technology roadmaps provide an inventory of technology, and thus they make it possible to increase the reusability of system components, leverage commodity components available in the marketplace, standardize techniques across multiple applications, and prevent the "disintegration" and proliferation of execution, development, and operations architectures.

It is interesting to note that no companies in the group were able to demonstrate the *financial* impacts attributable to their adoption of a technology roadmap. Perhaps more surprising was the fact that the companies had not been asked by senior management to produce such a benefit statement. The initial development of a technology roadmap is typically an initiative of the IT department. This suggests that IT departments understand the benefits of a technology roadmap and appear not to question the value of committing resources to this activity. Perhaps the internal benefits of building a technology roadmap—which are significant, judging from the preceding list—justify the exercise all by themselves. These benefits appear to be more tangible and immediate than external benefits.

ELEMENTS OF THE TECHNOLOGY ROADMAP

The process of developing a technology roadmap is depicted in Figure 8.1. It hinges on a gap analysis to assess the extent to which the current state of technology supports the current and forecasted needs of the business. From this are derived the organization's future technology requirements, which, coupled with a migration strategy, constitute the core of a technology roadmap. Participants identified seven important activities in developing and maintaining a technology roadmap. These are described below and are interspersed with strategies suggested by the group, based on their experiences. At the outset, it is important to dispel the notion that the development of a technology roadmap is a "once every five years" undertaking. Instead, there was strong consensus that a technology roadmap

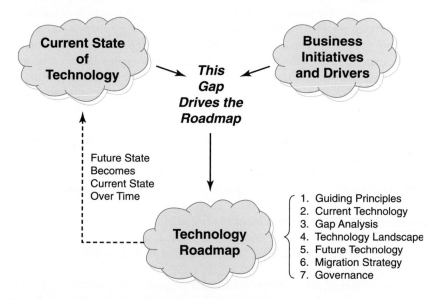

FIGURE 8.1 The Process of Developing a Technology Roadmap

should constitute a working instrument to be updated and revised annually. Otherwise it becomes inflexible, perhaps dated, and, as a result, unresponsive to the business.

Activity Number #1: Guiding Principles

When launching a technology roadmap, it is important to establish a set of principles that will guide its development and enhancement. First and foremost, this is a statement about the role and purpose of technology within the business that should clearly convey aspirations and purpose. It outlines how technology will support the business, stipulating the envisioned role for technology to play. This roadmap should be a statement about the *type* of technology support to be delivered to the business with a sense of performance. For example, contrast the following two statements: "We will provide technology that is proven, reliable, and cost effective" and "We will provide leading-edge technology."

In addition to establishing the role and purpose for the technology roadmap, it is important to outline its goals. One company's goal for its technology roadmap was "to increase the speed of developing, deploying, and productively executing future business models." It then outlined three strategies to accomplish this:

1. Decouple the business processes from the underlying IT applications.
2. Decouple business applications from the infrastructure.
3. Establish a new collaboration environment that supports the rapid introduction and productive use of the new business processes.

This signaled to the organization that IT was adopting a service-oriented architecture (SOA). Because SOA was not well understood by the business, the technology roadmap spoke to the desire to identify components of the business model, which could be designed as reusable software services; to adopt integrated and standardized processes for optimizing cost; to accelerate integrated data/information architecture to enable horizontal integration across the enterprise; and to provide a stable, secure, and ubiquitous workspace for employees to be more effective in their roles and efficient in their jobs by delivering information, applications, and people to easily collaborate within the context of business processes. This established the mandate, purpose, and goals of the technology roadmap, using language appropriate for the organizational context.

With the purpose and goals established, guiding principles can then be articulated to explain other key factors and decisions that would impact technology and, therefore, have a bearing on the technology roadmap. The following statements are examples of key principles used by focus group members:

- *Establish investment boundaries.* "We will invest in technology at a rate necessary to sustain our business growth."
- *Outline the role of technology for the organization.* "We will adopt a 'fast follower' strategy, aggressively adopting proven, architecturally compliant technologies."
- *Outline the role of technology within the industry.* "Technology is a core business competency."
- *Reinforce the role of standards.* "All components will adhere to open industry standards."
- *Specify the role of support.* "We will assist employees with technology problems that occur via call centers, desktop support, self-help, and/or service-level agreements."

- *Specify the impact on resident IT skills.* "We will draw technology expertise from our existing large skill base."
- *Outline development preference.* "We will buy first, build second."
- *Establish expectations.* "Service levels and availability are outlined for all production systems."
- *Adherence to standards.* "We will be security and privacy compliant."
- *Specify timeframe.* "The 'future' in our technology roadmap has a three- to five-year horizon."

Activity Number #2: Assess Current Technology

This is basically an inventory. It should outline what technologies the business currently has and describe their status (e.g., standard, unsupported, discontinued). The first task is to develop a classification scheme to assist in managing the inventory. For each type of technology domain (e.g., operating systems; hardware, desktops, servers, and storage; telecommunications and networks; applications; and databases), members recommended recording the following minimum information: business process area, platform, vendor, level of support, dependencies (products, applications), critical versus noncritical, and life cycle.

The next step is to assign a technology custodian/owner so someone within the firm is responsible for each technology domain. At one company, these individuals are referred to as technology "domain architects." Typical duties of such individuals include acquiring the technology, maintaining the relationship with the vendor, updating and enhancing the technology, facilitating in-house training for those working with the technology, accreditation regarding the technology, recording all applications of the technology, maintaining documentation (e.g., licensing; financing; and establishing service levels, guarantees, and warranties), and retiring the technology when appropriate. This can be a major responsibility as some individuals will have more than one domain assigned to them.

One of the key tools in managing the technology inventory is a framework to classify technologies. One such tool, the Application System Asset Management (ASAM) Decision Chart (Mangurian 1985), assesses the business importance (i.e., the application's overall value to the business), functional support (i.e., how well the system meets the business requirements), and technical support (i.e., the system's efficiency and effectiveness). This particular tool has been used successfully over a number of years by one firm. On an annual basis, all application systems are evaluated against these three criteria, leading to one of the following actions: maintain, renovate, replace, augment, or eliminate.

Another company uses a two-by-two matrix that evaluates applications on the basis of their criticality to the business (i.e., whether or not they support business processes deemed critical to the business units) and their strategic importance (i.e., those providing global functions that will not be replaced over the next two years). Placement within this matrix (i.e., maintenance classification) dictates service levels: strategic/critical applications receive "gold" service; critical/nonstrategic applications receive "silver" service; strategic/noncritical applications receive "bronze" service; and nonstrategic/noncritical applications receive "blue" maintenance. Yet another company uses the WISE chart to evaluate technologies on the basis of their strategic value and longevity, yielding four life cycle stages: watch, invest, support, and eliminate (McKeen and Smith 2003).

The focus group agreed that the specific classification scheme matters less than the fact that a company has a scheme to manage its technology inventory. The technology inventory also provides input to other processes such as risk management, team development, and skills planning.

Activity Number #3: Analyze Gaps

With a technology inventory in place, organizations can then perform a gap analysis between the technology that is currently available and that which is required. The first step is to identify the required technology. This ties the technology roadmap directly to the business and is perhaps the most crucial step in developing an effective plan. One manager made this point rather emphatically by saying, "Get this wrong, and the roadmap is junk." Others suggested that simply asking business leaders for their future requirements will not work for a number of reasons. First, business leaders do not think in terms of requirements; they think in terms of growth, customers, sales, markets, costs, suppliers, and shareholders. It takes a lot of work and skill to translate this view of the business into technology requirements. Second, the roadmap has to be ahead of the business—that is, it must reflect the fact that because business changes faster than technology, you have to build technology in anticipation of business change and growth. A technology roadmap cannot afford to be reactive; it must be proactive regardless of whether the technology vision is "quick second" or "late adopter." Third, business is driven by innovation and differentiation, while IT benefits from standards, common features, and universality. This will always put IT at odds with the business. According to one participant, it boils down to this question: When is a line of business so different that common systems don't make sense, and what criteria do you apply to test this?

Eliciting business drivers and building a composite picture of the technology required to support the business vision is more of art than science. It requires close cooperation between IT and the business. This cooperation happens at many levels within the organization and should be an ongoing activity. The annual IT planning cycle articulates the applications to be introduced over the next year, but attempting to derive a technology roadmap from this activity is a case of "too little, too late." IT has to be working with the business closely enough to be well ahead of the annual planning cycle. At one company, the domain architects are being reoriented to align them more closely with the business units to create a better early-warning system for application needs driven by growth and changes to the business model. Its manager stated the following:

> The enterprise has a vision, and each line of business has a vision, and the job of the domain architects is to put all these visions on the table to expose gaps. To do this, architects need to be 75 percent business and 25 percent technology. Today they are the reverse.

At another company, business analysts work together with enterprise architects to "get a fix on future business directions." We tend to think of architects and technical experts as playing the key roles, whereas the focus group pointed out that the best vantage point for performing a gap analysis between the existing technology and emerging business drivers is the CIO office, due to the fact that the CIO sits at the same table as other senior executives to set the strategy for the business. The focus group pointed out that having the CIO at these sessions provides a significant advantage in terms of forecasting the future for technology within the company.

With a "line of sight" to the business strategy coupled with an accurate technology inventory, all the tools to perform a gap analysis are in place. The outcome of the gap analysis is an articulation of the technology required to support the business's vision and strategy. Unfortunately, a technology roadmap cannot be simply created from this analysis because it must also be governed by trends in the external environment.

Activity Number #4: Evaluate Technology Landscape

The group was unanimous in its recommendation that firms must continuously invest in research and development (R&D) if they are to keep abreast of technology. The size of this investment, however, differs depending on how critical IT is to a firm. The roadmap should articulate how large this investment will be, how it will be enacted, who is responsible, and what guidelines are in place to assist this initiative. Setting these structures in place is the easy part; knowing when enough is enough is more difficult.

In the past much of a company's technology was dictated by its choice of vendor; if asked what its technology roadmap was, a firm could simply reply by naming a single vendor. Today's lock-in by vendors is much reduced, particularly with the widespread adoption of open standards, interoperability among various platforms, and Web services. Interestingly, this has probably resulted in the need for downstream firms to bear a greater portion of the R&D burden, whereas in the past they could leverage the vendor's R&D to a greater extent. Focus group members shared a number of different approaches to R&D, but all shared a common challenge: capital funding.

At some companies R&D flies "below the radar" as "skunkworks." Here the IT department uses its own money that it has squirreled away over time, treating R&D similar to a cost of doing business. In others R&D is financed by a technology investment fund (i.e., a tax to the business levied as a percentage of technology usage). This fund is governed by a committee composed of senior managers who guide the investment in R&D. In another firm, IT maintenance is reduced by 10 to 15 percent per year, and the dollars are reallocated to strategic IT investments, much of which are funneled to a "technology adoption program" described as a "sandbox where new technologies are tried, improved, tested, scaled, and assessed for business value." These latter approaches are preferable because they don't attempt to hide R&D. In fact, they make R&D transparent to the organization. Business leaders understand the need for reinvestment in the physical plant; IT is no different.

Activity Number #5: Describe Future Technology

This part of the IT roadmap should contain a description of the technologies to be adopted in the future. These future technology roadmaps should not be simple lists. They should also include the *logic* that was used in the decision to follow a certain path. If, for instance, the technology roadmap depicts a preferred vendor strategy, equally if not more important is the reasoning that was used in selecting this strategy. Making this explicit within the roadmap permits others to challenge the logic without challenging the actual decision. This is essential, particularly if you wish to obtain constructive input from business managers when creating your technology roadmap.

As important as the logic behind the roadmap are the assumptions built into the roadmap. IT professionals are frequently guilty of assuming that it is obvious to others why a certain strategy has been adopted. Hence, there is value in making all assumptions explicit. As with the need to present the logic of the roadmap, it is also vital to expose all embedded assumptions. These assumptions may reflect trends in the competitive market-place (e.g., vendor A will continue to dominate with its software offerings), the general environment (e.g., open standards adoption will accelerate), specific technologies (e.g., thin client architecture's time has arrived), or general trends (e.g., new development will move toward SOA). This exposure provides the basis for meaningful conversation to help clarify the roadmap's dependence on widely accepted (but perhaps not articulated) assumptions.

The group felt that describing the technology was fairly straightforward, using major technology domains such as hardware, software, applications, and networks. The difficulty often is in regard to the granularity of future technology. The question is this: How do you decide the level of detail in future technology platforms? According to one manager, "If your roadmap is severely impacted by business change, your roadmap is probably too tactical." The opposite, creating a technology roadmap that is too high level, is equally inadequate. The goal is to find the "sweet spot" between the two extremes, which is "more art than science," he said.

Activity Number #6: Outline Migration Strategy

A technology roadmap should also outline a migration strategy to get you from today's technology platforms to tomorrow's. At first glance, the implementation of a technology roadmap appears similar to the accomplishment of other major IT initiatives. The focus group, however, was quick to point out the differences. Of these, the primary one is that a technology roadmap is not a self-contained project; it affects *every* project as technologies are embedded within the entire spectrum of applications, many of which cross lines of business, geography, and generations. By positioning each technology domain on a life cycle (e.g., watch, invest, support, eliminate), two dominant migration strategies emerge: "gradual" versus "big bang."

The gradual strategy focuses on the application (i.e., as new applications are implemented or reworked, their technology is updated to fall in line with the new technology directions). The big bang strategy emphasizes the technology (i.e., all instances of a given technology are updated across all applications). The choice is not an either–or situation, nor is it a "technology only" decision. Rather the choice is (or should be) dictated by the business. There are few situations where the big bang approach is absolutely necessary simply because there are always means of staging the conversion over time, applications, business lines, and/or platforms. As one participant noted, "Even large architectural builds/deployments are typically done within a program across several phases." Sometimes, though, the big bang is a business necessity due to the need to reap advantages in a reduced timeframe.

A major challenge facing the migration strategy is the need to assign priorities to the various technology components that need to be changed. One organization uses the following criteria to assess the criticality of migration in order to assign order of execution:

- Technology elements that are inflexible
- Elements that do not meet the strategic direction
- Components that are expensive to maintain
- Components that do not meet nonfunctional requirements (e.g., scalability, extensibility)
- Architectural designs built to reflect obsolete business strategies (e.g., segmentation silos, line-of-business silos).

Once priorities are assigned, timelines can be established for the migration of various technologies.

A migration strategy should explicitly recognize a number of dominant trends within technology, such as the movement toward service-oriented applications and the deconstruction of applications into layers (e.g., presentation, business process, and data). Although such trends provide useful high-level guidance, they need to be augmented by more tactical guidelines (see Appendix A). Of particular interest here is the need for a migration strategy to explicitly plan for the migration of *people* skills in alignment with the future technology demands.

Activity Number #7: Establish Governance

Every organization should have an established process in place to articulate who is responsible for creating the technology roadmap, how and on what basis, by whom it is updated and enhanced, and finally who approves the technology roadmap. Most organizations in the group felt that the technology roadmap was legitimately the responsibility of the enterprise architecture function, which is responsible for mapping out the architectural platforms to support the various lines of business. The majority of companies recognized the need for two distinct levels of architecture governance within their organizations:

- *Strategic.* Individuals and groups at this level (typically, senior executives from IT and the business) set the overall architecture direction and strategy and ensure alignment with business objectives. They set standards and approve deviations from these standards. In addition, they monitor the overall attainment of the goals as articulated within the technology roadmap.
- *Tactical.* Members of this tactical group tend to be from the IT ranks, including architects, analysts, and managers. They typically work across lines of business as well as within lines of business with responsibility for the execution of the strategy (as opposed to its development). A key role is the provision of architecture consulting services to project teams.

At one company the key personnel of the tactical group are domain architects who have responsibility for broad categories of technology (e.g., server platforms), subdomain architects who have responsibility for technologies within a larger domain (e.g., desktops), and product stewards who have responsibility for specific products (e.g., Microsoft Windows XP). Accountability cascaded down this hierarchy with domain architects responsible for setting strategy, understanding the marketplace, and controlling proliferation of technology and product stewards responsible for new releases and versions of technologies as well as troubleshooting. At this organization, ultimate accountability rested with the executive architecture review board—a committee composed of senior business and IT architects—who ratify the technology roadmap and make final decisions regarding proposed deviations to the roadmap. If a need arises for an "off-profile" (i.e., "noncompliant") technology, it must be brought before the architecture review board for an "opinion." According to the manager, this is a very effective mechanism because "most people don't want their project elevated to the executive architectural review board!"

A major part of governance is enforcement. Effective enforcement requires IT to develop a new breed of "corporate" architect who is business focused and businesscentric.

According to one member, "Techcentric architects tend to be seen as police officers . . . there to enforce the law." It is better to have a businesscentric architect who can entertain business solutions that violate the preferred technology direction in light of increased technology risk (i.e., the risk of doing it) and business risk (i.e., the risk of not doing it) and arrive at a decision that best suits the business. The difference in approach is one of accommodation, as opposed to denial and prevention.

At one company the IT group did not want to ever have to "tell a business unit that they could not buy a specific package." The trade-off was to let the business specify the application's requirements and to let IT choose the product. Another firm tackled this problem by charging the business for the additional costs of a noncompliant application, such as extra in-house skills, application integration, conversions, and interfacing software. The overriding goal in all these firms was to achieve optimal decisions for the business, not rigid adherence to a technology roadmap.

A repository can be an aid to tracking decisions as well as a means of listing assigned responsibilities. At one company this "architecture library" lists all technology domains (e.g., hardware, applications, etc.) and all products within each domain. Product metadata include the following:

- Status (i.e., emerging, contained, mainstream, declining, retirement, obsolete)
- Proposed replacement product
- Name of product steward, subdomain architect, and architect
- Business impact analysis
- Interdependencies
- Total cost of ownership

Knowing that a specific product is "declining," who the product steward is, the name of the replacement product, and the business impact analysis demonstrating exactly where and how this product affects business processes all provide extremely valuable information to the organization. Such a resource requires a significant amount of work to build but, once built, greatly reduces the complexity of maintaining and evolving a technology roadmap.

PRACTICAL STEPS FOR DEVELOPING A TECHNOLOGY ROADMAP

As part of the meeting, focus group members were asked the following question: If you were a 'roadmap consultant,' what advice would you offer to management?" When their suggestions were combined and analyzed, the collective wisdom reduced to the following five recommendations. Interestingly, this advice would arguably apply to many, if not most, IT initiatives.

1. *Be bold and innovative when planning the roadmap.*
   - What you have done should not be the gauge by which you determine what you should do.
   - Innovation is key; start with a blank piece of paper.
   - Invent your future. Inspire others to help you build it.
2. *Align technology with the business.*
   - Determine what role technology will play in satisfying the business vision.

- Focus on using technology to solve business problems and deliver business value.
- Know when it is appropriate to choose leading-edge technology over being a late adopter/quick second.
- Ensure that the roadmap is flexible, extensible, and attainable to change with the business.
- Ensure that the organizational structure supports the delivery of a technology roadmap.

3. *Secure support for the roadmap.*
- Ensure that the funding model supports a technology roadmap.
- A migration strategy and roadmap require an executive sponsor, ownership, and accountability. Ensure that strategic decisions are made at the right level.
- Stay the course!

4. *Don't forget the people.*
- Every technology change requires changes in people's skills.
- Map new technologies to required skill acquisition.
- Take steps to ensure that IT personnel understand the technology roadmap and its logic, ramifications, and time frame.

5. *Control, measure, and communicate progress.*
- Measure progress along the way; use leading indicators.
- A successful roadmap must be measurable and updated at appropriate checkpoints.
- Communication of the roadmap is essential to success.
- Establish a governance process to manage technology and vendor choices.

Conclusion

The purpose of a technology roadmap is to guide the development of technology in an organization. But as pointed out in this chapter, it serves a much greater purpose for a business. It communicates the role that technology will play in advancing business goals. It outlines the explicit assumptions on which the roadmap is based and describes how these assumptions directly affect the rate and order of attainment of goals. It suggests the impact of future technology on the set of required in-house skills for the IT department. And it provides a vehicle for explaining the logic of technology-related decisions to business managers who otherwise interpret such decisions as overly rigid and unproductive. As such, a technology roadmap should be viewed as an important opportunity for IT to engage the business in meaningful and productive dialogue focused on furthering business goals. To limit this activity to simply forecasting technology is to miss a significant opportunity.

References

Carroll, L. *Alice's Adventures in Wonderland.* London: MacMillan & Co., 1865.

Mangurian, G. E. *Alternative to Replacing Obsolete Systems.* Cambridge, MA: Index Systems Inc., 1985.

McKeen, J. D., and H. A. Smith. *Making IT Happen.* Chichester, England: John Wiley & Sons, 2003.

APPENDIX A

Principles to Guide a Migration Strategy

One focus organization adopted the following four key principles to guide its migration strategy:

1. Migrate from productcentric to processcentric applications architecture using a service-based architecture that is grouped into layers such as presentation, business process, and data.

   • Maintain a sourcing strategy to develop strategic systems with competitive advantage in-house. Nonstrategic systems will be sourced through packages and services as available.

   • Maintain a technology skills base for critical technologies.

   • Utilize strategic partnerships to bring in leading-edge technology skills to accelerate implementation while, at the same time, transferring knowledge to your staff to permit in-house support and future development.

2. Deploy modular or component-based applications to minimize test and utility life cycle costs.

   • Adhere to a component-based and layered architecture with standardized, generic interfaces.

   • Ensure conformance of application development initiatives to the logical architecture specifications in order to engineer quality into the applications.

   • Build flexibility into the application components by allowing end-users to establish and change business rules.

3. Utilize components based on industry standards as the building blocks of architecture services.

   • Adhere to (or adopt) industry-accepted standards and methodology to promote ease of integration.

   • Minimize the complexity of application interfaces by adopting flexible data interface standards—for example, extensible markup language (XML).

   • Adhere to corporate technology and application development standards in order to improve the efficiency, effectiveness, and timeliness of application development initiatives.

4. Insulate applications from being affected by changes in other applications through middleware.

   • Use enterprise application integration (EAI) middleware services to integrate application services across and within business domains.

   • Define and document application interfaces well in a metadata repository that includes interface methods, purpose, and terms of usage.

   • Include in EAI services application interface services and work flow integration services, both within the department and in the extended enterprise.

   • Increase the degree of information and work flow integration across customer- and vendor-facing processes.

Delivering IT Functions:
A Decision Framework[1]

I n a recent article, the authors was pointed out how dramatically the list of IT responsibilities has grown over the past fifteen years (Smith and McKeen 2006). To the standard list of "operations management," "systems development," and "network management" have now been added responsibilities for "business transformation," "regulatory compliance," "enterprise and security architecture," "information and content management," and "business continuity management" as well as others. Never before has IT management been challenged to assume such diversity of responsibility and to deliver on so many different fronts. As a result, IT managers have begun to critically examine how they deliver their various functions to the organization.

In the past, organizations met additional demands for IT functionality by simply adding more staff. Although this option remains available today, several others are now at hand for delivering IT functionality. Software can be purchased, customized systems can be developed by third parties, whole business processes can be outsourced, technical expertise can be contracted, data center facilities can be managed, networking solutions (e.g., data, voice) are obtainable, data storage is available on demand, and companies will manage your desktop environment as well as all of your support/maintenance functions. Faced with this smorgasbord of delivery options, organizations are experimenting as never before. As with other forms of experimentation, however, there have been failures as well as successes, and most decisions have been made on a "one-off" basis. What is still lacking is a unified decision framework to guide IT managers through this maze of delivery options.

This chapter explores how organizations are choosing to deliver IT functions. The first section defines what we mean by an IT function and proposes a maturity model for IT function delivery. Following this, we take a conceptual look at IT delivery options, then we analyze actual company experiences with four different IT delivery options—(1) in-house, (2) insource, (3) outsource, and (4) partnership—in order to contrast theory with practice. The final section of the chapter presents a framework for guiding delivery decisions stemming from the shared experiences and insights of the managers in the focus group.

---

[1]McKeen, J. D., and H. A. Smith. "Delivering IT Functions: A Decision Framework." *Communications of the Association for Information Systems* 19, article 35 (June 2007): 725–39. Reproduced by permission of the Association for Information Systems.

A MATURITY MODEL FOR IT FUNCTIONS

Smith and McKeen (2006) list the overall responsibilities for which IT is held accountable. IT functions, in contrast, represent the specific activities that are delivered by IT in the fulfillment of its responsibilities. For instance, IT is held *responsible* for delivering process automation, which it may satisfy by delivering the following IT *functions* to the organization: project management, architecture planning, business analysis, system development, quality assurance and testing, and infrastructure support. Although an IT department provides myriad functions to its parent organization, a compendium of the key roles was created by amalgamating the lists provided by the members of the focus group (see Table 9.1).[2] This is meant to be representative, not comprehensive, to demonstrate how IT functions can form the basis of a decision framework.

Participants pointed out that not all IT functions are at the same stage of development and maturity, a fact that has ramifications for how these functions could be delivered. And although some functions are well defined, common to most companies, and commoditylike, others are unique, nonstandardized, and not easily shared. There was general agreement, however, that a maturity model for IT function delivery has five stages: (1) unique, (2) common, (3) standardized, (4) commoditized, and (5) utility.

1. *Unique.* A unique IT function is one that provides strategic (perhaps even proprietary) advantage and benefit. These IT functions seek to differentiate the organization in the marketplace. They are commonly, but not necessarily, delivered by internal IT staff due to the strategic aspect of the function being provided. Alternately, the function may be provided either by "boutique" firms that create special-purpose applications or by firms with in-depth industry experience that cannot be matched by internal IT staff (or even the internal business managers). Examples of unique IT functions might be business analysis, application integration, or knowledge-enabling business processes. Such functions depend on familiarity with the organization's internal systems combined with an in-depth knowledge of the business.

2. *Common.* This type of IT function caters to common (i.e., universal) organizational needs. Such a function has little ability to differentiate the business, but it provides a necessary, perhaps critical, component (e.g., financial systems, HR). Providers capitalize on commonality of function and are motivated to provide functions (e.g., customer relationship management [CRM], quality assurance, content management) to maximize market applicability. Most print operations are now common functions, for instance. Although they differ from firm to firm, they are required by most firms but are not considered to provide any competitive advantage.

3. *Standardized.* Standardized IT functions not only provide common tasks/activities but also adhere to a set of standards developed and governed by external agencies. Although multiple, perhaps competing, standards may exist, the attributes of such functions are well articulated, and as a result these functions enjoy wide applicability due to their standardization. Providers of such functionality (e.g.,

---

[2]We prefer the term *service* to *function*. We chose the term *function*, however, to avoid confusion with the current usage of *service* as in service-oriented architecture (SOA).

TABLE 9.1   List of IT Functions

IT Function	Description
Business Analysis	Liaison between IT and the business to align IT planning, match technology to business needs, and forecast future business directions
Systems Analysis	Elicits business requirements, designs process flow, outlines document management, and creates design specifications for developers
Strategy and Planning	Project prioritization, budgeting, financial planning/accountability, strategy development, policy development, and portfolio analysis
Data Management	Transactional data (e.g., invoicing, shipping), customer data (e.g., customer relationship management [CRM]), records management, knowledge management, business intelligence
Project Management	Managing the resources (e.g., money, people, time, equipment, etc.) necessary to bring a project to fruition in compliance with requirements
Architecture	Establishing the interaction of all system components (e.g., hardware, software, and networking), enterprise compliance with specifications and standards
Application Development	Designing, writing, documenting, and unit testing required code to enact specific functionality in compliance with a design specification
Quality Assurance and Testing	Testing all components of an application prior to production to ensure it is functioning correctly and meets regulatory and audit standards
Networking	Managing all networking components (e.g., hubs and routers) to handle all forms of organizational communication (e.g., data, voice, streaming video)
Operating Systems and Services	Operating systems for all hardware platforms and other devices (e.g., handhelds), upgrades, maintenance, and enhancements
Application Support	Provides enhancements, updates, and maintenance for application systems plus help and assistance for application users
Data Center Operations	Manages all operations of the production data center and data storage environment, including backup, DRP, security and access, and availability
Application Software	Manages all major applications (e.g., purchased or developed) to ensure viability of functionality and upgradability with a special emphasis on legacy systems
Hardware	Data servers, power supplies, desktops, laptops, Blackberries, telephones, and special equipment (e.g., POS, badge readers, RFID tags)

billing/payment functions, check processing, forms management, facilities management, disaster recovery planning) seek opportunities beyond common functions by promoting (i.e., developing, proposing, and/or adopting) standards to enhance the interoperability of their functional offerings.

4. *Commoditized.* These functions are considered commodities similar to oil and gas. Once attributes are stipulated, functions are interchangeable and indistinguishable (i.e., any barrel of oil will suffice). Furthermore, there may be many providers of the function. A good example is application service providers (ASPs) who deliver standard applications developed by third-party vendors to client firms without customization. Other commodity functions include network services, server farms, storage capacity, backup services, and universal power supply (UPS). What really distinguishes a commodity is the realization that the "risks

imposed by its absence outweigh the burdens of maintaining its availability" (Marquis 2006).

5. *Utility.* A utility function is a commodity (such as electricity) delivered by a centralized and consolidated source.[3] This source typically consists of an amalgam of suppliers operating within an integrated network capable of generating sufficient resource to fulfill continuous on-demand requests. *Private* utilities operate in competition with other providers, whereas *public* utilities tend to be single providers overseen by regulatory agencies that govern supply, pricing, and size. Examples of utilities include Internet service providers (ISPs) as well as other telecommunication services (e.g., bandwidth on demand).

These stages represent an evolutionary progression (or maturation) in IT functionality. The logic is straightforward: successful, unique functions are copied by other organizations and soon become common; commonality among IT functions paves the way for standardization; standardized functions are easily and effectively transacted as commodities; and finally, commoditized functions can be provided by utilities should an attractive business model exist. The group interpreted this progression as an ongoing process—that is, individual functions would be expected to advance through the sequence of stages as they matured. Furthermore, the continual discovery of new and unique IT functions, which are required by organizations to differentiate themselves and create strategic advantage in the marketplace, would guarantee the continuation of the whole evolutionary progression as depicted in Figure 9.1.

Using this maturity model, we then classified the IT functions listed in Table 9.1 according to their attained maturity stage. The results are represented in Figure 9.2. The differences among various IT functions are quite remarkable. Hardware (including servers and storage) was considered to reside at the commodity end of the maturity model due to its degree of standardization and interoperability, whereas business analysis remains a relatively unique IT function that differs considerably from organization to organization. Application software is more varied. As Figure 9.2 indicates, some application software is commoditylike, whereas other applications are highly unique to individual firms. The remaining IT functions vary similarly with respect to the maturity of their development and adoption industrywide.

The impetus for this discussion of function maturity was an implicit assumption that mature functions would be likely candidates for external delivery, and unique functions would be likely candidates for internal delivery. According to Figure 9.2, functions such as hardware, networks, common applications, and data center operations would be natural candidates for external provisioning, and IT planning, business and systems analysis, project management, and application development would be more likely provided by internal IT staff. The group agreed that these were indeed *general* trends. What proved to be somewhat of a surprise, though, was the degree that this generalization did not appear to hold as members of the focus group repeatedly shared examples of their specific sourcing activities that

---

[3]This concept has generated a significant amount of interest recently (Hagel and Brown 2001; Rappa 2004; Ross and Westerman 2004). Carr (2005), for example, speculates that not only is the utility computing model inevitable, but it will dramatically change the nature of the whole computing industry in like fashion to electrical generation of the previous century.

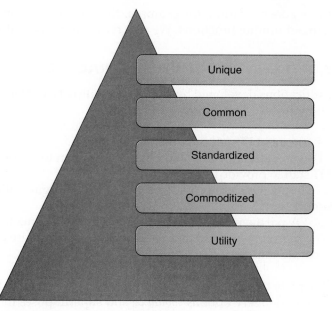

FIGURE 9.1   Maturity Model for IT Function Delivery

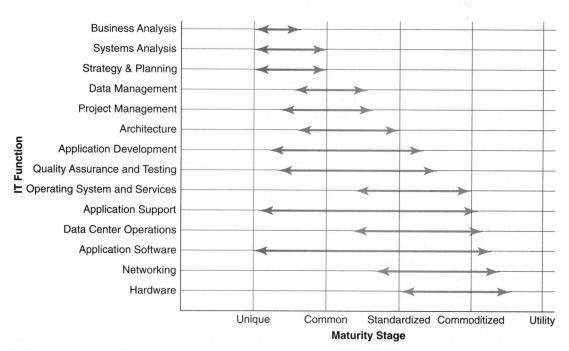

FIGURE 9.2   IT Functions Ranked by Maturity Stage

ran counter to this generalization; for example, they insourced commoditized functions and outsourced unique functions. We will return to this point later.

IT DELIVERY OPTIONS: THEORY VERSUS PRACTICE

Building on classifications developed by Lacity and Willcocks (2000), there are four different delivery options for IT functions:

1. *In-house.*   Permanent IT staff provide the IT function.
2. *Insource.*   IT personnel are brought into the organization to supplement the existing permanent IT staff to provide the IT function.
3. *Outsource.*   IT functions are provided by an external organization using its own staff and resources.
4. *Partnership.*   A partnership is formed with another organization to provide IT functions. The partnership could take the form of a joint venture or involve the creation of a separate company.

Figure 9.3 depicts the group's assessment of what the relationship between specific IT functions and delivery options *should be* and superimposes the four IT delivery options on the maturity grid. From this model it is clear that *in-house* staff should be assigned tasks that are in the unique–common maturity stages. Asking in-house staff to provide commoditylike functions would not be leveraging their unique knowledge of the business; because of their versatility, they can provide any IT function. As a result, their area of application was seen as being on the left of Figure 9.3 from top to bottom. *Insourcing* is basically a strategy of leveraging the in-house IT staff on a temporary basis. As such, contract staff should normally be assigned to work with permanent IT staff on a subset of the full range of tasks provided internally. *Partnerships* tend to exist in the lower part of Figure 9.3 because the truly unique tasks of business/systems analysis, planning, data management, and project management tend to be limited to a single organization and its strategy. Instead, partnerships were envisioned to focus on functions such as hardware, applications, software, and networking. Such partnerships could form regardless of maturity stage, which explains the left-to-right positioning of this IT delivery option in Figure 9.3 Finally, *outsourcing* should comprise a subset of partnerships much the same as insourcing comprises a subset of in-house functions. The reason is due to differences in governance; outsourcing arrangements are well articulated and governed by service-level agreements (SLAs), and partnerships are typically governed by memoranda of understanding (MOUs). If an organization is interested in a more flexible, innovative, and open-ended initiative, it would be better advised to seek a joint venture with another firm. Hence, partnerships were seen to have broader potential as a delivery option for IT functions.

Figure 9.3 represents the focus group's "generally accepted wisdom" regarding IT function delivery, yet the extent of the overlap of functions provided by the different delivery options is very pronounced. As such, Figure 9.3 provides limited guidance for managers tasked with choosing delivery options for specific IT functions. In order to gain more insight into decision behavior in practice, the group was asked to share recent examples of IT functions they were currently delivering by each of the four delivery options. In addition, they were asked to describe the

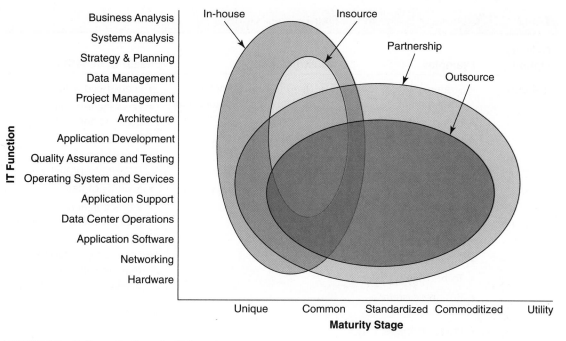

FIGURE 9.3   Delivery Options for IT Functions

justification criteria that their firm used in making these decisions as well as the benefits they felt they had realized. These examples were subsequently analyzed and the results used to create Table 9.2.

Perhaps the most surprising result based on the examples in column 2 of Table 9.2 is the lack of evidence of a relationship between IT function and delivery option. Such a relationship, were it to exist, would provide a natural basis for a decision framework. However, not only does it not exist, but there is considerable evidence to the contrary (i.e., the observation that identical IT functions are being delivered by all four delivery options). As a case in point, various types of systems development as well as application support/maintenance functions are provided by all four delivery options. Earlier we noted the generally accepted wisdom did not appear to hold up that commodity functions are ready candidates for outsourcing whereas unique functions are not. The data in Table 9.2 further corroborate this observation. Given this, one wonders what the operative criteria for choosing delivery options are if not the type (or maturity) of the IT function.

THE "REAL" DECISION CRITERIA

To explore this issue, participants were asked to review a recent business case and to share the *actual* criteria that were used to select the specific IT delivery option. Column 3 in Table 9.2 illustrates the justifications used for each of the four delivery options. This paints a much clearer picture of the decision criteria being used by IT managers when selecting delivery options.

TABLE 9.2   Example of Usage of the Four Delivery Options

Delivery Option	Examples	Justification	Realized Benefits
In-house	• Strategic system development • Legacy system support • New system development • Help desk/desktop support • Information/ document management • Application support • Intranet development • Technology support • Business systems analysis • Project management • Security services (change control) • Business intelligence and reporting	• Need to have complete control over the intellectual property • Need it *now* • Work is strategic • Skunkworks • Internal consulting to the business	• High-speed delivery • Leverage internal business and system knowledge • Ownership of intellectual property • Security of data • Protection and preservation of critical knowledge • Focus on core systems that are considered key assets
Insource	• Portal development • Specialized system (e.g., POS, CRM) development • Data warehouse development • Database development • Intranet development • Corporate systems development • Contract staff to provide key skills • Both local contractors and offshore company on retainer	• Need to have control over project delivery • Exposing intellectual property not an issue • Recurring program delivery such as ERP and CRM	• Highly flexible (e.g., personnel, engagement, and assignments) • Best of multiple vendors used • No need to expand internal IT staff • Staff easily meshed with existing teams • Semipermanent personnel if desired • Quick access to specific skill sets • Manage people as opposed to contracts • Evens out staffing "hills and valleys"

(continued)

TABLE 9.2 *(continued)*

Delivery Option	Examples	Justification	Realized Benefits
Outsource	• Infrastructure for new product • Business processes (e.g., billing, payroll) • Operations • Help desk • Field service support • Network management • Technology infrastructure (servers, storage, communications) • Web site development and hosting • Technology rollout • New stand-alone project delivery	• The work is not "point of differentiation." • Company does not have the competency in-house. • Deliverable is well understood, and SLAs are articulated to the satisfaction of both parties. • The outsourcer is "world class."	• Speed to market for specific products/systems • Acquire instant expertise as vendors are experts (often world class) • Business risk transferred to supplier • Outsourcer provides more "levers" for value creation (e.g., size, scope) • Lower cost than in-house
Partnership	• Common service (e.g., statement processing and payment services) • Emergency backup and support • Shared infrastructure • Special application development (e.g., critical knowledge requirement)	• Realize alignment on a benefit-sharing model • Enable collaborating partners to compete with others outside the partnership	• Future business growth and/or opportunities that arose from the partnership • Benefits not limited to a specific product or system deliverable • Decreased learning time and shared learning costs with partners

Decision Criterion #1: Flexibility

As a decision criterion, flexibility has two dimensions: response time (i.e., how quickly IT functionality can be delivered) and capability (i.e., the range of IT functionality). In-house staff rate high on both dimensions. Insourcing, as a complement to permanent IT staff, is also a highly flexible delivery option. Although outsourcing can *theoretically* provide just about anything, as a delivery option it exhibits less flexibility because of the need to locate an outsourcer who can provide the specific function, negotiate a contract, and monitor progress. Finally, partnerships enjoy considerable flexibility regarding capability but much less in terms of response time.[4] Within a partnership, the goal is to create value for the members of the partnership beyond what can be created by any single organization. How this value is created is up to the partnership, and as long as the parties agree, virtually anything is possible.

Decision Criterion #2: Control

This decision criterion also has two dimensions: delivery (i.e., ensuring that the delivered IT function complies with requirements) and security (i.e., protecting intellectual assets). Because they rank high on both dimensions of control, in-house and insourcing options are favored in cases where the work is proprietary, strategic, "below the radar" (i.e., skunkworks), or needed immediately (see Table 9.2). Outsourcing is the preferred delivery option when the function is not considered "a point of differentiation" and the deliverable is well understood and easily governed by means of a service-level agreement. Partnerships are designed to be self-controlling by the membership, and as previously observed, the functions provided by partnerships tend to be more open ended than those provided by other options.

In Table 9.2, column 4 presents the benefits of each delivery option. For the most part, this list is closely aligned with the list of justifications found in column 3. As such, it reinforces the existence of flexibility and control as key decision criteria. But in addition, a third key factor appears: *knowledge enablement*. Mentioned only tangentially within the list of justifications (e.g., "competence," "internal consulting," and "world class"), it is much more evident within the list of realized benefits (e.g., "leveraging internal business and system knowledge," "preservation of critical knowledge," "quick access to specific skill sets," "decreased learning time," and "sharing the learning costs with partners"). Marquis (2006) argues that "what is not easily replicable, and thus is potentially strategic, is an organization's intelligence and capability. By combining skills and resources in unique and enduring ways to grow core competencies, firms may succeed in establishing competitive advantage."

Decision Criterion #3: Knowledge Enhancement

Behind many delivery decisions is the need to either capture knowledge or retain it. One firm cited the example of developing a new business product. It "normally" would have been outsourced, but it was intentionally developed by in-house staff augmented by key contract personnel. The reason was to enable knowledge of this new business product to be transferred to internal IT personnel as well as to business personnel (who were also unfamiliar with this type of business offering). At another firm, the decision was made to insource key expertise "not to *do* the work, but to train internal staff *how* to do the work." The manager stated, "It would have been more logical and far cheaper to outsource the whole project." In another firm the support function for a key application was repatriated because the firm felt that it was losing an important learning opportunity that would keep staff abreast of developments in the market and develop new knowledge concerning a key line of business with growth potential. Furthermore, it is not just knowledge *development* that is the critical factor; knowledge *retention* is equally

---

[4]Response time within a partnership depends on two interdependent conditions holding: (1) a partnership must already exist, and (2) all partners must be committed to the same delivery timeline.

important. Whether implicitly or explicitly, knowledge enhancement appears to play a key role in most delivery decisions.

Decision Criterion #4: Business Exigency

Unforeseen business opportunities arise periodically, and firms with the ability to respond do so. Because of the urgency and importance of these business opportunities, they are not governed by the standard planning/budgeting processes and, indeed, most do not appear on the annual IT plan. Instead, a decision is made to seize the opportunity, and normal decision criteria are jettisoned in order to be responsive to the business. In these cases, whichever delivery option can produce results fastest is selected. The delivery option could be any of the four but is less likely to be a partnership unless the urgent request can be accommodated within the structure of an existing arrangement. Seen in a resource-planning context, business exigency demands constitute the "peaks" or "spikes." As one manager stated, "We have peaks and valleys, and we outsource the peaks."

The discussion also revealed the existence of two distinct sets of decision criteria: "normal" versus "actual." Manager after manager explained their decisions with the following preface: "*Normally* we would make the decision this way, but in this case we *actually* made the decision differently." When the participants referred to the normal set, they primarily cited issues of flexibility, control, and knowledge enablement. But when they described the actual decision criteria used to select the delivery option, a fourth factor emerged: "*business exigency.*"

It is difficult to ascertain the full effect of this last decision criterion. Certainly business exigency is a dominant factor. In an urgent situation, the fastest delivery option will take precedence. However, it is likely that the other three decision criteria play a significant role in the majority of delivery decisions regarding IT functionality. We are left to conclude that business exigency plays a more dramatic but less frequent role.

A DECISION FRAMEWORK FOR DELIVERING IT FUNCTIONS

Finally, the focus group was asked to outline a set of strategies for deciding how to deliver IT functions based on their collective experience and insights. The following step-by-step framework emerged.

Identify Your Core IT Functions

The identification of core functions is the first and most critical step in creating a decision framework for selecting delivery options. One manager captured this as follows:

> The days of IT being good at all things have long gone. . . . Today you have to pick your spots. . . . You have to decide where you need to excel to achieve competitive differentiation. . . . Being OK at most things is a recipe for failure sooner or later.

It was argued that the IT organization should approach the exercise of identifying its core functions by taking a page from the business handbook—that is, decide where competitive advantage lies, buttress it with the best resources, and divest all ancillary activities. In the case of IT, "divestiture" translates into seeking external *delivery* of functions because the responsibility and accountability for all IT functions will always remain with the IT organization.

Asked what constitutes a core function, the group suggested that it would depend entirely on where and how the IT organization decides it can leverage the business most effectively. Interestingly, what was considered *core* varied dramatically across the sample of organizations represented, spreading across the entire spectrum of IT functions including legacy system enhancement, business process design, enterprise system implementation, project management, and even data center operations. The only conclusion that resonated with the entire group was that "it matters more that the IT organization has identified core functions than what those functions actually are."

The articulation of core functions has major implications. First, the selection of core functions lays the cornerstone for the decision framework for delivery options. That is because, ideally, in-house functions reflect the organization's set of core functions. The assignment of permanent IT personnel to core IT functions, by default, assigns noncore activities to the remaining three IT delivery options (as we will see in the next strategy). Second, the selection of core functions directly impacts the careers of IT personnel. For example, one manager explained that at her organization "project management, business process design, and relationship management are key skills, and we encourage development in these areas." The implications for IT staff currently fulfilling "noncore" roles can be threatening as these areas are key targets for external delivery.

Create a "Function Delivery" Profile

One participant introduced the concept of a "function delivery" profile—a device that had been deployed successfully within his organization. It is reproduced in Table 9.3 and modified to accommodate the list of IT functions found in Table 9.1. This sample profile demonstrates (1) current core functions, (2) future core functions (additions and deletions), and (3) preferred delivery options for each IT function. What is most important is that this profile is built on an internal assessment of core IT functions. The justification provided by this particular organization for its specific delivery profile follows:

- Project management, business analysis, and architecture (both system and enterprise) are primarily provided in-house but may be augmented with insourced resources as required. In-house delivery is preferred for these functions for two reasons: First, project management and business analysis are recognized strengths within the organization, and second, this gives the organization more control over project direction.
- Because it is not recognized as a core function, development is primarily outsourced or insourced depending on the scope of the project.
- Quality assurance (QA) and testing are largely insourced as these are recognized as highly specialized skills, although not core functions. As a result, an entire division of IT is dedicated to these activities. Resources within this group are primarily contractors from a variety of vendors.
- Application support is a designated core function. Given the depth of business process knowledge needed as well as the in-depth knowledge of key applications required, this function is staffed entirely by internal IT personnel.
- Networking is currently provided by in-house staff augmented by insourced staff but is in transition. A recently formed partnership will eventually make this a noncore activity, and networking will eventually by provided entirely by the partner. This delivery option allows cost sharing and accommodates future growth. The partnership does not provide competitive advantage; it just makes good business sense.

TABLE 9.3   Sample Function Delivery Profile

Core Function?	IT Function	In-house	Insource	Outsource	Partnership
Yes	Business Analysis	✓			
	Systems Analysis		✓		
In Future	Strategy and Planning		✓	✓	
In Future	Data Management		✓		
Yes	Project Management	✓	✓		
Yes	Architecture	✓	✓		
	Application Development		✓	✓	✓
	QA and Testing		✓		
Now but not in future	Networking	✓			✓
	Operating Systems and Services		✓		
Yes	Application Support	✓			
	Data Center Operations			✓	
	Application Software			✓	✓
	Hardware			✓	

- The strategy and planning function as well as data management have been designated as future core functions. The firm is insourcing expertise from a top strategy consultancy to transition this skill to internal IT personnel. This explicitly recognizes the emerging importance of IT to the firm. Similarly, data management needs to become a key competitive strength in order to shorten product development cycles and time to market.

The sample profile depicted in Table 9.3 does not represent a "preferred" or even "typical" IT delivery strategy. Instead, it simply demonstrates how the four delivery options combine to satisfy the IT needs of a specific organization. Other organizations with a different mix of core functions (or even with the same mix) might well demonstrate a very different profile.

Evolve Full-time IT Personnel

Because of the alignment between core IT functions and in-house delivery, it is evident that delivery decisions should be based on leveraging an organization's full-time IT personnel. In fact, the focus group argued that this factor should be used to determine the majority of sourcing decisions. It is based on the realization that permanent IT personnel collectively represent a major investment by the organization and that this investment needs to be maximized (or at least optimized). This reinforces the previous discussion of "knowledge enhancement" as one of the key decision criteria in the selection of IT delivery mechanisms. One manager said the following:

> We choose a delivery option based on how it can build strength in one of our designated core competency areas. This may involve insourcing, outsourcing, a partnership, or any combination of these [but] . . . we have never outsourced a core competency.

The sample profile in Table 9.3 suggests how the three external delivery options (i.e., insourcing, outsourcing, and partnerships) can be used to supplement permanent IT personnel. Furthermore, the group suggested that a precedence for ordering should exist among the delivery options. Specifically, in-house and insourcing considerations should be resolved before outsourcing and partnerships are explored. The criteria to be used to decide between outsourcing and partnerships as delivery options should be flexibility, control, and business exigency (given that knowledge enablement is used to decide between in-house and insourcing). Insourcing, in particular, can be used strategically to bring in expertise to backfill knowledge gaps in core IT functions, address business exigency needs, and take on new (or shed old) core functions. Furthermore, insourcing represents variable costing, so there is usually maximal flexibility, which helps to smooth out resource "peaks and valleys."

The other method suggested to evolve internal IT staff, beyond supplementing them with the three external delivery options, is to hire strategically.[5] In other words, the range of IT delivery options permits "strategic" hiring as opposed to "replacement" hiring. In the past, IT organizations felt the need to "cover all the bases" with their hiring, and as individuals departed the organization replacements were sought. Today, however, there is no such impetus. In fact, attrition in noncore areas is considered advantageous as it permits hiring in designated strategic areas. This approach extends to permanent staff as well—that is, existing staff are strongly encouraged to develop their skills and expertise in alignment with designated core IT functions.

Encourage Exploration of the Whole Range of Delivery Options

Based on our sample of companies, it can be concluded that we are in the learning phase of IT function delivery. Some firms are clearly taking advantage of this opportunity and exercising their options in many different, often creative, ways. Others, perhaps more reticent, are sampling less broadly—choosing to stay within their "comfort zone"—and delivering IT functions predominantly with in-house resources. Most, however, are somewhere in the middle—that is, actively exploring different types of delivery options mostly for the first time. In all cases, exploration

---

[5]Although organizations continuously search for top IT talent, there appears to be a general aversion to increasing permanent staff among the focus group's companies. Reluctance to expand the IT staff naturally favors external delivery options. The consensus in the focus group was that this hiring aversion is fueling the growth of delivery options such as insourcing, outsourcing, and partnerships, but the group was reluctant to use this factor to explain IT delivery behavior. Instead, they claimed that the real driver was the existence of many alternative sourcing options, which have demonstrated the capability of providing superior results.

appears to be taking place without a strategy or guidelines; hence, decisions are taken one at a time. As a result, learning has been piecemeal—a phenomenon that may partially explain the lack of established trends in Table 9.2.

Combine Delivery Options Strategically

One of the key reasons for focusing on IT functions as opposed to another unit of analysis (e.g., projects, applications, or services) became clear by way of an example described by a manager. Satisfying her firm's data storage needs could involve using the provider's equipment, facilities, and staff. Or it could be the organization's hardware and staff in the provider's facilities, or basically any combination of the above. In each of these situations, the organization could justifiably claim that it had "outsourced" its data storage. Such a claim would be highly ambiguous. As a result, decisions need to be focused on the delivery of *specific* IT functions—that is a micro- versus a macroview.

Adopting a microview makes it possible to entertain the use of *combinations* of delivery options for the provision of IT functions. Participants pointed out that multiple delivery options are often used within a single project. In fact, they suggested that selecting a single delivery option for a project in its entirety is fast becoming nonstandard practice. The reality is that multiple providers are necessary to meet today's demands, particularly those of the business-exigency variety. This need for an amalgam of delivery options is easily understood with functions such as application development. Here requirements and design may be done in-house, coding may be outsourced to a third party, testing and quality assurance may be done by insourced experts, and implementation and rollout might be in partnership. Combining separate delivery options strategically can result in realizable benefits such as speed to market and quality of product or service. Speed to market results from parallel, synchronized development, and quality results from engaging delivery options based on demonstrated expertise and best practice.

Conclusion

Despite a steadily growing industry of third-party providers, IT organizations to date have ventured rather cautiously into this new area of IT function delivery. This chapter attempts to explain why this is so by examining the decision behavior and practices of a number of leading-edge organizations. From this analysis, four key decision criteria were identified: (1) flexibility, (2) control, (3) knowledge enhancement, and (4) business exigency. Today IT managers have an incredible range of available options in terms of how they choose to deliver IT functions. Clearly, the mistake is not to investigate the full range of these options. What has been lacking is greater direction and guidance in selecting IT delivery options. The concept of a maturity model for IT functions was also introduced as was a function-delivery profile to map delivery options onto core and noncore IT functions. These elements form the basis of a decision framework to guide the selection of delivery options. Following this framework, organizations can begin to move beyond the exploration stage to develop more strategic, nuanced, and methodological approaches to IT function delivery.

References

Carr, N. G. "The End of Corporate Computing." *MIT Sloan Management Review* Spring (2005): 67–73.

Hagel, J., and J. S. Brown. "Your Next IT Strategy." *Harvard Business Review* 79, no. 9 (October 2001): 105–13.

Lacity, M., and L. Willcocks. "An Empirical Investigation of Information Technology Sourcing Practices: Lessons from Experience." *MIS Quarterly* 22, no. 3 (2000): 363–408.

Marquis, H. A. "Finishing Off IT." *MIT Sloan Management Review* 47, no. 4 (Summer 2006): 12–16.

Rappa, M. A. "The Utility Business Model and the Future of Computing Services." *IBM Systems Journal* 43, no. 1 (2004): 32–42.

Ross, J. W., and G. Westerman. "Preparing for Utility Computing: The Role of IT Architecture and Relationship Management." *MIT Sloan Management Review* 43, no. 1 (2004): 5–19.

Smith, H. A., and J. D. McKeen. "IT in 2010: The Next Frontier." *MIS Quarterly Executive* 5, no. 3 (September 2006): 125–36.

Chapter 10

IT Sourcing

Outsourcing is now a widely accepted part of doing business. In IT, companies are outsourcing everything from operations and help desks to maintenance and development. What started as a mechanism largely to lower costs has become an integral part of a much larger IT strategy. IT departments are finding that outsourcing gives them access to a wider range of skilled resources, helps them focus on their core strengths, and speeds the time to market of products and services. Lower operational costs, reduced up-front investment, and the ability to convert fixed to variable costs also make outsourcing an attractive option for some IT services.

As IT organizations have gained experience with outsourcing, they have learned to do it more effectively—to better manage the relationships, risks, benefits, and outcomes involved. As a result, interest in outsourcing is growing, although a 2002 study found there is still considerable reluctance to use it (Mackie 2002). Clearly, outsourcing has found a place in the IT executive's toolkit.

The danger now is complacency. Thinking that they have a handle on outsourcing, IT managers could fail to consider newer forms of outsourcing, different options, different strategies, and/or changing economies. Certainly, there are new players on the horizon and new approaches to sourcing that will change yet again how IT sourcing decisions are made. Some of these include strategic sourcing practices; offshore contracting; and nearshore sourcing using companies based in India, Ireland, Asia, and Eastern Europe. Better connectivity, the availability of high-quality staff, and much lower costs are changing sourcing markets and expanding sourcing possibilities for companies.

In previous research, we examined outsourcing through application service providers (ASPs) and concluded the following:

> *The emerging external IT services marketplace offers rich opportunities and many possibilities for IT organizations to become more cost effective. . . . Strategic business applications development and management for mission-critical applications will [continue to] be in-house, but delivery for standard and meta-industry applications, processes and technology will be off-site. Thus . . . it is likely that external IT providers will form part of [a] future service delivery package. . . . However, as is so often the case in the IT industry, today's reality falls far short of what the industry promises. Companies wishing to take advantage now of what the external IT services marketplace can offer must evaluate [it] carefully and . . .*

proceed in full awareness of the risks involved. It is recommended that organizations articulate a sourcing strategy which balances internal versus external capabilities. (McKeen and Smith 2003)

This chapter first explores how sourcing strategy is evolving in organizations. Then it looks at emerging sourcing models, with particular emphasis on offshore/nearshore outsourcing. Next it discusses some new critical success factors for effective sourcing. Finally, it looks at how the role of IT itself is changing as a result.

THE EVOLUTION OF SOURCING

The concept of outsourcing IT services—that is, transferring some or all of a company's IT activities to a third party that performs them on behalf of the enterprise—has been a significant factor in IT decision making since the early 1990s (Lacity and Willcocks 2001). Globally, the outsourcing industry was estimated to be more than $1 trillion in 2000 (Kern et al. 2002). It is growing steadily as companies explore new possible sourcing models and outsourcing companies become better at what they do and expand the range of their services. At first, sourcing decisions were driven largely by economics, with outsourcers promising to remove millions of dollars from a firm's IT budget. However, today they reflect a significant shift in business strategy from diversification to a focus on core competencies. In turn, evolving sourcing models are transforming the underlying economics of IT (Lacity and Willcocks 2001).

As our understanding of sourcing has developed, three distinct yet complementary approaches have emerged:

1. *Outsourcing for operational efficiency.* This is the most well-established approach to sourcing, dating from the early 1990s, and is still by far the most common one, according to researchers (Lacity and Willcocks 2001). Here the "utility" functions of IT (e.g., computer operations, communications, infrastructure, and help desk) are transferred to an outsourcer, often along with company staff. The objective is to save money by sharing staff and resources with other companies in areas that do not make the company distinct and that have become routinized (Carr 2003). Outsourcing companies are typically autonomous entities that use their extensive experience in these areas, economies of scale, and the discipline of a contractual relationship to reduce the overall cost to a company while generating a profit for themselves. Many organizations have found that outsourcing to businesses that specialize in these services allows them to offer the same or better service at a reduced cost. Over time, this form of sourcing has become increasingly successful as companies have learned how to negotiate and manage contracts to make outsourcing work.
2. *Outsourcing for tactical support.* In the late 1990s, companies recognized that outsourcing could be used to help free up their own IT staff to perform selected support and development work and eliminate some of the peaks and valleys of the IT staffing cycle. "We are always under continual pressure to reduce the cost of our existing applications," stated one manager. "We spend 85 percent of our development budget on maintenance and support." Facing the dual challenges of Y2K and the dot-com bubble, and the resulting staff shortages they caused, many businesses began to use outsourcing in new ways. They offloaded their mature IT to an

outsourcer who could "keep the lights on" while company staff introduced new applications. They also used outsourcers as a way to introduce new technologies quickly (e.g., e-business) through such practices as managed hosting of a Web site and using outsourced staff to transfer their experience and skills to in-house staff. With this approach to sourcing, IT managers seek to rapidly add to their capacity to deliver applications and new technology to their organizations (Lacity and Willcocks 2001). Although cost is still important, the primary driver for using tactical outsourcing is to achieve flexibility and responsiveness. As tactical outsourcing has developed, contracts have become more flexible and outsourcers have come to be viewed increasingly as partners who can add other forms of value rather than simply reducing cost.

3. *Outsourcing for strategic impact.*   Over the last decade, sourcing has been increasingly recognized as a tool for achieving an organization's strategic objectives as well as driving costs down and adding capacity. As companies have become more focused on their core competencies, new possibilities for sourcing have opened up. With greater connectivity, it is now possible to outsource whole business processes that are not considered business critical. Noncore applications (e.g., accounting) can languish in-house because they cannot justify the same business value as other projects. By outsourcing these processes, companies can get full functionality without having to develop the applications themselves. Some organizations are using outsourcing to drive organizational change. "Today we consider outsourcing at a higher level," explained a manager. "We look at sourcing holistically. While you still need to outsource routine activities, you also need to look at it from the top down. Sourcing shouldn't be an ad hoc process." Companies are seeing that outsourcing can give them access to world-class capabilities, disciplines, quality, and innovation. To this end, some have established strategic alliances with a few vendors to take advantage of what they can offer. These preferred relationships are typically broad in scope and complex in nature and are designed to deliver significant business value (Smith and McKeen 2003). "Our supplier alliances are now part of getting any project approved," said another manager. "We must present the full continuum of sourcing options in any business case." Finally, organizations are learning that "right-sourcing" (i.e., choosing the right sourcing option for a given activity) can change with time. Certain functions that have been outsourced can become business critical, and others that were deemed core can now be outsourced. One manager explained, "In our company we are constantly testing what should be outsourced. The business has to be fully engaged in the process so they understand the implications." Strategic sourcing is a very recent trend, and companies have very little experience doing it. The focus group suggested moving carefully into this area until more is known about how to accomplish it successfully. Members also cautioned that customers should watch for hidden costs at this level (e.g., the need for integration by the customer) that can be quite expensive and could kill a business case for this type of sourcing.

Each of these three approaches to sourcing represents an increase in the size, scope, and impact of what is sourced. Table 10.1 summarizes these approaches. It should be stressed that one does not preclude the other. Companies tend to begin outsourcing for operational efficiency and move toward tactical and strategic approaches as they gain experience and confidence at each level.

TABLE 10.1   Three Complementary Approaches to IT Sourcing

Approach	Driver	Mode	Activities	Relationship
Operational Effectiveness	Cost reduction	Utility	Infrastructure, operations, support	Fee-for-service
Tactical Support	Capacity, flexibility	Service delivery	Mature technology, new technology	Partnership
Strategic Impact	Focus, business value	Toolkit	Processes, transformation, innovation	Strategic alliance

Companies have become quite good at basic utility, fee-for-service sourcing. In fact, by far the majority of sourcing is of this type (Lacity and Willcocks 2001). All of the companies in the focus group had some sourcing initiatives to improve operational efficiency, although none had completely outsourced their services, even at this level. Overall, studies show that about 38 percent of IT functions have now been outsourced to vendors (Barthelemy 2001).

Research has also identified five factors that are critical to the success of *current* outsourcing initiatives:

1. *Use selective sourcing.*   Careful selection of what to outsource and what to retain in-house is a demonstrably more effective approach than total outsourcing or total insourcing. Companies find it more controllable and satisfactory as well as considerably less risky (Chen et al. 2002).
2. *Have joint business–IT sponsorship.*   When both the business and IT executives are involved in making outsourcing decisions, the results are far more likely to meet expectations than when either group acts alone (Lacity and Willcocks 2001).
3. *Ensure a thorough comparison with internal operations.*   Too often companies don't get expected savings because they forget to include or identify the hidden costs involved in outsourcing when problems such as extra maintenance or consulting fees arise (Overby 2003b).
4. *Develop a detailed contract.*   Tighter contracts with carefully thought-out flexibility, evolution, and reversibility clauses lead to more successful sourcing (Barthelemy 2001).
5. *Limit the length of the contract.*   Short-term contracts (one to three years) are more likely to be successful than mid- or long-term contracts. This is because they involve less uncertainty, motivate supplier performance, help ensure a fair market price for services, and enable recovery from mistakes more quickly (Lacity and Willcocks 2001).

In spite of all that has been learned, between 14 and 78 percent of outsourcing functions are deemed failures (Barthelemy 2001; Overby 2003b), and repatriating functions are becoming more and more common (Overby 2003b). A major reason for this huge discrepancy in success rates is that companies are experimenting with increasingly more radical options to extend outsourcing models, thereby moving into areas of higher risk.

OFFSHORE AND NEARSHORE OUTSOURCING: EMERGING SOURCING MODELS

In addition to outsourcing larger and more complex chunks of work (e.g., innovation, business processes) and developing more complex relationships with vendors (i.e., strategic outsourcing), companies are also working with vendors at increasingly greater distances, typically in other countries. Known as *offshore outsourcing* (or simply *offshoring*), the primary driver for this sourcing model and its many variations is economic (Aron 2003; Kripalani and Engardio 2003). The increasing globalization of large companies and the need for global processes is also a factor (Chen et al. 2002). Vendors located in other countries, such as India, can charge a fraction of what it costs to provide the same service in the United States. Facilitated by ever-greater connectivity; ubiquitous, cheap bandwidth; and Web technologies, companies can afford to knit together people, processes, and platforms in different ways than have been possible previously (Aron 2003). Forrester Research has found that 44 percent of Fortune 1000 companies are offshoring some activities (cited in Blackwell 2003).

According to Chen et al. (2002), IT organizations are unclear about how offshoring fits into a company's overall sourcing strategy and are even less clear about how to make it successful. Undoubtedly, global outsourcing represents a significant shift in how organizations manage their IT activities (Elmuti and Kathawala 2000). Therefore, today's IT managers are approaching offshoring cautiously and building on what they have learned about other forms of outsourcing. "There is certainly a lot of hype about offshore outsourcing," said one, "but we're still skeptical about its benefits. We had a bad experience ten years ago. The level of professionalism and understanding just wasn't there, so it didn't work." Nevertheless, the cost differentials and the "hype" are forcing everyone to look seriously at offshoring as part of their sourcing strategy.

Offshore Outsourcing Benefits

It is cheaper to do IT work outside the United States. Even doing work in Canada can reduce costs for many United States–based firms. However the big savings come from sending work to Third World countries, where salaries are 40 to 60 percent lower than in North America. Most Third World countries have significant numbers of well-trained professionals and offer considerable tax breaks.[1] As a result, even with additional travel and connectivity charges, companies are expecting to save 20 to 40 percent on costs such as managing infrastructure or operating a help desk (Bhandari 2003). The differentials are so significant that the increased competition is also driving down the rates of traditional North American outsourcing vendors (Blackwell 2003). These vendors are also setting up centers in India so they can compete more effectively (Kripalani and Engardio 2003).

Typical activities that are being sourced offshore include help desk, personal computer repair, disaster recovery, back office processes, application maintenance, network management and operations, application and IT support, and problem resolution (Chordas 2003). These are relatively routine and straightforward utility types of functions

---

[1]There are more IT engineers in Bangalore, India, alone than there are in Silicon Valley, California (Kripalani and Engardio, 2003).

that many companies feel very comfortable in outsourcing. Thus, in moving these functions offshore, they are limiting risk while taking advantage of the resulting cost benefits. However, many offshore outsourcers, especially in India, are also seeking to scale up the types of activities in which they are involved. Quality standards in India, for example, are often higher than in North America (Blackwell 2003). In many cases Indian companies have better software and risk management processes and have been among the first in the world to achieve the highest SEI CMM rating of five (Satyam 2003). These firms are seeking a larger presence in the high-end software development and consulting areas of the market (i.e., tactical and strategic outsourcing). Big vendors, such as Oracle, Accenture, and Microsoft, are also establishing partnerships and software development centers in India to take advantage not only of the cost savings involved but also the skills available (Blackwell 2003).

Offshore Outsourcing Locations

Although 85 percent of offshore outsourcing work currently goes to India, several other countries are looking to increase their share of this work. China, Russia, and the Philippines are the most serious competition, although they are far behind India at present (Overby 2003a). Canada is also involved in this market because of its proximity to the United States, even though it is more expensive than other offshore vendors. Ireland, Israel, Mexico, and South Africa are also positioning themselves in this market. Forrester Research predicts that by 2015, about 3.3 million jobs will have moved offshore—70 percent to India, 20 percent to the Philippines, and 10 percent to China (cited in Chordas 2003).

All of these countries offer reduced or substantially lower costs, but they are not considered equal in other important characteristics, which should be considered before a company makes a significant outsourcing decision. These factors include language, cultural similarities, time differentials, political stability, quality, project management skills, education, and infrastructure. Table 10.2 summarizes these for the five main countries involved in offshore sourcing with the United States.

TABLE 10.2   A Comparison of Offshore Outsourcing Nations

Country	Language	Cultural Similarities	Time Differential	Political Stability	Project Management Skills	Education	Infrastructure
Canada	English	Many	None	Excellent	Very good	Excellent	Excellent
India	Good English	Some	Large	Good	Excellent	Excellent	Improving
China	Limited English	Few	Large	Good	Unknown	Good	Good
Philippines	Good English	Some	Large	Good	Unknown	Good	Very good
Russia	Limited English	Few	Large	Fair	Poor	Good	Unknown

Source: Based on Chordas 2003; Damsell 2003; Gallagher 2002; Overby 2003a.

Offshore Outsourcing Risks

As Table 10.2 shows, offshoring involves considering a number of factors, such as language and political stability, which have not traditionally been part of outsourcing decision making. Comments from practicing IT managers clearly illustrate some of the risks involved.

> *"We outsourced a call center to India and then brought it back. There were problems with the time to transfer calls, language, and spelling. The accents weren't bad, but there was often poor understanding on the phone."*
>
> *"We outsourced project management and then lost all their interfaces with the users when they left. Now we have 100 percent internal project management."*
>
> *"We outsourced our help desk. It was brutal. We had the mix wrong. We needed more decomposition of activities and a more granular understanding of what we were doing."*

A number of additional risks must also be addressed as part of the offshore outsourcing decision-making process:

- *Hidden costs.* These include the cost of finding a vendor, drafting the contract, and managing the effort, as well as the cost of transitioning to a new vendor if the first doesn't work out. Monitoring, bargaining, and negotiating needed changes to a contract typically add up to about 8 percent of the yearly contract amount (Barthelemy 2001). Travel and visa costs are also often substantial (Blackwell 2003). As a result, many companies are finding they are not achieving the savings they anticipated (Elmuti and Kathawala 2000).
- *Reduced control.* Although outsourcing in general reduces an organization's control over how its services are delivered, offshore sourcing can greatly increase these risks because the vendors operate in substantially different business environments. A company may, therefore, have greater liability exposure and face problems with such issues as confidentiality, security, and time schedules (Elmuti and Kathawala 2000).
- *Legal and political uncertainties.* Working in other countries means dealing with a wide variety of unfamiliar government regulations and restrictions, legal systems that may be unable to cope with the types of disputes that may arise between companies or between companies and the government, and weak intellectual property rights (Overby 2003b). Furthermore, governments in Third World countries may be considerably less secure than in North America or Europe. India has lost work recently due to the instabilities in that part of the world following the attacks of September 11, 2001.
- *Cultural differences.* Different cultural backgrounds can cause numerous difficulties. In addition to language problems, such matters as the pace of daily life, employees' relationship to authority, attitudes to security, and adherence to socialist principles can lead to misunderstandings that can be daunting (Overby 2003b).
- *Social justice.* Practicing IT managers were also very aware of the "optics" of offshore outsourcing. "Public perceptions are important to us," stated one. Another manager noted that his company has a labor code of conduct and a risk rating for different countries that assesses their labor practices and other dimensions of risk. Government organizations in particular are especially sensitive to the issues of moving jobs out of the country. For example, a recent public outcry forced the state of Indiana to cancel a $15 million contract with a firm in India (Kripalani and Engardio 2003).

Variations in Offshore Outsourcing Models

Some of the risks and concerns cited above are forcing vendors and companies to rethink the basic offshore outsourcing model. Some are distinguishing between offshore and nearshore sourcing. Not only are some U.S. vendors setting up sourcing centers in Canada, but some Indian firms are doing so as well. For example, Satyam Computer Services has recently opened a development center in Toronto to ensure that North American clients can "deal with a company that's always close to home, close to their unique needs" (Satyam 2003). Although much work actually can be completed in India, having relationship managers and business analysis in closer proximity to their customers provides additional security and mitigates many of these risks.

Other companies are looking at nearshore opportunities in lower-cost areas of their own countries. One Canadian firm is using nearshore sourcing to move development work to New Brunswick—a province with cheaper labor. Several Native American reservations have gone into the sourcing business as well. They argue that they can offer the same low-cost, high-value work that is done offshore but without the headaches of language barriers, remote management, or security concerns (Field 2001). These options are particularly attractive for sensitive legal and government work that should not be sent overseas.

Other firms are finding that they can get many of the benefits of offshore sourcing by working with a major vendor who will undertake to manage the offshore work and relationships. "You can have global options if you pick your vendor carefully," said one. "We triage our projects with our partner to find the best sourcing choice possible."

Sourcing today is actually a continuum of practices that can be "sliced and diced many different ways," depending on the needs of the company and the particular activity involved. Partnerships with key vendors are especially important in these situations so they can optimize the blend of internal and external staff appropriately. "You shouldn't go with a one-off project offshore," one manager explained, but rather with a carefully designed strategy that enables experimentation with different sourcing models and includes the ability to reverse a sourcing decision if it doesn't work out.

SUCCESSFUL SOURCING

As experience with sourcing increases, organizations are learning more about what it takes to manage sourcing successfully. However, although some critical success factors are well established (see above), as new models of sourcing emerge and as sourcing takes on a more central part of IT and organizational strategy, understanding what is involved in successful sourcing is still evolving. The focus group identified several factors that are essential in its effective management.

Sample Sourcing Criteria

What are our industry dynamics, and where are we in the food chain?

What are we good at?

What do we want to be good at?

What should we be good at?

Do we want to invest in this function/activity?

How many vendors do we want to deal with?

Sourcing Strategy

Whether a company uses sourcing strategically or not, every organization should have an overall sourcing strategy. This helps it determine what to source, where to source, and to whom to source. Experts have suggested many different ways of determining what to source—what's core and what's not, contribution to business value, maturity of technology, activities that are routine and less knowledge intensive, and entry-level functions (Aron 2003; Barthelemy 2001; Lacity and Willcocks 2001). In practice, however, numerous approaches to "right-sourcing" are possible. What is right for one organization is not necessarily right for another. Companies should consider the following:

1. First develop an in-depth understanding of business drivers and strategy before developing a sourcing strategy.
2. Then IT managers should develop a detailed understanding of the IT functions, processes, and overall portfolio. Without this, it is possible that too much or too little could be outsourced, leading to significant problems.
3. Then they should apply their particular sourcing criteria to IT activities (see "Sample Sourcing Criteria") to determine which parts of IT can be successfully sourced.
4. Finally, the sourcing strategy must be continually tested and reevaluated as the industry, business strategy, and sourcing possibilities change frequently.

Risk Management/Mitigation

"War stories" abound. Every firm can cite examples of activities that had to be resourced to a different vendor, tasks that needed to be reinsourced, or contracts that were renegotiated because of problems. The fact is sourcing introduces new levels of risk to the organization. Loss of control, security and privacy problems, poor-quality work, hidden costs, lack of standards, unmet expectations, and bad publicity are just some of the problems that have been experienced. When moving into new forms of sourcing, it is important to incorporate risk management and mitigation into every aspect of sourcing.

- Detailed planning is essential. Precise definitions of roles, responsibilities, and expectations must be developed. Specialists in outsourcing are now available to provide advice on how to select a vendor and plan the work involved. The specialists can assist—but not replace—the IT sourcing team in understanding how to assess and engage a vendor. This is especially important when considering offshore sourcing because of the additional complexities involved.
- Monitoring and an audit trail must be incorporated into the contract to both encourage self-correction and ensure all parties live up to their commitments.
- All potential risks should be rated as to both the likelihood of occurrence and their impact if they do occur (Aubert et al. 2001). Appropriate steps should be explicitly taken to reduce and/or manage these risks.
- An exit strategy must be devised. "Any well-designed sourcing strategy must retain alternatives to pull activities back in-house," explained one manager.
- Finally, exercise caution when moving into new avenues of sourcing. The hype in the popular press, often originating from vendors, greatly inflates the benefits that

can be achieved while minimizing the risks. It is recommended that managers experiment with a "simple, substantial pilot" before committing the company to a significant new outsourcing initiative.

Governance

"With any sourcing initiative, governance must be super-good," said a manager. Most IT functions now recognize the importance of relationship management at all levels (i.e., the frontline, middle, and senior management) in delivering value. Nevertheless, it cannot be underestimated. "When the relationship between the client and its vendor is adversarial, the vendor will take advantage of gaps in the agreement. When there is mutual trust, vendors often work hard to deal fairly with the gaps" (Barthelemy 2001). "Layers of governance are critical to successful sourcing relationships," said one manager. Others also suggested retaining strong internal project management and ensuring that vendors also have these skills. "You can't outsource project management or the relationship with the customer," they agreed. Governance problems are exacerbated when offshore sourcing is undertaken because of the difficulties of managing relationships at a distance (Chordas 2003). This is one reason the larger offshore vendors are setting up local development centers. At minimum, an offshore outsourcer should name an internal manager who will act as the organization's champion and be responsible for quality assurance. Ideally, an outsourcing relationship should be structured to ensure shared risk so both parties are incented to make it work (Garr 2001).

Cost Structures

One of the most important elements of successful sourcing is a complete understanding of the cost structures involved. Previously, vendors have profited from their ability to squeeze value from outsourced activities because they had a better and more detailed appreciation of their costs. Furthermore, they were able to apply disciplines and service-level agreements to their work, which IT organizations were often prohibited from doing (Lacity and Willcocks 2001). Today this is changing. Companies are applying the same standards to their own work, enabling them to make more appropriate comparisons between the costs of doing an activity in-house and outsourcing it. They also have a better understanding of the true costs of outsourcing, including relationship management and contract management, which have frequently been underestimated in the past. "We need to thoroughly understand our economic model," said one participant. "Vendors have the advantage of knowing best practices and economies of scale, but they are at a disadvantage from a profit and knowledge point of view. If we can't compete in-house, we should outsource." Interestingly, many companies believe they can compare favorably in many areas with outsourcing vendors. Ongoing cost comparisons are ideal, according to researchers, because they motivate both parties to do their best and most cost-effective work (Lacity and Willcocks 2001). The reduced cost of labor is simply one element of the outsourcing value proposition. "We must learn to understand and track *every* cost involved," said an IT manager. "There are new governance costs; privacy, legal, and regulatory costs; and other hidden costs that have to be articulated and monitored." The need to better understand the total cost of ownership of each IT activity is forcing managers to become considerably more aware of the financial implications of their decisions and develop a whole new set of skills as a result.

THE CHANGING ROLE OF IT

New IT Roles and Responsibilities

- Solution delivery
- Task decomposition
- Task costing analysis
- Right-sourcing decision making

- Designing for collaboration and connectivity
- Supplier relationship management
- Contract management and monitoring
- Sourcing marketplace analysis

The growth of sourcing over the past decade has led to a number of new roles for IT managers and has changed the relative importance of key IT skills. As lower-level IT activities are outsourced, what is increasingly left behind is the high-value-added work that only knowledgeable, in-house IT practitioners can provide. "The development skills we need these days are not coding, but integration, business analysis, and project management. We need to hone these skills to do the jobs that are difficult to outsource," explained one manager. Although important pieces of development can be done off-site, it is still IT's job to put all the pieces together and make technology work for the enterprise. In short, organizations need to improve their solution delivery skills, which is by no means a straightforward or simple task.

Systems thinking skills are becoming increasingly critical as well. They are fundamental to the detailed decomposition of tasks, which is the first step in better understanding both cost structures and the relative strategic importance of each task. IT organizations also need more formal processes and decision-making frameworks within which to tackle the key sourcing questions of what to outsource and how it should be done. These should include the parts of the business that will be affected by outsourcing and involve both tactical and strategic discussions with business management.

Emerging sourcing models will also need to be incorporated into the organization's technology plans as well as its business strategies. IT architectures must be designed for greater connectivity and collaboration across organizational boundaries. Companies should anticipate a wide variety of possible options in how their processes and transactions will be undertaken.

Finally, IT organizations are recognizing that they need new management skills, governance structures, and organizational processes to make outsourcing work effectively. Several companies now have a "supplier relationship management" function, at a mid to senior management level, responsible for ensuring that outsourcing arrangements are working well. Similarly, some companies are learning how to develop effective sourcing contracts and monitor them, both for supplier compliance and for internal satisfaction (Smith and McKeen 2003). In the future, companies will also need skills to better analyze the external sourcing marketplace and their industry to select the most appropriate options for their organizations.

Conclusion

Sourcing has become an integral part of almost all IT organizations today. Originally a straightforward mechanism for reducing operational costs, sourcing is rapidly evolving into a strategically important means of delivering optimal IT value. At present, companies and vendors are experimenting with new models of sourcing, only some of which will be sustainable. Increasingly, it is IT's job to guide the organization in making the best sourcing decisions possible and to ensure that the anticipated value is obtained from vendor relationships. This involves developing new IT skills that incorporate an understanding of technology with strong business knowledge and analytic capabilities. As a result, despite the fact that sourcing is changing the nature of

the work that is done internally in IT, it is unlikely that sourcing will eliminate internal functions altogether or reduce their value to that of a utility, as has been suggested by some (e.g., Carr 2003). To the contrary, more and more organizations will need the systems thinking, architectural understanding, and strategic awareness embodied in a modern IT department in order to ensure that they don't end up with a hollow shell of an organization that provides limited added value.

References

Aron, R. "Sourcing in the Right Light." *Optimize* June (2003): 26–34.

Aubert, B., M. Patry, S. Rivard, and H. A. Smith. "IT Outsourcing Risk Management at British Petroleum." Proceedings of the 34th Hawaii Conference on System Sciences, Maui, Hawaii, January 5–8, 2001.

Barthelemy, J. "The Hidden Costs of IT Outsourcing." *MIT Sloan Management Review* 42, no. 3 (Spring 2001): 60–69.

Bhandari, A. "'Near-shoring' India's IT Companies." *Toronto Star,* June 2, 2003.

Blackwell, G. "Sending It Offshore." *Edge* 2, no. 2 (February 2003).

Carr, N. "IT Doesn't Matter." *Harvard Business Review* May (2003).

Chen, Q., Q. Tu, and B. Lin. "Global IT/IS Outsourcing: Expectations, Considerations and Implications." *Advances in Competitiveness Research* 10, no. 1 (2002): 100–11.

Chordas, L. "Eyes on India." *Best's Review* 104, no. 1 (May 2003): 98–103.

Damsell, K. "Offshore Outsourcing Seen Reshaping the Tech Sector." *The Globe and Mail,* November 11, 2003.

Elmuti, D., and Y. Kathawala. "The Effects of Global Outsourcing Strategies on Participants' Attitudes and Organizational Effectiveness." *International Journal of Manpower* 21, no. 2 (2000): 112–28.

Field, T. "How to Get In and Out of an Outsourcing Deal." *CIO* 15, no. 6 (December 15, 2001–January 1, 2002): 85–86.

Gallagher, J. "Canada: New Outsourcing Option?" *Insurance and Technology* 27, no. 10 (September 2002): 9.

Garr, D. "Inside Outsourcing." *Fortune: Technology Review* 143, no. 13 (Summer 2001): 85–92.

Kern, T., M. Lacity, and L. Willcocks. *Netsourcing: Renting Business Applications and Services over a Network.* Upper Saddle River, NJ: Pearson Education, 2002.

Kripalani, M., and P. Engardio. "The Rise of India." *BusinessWeek,* December 8, 2003.

Lacity, M., and L. Willcocks. *Global Information Technology Outsourcing: In Search of Business Advantage.* Chichester, England: John Wiley & Sons, 2001.

Mackie, A. "Outsourcing Outlook." *Computer Dealer News* 18, no. 19 (October 18, 2002).

McKeen, J., and H. Smith. *Making IT Happen: Critical Issues in IT Management.* Chichester, England: John Wiley & Sons, 2003.

Overby, S. "Passages Beyond India."*CIO* 16, no. 6 (January 1, 2003a): 60–61.

_____. "Bringing IT Back Home." *CIO* 16, no. 10 (March 1, 2003b): 54–56.

Satyam Computer Services Limited. Internal company document. Secunderabad, India, 2003.

Smith, H., and J. McKeen. "Strategic Sourcing at the Bank of Montreal." *The CIO Brief* 9, no. 2 (2003).

Chapter 11

Application Portfolio Management[1]

According to many industry assessments, the typical IT organization spends as much as 80 percent of its human and capital resources maintaining an ever-growing inventory of applications and supporting infrastructure (Serena 2007). Although no one argues with the importance of maintaining applications (after all, they do run the business), everyone is concerned with rebalancing the IT budget allocation to increase the discretionary spend by decreasing the maintenance spend, ensuring that the set of applications is well-aligned with business needs, and finally, positioning the organization technologically to respond to future initiatives. Collectively, this activity has come to be known as "application portfolio management" or APM.

Formally, APM is the ongoing management process of categorization, assessment, and rationalization of the IT application portfolio. It allows organizations to identify which applications to maintain, invest in, replace, or retire, and it can have significant impact on the selection of new business applications and the projects required to deliver them. The overall goal of APM is to enable organizations to determine the best approach for IT to meet business demands from both a tactical and strategic perspective through the use of capital and operating funds allocated to building and maintaining applications. APM typically includes an analysis of operating and capital expenses by application, demand analysis (i.e., assessing business demand at the application level to determine its strategic and tactical business drivers), and application portfolio analysis (i.e., the current versus the desired state of the application portfolio in terms of both technology and business value).

Although APM is not a new idea, it may be one whose time has come. There are many espoused benefits of APM, including the following: reduction of the cost and complexity of the applications portfolio, reduction or elimination of redundant functionality, optimization of IT assets across different applications and functions, greater alignment with the business, better business decisions regarding technology, and an effective means of communicating the contribution of IT to the overall organization.

This chapter begins by examining the current status of IT applications in organizations. It then examines the notions of a portfolio perspective as it applies to applications (as opposed to a

---

[1]McKeen, J. D., and H. A. Smith. "Application Portfolio Management." *Communications of the Association for Information Systems* 26, article 9 (March 2010): 157–70. Reproduced by permission of the Association for Information Systems.

portfolio of financial assets) and outlines the specific benefits of such a perspective. Implementing a successful APM initiative requires three key capabilities—strategy and governance, inventory management, and reporting and rationalization—which are described in detail. The chapter concludes with some key lessons learned by organizations having invested in APM.

THE APPLICATIONS QUAGMIRE

According to a recent industry report, the

> "typical IT organization expends as much as 80% of its human and capital resources maintaining an ever growing inventory of applications and supporting infrastructure. Born of autonomous business-unit-level decision making and mergers and acquisitions, many IT organizations manage multiple ERP applications, knowledge management systems, and BI and reporting tools. All are maintained and periodically upgraded, leading to costly duplication and unnecessary complexity in IT operations. Left unchecked, the demands on the IT organization to simply maintain its existing inventory of applications threatens to consume the capacity to deliver new projects" (Serena 2007).

The proliferation of application systems within organizations is legendary. Built over time to serve an ever-changing set of business requirements, such systems span generations of technologies (e.g., hardware, software, systems, and methodologies), many of which are now obsolete and unsupported by any vendor community, are host to countless "workarounds", remain poorly documented, depend on the knowledge of a rapidly retiring workforce, and yet continue to support the key operations of the organization. Some (if not many) of these application systems have never been revisited to ascertain their ongoing contribution to the business. Based on decisions made by separate business units, many applications duplicate the functionality of others and are clearly redundant, and others have become unnecessary but have managed to escape detection. Accounts of organizations continuing to pay licensing fees for decommissioned software and supporting 27 different payroll systems all attest to the level of disarray that typically exists in a large organization. The full impact of such a quagmire becomes apparent either when virtually the entire IT budget is consumed by maintenance and/or when an organization attempts to integrate its suite of applications with those of an acquiring firm—whichever comes first.

Cause and effect are straightforward. The number of applications grows due to the practice of continually adding new applications without eliminating old ones. As it grows, the number of interfaces increases exponentially as does the number of complex and often proprietary enterprise application integration (EAI) solutions to "bridge" these disparate systems. The combined effect is to increase the frequency of (and costs of supporting) redundant systems, data, and capabilities across the organization. As their number and complexity grow, so does the workload and, without expanding IT budgets and headcounts commensurably, so does the portion of the IT budget devoted to maintenance and operations. From a management perspective, organizations are left with shrinking discretionary funds for new IT development and find themselves unable to assess the capability or measure the adequacy and value of current application support structures, track dependencies of business processes on applications, determine where money is being spent, and map IT investments to business objectives. Thus, in many organizations, the suite of IT applications has become close to unmanageable.

But while the cause and effect are identifiable, remedies are not easily obtained. The first obstacle is resources:

> After years of acquiring software systems and not getting rid of anything, companies have severe application clutter. As a result, given their limited financial resources, they can't meet the current demand for IT unless they "turn off" some applications. . . . The practice of continually adding to the IT burden while holding IT budgets and head counts relatively flat is obviously problematic. Yet that's exactly what many companies have done since the early 2000s. And this practice is one of the reasons why many CIOs feel that they simply don't have enough resources to meet internal demand for IT. (Gomolski 2004)

A second barrier is that few line-of-business managers want to give up any application once it's installed. In their minds, the agony of change is clearly not worth the rewards. "Some applications are so old that nobody remembers who ordered them" (Gomolski 2004, 29). The third impediment, and perhaps the most severe, is the fact that IT often lacks the political clout to make business managers engage in an exercise to rationalize applications across the enterprise in order to decommission some applications.

THE BENEFITS OF A PORTFOLIO PERSPECTIVE

A part of the application dilemma is the lack of a portfolio perspective. Historically, organizations have opted to evaluate applications exclusively on their own merits—a practice that can easily promulgate unique systems across any business unit that can justify the expense. One manager claimed that this practice results in "a stream of one-off decisions . . . where each decision is innocent enough but, sooner or later, you are in a mess . . . sort of like walking off a cliff using baby steps." In contrast, adopting a "portfolio" perspective means evaluating new and existing applications collectively on an ongoing basis to determine which applications provide value to the business in order to support decisions to replace, retire, or further invest in applications across the enterprise.

The portfolio approach is universal in finance and provides a point of comparison. Boivie (2003) presents the following analogy:

> Just imagine you bought stock a decade ago for a lot of money, a good investment at the time, but then you did not review its value over the intervening years. Merely sitting on the stock may have been the right thing to do. Then again, you may have missed opportunities to invest more profitably elsewhere if the company was not doing well, or to invest more in the stock if it was profitable. Obviously this is not a wise way to handle your investment, but it's exactly what many companies are doing when it comes to investments in their IT applications!

TABLE 11.1   Managing IT Applications as a Financial Portfolio

Investment Portfolio Management	Application Portfolio Management
Professional management but the client owns the portfolio.	Professional management but the business owns the portfolio.
Personal financial portfolio balanced across investments in: • equities • fixed income • cash	Application portfolio balanced across investments in: • new applications • currency (maintenance, enhancements, upgrades) • retiring/decommissioning
Client directs investment where needed (e.g., 50% equities, 40% fixed, 10% cash).	Business directs investments where needed (e.g., 40% new applications, 30% currency, 30% decommissioning).
Client provides direction on diversity across investments (e.g., investment in one fund would exclude/augment investment in other funds).	Business provides direction on diversity of investment (e.g., investment in one business capability might exclude/augment investment in another).
Client receives quarterly updates on their portfolio health and an annual report.	Business receives quarterly updates on application portfolio health and an annual report.
New investments are evaluated on their impact on the overall portfolio as well as on their own merits.	New applications are evaluated on their impact on the overall portfolio as well as on their own merits.

Kramer (2006) concurs that application portfolio management is similar to the approach used by portfolio managers at money management firms where "investment officers continually seek to optimize their portfolios by assessing holdings and selling off assets that no longer are performing." It is suggested that "the same approach can be used by technology executives, especially when evaluating the applications in their portfolios and deciding which ones to continue funding, which to pull back on and which to sunset or kill." One firm mapped investment portfolio management against applications portfolio management (see Table 11.1) in order to highlight the similarities and advocate for adopting this approach for IT applications.

The ensuing discussion of the focus group suggested that the requirement for all new investments (i.e., IT applications) to be evaluated relative to all existing (i.e., past) investments within the portfolio is arguably the critical benefit provided by adopting a portfolio perspective. The group also urged caution, however, due to the differences between a portfolio of financial assets (e.g., stocks and bonds) and one of applications. With the former, we assume a degree of independence among assets that rarely exists with applications. According to one writer (Anonymous 2008), "while financial planners can sell an underperforming stock, CIOs will likely find it far more difficult to dispose of an unwieldy application." Applications are rarely stand-alone; business functionality is often delivered by an integrated web of applications that cannot be separated piecemeal. As a result, diversification strategies can be difficult where IT assets are highly interdependent and deliver returns only collectively (Kasargod and Bondugula 2005).

A portfolio perspective forces the linkage between the set of existing applications (i.e., the applications portfolio) and the set of potential applications (i.e., the project portfolio). The linkage is bi-directional—that is, potential applications must be evaluated against existing applications and vice versa. Caruso (2007) differentiates these as follows:

- *Application Portfolio.* The focus of the application portfolio is on the spending for established applications, trying to balance expense against value. These applications may be assessed for their contribution to corporate profitability and also on nonfinancial criteria such as stability, usability, and technical obsolescence.
- *Project Portfolio.* Management of the project portfolio focuses on future spending, attempting to balance IT cost-reduction efforts and investments to develop new capabilities with technology and application upgrades.

The focus group suggested that organizations have focused most of their attention on new projects which has, in part, resulted in the applications quagmire previously described. The focus of this chapter is on application portfolio management. It argues that the effectiveness of the project portfolio can be enhanced substantially by managing the application portfolio much more effectively. This linkage is made explicit later in the chapter.

The benefits to be realized by adopting an applications portfolio perspective are significant. The focus group was polled to solicit the benefits that their organizations had identified. These benefits were then grouped into the three categories, as established by Caruso (2007) and are presented in Table 11.2.

The list of benefits is impressive. To put them into perspective, a number of comments are in order. First, if the benefits to be realized are this substantial, why haven't organizations moved more aggressively to enact APM practices? The short answer is that APM has been difficult to fund and, once funded, represents an enormous management challenge. Second, the majority of these are "anticipated" benefits as they have yet to be reaped by focus group firms. Third, APM requires the development of a number of related activities (described in the latter sections of this chapter). Although benefits are realized during individual activities, the most significant benefits are not realized until most, if not all, of these capabilities have been completed. Finally, APM involves a different way of approaching IT investments—a collective view of all IT applications across the enterprise—which has cultural and political ramifications for organizations. The good news is that organizations that are well advanced in APM have realized significant benefits. We highlight one such firm in Table 11.3.

MAKING APM HAPPEN

As the focus group discussion evolved, it became apparent that application portfolio management presents a significant management challenge and success requires the commitment of considerable organizational resources. Furthermore, APM involves the development of three interrelated capabilities. The first capability is the articulation of a strategy including goals, deliverables, and a set of governance procedures to guide the management of the application portfolio. Next is the creation of an applications inventory to monitor key attributes of existing applications. The third capability involves building an analysis and reporting capability in order to rationalize the applications

TABLE 11.2   A List of APM Benefits

1. Visibility into where money is being spent, which ultimately provides the baseline to measure value creation
   a. Increasing the ease of determining which legacy applications are to be retired.
   b. Simplifying the technical environment and lowering operating costs.
   c. Reducing the number of applications and optimizing spending on application maintenance.
   d. Increasing the predictability of measuring service delivery for project selection.
   e. An enterprise view of all applications allowing for ease of reporting (e.g., How many applications use Sybase? How many systems support sales reporting?)
   f. A common view of enterprise technology assets improving reuse and sharing across the enterprise.
   g. Clarity over maintenance and support spending.
   h. Ability to manage and track business controls and regulatory compliance of all applications.

2. Prioritization of applications across multiple dimensions, including value to the business, urgency, and financial return
   a. Funding the right application effort by providing quick access to validated information in support of business cases for investment.
   b. Providing better project solutions by identifying available capabilities for reuse.
   c. Providing criteria to drive application rationalization and monitor impacts.
   d. Providing an "end state" view for all applications, which helps direct roadmaps and enables progress reporting.
   e. Expediting prioritization discussions and executive decision making.
   f. Driving IT refurbishment initiatives.

3. A mechanism to ensure that applications map directly to business objectives
   a. Aligning business and IT efforts with business processes by providing (1) clarity of the application landscape, leading to synergies across different business units and the pursuit of a global systems architecture; and (2) insight into gaps or redundancies in the current portfolio, thereby enhancing the ability to manage risk effectively and efficiently.
   b. Enabling productive discussion with senior management regarding IT's contribution to business value.
   c. Identifying the strategic and high business value applications, thereby allowing the redirection of some of the funding previously used for nonstrategic applications.
   d. Enabling easy and effectively analysis of impacts to applications from changing business conditions.
   e. Improving the focus and direction of investments.
   f. Developing a vehicle to drive the technical portfolio to the "right" mix, based on strategy, architecture, TCO, and internal skill sets.
   g. Prioritizing efforts and focus for IT delivery—ensuring the right skills are in place to support business requirements.

TABLE 11.3   An APM Case Study

Vision
- Reverse the rising tide of application maintenance costs.
- Fund strategic development efforts from reduced support and maintenance costs.
- Align IT with business goals.

Challenge
- Assess current portfolio of applications.
- Establish targets, savings strategies, and supporting plans.
- Data currency and accuracy.

Solution
- Identify redundant or obsolete applications and set end-of-year targets for retiring a committed percentage of the total.
- Classify applications by their strategic value and shift maintenance support focus to highly strategic applications.
- Rank applications with a quality score; applications failing to meet a baseline are selected for preventive maintenance, code simplification, maintainability.
- Migrate an increasing share of maintenance work to lower-case geographies.

Value
- Cut applications by 70%.
- Establish rigorous priorities—SLAs now vary based on objective business criteria.
- Reengineered applications—defects down 58% and maintenance costs down 20%.
- Relocated work—significant maintenance is now performed in countries with costs 60–70% lower than previously.

portfolio according to the strategy established. These capabilities (depicted in Figure 11.1), although distinct, are also closely interrelated and build on each other.[2] To deliver value with APM, organizations must establish all three capabilities. Experience suggests that organizations tend to start by inventorying applications and work from the middle out to refine their APM strategy (and how it is governed) as well as to establish efforts to rationalize their applications portfolio. As such, APM represents a process of continual refinement. Fortunately, experience also suggests that there are real benefits to be reaped from the successful development of each capability. These capabilities are described in detail below.

Capability 1: Strategy and Governance

There are many different reasons to adopt application portfolio management. At one firm, the complexity of the IT application portfolio had increased to the point of becoming unmanageable. The firm viewed APM as the means to gain some measure of control

---

[2]The focus group did not see APM as a "stage" model where organizations advance through a prescribed set of stages. Instead they identified three highly interrelated "capabilities" that organizations need to establish in order to advance their application portfolio management.

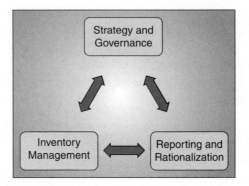

FIGURE 11.1   Key APM Capabilities

over a burgeoning collection of disjointed IT applications. Another firm had set an architectural direction and established an IT roadmap and saw APM as a way to "put some teeth" into the enforcement of these policies. At a third firm, the manager of a strategic business unit was frustrated over escalating annual IT costs and the "pile of applications" that seemed to have "little connection to actual business services." A simple poll of the focus group, however, suggested that APM tended to be an IT-led initiative as opposed to a business initiative—a fact that has implications for launching and funding APM.

To get an APM initiative underway, it is necessary to build a business case. How this is done depends on the firm's strategy. According to one manager, "[I]f APM is positioned as inventory management, you'll never get the business to pay for it." In his organization, APM was promoted as a cost-reduction initiative focused on the elimination of unused (or underused) applications, unnecessary software licenses, duplicated data, and redundant applications. The business case included an aggressive schedule of declining IT costs to the business. In another organization, the APM initiative is supported internally by the IT organization and driven largely by the enterprise architecture group. In fact, the business is unaware of its APM program. In a third example, APM was couched within the overall strategy of transforming the business. The argument was that APM could "reduce ongoing support costs for existing applications in order to re-direct that IT spend into business transformation." The business case included metrics and a quarterly reporting structure to ensure that savings targets were obtained. The conclusion reached by the focus group was that each organization is unique and, given the wide variety of potential APM benefits, the best strategy is to attach APM to a broader enterprise goal. The focus group felt that, if APM is attempted solely within the IT organization without business backing, it is less likely to produce the full range of benefits.

The strategy selected to launch APM has direct ramifications for the information collected about each application (i.e., the second capability—inventory management) as well as what information is reported and tracked by senior management (i.e., the third capability—reporting and rationalization). In the next section of this chapter, we present a comprehensive set of information that could be collected for IT applications within the portfolio. Organizations, depending on their APM strategy, may focus on a subset of this information and develop a reporting and rationalization capability built on this information.

APM strategy and governance are linked; if strategy is the destination, then governance is the map. According to one manager, governance is "a set of policies, procedures, and rules that guide decisions and define decision rights in an organization." Application portfolio governance answers three questions:

1. *What decisions need to be made?*   This addresses the types and/or categories of decisions often referred to as decision domains. It also links the decisions with the processes that are needed to manage the application portfolio.
2. *Who should make these decisions?*   This addresses the roles and accountabilities for decision makers (e.g., who provides input, who approves and has final authority). This links the decisions to be made (the "what") with the decision makers (the "who").
3. *How are these decisions made?*   This addresses the structures and processes for decision making (e.g., the architecture review board). This links the decisions to be made (the "what") with the people/roles (the "who") involved in decision making with the timelines and mechanisms for making those decisions (the "how").

On an ongoing basis, organizations introduce new applications and (less frequently) retire old applications. The key difference with APM is that these applications are managed holistically across the enterprise on a much more formalized and less piece-meal basis. The goal is to discover synergies as well as duplication, alternative (and less costly) methods for providing business services, and rebalancing (or rationalizing) the portfolio of applications with regard to age, capability, and/or technical health. This represents a significant organizational change that impacts governance procedures directly. According to one IT manager, "no longer can business units acquire an IT application that duplicates existing functionality without scrutiny by the APM police." With the adoption of APM governance procedures, such actions become visible at high levels within the organization.

How new governance procedures are actually implemented varies by organization. However, the focus group suggested that effective APM governance must be both free-standing (in order to have visibility and impact) as well as closely integrated within the framework of existing governance mechanisms (in order to effect the status quo). As an example, the IT project selection committee must consider the impact of prospective IT projects on the existing portfolio of enterprise applications if the organization is to achieve its APM rationalization goals regarding architecture and/or functionality. That is, the APM governance processes must leverage existing organizational governance processes, including architectural reviews, exception process handling, IT delivery processes, strategic planning and annual budgeting, and technology reinvestment and renewal. One manager shared his enterprise IT governance framework to demonstrate where and how APM was situated within other established processes (see Figure 11.2).

Effective governance starts with ownership, which entails responsibilities and accountabilities. At a tactical level, each IT application should have an owner. This individual is held responsible for the ultimate disposition of the application—that is, when it is enhanced, refurbished, or decommissioned. The sense of the focus group was that the application owner should be a business manager—except for internal IT applications. Each application should have a business owner, and it is common to also appoint a custodian whose key duty is to keep the information up to date. Given the technical

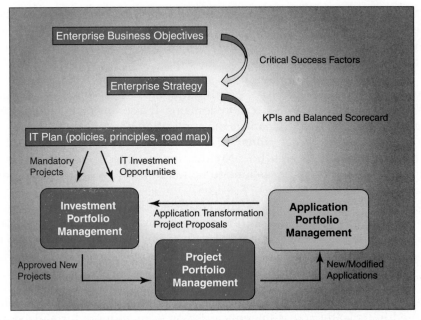

FIGURE 11.2   Positioning APM Within an Enterprise IT Governance Framework

nature of the application information (see Appendix A), the custodian is typically an IT employee, perhaps an account manager or someone within the enterprise architecture group. With stewardship (i.e., owner and custodian) in place at the application level, the next level of governance is the portfolio level. A management committee comprised of application owners, senior enterprise architects, and IT planners/strategists should meet regularly, perhaps quarterly, to make decisions regarding the disposition of applications within the overall portfolio. This committee would report to the senior executive on portfolio activities, performance toward goal achievement, and establishment of linkages to fiscal planning and strategy. In very large organizations, an additional committee of portfolio owners might also be required.

Effective governance is critical for overcoming a number of problems common during the initial phases of APM. Some of the challenges experienced by the focus group included the following:

- Application owners are accountable to execute the process, but no one has defined who (or what body) is accountable for the process itself or what governance practices should be applied to make it happen.
- Managing applications requires additional maturity for defining, a roadmap for the portfolio. Without this, some applications are well-planned while the overall portfolio is not.
- The classification criteria for applications are in flux and lack an executive process for validating the ratings.
- Application assessments are not taken seriously by executive owners ("Everything is important if not critical"), and this erodes the credibility of the process and the overall value of the exercise of managing applications as a portfolio.
- Business managers lack awareness and accountability.

- There is difficulty from the "supply" side—that is, there is reluctance to take owner-ship of the data to ensure its integrity, quality, and timeliness.
- Demand-side aggression pushes for more and more application attributes.

The focus group felt that each of these problems requires effective governance procedures. But like all organizational initiatives, changes to existing routines and methods take time to mature.

Capability 2: Inventory Management

Before building an inventory of applications, organizations first need to know what appli-cations they are going to inventory. One firm started by defining an application as a com-puter program or set of computer instructions that allows end-users to accomplish one of more specific business tasks and is able to operate independently of other applications. An application can also be a distinct data store used by multiple other applications. Examples include commercial off-the-shelf packages, applications written in Excel that perform spe-cific business functions, custom-developed computer software programs, a data ware-house and/or the reporting applications accessing it, and/or modules, services, or components, either purchased or custom built to perform a specific business function. This definition excludes system software or platform software (e.g., operating systems, device drivers, or diagnostic tools), programming software, and user-written macros and scripts.

What is most important is that organizations identify which specific applications will be included in the portfolio to be actively managed. One firm excluded all applications not explicitly managed by IT (e.g., Excel spreadsheets developed by managers for analytical purposes), another focused only on "major" applications according to size, and a third firm only included "business-critical" applications. This decision has direct implications for the size of the APM effort. The organization that limited its portfolio to business-critical applications reduced the portfolio to 180 applications from 1,200—a significant reduction in the amount of effort required. The organization's decision to limit (and therefore focus) its application portfolio depends on the strategy outlined in Step 1 above.

With inclusion criteria established, organizations must then identify what specific information about applications will need to be captured. A list of possible information items gathered from the members of the focus group is presented in Appendix A. These items are categorized according to the following five headings:

- *General application information* is the information used to explicitly and clearly identify an application, distinct from all other applications, and provide a basic understanding of its functionality.
- *Application categorization* is the information providing criteria used to group applications for comparison and portfolio management purposes (e.g., business capability provided, life cycle status).
- *Technical condition* provides the overall rating of the technical quality of the application, including various elements of risk (e.g., development language, oper-ating system, architecture).
- *Business value* provides an overall rating of the value of the application to the business (e.g., business criticality, user base, effectiveness).
- *Support cost* captures the order of magnitude of the overall cost of an application after deployment. It includes maintenance and support costs (including upgrades) but not the initial purchase, development, or deployment costs.

The focus group could not overstate the importance and criticality of selecting the information to be maintained as part of the application inventory as this information dictates the types of analyses that can be performed after the fact (as outlined in the next section). Once selected, the task of capturing application information and keeping it current is a monumental effort. The focus group suggested that, without clear ownership of the information and assigned responsibilities for a custodial function, attempts at application portfolio management would falter. One of the key motivations for establishing a strict information regime is the delivery of demonstrable benefits from the exercise. These are discussed in the next section.

Capability 3: Reporting and Rationalization

With an application inventory established, a set of standard parameter-driven reports can be produced to monitor the status of all existing applications so management can readily ascertain the health of any specific application or the overall health of the portfolio of applications. One firm has a collection of standard reports that analyze the number of applications and their costs, how business capabilities are supported and where duplication exists, breakdowns of annual application costs, application life-cycle patterns, and reuse options for future projects. One widely adopted report compares applications on the basis of business value, technical condition, and cost (see Figure 11.3). As depicted, this chart helps organizations rationalize their IT application portfolio by tracking applications over time as they become less important to the business and/or lose technical currency. One organization found that eliminating those applications in the bottom left of the quadrant—which provide limited business benefit, often at a significant cost—can be a "combination of quick hits and longer-term initiatives." Even managers reluctant to retire a business application can be convinced with evidence of the full support costs.

Once the application inventory is assembled, the number of ways to "slice and dice" the information is unlimited and the value obtained is commensurate. One manager

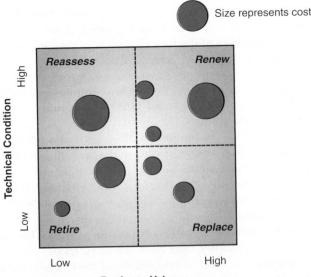

FIGURE 11.3 Application Portfolio Highlighting Business Value, Technical Condition, and Cost

claimed that, for the first time her organization is able to answer questions such as "How many applications use Sybase?" and "How many systems support sales reporting"? The provision of ad hoc reporting capability is a quick way to discover the number of current licenses with a specific vendor and/or to assess the costs of providing specific business services. Ultimately, organizations need to know their true costs of doing business in order to explore options for providing different customer services. The information produced by analyzing the IT application portfolio takes organizations a huge step closer to this level of understanding and optimization.

The information needs supported by an application inventory vary by stakeholder. The IT organization wants to map business functionality against applications; the risk, audit, and security teams are most interested in regulatory compliance and a risk management perspective; and business teams are interested in understanding the costs and business value of the applications they use. Even within IT, different groups (e.g., solutions delivery, information security, production support, executive management, regulatory compliance, infrastructure, architecture, and planning) have information needs that are unique from the application portfolio. For this reason, most firms mandate a single application portfolio capable of supporting many different views at different levels as well as a composite view of the entire portfolio. One manager explained this by claiming that, although different views of the portfolio satisfy individual groups within her organization, the "consolidated view ultimately demonstrates the effectiveness of monitoring and tracking business performance of the assets across the entire IT application portfolio."

KEY LESSONS LEARNED

The following represent some of the lessons learned based on the collective experience of the members of the focus group:

- *Balance demand and supply.* Managers tend to push for the inclusion of more and different application attributes as well as more reports of infinite variety (the "demand" side) while balking at assuming ownership of this data in order to ensure its integrity, quality, and timeliness (the "supply" side). When launching an APM initiative, clear governance procedures should be established to govern regular enhancements and releases for APM reporting.
- *Look for quick wins.* Gaining awareness and acceptance of an APM initiative can be an uphill struggle. This effort is aided greatly by capturing a number of "quick wins" early on. Organizations should look carefully at the possibility of decommissioning applications as a ready source of immediate and visible wins that impact the bottom line directly. Reuse provides midterm wins, and rationalization provides longer-term wins.
- *Capture data at key life stages.* It is a mistake to wait to capture data when applications are already in production. Data should be captured at multiple stages—when the application is first approved, when in testing during development, when promoted to production, during significant modifications, and when retired. As soon as data are captured and made available, the organization can benefit. For example, knowing the attributes of applications under development can be valuable for planning/budgeting purposes and ultimately enables better project solutions.

- *Tie APM to TCO initiatives together.*   If a total cost of ownership (TCO) initiative is underway, ensure that the APM is closely tied to the TCO initiative. Much of the information captured as part of the APM initiative will support the TCO initiative—and vice versa. Knowing this relationship in advance will ensure that the data are captured to facilitate both purposes. The long-term savings can be significant.
- *Provide an application "end-state" view.*   It is important to provide current information about applications, but it is equally important to provide an end-state view indicating the application's future trajectory. This facilitates a planned and orderly evolution toward retirement for applications as well as key information for business planning (e.g., roadmaps, gap reporting, and progress reporting).
- *Communicate APM benefits.*   Gaining awareness and acceptance of an APM initiative is a constant struggle. Organizations must seek opportunities to communicate why this initiative is underway, what results have been realized, and what the next stages to be accomplished are. Effective communication is even more important in situations where the APM initiative is being driven internally by the IT organization.

Conclusion

This chapter, based on the collective experience and insights of senior IT managers from a number of leading organizations, provides guidance to those investigating APM and/or planning to launch an APM initiative. Application portfolio management promises significant benefits to adopting organizations. Obtaining those benefits, however, requires the development of three mutually reinforcing capabilities. The first capability is the development an APM strategy buttressed with governance procedures, the second is the creation of an application inventory, and the third is a reporting capability built to align the application portfolio with the established strategy. Each of these capabilities provides stand-alone benefits, but together they enable an organization to optimize its IT assets, reduce the cost and complexity of its portfolio, reduce or eliminate redundant functionality, facilitate better business decisions regarding technology, and effectively communicate the contribution of IT to the overall organization.

References

Anonymous. "Maximizing IT Investment." *Wall Street & Technology,* April 2008.

Boivie, C.A. "Taking Stock of Your Portfolio: Do You Have a Good Idea of the Value of Your IT Applications, Both Old and New?" *CIO Canada* 11, no. 10 (October 2003).

Caruso, D. "Application Portfolio Management: A Necessity for Future IT." *Manufacturing Business Technology* 25, no. 10 (October 2007): 48.

Gomolski, B. "Cleaning House." *Computerworld* 38, no. 51 (December 2004).

Kasargod, D., and Bondugula, K. "Application Portfolio Management." *Infosys* (April 2005): 1–8. Originally published in www.gtnews.com.

Kramer, L. "CIO Challenge: Application Portfolio Management." *Wall Street & Technology,* May 2006.

Serena Software Inc. "Application Portfolio Management (APM): Solving the Challenges of APM with Serena® Mariner®," 2007. www.serena.com/docs/repository/products/mariner/datasheet-apm-mariner.pdf (accessed March 12, 2011).

APPENDIX A

Application Information

A) *General application information* is the information used to explicitly and clearly identify an application, distinct from all other applications, and provide a basic understanding of its functionality.

- Name—the name that uniquely identifies the application
- Short Name—an abbreviation or acronym that is likely a unique identifier of the application and is used for reporting when there is not room to use the application's full name
- Description—a more extensive description of the application typically focusing on its functional scope
- Portfolio Owner—the title of the portfolio owner of the application and the name of the person currently filling that role (The portfolio owner is typically filled by someone at VP level or higher.)
- Stakeholders—key people (by name and title) that could have been identified as a portfolio owner if multiple portfolio owners were allowed
- Application owner—the title of the portfolio owner's delegate (if there is one) and the name of the person currently filling that role (The application owner is typically someone reporting to the portfolio owner and empowered to make decisions relating to the ongoing use and evolution of the application. The application owner role is typically filled by someone below the VP level.)
- Business consultant—the name of the IT-business liaison (This person is part of the IT organization but is responsible for the relationship with the business unit/
- Internally versus externally developed—states whether the application was developed internally (by any business or IT organization)

or whether it was purchased from an external vendor

- Vendor—the name of the vendor that owns the application (For internally developed applications, this should be the business unit or IT unit that is responsible for maintaining the application, i.e., provides the resources and funding.)
- Product name—the name of the product (Only required when a product has an explicit name that is not the vendor name.)
- Version number—the complete version number of the application that is in production
- Current version—the most current version number in full release by the vendor
- Implementation date—the year and month that the solution went into production
- Last major upgrade—the year and month that the last major upgrade went into production (Major upgrades typically require a project approach, explicit funding, training, and planning to avoid downtime, etc. This field is blank if there has not been a major upgrade after the implementation date.)
- Last minor upgrade—the year and month that the last minor upgrade went into production (Minor upgrades are typically upgrades that can be performed during regularly scheduled maintenance windows and can be performed as part of routine application maintenance. This field is blank if there has not been a minor upgrade after the last major upgrade, e.g., point releases, security patches.)
- Next scheduled review—the year and month that the application profile should next be reviewed (By default, this should be one year from the current review, but will be updated as assessment schedules are developed.)

B) *Application categorization* is the information providing a variety of criteria/data used to group applications for comparison and portfolio management purposes.

- Application scope—identifies the breadth of use of the application across the organization (e.g., enterprise, multidivisional, divisional, multidepartmental, departmental, individual users)
- Life-cycle status—identifies the life-cycle stage that the application is in (e.g., emerging, standard, contained, retirement target, retired)
- SBUs used by—a choice of one or more business divisions that use the application
- SBUs used for—a choice of one or more business divisions that the application is used on behalf of
- Application capability—broad categories of capability that applications provide (e.g., supply chain management [SCM] planning, SCM execution, SCM procurement)
- Application subcapabilities—subcapabilities of functionality that applications provide (A single application will often provide functionality covering multiple subcapabilities.)
- Support organization—identifies the organizational support for the application (e.g., IT organization, third party, business unit)
- Recoverability—the requirement to be able to recover the application in the event of a disaster and the ability to perform that recovery
- Application type—a genera l categorization of the application's use of data (e.g., analytical/reporting, transactional, collaborative, hybrid)
- Application profile—a general categorization of the application's functional profile (e.g., suite, best of breed, in-house.)

C) *Technical Condition* provides the overall rating of the technical quality of the application, including various elements of risk.

- Development language—the programming languages that the application is developed with (The language element should address programming code running on the server, client, database, middleware, etc.)
- Operation system(s)—the operating systems required for all layers of the application where there are application-specific requirements (This can be applied to the server, database, middleware, client, etc. This evaluation categorization does not address the Web browser in a Web-based application.)
- Hardware platforms—the hardware platforms required for all layers of the application where there are application-specific requirements (This can be applied to the server, database, middleware, client, etc.)
- Database/data model—the database platform and database model (i.e., data architecture) that the application is tied to (or built on)
- Integration—the integration tools and model used to integrate the applications with other applications (The "model" aspect of this criterion is closely related to the overall architecture of the systems but specifically looks at the framework/approach used for integration.)
- Architecture—the application architecture, technology patterns, etc. that define "how" different elements of technology were put together to create the application, e.g.,. NET, J2EE, J2SE, OO, Client/Server, Web-based, thin-client, etc. (This criterion also addresses the extensibility of the application—the ability of the applications to be modified to meet future/changing functional requirements.)
- Security—the capability of the application to (1) limit access to data and functionality to specific users and/or groups and (2) provide audit information related to functions performed (or attempted to be performed) on the data viewed (or attempted to be viewed) by specific users (This metric addresses the application's native capabilities, the specific implementation/modification of those capabilities, and the security requirements of the organization.)
- Vendor viability—the likelihood that the vendor will remain strong in the relevant application market and industry vertical
- Vendor support—the ability and commitment of the vendor to provide support for the applications. (This includes the ability and commitment to provide new releases and patches to the application.)
- Key abilities—(1) availability of the application relative to user requirements identified in service level agreements (SLA), (2) scalability

of the application to meet current and future user and transaction volumes, and (3) performance of the application in starting, retrieving information, and performing transactions

- User interface—the overall usability/intuitiveness of the application's interface (This is often reflected by training requirements, support requirements, on-line documentation, etc.)

D) *Business value* provides an overall rating of the value of the application to the business.

- Competitive advantage—the extent to which the application enables a capability that (1) increases revenue, (2) lowers cost, or (3) differentiates the company in the marketplace
- Business criticality—the extent to which the application materially affects the company's ability to conduct core business processes (i.e., sell, deliver, close financial books) (This includes the ability to meet regulatory requirements.)
- User base—the number and variety of users that use the application (This measure is adjusted to reflect the difference between causal/occasional users and power users, as well as internal versus external users. This

measure also includes transaction volumes that the application performs to account for essential applications with few users but large transaction volumes that the business is dependent on.)

- Current effectiveness—ability of the application to meet current business requirements within the scope of the functionality it was intended to provide
- Future effectiveness—ability of the application to meet future business requirements within the scope of the functionality it was intended to provide and logical/reasonable extensions of that functionality.

E) *Support cost* captures the order of magnitude of the overall cost of an application after deployment. It includes maintenance and support costs (including upgrades) but not the initial purchase, development, or deployment costs.

- Elements included—license maintenance, other licensing fees, vendor/external support, internal support, and hardware
- Elements not included—PCs, network, telephony, or other shared services; end-user costs, such as time lost to support calls, downtime, etc. (Typically these data are not readily available at the level of granularity required.)

MINI CASE
Building Shared Services at RR Communications[3]

Vince Patton had been waiting years for this day. He pulled the papers together in front of him and scanned the small conference room. "You're fired," he said to the four divisional CIOs sitting at the table. They looked nervously at him, grinning weakly. Vince wasn't known to make practical jokes, but this had been a pretty good meeting, at least relative to some they'd had over the past five years. "You're kidding," said Matt Dawes, one of the more outspoken members of the divisional CIO team. "Nope," said Vince. "I've got the boss's OK on this. We don't need any of you anymore. I'm creating one enterprise IT organization, and there's no room for any of you. The HR people are waiting outside." With that, he picked up his papers and headed to the door, leaving the four of them in shock.

"That felt good," he admitted as he strode back to his office. A big man, not known to tolerate fools gladly (or corporate politics), he was not a cruel one. But those guys had been thorns in his side ever since he had taken the new executive VP of IT job at the faltering RR Communications five years ago. The company's stock had been in the dumpster, and with the dramatically increased competition in the telecommunications industry as a result of deregulation, his friends and family had all thought he was nuts. But Ross Roman, RR's eccentric but brilliant founder, had made him an offer he couldn't refuse. "We need you to transform IT so that we can introduce new products more quickly," he'd said. "You'll have my full backing for whatever you want to do."

Typically for an entrepreneur, Roman had sketched the vision swiftly, leaving someone else to actually implement it. "We've got to have a more flexible and responsive IT organization. Every time I want to do something, they tell me

'the systems won't allow it.' I'm tired of having customers complaining about getting multiple bills for each of our products. It's not acceptable that RR can't create one simple little bill for each customer." Roman punctuated his remarks by stabbing with his finger at a file full of letters to the president, which he insisted on reading personally each week. "You've got a reputation as a 'can do' kind of guy; I checked. Don't bother me with details; just get the job done."

Vince knew he was a good, proactive IT leader, but he hadn't been prepared for the mess he inherited . . . or the politics. There was no central IT, just separate divisional units for the four key lines of business—Internet, mobile, landline, and cable TV service—each doing its own thing. Every business unit had bought its own hardware and software, so introducing the common systems that would be needed to accomplish Roman's vision would be hugely difficult—that is, assuming they wanted them, which they didn't. There were multiple sales systems, databases, and customer service centers, all of which led to customer and business frustration. The company was in trouble not only with its customers but also with the telecommunications regulators and with its software vendors, who each wanted information about the company's activities, which they were legally entitled to have but which the company couldn't provide.

Where should he start to untangle this mess? Clearly, it wasn't going to be possible to provide bundled billing, responsiveness, unified customer care, and rapid time to market all at once, let alone keep up with the new products and services that were flooding into the telecommunications arena. And he hadn't exactly been welcomed with open arms by the divisional CIOs (DIOs), who were sus-

[3]Smith, H. A., and J. D. McKeen. "Shared Services at RR Communications," #1-L07-1-002. Queen's School of Business, September 2007. Reproduced by permission of Queen's University, School of Business, Kingston, Ontario, Canada.

picious of him in the extreme. "Getting IT to operate as a single enterprise unit, regardless of the product involved, is going to be tough," he admitted to himself. "This corporate culture is not going to take easily to centralized direction."

And so it was. The DIOs had fought him tooth and nail, resisting any form of integration of their systems. So had the business unit leaders, themselves presidents, who were rewarded on the basis of the performance of their divisions and, therefore, didn't give a hoot about "the enterprise" or about anything other than their quarterly results. To them, centralized IT meant increased bureaucracy and much less freedom to pick up the phone and call their buddy Matt or Larry or Helen or Dave and get that person to drop everything to deal with their latest money-making initiative. The fact that it cost the enterprise more and more every time they did this didn't concern them—they didn't care that costs racked up: testing to make sure changes didn't affect anything else that was operational; creation of duplicate data and files, which often perpetuated bad data; and loss of integrated information with which to run the enterprise. And the fact that the company needed an army of "data cleansers" to prepare the reports needed for the government to meet its regulatory and Sarbanes-Oxley requirements wasn't their concern. Everyone believed his or her needs were unique.

Unfortunately, although he had Roman's backing in theory, in practice Vince's position was a bit unusual because he himself didn't have an enterprise IT organization as yet and the DIOs' first allegiance was clearly to their division presidents, despite having a "dotted line" reporting relationship to Vince. The result was that he had to choose his battles very, very carefully in order to lay the foundation for the future. First up was redesigning the company's internal computer infrastructure to use one set of standard technologies. Simplification and standardization involved a radical reduction of the number of suppliers and centralized procurement. The politics were fierce and painful with the various suppliers the company was using, simultaneously courting the DIOs and business unit leaders while trying to sell Vince on the merits of their brand of technology for the whole company. Matt Dawes had done everything he could to undermine this vision, making sure that the users caused the maximum fuss right up to Roman's office.

Finally, they'd had a showdown with Roman. "As far as I'm concerned, moving to standardized hardware and software is nondiscussable," Vince stated bluntly. "We can't even begin to tackle the issues facing this company without it. And furthermore, we are in serious noncompliance with our software licensing agreements. We can't even tell how many users we have!" This was a potentially serious legal issue that had to be dealt with. "I promised our suppliers that we would get this problem under control within eighteen months, and they've agreed to give us time to improve. We won't have this opportunity again."

Roman nodded, effectively shutting down the argument. "I don't really understand how more standardization is going to improve our business flexibility," he'd growled, "but if you say so, let's do it!" From that point on, Vince had moved steadily to consolidate his position, centralizing the purchasing budget; creating an enterprise architecture; establishing a standardized desktop and infrastructure; and putting tools, metrics, and policies in place to manage them and ensure the plan was respected by the divisions.

Dawes and Larry Hughes, another DIO, had tried to sabotage him on this matter yet again by adopting another manufacturer's customer relationship management (CRM) system (and yet another database), hoping that it could be up and running before Vince noticed. But Vince had moved swiftly to pull the plug on that one by refusing the project access to company hardware and giving the divisional structure yet another black mark.

That episode had highlighted the need for a steering committee, one with teeth to make sure that no other rogue projects got implemented with "back door funding." But the company's entrepreneurial culture wasn't ready for it, so again foundational work had to be done. "I'd have had a riot on my hands if I'd tried to do this in my first few years here," Vince reflected as he walked back to his office, stopping to chat with some of the other executives on his way. Vince now knew everyone and was widely respected at this level because he understood their concerns and interests. Mainly, these were financial—delivering more IT for less cost. But as Vince moved around the organization, he stressed that IT decisions were first and foremost business decisions. He spoke to his colleagues in business terms. "The company wants one consistent brand for its organization so it can cross-sell services. So why do we need different customer service organizations or back-end systems?" he would ask them. One by one he had brought the "C"-level executives around to at least thinking about the need for an enterprise IT organization.

Vince had also taken advantage of his weekly meetings with Roman to demonstrate the critical linkage between IT and Roman's vision for the enterprise. Vince's motto was "IT must be very visible in this organization." When he felt the political climate was right, he called all the "Cs" to a meeting. With Roman in the room for psychological support, he made his pitch. "We need to make all major IT decisions together as a business," he said. "If we met monthly, we could determine what projects we need to launch in order to support the business and then allocate resources and budgets accordingly."

Phil Cooper, president of Internet Services, spoke up. "But what about our specific projects? Won't they get lost when they're all mixed up with everyone else's? How do we get funding for what we need to do?"

Vince had a ready answer. "With a steering committee, we will do what's best for the organization as a whole, not for one division at the expense of the others. The first thing we're going to do is undertake a visioning exercise for what you all want our business to look like in three years, and then we'll build the systems and IT infrastructure to support that vision."

Talking the language of business had been the right approach because no one wanted to get bogged down in techno-jargon. And this meeting had effectively turned the tide from a divisional focus to an enterprise one—at least as far as establishing a steering committee went. Slowly, Vince had built up his enterprise IT organization, putting those senior IT managers reporting to him into each of the business divisions. "Your job is to participate in all business decisions, not just IT ones," he stated. "There is nothing that happens in this company that doesn't affect IT." He and his staff had also "walked the talk" over the past two years, working with the business to identify opportunities for short-term improvements that really mattered a lot to the divisions. These types of quick wins demonstrated that he and his organization really cared about the business and

made IT's value much more visible. He also stressed accountability. "Centralized units are always seen to be overhead by the business," he explained to his staff. "That's why we must be accountable for everything we spend and our costs must be transparent. We also need to give the business some choices in what they spend. Although I won't compromise on legal, safety, or health issues, we need to let them know where they can save money if they want. For example, even though they can't choose not to back up their files, they can choose the amount of time it will take them to recover them."

But the problem of the DIOs had remained. Used to being kings of their own kingdoms, everything they did appeared to be in direct opposition to Vince's vision. And it was apparent that Roman was preaching "one company" but IT itself was not unified. Things had come to a head last year when Vince had started looking at outsourcing. Again the DIOs had resisted, seeing the move as one designed to take yet more power away from them. Vince had offered Helen a position as sourcing director, but she'd turned it down, seeing it as a demotion rather than a lateral move. The more the DIOs stonewalled Vince, the more determined he became to deal with them once and for all. "They're undermining my credibility with the business and with our suppliers," Vince had complained to himself. "There's still so much more to do, and this divisional structure isn't working for us." That's when he'd realized he had to act or RR wouldn't be able to move ahead on its next project: a single customer service center shared by the four divisions instead of the multiple divisional and regional ones they had now.

So Vince had called a meeting, ostensibly to sort out what would be outsourced and what wouldn't. Then he'd dropped the bombshell. "They'll get a good package," he reassured himself. "And they'll be happier somewhere else than always fighting with me." The new IT organizational charts, creating a central IT function, had been drawn up, and the memo appointing his management team had been signed. Vince sighed. That had been a piece of cake compared to what he was going to be facing now. Was he ready for the next round in the "IT wars"? He was going to have to go head to head with the business, and it wouldn't be pretty. Roman had supported him in getting the IT house in order, but would he be there for the next step?

Vince looked gloomily at the reports the DIOs had prepared for their final meeting. They documented a complete data mess—even within the divisions. The next goal was to implement the single customer service center for all divisions, so a customer could call one place and get service for all RR products. This would be a major step forward in enabling the company to implement new products and services. If he could pull it off, all of the company's support systems would, for the first time, talk to each other and share data. "We can't have shared services without common data, and we can't have good business intelligence either," he muttered. Everything he needed to do next relied on this, but the business had seen it differently when he'd last tried to broach the subject with them. "These are our data, and these are our customers," they'd said. "Don't mess with them." And he hadn't

. . . but that was then. Now it was essential to get their information in order. But what would he have to do to convince them and to make it happen?

Discussion Questions

1. List the advantages of a single customer service center for RR Communications.
2. Devise an implementation strategy that would guarantee the support of the divisional presidents for the shared customer service center.
3. Is it possible to achieve an enterprise vision with a decentralized IT function?
4. What business and IT problems can be caused by lack of common information and an enterprise IM strategy?
5. What governance mechanisms need to be put in place to ensure common customer data and a shared customer service center? What metrics might be useful?

MINI CASE
Creating a Process-Driven Organization at AgCredit[4]

Kate Longair knelt on the floor of the CEO's office as she unrolled the twenty-foot-long diagram of all of the processes and systems in the company and how they interconnected. Dressed in "Saturday casual" jeans, white shirt, and boots, she looked more like a suburban soccer mom than a high-powered, up-and-coming banking executive. But Saturday was the only day she could get a couple of uninterrupted hours with her boss, Jim Finney. "I never thought business transformation would be such physical work," she joked as the two of them struggled to move the furniture so they could spread out the huge document and pin it down so it wouldn't roll up again.

This was the culmination of three months of nonstop work for Kate and her team, and she knew it would be a key decision point for AgCredit. Would Finney get it? He wasn't a technical person, and although he had agreed to be the corporate sponsor of her Enterprise Integration Program (EIP), there was a chance he'd be overwhelmed with the detail on this chart and simply abdicate responsibility to his chief of operations. That would be the kiss of death for EIP. The COO, Steve Stewart, was a great guy, but only the CEO would have the clout to push through the radical changes Kate was proposing for the company.

Kate began her spiel by reminding Finney why she was here. "Three months ago you asked me to fix AgCredit's 'systems problems'." Briefly, she took him back through her mandate. AgCredit, the MidWest Agriculture Credit and Loan Company—a midsize financial institution focusing on agribusiness—had grown significantly in the past few years and was holding its own against other, much larger banks because of its extensive customer knowledge. But Finney had recognized that its people and processes were taxed to the hilt.

"We can't keep throwing people at our problems," he'd said to his executive team at the time. "We've got to get some better technology in here to support them."

That comment had opened a can of worms. "IT's a mess," complained Stewart. "Nothing works well and nothing talks to anything else. Whenever I ask anyone to do anything, they tell me it's going to cost a million bucks. I vote we outsource the whole thing." Paul Manley, the senior vice president of e-business, agreed. "Our IT is completely broken. I wouldn't ask any of them to solve our business problems. I could do a better job!" The others chimed in with their war stories of project delays, bad information, customer complaints, and IT staff who didn't know which end of the business was up. The upshot of the meeting was that all of the business executives wanted much better systems integration, but not one of them had any idea where to start or the time and skills to do the job. So Kate had been given the mandate to form a team and figure out the best approach to achieving systems integration.

"We began by interviewing the executive team about their business strategy and the barriers they saw in achieving it," she explained to Finney. "The first thing we noticed was that everyone knew what he wanted to do and how it would add value to the company, but no one understood how their business strategy would fit with everyone else's to deliver enterprise value. The second thing we realized was that we didn't understand our business processes and how they worked together. And if we didn't understand these, it was going to be impossible to get the right systems in place to support them." IT had been saying this for quite a while, she reflected silently, but it simply didn't have the credibility with the business to be believed.

[4]Smith, H. A., and J. D. McKeen. "Creating a Process-Driven Organization at AgCredit," #1-L07-1-001. Queen's School of Business, September 2007. Reproduced by permission of Queen's University, School of Business , Kingston, Ontario, Canada.

"That's when we realized we had to understand our key strategic drivers and how our current business processes worked to enable them." These processes had never been written down before, so most of the previous months had been spent trying to understand and document them in workshops with key business subject matter experts. At the same time, some members of her team had documented AgCredit's systems and what they did. The result was the twenty-foot chart at their feet. The top part showed all the current business processes, and the bottom part showed all the systems that supported these business processes. When the north–south linkages between systems and processes were added to the chart, the problems became readily apparent.

Using a laser pointer, Kate walked Finney through just how many systems the frontline staff had to access for a simple business process, such as renewing a loan. All these connections made the diagram look like a plate of spaghetti. "What a mess!" he commented when the presentation was finished. "We've got to do something to fix this. What do you recommend?"

"Well . . ." she began hesitantly. "This is a bit radical, but I'd like to stop all new systems development for at least six weeks until we get a better handle on what our desired future business processes will look like. We've got about $40 million worth of projects on the books, but until we know where we're going as an enterprise, it's hard to tell what's worthwhile and what isn't." Because each of the four business divisions had its own pet projects, the only person who could make this call was Finney. "Let's do it," he said. "We've got to get this situation under control if we're going to be able to compete the way I want us to." Finney was referring to AgCredit's key strategic drivers, which included continuous growth, expanded customer relationships, the ability to spend more time with the customer, the ability to cross-sell between business divisions, and the ability to provide a consistent customer experience across all delivery channels.

With Finney's unconditional support, Kate was able to avoid much of the political fallout of the system development halt. "I wouldn't have survived without it," she commented to a colleague over lunch a few weeks later. "If he'd thrown me to the wolves, we'd have been toast. Everyone would have sat on the fence and waited

for me to fail. At least this way, they have to work on this with me." Over the next few weeks, Kate and her team developed a high-level vision of AgCredit's future business processes that fully supported Finney's enterprise strategy and led to the creation of a roadmap for transforming how the business operated, but the IT portion of the chart remained a problem.

It was clear to Finney that he needed a CIO who could work with and support the EIP team with technology, someone who had the complete trust of the business and who was a highly effective executive capable of driving both a business and an IT transformation agenda forward.

No sooner was the need articulated than the answer walked by his office. "Paul, have you got a minute?" Finney called. As Manley entered the office, stepping carefully around the chart still spread across the floor, Finney dropped his bombshell. "You've often said you could do a better job of running IT if we gave you the chance. Now you can put your money where your mouth is!" This was said as a joke, not a challenge. If anyone was up to the job, it was Manley. "Wow!" said Manley. "I guess you're desperate." It was a gutsy move because Manley had little formal technical expertise, although he had masterminded AgCredit e-business initiatives for the past three years. Both Finney and Manley knew it. This move would be watched very carefully, and both of their personal reputations were on the line. But Manley relished the challenge and accepted the offer without hesitation, wasting no time diving into the confusion and disarray.

The first problem Manley faced was buying some time to figure out what needed to be done in IT, so after consultation with Kate and Finney, the stoppage on all systems development was extended for an additional forty-five days. This was not a popular decision, but it underscored the importance of making some changes in IT and also getting some agreement on the new key business processes and the transformational roadmap— which was proving to be a challenge—before spending any more money on IT solutions. "At least," he said wryly to Kate, "working on their priorities will distract the business from what I'm going to be doing in IT."

Manley's first survey of his new "empire" was discouraging. IT was in a significant state of disarray. IT governance was nonexistent, and there was no architecture plan. IT was organized in silos to mirror AgCredit's divisional structure, and each business unit owned and governed its own IT projects. This resulted in business unit leaders making IT decisions based on their current needs and essentially "mortgaging the future" because they wouldn't fund the foundational work needed to operate IT at an enterprise level. Furthermore, because IT was considered a necessary evil, the company had outsourced chunks of it, sometimes for the wrong reasons. As a result, Manley's IT staff felt highly disengaged from the company, scoring 30 percent versus the overall company engagement score of 69 percent. Many staff were unclear of their roles or were performing roles for which they were unqualified. There was a significant lack of technical skills in certain areas, and the organization was also missing senior IT managers who could be "thought leaders." Finally, many vacancies remained unfilled because the company couldn't find qualified staff for what it was willing to pay.

A key problem was the applicationcentric approach the organization took to its work. Businesspeople would come to IT and say "I need a new system." Most businesspeople had been trained by IT to think in terms of existing systems. And IT staff were always injecting "IT reality" into business thinking, telling others that they couldn't do something because "the system wouldn't allow it." This had led to a complete data mess, among other things. AgCredit had four major systems, each with its own database, and special interfaces had been built to enable each to communicate with the others. As a result, the company now had a Tower of Babel where the same information appeared in different formats, which were difficult to reconcile. This was a significant challenge when creating accurate reports for banking and other government regulators.

Now Manley had the high-tech guru he'd hired in his office telling him that going to a service-oriented architecture (SOA) was going to solve all his problems! Dirk Schader's eyes gleamed as he laid out the benefits of this latest technological panacea. "If we adopt SOA principles in IT, everything will be deconstructed into separate 'services.' We'd have foundational services, such as forms management and identity management; internal services, which would decompose applications into small pieces of functionality, such as

loan servicing or changing customer address; and finally, we could buy external services, like credit rating. I think this is just what AgCredit needs!"

Manley struggled to get his thoughts together about this. Theoretically, the case for SOA was compelling, but would it really work? Schader was a highly reputable consultant, and services would match with processes quite well, but was the company ready for this? Was IT? Was the technology ready for prime time? "I think you've got something here," he said cautiously, "but I want to think this through carefully. First, we have to make sure it's the right technical approach and not just another high-tech fad."

Schader interrupted. "I don't think there's any other way, to be frank. You need to integrate different technologies and platforms without completely replacing them, right?" Manley nodded. "So SOA is technology neutral. It's really an approach and principles for technology design, and it supports Web services, which is a language that works across all technologies."

"We've traditionally bought and customized software packages and integrated them at the back end," stated Manley, showing off his newly acquired technical knowledge. "How would SOA be different, and would our existing packages work with SOA?"

"Good questions," answered Schader. "Almost all vendors say they can handle SOA, but many of them can't. We're going to have to be very careful about who we choose to buy components from. Some of these guys say their stuff is based on open standards, but when you get into the guts of it, you find it's got some proprietary code built in. SOA is tough to do—no question—but given all the good business process work you've done and the fact that you are going to completely redesign and restructure IT, I think you've got a shot at making it a success."

"I agree," said Manley, "but we're going to have to prove it to the executive team, and we're going to need some basic foundational work on our data. Before we even start this SOA stuff, we have to get a handle on that. Can you work with Kate to put a plan together for creating a single set of customer information that would work with each of our systems temporarily? Maybe if the two of you 'bang a few heads' in the business, and now that we've got Finney's support, we can finally make some progress in this area. Then you could get started on creating a single customer information file. If we can get this far when no one else has been able to, I bet they'll trust us to try out SOA with a small business process."

Schader nodded. "Sure thing, and I'd like to get Samantha Secord involved with this. She's got some really good business analytical skills, which I think could be developed. She's been stuck coding, and it's not really her thing."

Manley groaned at the reminder that his staffing was a mess. "Go for it," he agreed. "I'll work something out with HR." SOA and customer information were great ideas for the future, but his bigger problems were going to be getting at the nuts and bolts of IT transformation. He now understood the function's current problems, but without a new IT organizational structure and governance, agreement from the business, and supportive corporate processes, nothing was going to get fixed permanently and they'd have no hope of supporting Kate's business transformation. "We've got to develop our capabilities, and the business has to see we can do what we say we'll do," he muttered to no one in particular. "And we've got to do it quickly." He turned to his PC and began to sketch out a plan.

Two days later Manley called a meeting of all his managers to explain the need for the new IT organizational structure. "Our first critical success factor is not going to be whether we can develop new systems or use new technologies, although those are important. It's about how to position IT to be successful in a processcentric organization. I'm going to need all your help to do this properly. We've got to work in partnership with the business, but we've also got to recognize the strengths we bring to the table. This won't happen overnight. Here's what I have in mind. . . ."

Discussion Questions

1. Propose an organizational structure for the IT department that you feel would support the transformation of AgCredit into a processcentric organization.

2. Outline a project selection process for AgCredit to ensure alignment with the enterprise business vision.

3. How should Manley "make the case" for SOA to ensure that the executive team at AgCredit buys in?

4. What new internal IT capabilities will have to be developed in order to create an IT department to support AgCredit's future business architecture?

5. What aspects of IT governance do you think would be important in supporting this transformation?

MINI CASE
IT Investment at North American Financial[5]

Caroline Weese checked her makeup and then glanced at her watch for the tenth time. Almost 10:45. Showtime. As North American Financial's (NAF) first female CIO, she knew she had to be better than good when she met with the company's senior executives for the first time to justify her IT budget. They had shown their faith in her three months ago by giving her this position, when NAF's long-serving senior vice president of IT had had to retire early due to ill health. But women were just beginning to crack the "glass ceiling" at the bank, and she knew there was a lot more riding on this presentation than just this budget.

That said, the budget situation wasn't great. As she well knew from her earlier experience in more subordinate roles, the CIO had the unenviable task of justifying the company's $500M budget to a group of executives who only saw the expense of IT, not its value. This was especially frustrating because NAF's IT management was excellent, when looked at by any standard. NAF's IT group consisted of almost 7,000 professionals who followed all the recommended standards such as CMM, CMMI, ISO9001, and ITIL to ensure that its IT processes were efficient, cost effective and on par with, if not higher than, industry standards. It had been certified at a minimum Level 3 CMMI and was an industry leader in delivering projects on time, on budget, and in scope. But in the past few years, NAF executives had implemented rigorous cost containment measures for IT, leaving the CIO to struggle to be all things to all people.

"They want innovation, they need reliability and stability, and we're required by law to meet ever-more stringent government regulations, but they're still nickel-and-diming us!" Caroline thought indignantly. She envied the bank's business units that could clearly show profit-and-loss statements, and their ability to make strategic decisions about what to do with the excess capital they often had. In her world, business strategies changed regularly and, thus, IT's goals had to as well. But strategies were not linked to budgets, which were typically set six to nine months in advance. As a result, IT was always struggling to keep up and find the resources to be flexible.

She squared her shoulders, took a deep breath, pasted a smile on her face and pushed open the door to the executive conference room to face her colleagues and her future. The room was full of "suits"—a few females here and there, but mostly tough, middle-age males who expected answers and action. Following a few pleasantries about how she was adjusting to her new role, they got down to business. "The thing we're most concerned about, Caroline," said Bill Harris, NAF's CEO, "is we simply don't see where we're getting value from our IT investments. There's no proof in the bottom line." The CFO added, "Every year we approve hundreds of millions of dollars for IT projects, which are supposedly based on sound cost–benefit analyses, but the benefits never materialize." Heads around the room began nodding.

Caroline's mind was whirling. What did they really want from her? Pulling her thoughts together quickly, she responded. "If you're looking for IT to tell you which projects will deliver the most business value, or if you want me to monitor the business units after the projects they asked for are implemented to see if they are delivering value, you're asking me to do something that's well beyond IT's scope of expertise. We're not the experts in your business case, and it

[5]Smith, H. A., and J. D. McKeen. "IT Investment at North American Financial," #1-L09-1-001. Queen's School of Business, October 2009. Reproduced by permission of Queen's University, School of Business, Kingston, Ontario, Canada.

shouldn't be up to us to monitor how you use the technology we give you. I'll take full responsibility for the quality of our work, its timely delivery, and its cost, but we really have to work together to ensure we're investing in the right projects and delivering benefits."

"What do you recommend then?" asked Sam Patel, head of Retail Banking. "I think we need an IT Investment Committee that I would co-lead jointly with you, Matt," Caroline said while looking pointedly at the CFO. "We need a strong partnership to explore what can be done and who should be responsible for doing it. Finance is the only place where all the money comes together in this organization. Although I have to pull together an IT budget every year, it's really contingent on what each business unit wants to spend. We don't really have an enterprise IT budgeting process that looks across our business silos to see if what we're spending is good for NAF as a whole." Matt Harper looked thoughtful. "You could be on to something here, Caroline. Let's see if we can figure this out together."

The rest of the meeting passed in a blur, and before Caroline knew it, she and Matt were trying to identify who they should assign to help them look at their IT investment challenges. These were significant. First, there was inconsistent alignment of the total IT development budget with enterprise strategies. "We have enterprise strategies but no way of linking them to enterprise spending," Caroline pointed out. IT budgets were allocated according to the size of the business unit. Smaller lines of business had smaller IT budgets than larger ones. "For some small business units like ours, government mandatory projects eat up our entire IT budget," complained Cathy Benson, senior vice president of Business Banking Product Management. This made it extremely difficult to allocate IT resources strategically—say, for example, to grow a smaller business unit into a larger one.

Second, project approvals were made by business units without addressing cross-unit synergies. Looking at the projects IT had underway revealed that the company had eighteen separate projects in different parts of the business to comply with anti–money laundering regulations. "We've got to be reinventing the wheel with some of these," complained Ian Ha, senior director of NAF's Risk and Compliance department.

Third, although business cases were required for all major projects, their formats were inconsistent, and the data provided to justify the costs lacked rigor. "There seems to be a lot of gaming going on here," observed Michael Cranston, director of Financial Strategy. "A lot of these numbers don't make sense. How come we've never asked the business sponsors of these projects to take ownership for the business benefits they claim when they ask for the money in the first place?"

Fourth, once a project was approved, everyone focused on on-time, on-budget delivery. No one ever asked whether a project was still necessary or was still on track to deliver the benefits anticipated. "Do we ever stop projects once they've started or review the business case 'in-flight'?" mused Matt. Finally, no one appeared to be accountable for delivering these benefits once an IT project was developed and implemented; rather, everyone just heaved a great sigh of relief and moved on to the next project.

Because the total IT budget for new development work was allocated by business unit, the result was a prioritization process that worked reasonably well at the business unit level but not for NAF as a whole. Enterprise executives created enterprise strategies, but they didn't get involved in implementing them in the business units, which left the business unit heads to prioritize initiatives within their own silo. In prioritization meetings, leaders would argue passionately for their own particular cause and focusing on their own needs, not on NAF's overall strategies. "We really need to align this process with our enterprise priorities," said Caroline. Matt agreed. "There's got to be a process to bring all our investment decisions for new projects together so we can compare them across business units and adjust our resourcing accordingly."

Looking deeper into these matters revealed that there was more to IT spending than simply prioritizing projects, however. Almost 60 percent of the bank's IT budget was spent not on strategic new development projects but on maintaining existing systems, interfaces, and data. And another 20 percent was work that had to be done to meet the demands of government legislation or the bank's regulators. "How is this possible?" asked Sam. "No wonder we're not getting much 'bang for our buck'!" Caroline exclaimed. "Every time we develop or acquire a new system without getting rid of something else, we add to our 'application clutter.' When we continually add new systems while holding IT budgets and head counts relatively flat, more and more of our resources have to be devoted to supporting these systems." New systems meant new interfaces between and among existing systems, additional data and dependencies, and increasing risk that something could go wrong. "We've tried to get the business units interested in sponsoring an initiative to reduce duplication and simplify our applications portfolio, but they're not interested in what they call 'IT housekeeping.' They don't see how dealing with this will help them in the long run. I guess we haven't explained it to them very well."

Brenda Liu, senior director of IT Infrastructure, added, "We also have to keep our IT environment up to date. Vendors are continually making upgrades to software, and there are also license fees to consider. And, as you know, we have to build in extra reliability and redundancy for our critical systems and data, as well as privacy protection for our banking customers. It's an expensive process." "I get all this," said Benson, "but why can't you explain it to us properly? How can you just expect us to accept that 80 percent of your budget is a 'black box' that doesn't need justification? Although every dime you spend may be critical to this company, the fact remains that IT's lack of transparency is damaging its internal credibility with the business."

Round and round the issues they went. Over the next two months, Caroline, Matt, and their team hammered away at them. Eventually, they came up with a set of five principles on which their new IT investment process would be based:

1. Alignment of the IT development portfolio with enterprise strategies
2. Rigor and common standards around IT planning and business casing
3. Accountability in both business and IT for delivering value
4. Transparency at all levels and stages of development
5. Collaboration and cross-group synergies in all IT work.

In their team update to the bank's executive committee, Caroline and Matt wrote, "Our vision is for a holistic view of our IT spending that will allow us to direct our resources where they will have the greatest impact. We propose to increase rigor and discipline in business casing and benefits tracking so NAF can invest with confidence in IT. The result will be strategic partnerships between IT and business units based on trust, leading us to surprise and delight our customers and employees and amaze our competitors."

With the executive committee's blessing, the IT Investment Office was created to design and implement a detailed investment optimization process that could be implemented throughout the bank in time for the next budget cycle. Cathy Benson was named its new director, reporting to Matt. Speaking to her staff after the announcement, Caroline stated, "I really believe that getting this work out of IT and into the business will be critical for this process. We need to make the decision-making process clearer and more collaborative. This will help us learn how to jointly make better decisions for the enterprise."

With the hand-off from IT officially in place, Cathy and Matt knew they had to move quickly. "We've got three months before the next budget cycle begins," said Matt. "You've got to make it real by then. I'll back you all the way, but you're going to have to find some way to deal with the business unit heads. They're not going to like having their autonomy for decision making taken away from them. And you have to remember they need some flexibility to do work that's important to them." Cathy nodded. She had already heard some of the negative rumors about the process and knew she was going to have to be tough if it was going to be successful and not torpedoed during its implementation.

Calling her project team together for its first meeting, she summarized their challenge. "We have to design and implement three interrelated practices: a thorough and rigorous method of project categorization and prioritization, comprehensive and holistic governance of IT spending and benefits delivery at all levels, and an annual IT planning process that provides transparency and accountability for all types of IT spending and which creates an integrated and strategically aligned development portfolio. Then we have to roll it out across the organization. And the change management is going to be massive. Now, who has any ideas about what to do next?"

Discussion Questions

Cathy Benson, the director of the newly created IT Investment Office, is tasked with the "design and implementation of a detailed investment optimization process to be implemented throughout the bank in time for the next budget cycle." She has three months to do this and it must be in accordance with the five established principles to guide the bank's IT investment process. Your task is to design and implement the following:

1. A thorough and rigorous method of project categorization and prioritization
2. A comprehensive and holistic governance of IT spending and benefits delivery at all levels
3. An annual IT planning process that provides transparency and accountability for all types of IT spending and that creates an integrated and strategically aligned development portfolio

Chapter 12

Strategic Experimentation with IT[1]

The role of IT is changing. According to Smith and McKeen (2006), it is bifurcating into separate roles: commodity service and competitive differentiation. Seemingly schizophrenic, these dual perspectives simply reflect the fact that organizations need to balance their bottom-line focus with their top-line focus—that is, they need to take the costs out of the business while growing revenues through IT-enhanced products and services. Although IT is experienced at reducing internal costs, a top-line focus is new and different. It requires a customercentric orientation. Developing systems for employees is not the same as for real customers who lack allegiance, skill, and/or patience. A top-line focus also requires experimentation with new products and services that are predominantly technology enabled. Such experimentation (e.g., trying new offerings) is well established in most organizations, but it is new terrain for the IT function. It means new collaborations (e.g., marketing, business development, research and development), and it entails new skills and roles (e.g., forecasting, marketing timing). The upshot is to put IT front and center. With services Web enabled and products downloadable, most of what customers know and think about an organization is now based on its Internet presence. As an anonymous CEO quipped to a group of IT executives, "Welcome to the world of consumer behavior."

This chapter explores how IT is being used for strategic IT experiments (e.g., where IT is being used to drive a new business venture), as opposed to "experiments with new IT" (e.g., where promising new technologies are examined). It is clear that strategic IT experimentation cannot be examined in isolation. In most firms, strategic experimentation occurs within a larger organizational framework of innovation—an organization's need to reinvent its products and services and occasionally itself—and, as a result, is best understood within this context. Therefore, in the next section we describe the nature of innovation and the role of strategic experimentation. Following this, we present a typical innovation life cycle and show where experimentation fits within this model. In the final section of this chapter, we offer advice for managing strategic IT experiments.

---

[1]McKeen, J. D., and H. A. Smith. "Strategic Experimentation with IT." *Communications of the Association for Information Systems* 19, article 8 (January 2007): 132-41. Reproduced by permission of the Association for Information Systems.

INNOVATION AND STRATEGIC EXPERIMENTATION

The need to innovate is well established as necessary for long-term organizational survival (Christensen and Raynor 2003; Hamel and Välikangas 2003). According to Christensen (1997), there are two types of innovation: sustaining and disruptive. *Sustaining* innovation improves an existing product or enhances an existing service for an existing customer. In contrast, *disruptive* innovation targets noncustomers and delivers a product or service that fundamentally differs from the current product portfolio. Sustaining innovation leaves organizations in their comfort zone of established markets, known customers, and realizable business models. Disruptive technologies enjoy none of these benefits. To be successful for the initiating organization, the disruptive innovation must meet two basic requirements: it must create value as perceived by customers, and it must enact mechanisms to appropriate or capture a fair share of this new value (Henderson et al. 2003). For other organizations and particularly dominant players, disruptive innovation can be devastating. Christensen (1997) refers to this as "the innovator's dilemma." For an excellent discussion of disruptive technologies and a review of six leading theories of innovation, see Denning (2005).

Innovation comes about through organizational change, and here, too, we see two dominant forms: continuous change versus punctuated equilibrium. Brown and Eisenhardt (1997) describe *continuous change* as "frequent, relentless, and perhaps endemic to the firm," whereas the *punctuated equilibrium* model of change "assumes that long periods of small, incremental change are interrupted by brief periods of discontinuous, radical change." In this latter case, change is primarily seen as "rare, risky, and episodic." Although it is tempting to equate sustaining innovation with continuous change and disruptive innovation with punctuated equilibrium, it is not so simple. In fact, Brown and Eisenhardt (1997) as well as Meyer (1997) cite examples of firms that have successfully reinvented themselves through continuous change as opposed to abrupt, punctuated change. In fact, these authors suggest that "in firms undergoing continuous change, innovation is intimately related to broader organization change."

Innovation frequently involves experimentation (Govindarajan and Trimble 2004). Experimentation invokes the notion of testing or trying something new. Learning is paramount; whether the experiment succeeds or fails is secondary to what is learned during the conduct of the experiment. Experiments also conjure up a sense of the unknown, trying something that no one has actually tried before. The juxtaposition of the word *strategic* with *experiment* introduces direction, purpose, importance, and future criticality for the organization. Strategic experiments are not happenstance. Although distinctions are sometimes fuzzy, many authors differentiate strategic experiments from process and product innovations that tend to be narrower and more focused on existing offerings. Nicholls-Nixon et al. (2000) define *strategic experimentation* as:

> a series of trial-and-error changes pursued along various dimensions of strategy, over a relatively short period of time, in an effort to identify and establish a viable basis for competing.

Govindarajan and Trimble (2004) further highlight the inherent risky nature of strategic experiments, which they characterize as:

> a multiyear bet within a poorly defined industry that has no clear formula for making a profit. Potential customers are mere possibilities. Value propositions are guesses. And activities that lead to profitable outcomes are unclear.

As such, strategic experiments represent a rather unique management challenge. According to Govindarajan and Trimble (2005), strategic experiments constitute the "highest-risk, highest-return category of innovation and require a unique managerial approach." Where the goal is learning, results are vastly different from those normally monitored and measured within organizations. Even expectations take on altered meaning—sometimes heretical—where failure is tolerated and perhaps even expected. There is also a strong element of trying to manage the unmanageable. Strategic experiments benefit from none of the controls easily imposed in a laboratory setting; for instance, control groups may not be available, results may be ambiguous, it may not be possible to shield experiments from outside influences, experiments may not be repeatable and/or verifiable. Furthermore, attempts to manage these experiments may destroy them. Management is a delicate balance where:

> successful multiple-product innovation blends limited structure around responsibilities and priorities with extensive communication and design freedom to create improvisation within current projects. This combination is neither so structured that change cannot occur nor so unstructured that chaos ensues. (Brown and Eisenhardt 1997)

Of interest for our purposes is the fact that IT often plays a key role in innovation and change. In fact, many recent innovative products (e.g., Blackberries, iPods) and services (e.g., eBay, VoIP) are clearly enabled by information technology. One pundit suggests that innovation and transformation are becoming the new *I* and *T* in IT (Slofstra 2006). The term *strategic IT experimentation* focuses on the subset of strategic experiments that are based on information technology similar to the above examples. Interestingly, very little attention has been paid to strategic IT experimentation. Henderson et al. (2003) introduce the concept of "platforms" (e.g., technology platforms, capability platforms, and business platforms) as enabling conditions offered by IT to support innovation. Sambamurthy et al. (2003) suggest a role for IT as a "digital options generator." Both of these studies look at IT from the standpoint of its role as a facilitator and/or enabler of innovation and agility. In this chapter we examine the management issues and challenges involved with actually conducting strategic IT experimentation. To do so, we first describe the innovation life cycle as the context for strategic IT experimentation.

STRATEGIC EXPERIMENTATION WITHIN THE INNOVATION PROCESS

Organizations typically do not assign responsibility for strategic experiments to individual departments. In fact, few organizations even use the term *strategic experiment*. Instead, organizations commit resources (space, funds, and people), build infrastructure, articulate procedures, and provide incentives, all in an effort to instill a culture of innovation. We refer to this collection of activities as the *innovation process*. Strategic IT experiments exist within such a process and must be understood in this context. Two examples of how companies incorporate strategic experimentation into their innovation processes are as follows:

- Oilco challenged its lines of business to use IT as a source of innovation. Because the rate of change is so much faster with IT as compared to other forms of technology, Oilco realized that its traditional approaches for assessing and adopting new technology wouldn't work. As a result, the company created an abbreviated innovation process. New ideas/opportunities (arising from employees, suppliers, universities, partners, and/or venture capitalists) must now pass three filters: (1) relevance, (2) technical readiness, and (3) economical viability. Once passed, a line of business must then be willing to sponsor an experimental pilot. If this is successful, the idea/opportunity becomes part of an "upscale pilot," which greatly expands its range and reach. Success here leads to adoption by a line of business. The whole process, from idea to adoption, happens within a year.

In this process strategic IT experimentation begins with business sponsorship of the experimental pilot and continues into the upscale pilot (as various features of the innovation are tried). Often experiments involve Oilco's partners. In essence, Oilco "provides the business milieu within which its technology partners can hold large-scale, real-life experiments" (Smith 2006).

- Telco has a somewhat different innovation process centered on the fact that all its products and services involve technology. It consists of four stages:

  1. *Idea.*   Ideas are generated through informal processes (e.g., brainstorming sessions or competition activity) as well as formal processes (e.g., market research or industry trend analysis), and the sources of ideas are varied (e.g., vendors, peers, product and marketing, customers, laboratories). Ideas must meet certain requirements to pass to the next stage, including specific and targeted objectives that address "pain points" or core business offerings, technical measurement, and identification of business sponsors and champions. On an annual basis, about forty to fifty ideas are approved for the next stage.

  2. *Proof of concept.*   At this stage, teams are assigned to specific ideas in order to conduct the proof of concept. Testing is done within a formal or informal laboratory setting using typical controlled experimentation. The process is very agile and adaptive, and the original idea can morph substantially. The team is highly focused and intentionally kept small. The entire proof-of-concept stage occurs over one to four weeks. Of the forty to fifty original ideas, only five to ten make it successfully through this stage. Requirements for passage to the next stage include addressing issues of intellectual property protection as well as providing a service description for the new idea.

  3. *Trial or pilot stage.*   This stage is described by the firm as "contained production exposure" as the idea is exposed to the market in a limited and measured way. A market segment is defined, and certain customers (who may be employees) are offered the chance to experiment with the product or service. Measurements are taken to reveal the marketing/branding issues, the financial "price points," and the operational impacts. The trial/pilot occurs within a window of four to twelve weeks, but occasionally it is extended. In addition to favorable results (i.e., marketing, financial, and operational), requirements for the next stage include complete product designs and business and system requirements. Many ideas are killed at this stage.

  4. *Transition stage.*   This stage is the "go to market" stage, and the idea now enters the full system development life cycle to ensure that the product or service is "industrial strength." Many shortcuts (i.e., "duct tape" solutions), which served well enough for the pilot, must now be engineered to meet production standards. It is interesting to note that IT has some unique opportunities and

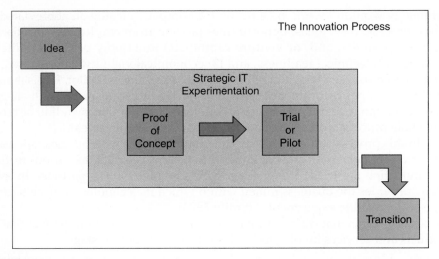

FIGURE 12.1   Strategic Experimentation Is Part of the Innovation Process

dangers when transitioning from an experiment to a full-fledged offering. One Telco manager suggested that "you can sometimes go too fast from concept to the one you actually drive."

In both these innovation processes, strategic experimentation begins *after* an idea has been vetted and deemed relevant and *before* it is transitioned into a full component of the business—whether product, service, new technology, or new process. Thus, strategic IT experimentation begins at the proof-of-concept stage (corresponding with Oilco's experimental pilot) and continues through the trial/pilot stage (corresponding with Oilco's upscale pilot). A feedback loop may be involved at the trial or pilot stage (see Figure 12.1).

STRATEGIES FOR SUCCESSFUL IT EXPERIMENTATION

Three conditions are necessary for strategic IT experimentation to be successful: (1) motivation, (2) support, and (3) direction. As one manager stated, "Without motivation, little will happen; without support, little can happen; and without direction, anything can happen." The focus group's recommendations to others seeking to improve strategic IT experimentation include the following:

1. *Motivate: Establish rewards for strategic IT experimentation.* Although many individuals are naturally drawn to experimentation, the demands of everyday work often drive this interest and inclination into remission. Furthermore, experimentation is risky, and not all people are willing to risk their reputations. As a result, experimentation and innovation do not flourish without intervention. According to focus group members, the way to create an innovation-enabled organization is twofold: provide incentives and rewards to support experimentation and risk taking, and make it everyone's job. Good ideas are good ideas, and experience

shows that they are as apt to originate at the customer interface as they are within the laboratory or the executive ranks.

Taking this a step further, one company has made innovation a component of everyone's annual performance measurement. In addition, it also offers five specific types of formal rewards for innovation ranging from patentable ideas to emerging business opportunities. Not all rewards need be formal. One firm uses a system of frequent informal rewards (e.g., books, tickets, cards, recognition days, and executive citations) to recognize innovative IT ideas and encourage and reward strategic experimentation with IT. Another company discovered that the best reward for IT personnel is simply the opportunity to work and play with new technology! In this company enterprising IT personnel win the right to experiment with new technology without the need for champions or sponsors. According to the manager involved, this activity is funded by "skunkworks" and "beg and grovel."

2. *Support: Create infrastructure to support experimentation.*   Offering rewards for experimentation sends employees the signal that experimentation and innovation are encouraged and will be recognized. This provides the motivation for individuals to experiment, but organizations need to provide support for such experimentation if they want it to happen. Over time, the combination of recognition and support builds a culture of innovation.

However, notwithstanding this, many firms believe it is also necessary to build some infrastructure around IT innovation and experimentation. One company, for instance, created the position of "chief scientist" and provided that office with a budget and resources. This was the organization's "way to signal to everyone that the lifeblood of the organization is discovery . . . not just innovation," said the manager involved. At this company, "innovation is a given" and expected in all parts of the business. "Discovery," however, conveys a sense of urgency as well as the notion that the company needs to continually reinvent itself to survive in the marketplace.

Many companies have formal centers (or laboratories) to support innovation and experimentation. Depending on the firm, the roles of these centers vary from "new product introduction" to "new technology introduction" to "business venturing" to "incubation centers." Where IT is considered a key business driver, they usually focus almost exclusively on strategic IT experimentation. The critical aspect of their creation is the provision of support and infrastructure to enable idea review and experimentation. Most centers are formally entrenched within the organization with ongoing funding, permanent staffing, and well-developed procedures and processes to encourage, guide, and support innovation. According to one manager, the key element is "to link sponsorship to innovation," reflecting the fact that "good ideas don't make it on their own."

Companies in the group reached consensus on the mandate for innovation centers, but they disagreed about their governance. Two distinct strategies surfaced:

- *Insulate.*   This strategy creates innovation centers as places where "all lines of business can come together to address common problems." According to proponents, the key benefit of this approach is the ability to foster synergies across the business in the belief that innovation is best "nurtured away from the mainstream business."

- *Incubate.*   Those following this strategy place their innovation centers within specific lines of business (LOBs). Proponents suggested that forcing innovation to be housed within a single LOB leads to IT experimentation focused on "real" problems and opportunities and committed local ownership.

The innovation infrastructure that was common to virtually all organizations in the group was the maintenance of an intranet for launching ideas. These sites are considered to be effective for soliciting, vetting, and sharing ideas and/or opportunities. According to one manager, an intranet's chief value is that "anyone can input and everyone gets access" to build on ideas. In firms with innovation centers, intranets are effective "feeder" systems. In organizations lacking the formal support of an innovation center, ideas identified on the intranet require a sponsor to marshal support to turn them into realizable products and/or services.

A common form of financial support is the establishment of internal venture funds. In about half of the participating organizations, funding mechanisms had been set up to support IT experimentation. Typically, such funds are made available on a competitive basis with an oversight committee in place to award resources and to monitor progress and completion.

3. *Direct: Manage innovation strategically.*   One manager pointed out that "experimentation never fails as long as there has been learning." Strictly speaking, the focus group agreed *but* felt that "any such learning would have to be strategically important for the organization" for it to be considered successful. According to the group, learning for the sake of learning was "an activity enjoyed by academics"— much to our chagrin! They suggested that providing motivation and support for individuals to experiment freely would be a recipe for disaster. Organizations must provide *direction* for these activities. Strategic IT experimentation does not occur by happenstance. Some participant suggestions for directing IT experimentation in order to ensure that it was strategically relevant include the following:

    a. *Link experimentation and innovation to customer value.*   A simple yet effective way to accomplish this is to focus on emerging pain points. At one company all new ideas had to articulate the specific customer pain point (CPP) that would be addressed. This requirement, in and of itself, produced results. As the manager involved related, "The identification and surfacing of CPPs stimulated considerable and sometimes heated discussion. Many people were surprised to learn of CPPs, and many potential solutions emerged. It was a case of 'if only I had known.'" Unfortunately, failure to articulate business value to the customer is a common phenomenon.

    b. *Link experimentation to core business processes.*   The opposite approach focuses IT experimentation internally on core business functions. One participant, whose organization is "currently reluctant to experiment in the market," focuses all its experiments on core business activities. "Our belief is that IT experimentation is strategic only if it produces significant efficiencies for internal operations in a way that can be captured on the bottom line," she said.

    c. *Use venture funds to guide strategic initiatives.*   Although establishing venture funding for IT experimentation is a form of support (see above), the governance of such funds can be instrumental in achieving strategic alignment. Venture funds are typically given for initiatives that do the following:

- Make greater use of innovation resources
- Focus on new business models
- Explore new/disruptive technologies
- Focus on penetrating new markets
- Leverage cross-organizational capabilities
- Streamline decision making
- Focus on opportunities that can be scaled.

FROM EXPERIMENTATION TO INNOVATION: LESSONS LEARNED

Focus group members shared examples of both successful and unsuccessful IT experiments. Of the three dramatic failures mentioned, all involved not the experiment itself but, rather, the transition from successful experiment to broader practice or to the marketplace. Since the goal of a successful experiment is to ultimately become an innovation from which the business derives value, navigating the transition from experiment to innovation is especially important. Although three is a small sample on which to draw conclusions, these failures had several elements that were common. From these experiences, the group reached consensus about how to approach this critical transition point:

- *Focus on achievable targets.*   Strategic IT experiments should be manageable and targeted but, at the same time, built so they can scale up easily. According to one manager, "It is far easier to ramp up a proven venture than to plan, build, and deliver a winner." At one company an experiment involved a "proof of concept" for a new technology involving six sites. Management then rapidly decided to expand the experiment to three hundred sites! This action literally ended experimentation, and the task immediately became one of a large-scale implementation.
- *Don't rush to market.*   Positive results from an experiment should be viewed as justification for further experimentation, not as a "license to launch." At one company, a decision to go to market based on very favorable results from a strategic IT experiment quickly ran into difficulty. The customers involved in the experiment turned out to be unrepresentative of the overall customer base, and the uptake in the market plummeted as the rollout broadened its base.
- *Be careful with "cool" technology.*   Because IT experimentation deals with technology, it is sometimes easy to be misled by cool technology. The buying public may not understand what the technology does (e.g., it's an Internet pen), may have no need for the things that the technology does (e.g., it tracks unvisited sites), and/or may not find the technology appealing (e.g., it's a mouse with arms and hands). On the other hand, this same technology may become the item that every teenager on the planet must have! Therefore, exercise caution.
- *Learn by design.*   The goal of an experiment is to learn. The group provided several examples of experiments where nothing was learned. In these cases insufficient controls were designed into the experiment to enable the organization to ascertain after the fact what had happened. Was failure due to product features or due to functioning? A lack of effective marketing? The price point? Thus, the first step in a strategic IT experiment should be to identify the critical questions that need to be answered, then to design these into the experiment.

Conclusion

Stressing top-line growth brings IT into the mainstream of product and service innovation, which, in turn, means that the IT function must become more customercentric, assimilate new skills, and work collaboratively with the business development arm of the organization. It also leads a company into the realm of strategic IT experimentation. This reflects the ubiquitous nature of information technology and represents a new and exciting role for IT. This chapter has outlined some of the issues and challenges IT managers are experiencing as they begin to move into the uncharted waters of innovation. At present, in most organizations, strategic experimentation is merely a collection of activities and procedures for testing out new ideas. As managers become more experienced in this area, however, it can be expected that many of the practices outlined above will become better understood and IT will be able to use strategic experimentation more effectively to successfully spin good ideas into innovation gold.

References

Brown, S. L., and K. M. Eisenhardt. "The Art of Continuous Change: Linking Complexity Theory and Time-Paced Evolution in Relentlessly Shifting Organizations." *Administrative Science Quarterly* 42, no. 1 (March 1997): 1–34.

Christensen, C. *The Innovator's Dilemma: When New Technologies Cause Great Firms to Fail.* Boston: Harvard Business School Press, 1997.

Christensen, C., and M. Raynor. *The Innovator's Solution: Creating and Sustaining Successful Growth.* Boston: Harvard Business School Press, 2003.

Denning, S. "Why the Best and Brightest Approaches Don't Solve the Innovation Dilemma." *Strategy & Leadership* 33, no. 1 (2005): 4–11.

Govindarajan, V., and C. Trimble. "Strategic Innovation and the Science of Learning." *Sloan Management Review* 45, no. 2 (2004): 66–75.

———. "Building Breakthrough Businesses within Established Organizations." *Harvard Business Review* May (2005): 59–68.

Hamel, G., and L. Välikangas. "The Quest for Resilience." *Harvard Business Review* September (2003).

Henderson, J. C., N. Kulatilaka, N. Venkatraman, and J. Freedman. "Riding the Wave of Emerging Technologies: Opportunities and Challenges for the CIO." Working paper, Boston University, School of Management, 2003.

Meyer, M. H. "Revitalize Your Product Lines Through Continuous Platform Renewal." *Research Technology Management* 40, no. 2 (March/April 1997): 17–28.

Nicholls-Nixon, C. L., A. C. Cooper, and C. Y. Woo. "Strategic Experimentation: Understanding Change and Performance in New Ventures." *Journal of Business Venturing* 15 (2000): 493–521.

Sambamurthy, V., A. Bharadwaj, and V. Grover. "Shaping Agility Through Digital Options: Reconceptualizing the Role of Information Technology in Contemporary Firms." *MIS Quarterly* 27, no. 2 (June 2003): 237–63.

Slofstra, M. "CEOs Who Get It." *Edge* 5, no. 2 (May/June 2006): 4.

Smith, H. A. Notes from a private presentation, Society for Information Management's Advanced Practices Council, Chicago 2006.

Smith, H. A., and J. D. McKeen. "IT in 2010: The New Frontier." *MIS Quarterly Executive* 5, no. 3 (September 2006): 125–36.

Enabling Collaboration with IT[1]

O ur increasing connectedness is driving new ways of working together to deliver business value. Globalizing organizations, outsourcing, mobile work, innovation, interorganizational teams, innovation, and reaching out to suppliers and customers are driving today's need to improve collaboration within firms. And, of course, IT is at the center of these trends. A study on what makes widely dispersed virtual teams effective found that, contrary to expectations, technology was a significant factor in facilitating their success (Majchrzak et al. 2004). However, literally hundreds of software packages are being promoted for improving collaboration. These technologies, such as virtual worlds, Web 2.0 applications, social networking, content management, and new ways of communicating (e.g., blogs, wikis, instant messages, tweets) appear almost daily and are being adopted and adapted rapidly in the wider society. They are challenging many of the traditional conventions of how work is done and the role of IT functions themselves.

As the menu of available technologies widens, becomes virtually free, and employees clamor to use them anywhere, anyplace, and anytime, IT managers are asking many questions including these:

- What is the business value of these technologies?
- What is the best way to assess them and make decisions about their use?
- How can these technologies best be managed and adapted for organizational purposes?

Furthermore, as new technologies appear, businesses are experimenting with different types of collaboration, such as those listed above, and IT functions are often expected to make collaboration happen through the implementation of technology, even though technologies are only one piece of any collaboration initiative. Certainly IT functions provide the "heavy lifting," such as connectivity and information integrity, without which most collaboration efforts would not be effective, and a well-designed IT architecture is a key enabler of collaboration (Johansen 2007). And, at the most basic level, IT also protects the privacy and security of information and users. But how new applications are implemented is often as important as the

[1]Smith, H. A., and J. D. McKeen. "Enabling Collaboration with IT." *Communications of the Association for Information Systems* 28, article 16 (March 2011): 243–254. Reproduced by permission of the Association for Information Systems.

technology itself in delivering business value. As one IT manager stated, "We some-times jump directly to the tool without thinking through the strategy and tactics involved." As a result, IT managers can sometimes feel that the deployment of collabo-ration is less than optimal.

This chapter explores IT's role in enabling collaboration in organizations, and at the same time what IT's role should not be (i.e., what responsibilities and account-abilities should properly be the function of the business). It accomplishes this by identi-fying the principal forms of collaboration used and the primary business drivers involved in them, how business value is measured, and the roles of IT and the business in enabling collaboration. The chapter first looks at some of the reasons why collabora-tion is becoming so important in organizations and the business value it enables. Next it examines some of the different characteristics of collaboration in various organizations. Focus then switches to the key components of a collaboration program, how these influ-ence its effectiveness, and IT's role in promoting collaboration. The chapter concludes with a series of recommendations for IT managers to use as a guide for how they can best facilitate collaboration in their organizations.

WHY COLLABORATE?

There is no doubt that information and communications technologies are enabling differ-ent ways of working—within organizations and between them. Who could imagine life without e-mail? Without Google? Without cell phones? These technologies and others have changed forever how we interact with others both personally and professionally, how we share information, and where work gets done. Thus, it should be no surprise that there's strong interest in collaboration among business practitioners and academics alike. A simple Internet search on this topic yields literally thousands of articles. And it is no secret that what we are seeing now is just the tip of the technology iceberg. Whether we do or do not yet actually use the next generation of collaboration/social networking tech-nologies in our work, everyone has heard about them, including instant messaging, Twitter, Facebook, webcams, and others, and no one is a stranger to speculation about how these technologies are going to change the face of organizations yet again.

Almost any business or IT journal these days contains speculative "think pieces" or case studies about how essential it will be to collaborate (in various ways) in the future and how failing to do this will result in the organization becoming a dinosaur (Amabile and Khaire 2008; Lynch 2007; Romano et al. 2007). And it is certainly without question that hundreds of new technologies—including hardware, software, applica-tions, and services—are currently being promoted to businesses as enabling collabora-tion and all of the benefits it will bring. Yet business and IT managers are struggling to cut through the hype to get at the real value collaboration will bring. They have seen this before in both the "Internet bubble" and the knowledge management fad and know from bitter experience with previous generations of groupware, knowledge manage-ment, and collaboration investments that achieving positive results is not as easy as plugging in a piece of technology (Iandoli 2009a). Many have a long history of deploy-ing collaboration technology and seeing it gather dust (McAfee 2006).

It is therefore no surprise that the focus group reported a great deal of conflicting feelings in their organizations about collaboration, from wildly enthusiastic to highly skeptical. One company has invested substantial amounts of time and money in collaboration technologies and in adapting its organizational culture and behaviors accordingly and believes that they have become more productive, effective, and successful as a result. On the other hand, another manager reported his company's senior executives were grumbling that no one has yet given them a real business need for collaboration. Some members reported that there's a lack of business push for collaboration in their organization, and others stated that their business units were "coming around in some areas because they feel they need to be where their customers are." Most agreed that virtual interaction is becoming increasingly commonplace and that the percentage of time employees work virtually (and therefore need collaboration technology) is increasing (Drakos et al. 2009; Romano et al. 2007). One study found that spending on collaborative software represents one-fifth of most organizations' technology budgets, but business leaders are still uncertain if these investments are improving either collaboration or the quality of work (Cross et al. 2005). This sentiment was reflected by most of the focus group participants. "We're still experimenting with collaboration," explained one. "We don't have a business project, but we're developing a collaboration strategy."

Because collaboration is evolving so rapidly, it's difficult to definitively articulate the business drivers and benefits involved. However, there appear to be five main categories of potential business value:

1. *Top-line value.*   A great deal has been written about the importance of collaboration in improving and/or increasing creativity and innovation in organizations. One study found that collaboration technologies play a critical role in improving knowledge creating and sharing practices and in developing new processes, products, and services (Fink 2007). Another noted "great ideas can come from anywhere and IT has dramatically reduced the cost of accessing them" (Pisano and Verganti 2008). The expectation is that collaboration both across an organization and with customers, suppliers, and other third parties, will strengthen an organization's ability to identify new business opportunities and formulate creative solutions (Fink 2007). The goal is "real time, rich, location independent collaboration" by creative teams that can rapidly process and assimilate knowledge from many different sources and apply it in practical ways (Gordon et al. 2008). This type of value is especially important in highly dynamic and competitive industries where the generation of a large number of new, good ideas is critical to competitive advantage. Within the focus group, most organizations were just beginning to recognize how technology, collaboration, and innovation could be harnessed to change their business models, products, and services. "We're beginning to see our executives more open to these concepts and how changing how we work together and with our customers can make a difference," said one. One firm has included collaboration and innovation in its performance review criteria. Nevertheless, these appear to be the exceptions, and focus group managers mainly commented that their business leaders were not yet really thinking about how technology could help them in this area.

2. *Cost savings.*   In a number of focus group companies, collaboration is seen as having real cost savings potential in such ways as reducing travel costs through virtual meetings, improving communications, and enabling remote access to documents. Participants noted that collaborative technology facilitates the work of global and virtual teams by compressing work flow, reducing development costs, increasing communication, minimizing misunderstandings, improving coordination between groups, and enabling linkages with vendors, suppliers, and customers that speed up the supply chain and other work processes.

3. *Effectiveness.* There is wide recognition that collaboration technology, used properly, can make group work more effective. This is particularly true for virtual teams. For example, one focus group company uses social networking technologies (behind its firewall) to enable team members from around the world to learn about each other, have fun events, and understand each others' customs and culture. "This has been really useful for us in building strong global teams," said the manager involved. Collaboration technology, particularly unified communications, is especially useful in integrating remote and mobile workers seamlessly into team or project activities. It enables them to "touch down" in an office and plug into the applications and information they need, wherever they are in the world. Increasingly, too, for many professionals, whose work consists of participation in a number of ad hoc projects, collaboration technology enables them to more effectively juggle a variety of commitments. One firm uses it extensively for its multidisciplinary projects, such as pandemic planning. Finally, online education is a big application of this technology, allowing employees to participate from a variety of locations, have virtual and real-time discussions, and incorporate learning into the demands of their workday.

4. *Accessibility of people.* A key feature of collaboration and its associated technology is that it provides a company with access to a much broader range of skills, capabilities, resources and services than have been traditionally available. Collaboration technology significantly expands the number of potential partners and expertise available to a company (Pisano and Verganti 2008), and in recent years different types of interorganizational alliances—from supply chain integration to design coordination to innovative partnerships—have become commonplace (Attaran 2007). However, it is the ability to access internal expertise that is currently of most interest to the focus group companies. Only one firm had successfully implemented a comprehensive enterprise directory, including phone book, expertise location anywhere in the organization, reporting structures, and connection with social networking information. Yet even this firm recognized how difficult building such a capability can be. "Over the years, it has been a huge stumbling block for us," one focus group member said. Other members were envious. "We're trying to build this facility," said one, "because right now it's really hard for us to find people in our organization." Ideally, this type of accessibility also enables the development of communities of interest within the organization—either work focused or built around personal interests. In our virtual, networked world that is rapidly losing the "human touch" and is characterized by "ephemeral relationships," these communities can help build staff morale and create a sense of belonging (Tebbutt 2009; Thomas and Bostrom 2008).

5. *Accessibility of information.* One of the biggest benefits of collaboration and its associated technology is that it makes information much more accessible than in the past. Information repositories, such as the intranet, enable the management and sharing of digital content on an as needed basis (Chin et al. 2008). Other technologies, such as wikis, support the creation of new content and its publication. These tools enable information and knowledge sharing across time and space in ways that were unheard of a mere decade ago (Fink 2007). Many focus group members believe that portal and content management applications will be the biggest value of collaboration. But they also feel it will take a lot of work to get

there. "Our intranet is just a garbage scow of information," sighed one manager. "The same document can exist in literally hundreds of places." Another noted, "While our corporate level content is well managed, it gets messier and messier the lower down in the organization you go. We need much more information management and filtering to make our Intranet really useful." Finally, although everyone agrees that collaboration will only be successful if more information is made more widely available, there is still a great deal of fear that "someone will do something bad with it," which explains why in many organizations the default position is not to share.

6. *Flexibility.*   The world is becoming increasingly volatile, uncertain, complex, and ambiguous and this is creating a highly dynamic business environment for many companies (Johansen 2007). Flatter, more networked, and collaborative structures create the right work and leadership environment, facilitating fluid workforces and speedy decision making and providing transparency of information and capabilities while retaining clarity around the organization's beliefs, values, and responsibilities (Reeves et al. 2008). A networked organization, with situational leadership, less structure, and the ability to create new capabilities through its networks, will be much more able to cope with these challenges. Flexibility will involve space, technology, and protocols for working in networks and will exist at the intersection of real estate, HR, and IT (Johansen 2007). Flexibility underlies many of the reasons why focus group members are interested in collaboration. Although most are still seeing this as a need within a more traditional, hierarchical organizational structure, some recognize that their structure and governance practices will have to change substantially.

CHARACTERISTICS OF COLLABORATION

Although there is much talk about the benefits of collaboration and the need for more of it in organizations, clarity is significantly lacking about what collaboration actually is. As one focus group member put it, "If you asked a hundred people to describe collaboration, you would get a hundred different answers. There's a huge disparity in understanding about this topic." There is also significant confusion about collaboration, which is a human activity, and collaboration technology, which is the hardware, software, and applications that enable the work of collaboration (Camarinha-Matos et al. 2009). Finally, the group noted that collaboration is often used interchangeably with such terms as networking, social networking, and cooperation. It is therefore important to be clear about the range and scope of collaboration in organizations these days, including who is involved in collaboration, what type of work is being done, and where it is being done since these have a direct bearing on how the IT function can best support collaboration with technology (see Figure 13.1).

• *Who is collaborating?*   At its simplest, *collaboration* describes work that is done jointly with others (Wikipedia 2011). In modern organizations, this covers a lot of territory. Sometimes, collaboration can be as basic as two people working together to achieve a goal, but it also refers to a wide spectrum of different types of collaborative participants. In organizations, there can be collaboration within teams (both formal and ad hoc), between business units, and within communities of interest.

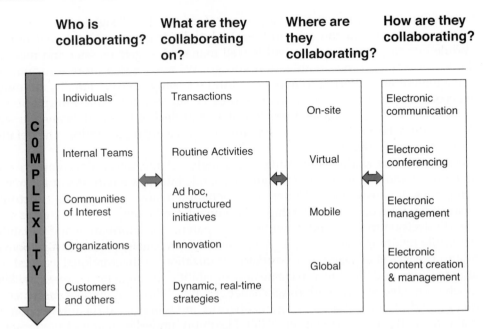

Who is collaborating?	What are they collaborating on?	Where are they collaborating?	How are they collaborating?
Individuals	Transactions	On-site	Electronic communication
Internal Teams	Routine Activities	Virtual	Electronic conferencing
Communities of Interest	Ad hoc, unstructured initiatives	Mobile	Electronic management
Organizations	Innovation	Global	Electronic content creation & management
Customers and others	Dynamic, real-time strategies		

FIGURE 13.1   The Range and Scope of Collaboration

Collaboration can also occur beyond a firm's boundaries, including between an organization and its customers, between one or more organizations (as in a supply chain or an innovative partnership), and, as we are beginning to see, with the world at large (also known as "mass collaboration"). As organizations have become more comfortable with collaborative work, they are extending it in new ways and to more and more types of participants. Most focus group organizations still focus on internal collaboration, yet there was general agreement that the trend is toward opening up collaboration beyond organizational boundaries. At present, most organizations are fairly "locked down" but have practices in place to enable key suppliers and trusted third parties to access internal company data and to work collaboratively with internal participants.

• *What are they collaborating on?*   Collaboration can take many forms. The early wins in organizations, according to the focus group, were simple transactions. These included e-mails, conferencing, extranets with partners, and basic workflow. Next came collaboration around routine activities, such as access to information and its reuse, ease of information creation and publishing; coordination of experts to solve common problems and to reduce the work involved in mundane tasks, such as coordination and planning (Cross et al. 2005; Edmonston 2008; Fedorwicz et al. 2008). Most organizations in the focus group have substantial initiatives in this area, although they believe there's more work to be done, especially in such matters as improving content management and creating enterprise directories. A third type of collaboration is more unstructured in nature and includes the development of communities for various purposes, creating collaborative work environments where innovation can occur, and collaboration for issue and infor-

mation management. Most focus group members had only just begun to understand how best to leverage this type of collaboration, and their efforts in this area
are still mainly experimental. However, one firm has created a new technology
adoption environment, where any technology innovation can be shared and where
others can use and provide feedback about its utility and effectiveness. The most
challenging form of collaboration is probably best epitomized at present by the
online gaming community. Here, various participants work together in real time to
achieve structured goals under rapidly changing conditions. Dynamic collaboration is characterized by speed of decision making with incomplete information,
the ability to modify decisions in response to changing conditions, trial and error,
the continual need to address and deal with risk, hyper-transparency of information, and situational leadership (Reeves et al. 2008). None of the organizations in
the focus group had achieved this type of collaboration, but all recognized that this
is increasingly the way members of the younger generation expect to work and
also felt that, as business challenges become more complex, organizations will
have to find better ways of collaborating in this way.

- *Where are they collaborating?*   Increasingly, collaboration needs to take place on
an anywhere, anytime basis. Inside organizations, members noted the need for
more meeting spaces and meeting rooms as well as "touch down" areas where contractors and outside staff can temporarily set up office. Almost all focus group
organizations already support virtual and mobile work, at least to some extent.
Several members of the focus group also routinely utilize international or global
teams where collaboration takes place across time zones, national boundaries, cultures, and language groups. Some were also beginning to experiment with different
forms of collaboration with individuals and enterprises beyond their organizational boundaries, which requires dealing with different organizational cultures,
practices, processes, systems, and data.

- *How are they collaborating?*   Collaborative technology comprises the tools that
are used to facilitate the work of collaboration. These fall into four main categories:
electronic communication (such as e-mail, instant messaging, blogs), electronic conferencing (e.g., video conferencing, meeting software), electronic management (e.g.,
file sharing, activity assignment, task management), and electronic content creation
and management (e.g., publishing tools, enterprise directories). However, newer
collaborative technologies, such as social networking applications, tend to fall into
multiple categories depending on how they are used (e.g., for communication or
information creation). As a result, the boundaries between the categories are blurring with the rapid evolution of this technology.

COMPONENTS OF SUCCESSFUL COLLABORATION

Understanding what collaboration and its potential benefits are is important to achieving an awareness of how collaboration can be effectively used in an organization, but
the high failure of collaboration projects suggests that successful collaboration requires
mastering how to implement and manage it (Schuh et al. 2008). The key challenges for
managers (both business and IT) are to create a supportive working environment and
motivational conditions and to develop the skills and organizational arrangements
within which collaboration can flourish (Fedorwicz et al. 2008; Thomas et al. 2007).

Four components of collaboration must work together to ensure successful collaboration of any type (MacCormack and Forbath 2008):

1. *People.*   Collaborative work requires different skills than more traditional forms of work. In particular, strong communication skills are essential. This is especially true the more work is mediated through technology, virtual, and across organizational and cultural boundaries (Romano et al. 2007). Cultural differences around social expectations, the need for more openness, flexibility, and interdependence in work assignments; the need to develop trust in an "opaque" environment (i.e., one that lacks many traditional social cues); and differences in organizational practices all add up to a requirement for managers to rethink how people will work together in this new world of work (Evans and Wolf 2005; Fiore et al. 2008). Inexperienced teams, lack of management attention, and different expectations of partners are some of the major reasons why collaboration initiatives can fail (Schuh et al. 2008). Thus when implementing collaboration, managers should be aware that it is not "business as usual" and should pay more attention to the social and behavioral changes that will be necessary (Edmonston 2008; Thomas and Bostrom 2008). One focus group manager noted, "You cannot overemphasize the importance of culture. It will make or break you." Finally, as the complexity of the tasks involving coordination increases, so does the need for management attention to coordination (Schuh et al. 2008). In short, creating the working environment within which collaboration occurs becomes the primary role of the manager, rather than monitoring individual productivity or performance. Signs that these efforts have been successful are engaged, satisfied, and committed staff who fully participate in collaborative processes (Nohria et al. 2008). Conversely, managers who cultivate a fear of failure or who do not protect their staff from what is often a larger, hostile corporate environment, are likely to see collaborative initiatives fail (Amabile and Khaire 2008).

2. *Program.*   Collaboration needs to be part of a coherent program to create and capture value, not a series of stand-alone efforts (Schuh et al. 2008). It is highly unlikely that collaboration initiatives will achieve an organization's goals unless they are managed holistically (MacCormack and Forbath 2008). Furthermore, it is essential that managers understand the strategic trade-offs involved in collaboration and make conscious decisions about how to structure and govern it. This is especially true when external partners are involved (Pisano and Verganti 2008). Most important, organizations need to understand comprehensively how to use their knowledge and information assets. Focus group members stressed that well-organized, searchable information is the foundation for any type of collaboration, and this resource requires a significant investment to develop and maintain. As a result, many companies are working primarily on content management strategies. In addition, high-level decisions need to be made about how to develop new collaboration capabilities, determine what types of collaboration the organization seeks to engage in, what policies are needed, and how to create an environment where the desired collaboration can thrive. Two key principles of any collaboration program are emergence (i.e., the recognition that we don't always know who will make the greatest contribution to a problem in advance) and planned serendipity (i.e., designing a working environment where underexplored relationships between people, data, and applications can become visible) (Majchrzak 2009).

3. *Processes.*   Within a strategic and holistic approach to collaboration, it is important to develop processes that support or help manage this type of work. Since collaboration is a moving target in the modern enterprise, managers need ways to rapidly learn what is working and what isn't and to make changes as the work unfolds (Edmonston 2008). Managers also need a process to take advantage of successful innovations and a way of recognizing failures and killing them off quickly (Amabile and Khaire 2008). Effective processes are also required to support collaborative teams and partnerships, to help them know what they know and coordinate their thinking (Johansen 2007). Specific processes that the focus group identified as being supportive of collaboration include administrative practices that recognize the convergence of many different types of communication (the management of which is often separated), content management processes, the ability to identify a "single source of truth" (i.e., the official documents pertaining to any topic), and the creation of parameters to help staff understand how and under what conditions they can collaborate. Conversely, a siloed focus and an emphasis on process efficiency above all else will likely stifle collaboration (Kleinbaum and Tushman 2008).

4. *Platforms.*   These are the tools, technologies, and standards that enable people to share data and to work together seamlessly from a variety of locations. The advent of cheap connectivity has been the driving force behind many new ways of collaborating in recent years (Smith and McKeen 2008), yet efforts to promote collaboration have focused largely on connectivity with little recognition of the other factors that make it effective (Cross et al. 2005). Technology is a key resource in enabling collaboration, but it must be designed to achieve the organization's goals and fit with its culture and practices. As with the other components of collaboration, the objective of a platform is to create an environment within which collaboration can take place, rather than the traditional systems approach of hardwiring specific information and work processes (Iandoli 2009b). An effective technology platform should support plug-and-play communications, provide access to information, and enable the transformation of information into knowledge. It should also provide tools for the rapid creation of communities, teams, and networks, be based on open standards, and be flexible and adaptive (Camarinha-Matos et al. 2009; Iandoli 2009b). However, most focus group organizations are nowhere near creating such a platform. Most are still questioning whether they should invest in collaborative technologies rather than look for ways to coherently manage a set of business tools for collaborative work (Drakos et al. 2009).

THE ROLE OF IT IN COLLABORATION

Clearly, the IT function alone cannot make collaboration happen, even if it provides robust collaboration technology. The business plays a critical role in determining its strategy and creating processes and a working environment that make it possible to collaborate for business value. That said, there is still no answer to where an organization's collaboration strategy "belongs." In most, IT still owns it and, as a result, the whole field of collaboration is an opportunity for IT managers to demonstrate real business leadership (Lynch 2007; Mann 2008). CIOs can work with business executives to identify and orchestrate collaborative capabilities, coordinate enterprise services, and educate leaders about opportunities and possibilities.

In addition, IT leaders have some very specific technology responsibilities that must be put in place to enable collaborative work to occur. At present, four major technology areas must be addressed iteratively and concurrently. These are merely the fundamentals, however. Since this field is evolving rapidly, IT leaders must be prepared to continually reassess all aspects of collaboration technology, its governance, and policies and to rebalance these as necessary (Smith et al. 2007).

1. *Communication.*   A significant and growing area of collaborative technology is enabling a wide spectrum of communications options, from voice mail to video and everything in between. "Users increasingly see communications and collaboration not as separate activities but as a smooth continuum of modalities where the difference between talking on the phone and posting on a wiki becomes a matter of choice and preference" (Mann and Elliot 2007). As such unified communications become a technological reality, IT leaders will need to develop an architecture that supports them as a single technology spectrum rather than as separate components. Gartner Group predicts that phone directories, e-mail, voicemail, instant messaging, presence awareness, computer telephony, and conferencing technologies will increasingly converge over the next five years, leading to serious organizational challenges in how these services are managed (Mann and Elliot 2007). However, other types of communication and collaboration software, such as voice, call centers, mobile, team workspaces, and social software will not be part of this convergence and will have to be appropriately managed as they too evolve. Ultimately, communications technology will be embedded in all business applications and will need to be ubiquitous, reliable, secure, and integrated (Andriole 2006).

2. *Information Access and Management.*   Developing an improved information processing capability, including accurate and visible information, manipulability, exchangeability, and ease of information transfer is a primary goal for all IT functions in supporting collaboration. One focus group member explained his mandate as follows: "We want to make it easy for anyone to share information via the intranet, to support collaboration with information, and to link people to documents and vice versa." To accomplish this goal, it is important for organizations to reduce the number of databases and data management platforms they maintain and to develop the intranet into a robust information sharing platform. Typically, organizations also need a document management system with proper versioning and access controls, although these systems are notoriously difficult to integrate with other information management tools. We're finding it really hard to upload and share documents," said one manager. "It's a big headache for us." Content management, particularly at the business unit and team levels is also challenging as the use of many separate tools tends to replicate information in a relatively unmanaged fashion. At present in most companies, attention needs to be paid to integrating fragmented information resources, improving information visibility, filtering and navigation, and establishing principles for information access (Cain 2008; Thomas et al. 2007).

   Several focus group companies commented that perception is still widespread in their organizations that if information is made more widely available "bad things will happen." "We instinctively don't want to share," said one manager. Managing the tension between the need for information availability to facilitate collaboration and protecting the organization from the associated risks is an area where IT managers should be working proactively to ensure they deliver the optimal value (Gordon et al. 2008; Smith et al. 2007).

3. *Security and Risk.* It is a primary responsibility of the IT function to protect the integrity of its systems and data. This is becoming increasingly more challenging as both internal and external organizational boundaries break down and new forms of collaboration are introduced (Smith et al. 2007). IT managers recognize that removing the traditional layers of separation between departments and enterprises makes the organization more vulnerable and their job more difficult. Therefore, IT departments can often be viewed as obstacles to collaboration (Gordon et al. 2008). There is no easy answer to this dilemma. Companies need safe and secure communications, but it is no longer possible to use "stovepipe" security to ensure this. Instead, IT functions must improve security architectures and infrastructures and continually assess the balance between the openness required by collaboration and the risks involved. Focus group members noted that security must become more granular and principles based. "We are beginning to develop a policy for how we as a company use social networking tools," said one manager. "The broader the team, the greater the risks involved." Another added, "We need better authentication tools, and we must be clearer about the types of information that can be shared." Others noted that security must be commensurate with the risks involved. "We must use the most appropriate tools for the particular task at hand." Finally, they pointed out that this task is about to get much more difficult as companies begin to open themselves up to collaboration with their end customers. "This is a huge challenge that we have not yet faced up to," said one.

4. *Technology Integration.* The more IT can achieve integration of data, applications, hardware, and software, the easier it will be to provide the information and tools needed to facilitate collaboration. Thus, focus group members recommended the massive simplification and rationalization of applications, databases, and software as a precursor to any significant collaboration initiative. The drive to collaboration is also behind the increasing interest in industry neutral and global IT standards of all types (Chituc et al. 2009). "Technology should be a facilitator of collaboration, not an obstacle," said one manager. "Our users want to plug and play in this area, and we can only achieve this through standardization." Some organizations in the focus group provide "canned" collaboration tools, such as blogs, personal Web sites, team sites, and wikis that allow the rapid formation of ad hoc teams and ease of social networking. These can then be tailored to particular needs requiring just enough information so they can be effectively managed and decommissioned in the longer term.

In addition, centralized and integrated structures within IT for developing enterprisewide communications and collaboration capabilities can facilitate synergistic interactions between these tools and create useful cross-technology opportunities that might not previously have been obvious (Sanders 2007). Focus group organizations varied widely in this area. Some assigned IT a leading role in delivering collaboration technology, and others are implementing it on a more piecemeal basis. All agreed, however, that without centralized support for this technology, it is unlikely to deliver enterprise-level value.

These four collaborative technology building blocks are the most critical elements to which IT should pay attention at present. However, new technologies are already on the horizon, and these will require continual assessment from IT managers as to their usefulness and how they can be integrated into the existing organizational infrastructure and collaboration architecture. Some of these technologies include dynamic modeling tools, simulation engines, visualization tools, data reduction and summarization applications, and intelligence gathering tools. In short, IT managers are going to have to remain aware in this very rapidly changing market and be willing to adapt quickly to changing conditions. Paying attention to these four fundamental building blocks now will enable them to do this more easily and effectively in the future.

FIRST STEPS FOR FACILITATING EFFECTIVE COLLABORATION

Given the multifaceted nature of collaboration and its many potential but as yet unproven benefits, IT managers could understandably adopt a wait-and see approach. In fact, this is what many members of the focus group are doing: talking about strategy and planning small pilots to test the waters. However, amid all the confusion, they also had some practical ideas for ways that organizations could begin to approach this complex and dynamic new way of working and using technology.

1. *Develop a coherent vision.*   Effective collaboration requires a multidisciplinary approach and a shared business–IT vision (Lynch 2007). It is essential that such a vision begin with understanding the organization's values, legal requirements, and core intellectual property. From this, a strategic perspective can be developed about what the business wants to accomplish with collaboration and what types of technology would best support it. Focus group members suggested that developing a vision for collaboration must be carefully approached because "the judgment line is shifting rapidly" and our static paradigms of work are rapidly becoming much more dynamic. These factors will change business models and strategies and affect how companies will need to manage the complex business environment of the near future. Ideally, a vision for collaboration should include a unified strategy and business models, tools, and experiments to help the organization gain further insights. The vision's ultimate goal should be to nurture an internal working environment (and in the longer term a broader business ecosystem) that will enable productive collaboration to emerge. At this early stage, both business and IT leaders should play a key role in articulating a collaboration vision and in connecting it to the right people who can make it happen.

2. *Plan for adaptation.*   If there's one aspect of collaboration about which everyone agrees, it's that collaboration is evolving and complex and will require significant and ongoing management attention (Schuh et al. 2008). Organizations, and particularly IT functions, therefore need to develop the "flexing skills" needed to cope with the rapid development of collaboration and its associated technologies (Iandoli 2009b). Focus group members noted that their organizations are already becoming flatter and more complex as collaboration and networks emerge. "Business is speeding up, and we will need new skills for coping and adapting rapidly," said one. It is therefore essential that organizations develop processes for learning what is working with collaboration and what isn't and mechanisms for sharing these lessons. Above all, the management of collaboration needs to be multidisciplinary and responsive to change.

3. *Start with specific fundamentals.*   Facilitating effective collaboration will take time—both to build a strategy and to get the technology fundamentals in place. Many organizations have specific "pain points" that could be worthwhile places to

start putting energy into collaboration. In the focus group, these were clearly around information management and access. "Our Intranet is unmanaged and not relevant," complained one manager. Another noted that it was very hard finding people in his organization. "We'd love to have a 'blue pages' to enable us to start internal social networking," he said, referring to one firm's internal company directory. In addition, several participants noted that their office space doesn't support collaboration. "We need to have many more collaborative workspaces," she noted. A simple assessment of these gaps and some management attention to them could lead to a great improvement in how people are able to collaborate.

4. *Establish principles of behavior.*   As noted above, much of the governance of collaboration is based on principles, rather than rules. The most basic principle is transparency, not only of information but also of behavior (Majchrzak 2009). Some focus group companies have already established a code of conduct to govern electronic communication and collaboration, and others are working on one. A big fear is that providing improved communication will enable employees and customers to post negative comments about the organization. One important way of allaying these fears is to eliminate online anonymity. "Anonymity results in bad behavior," said one manager. "With a clear online identity, negativity is quickly found out and is usually self-policed by others in the community." Another noted, "In a business environment where all posts are traceable, abuse is unlikely." As social networking takes hold in our culture, and organizations explore ways they can use it to connect with their customers, they are realizing that establishing rules of etiquette for how to do this is important. "We have a hard and fast rule that if you are using social networking to do business, you must state your company affiliation," said a manager.

    Cultural and behavioral practices are changing as a result of collaboration, and agreement is widespread that these will require serious management attention. For example, as staff become empowered to innovate and make real-time decisions, organizations will need to foster increased psychological safety so people don't fear being penalized if they make a mistake (Edmonston 2008). Similarly, work will need to be done to align work management and human resources practices, as well as incentives, if collaboration is to really make a difference (Cross et al. 2005). Finally, as connectivity becomes more pervasive and global, companies will have to develop policies and practices that enable staff to achieve an effective work–life balance. For example, one global firm has developed a small scheduling application to determine the least invasive time to have a meeting across different time zones. Tools can also be used to assist staff with controlling their accessibility and protecting their privacy (Mann 2008).

5. *Gradually move beyond the firewall.*   None of the focus group companies was comfortable as yet extending collaboration beyond their firewalls, unless in very tightly controlled circumstances (e.g., with vendors or third-party service providers). Major concerns about risk, privacy, and corporate liability remain. These issues need to be discussed and managed so that the power of collaboration can be realized. For example, one firm's privacy officer is now involved in determining what information can and cannot be shared. Some initial external target groups will include retirees, clients, and business partners. "We are gradually working through our concerns because of the unbelievable power of these tools," one manager said.

Conclusion

Collaboration is a complex concept with uncertain benefits and requires major organizational change. The drive to adopt collaboration is being accelerated by the possibilities enabled by information technology, which support real-time, global communication and anytime, anywhere access to information. In addition, companies are feeling considerable pressure to adopt collaboration technology because of their increasingly widespread use among individuals, many of whom are becoming their employees. There is no question that collaboration will play a major role in how we work and live in the future. However, as we move into this new era, companies are taking their time to determine how best to take advantage of what collaborative technology has to offer. This chapter has identified the major ways companies might want to collaborate and the benefits that are anticipated from each. It has also explored some of the major characteristics and components of collaboration in order to clarify concepts and to distinguish between the work of collaboration, which is a human activity, and collaboration technology, which facilitates it. It has shown that effective collaboration will not result from simply implementing more collaboration software. Instead, it will require a proactive and holistic strategy that integrates business goals and technology potential. At present, all aspects of collaboration and collaboration technology are in their infancy, so it is understandable that many companies are proceeding cautiously into this new world. Nevertheless, the speed with which both technology and practice are moving suggests strongly that it is time for managers to put some collaborative fundamentals in place. Furthermore, IT managers have an opportunity to provide business leadership around collaboration if they can clearly articulate its business potential and benefits, rather than focusing on the technology itself.

References

Amabile, T., and M. Khaire. "Creativity and the Role of the Leader." *Harvard Business Review* 86, no. 10 (October 2008).

Andriole, S. "The Collaborate/Integrate Business Technology Strategy." *Communications of the ACM 49*, no. 5 (May 2006).

Attaran, M. "Collaborative Computing: A New Management Strategy for Increasing Productivity and Building a Better Business." *Business Strategy Series* 8, no. 6 (2007): 387–93.

Cain, M. "Key Issues for Unified Communications and Collaboration, 2008." Gartner Inc., ID Number: G0015672, April 10, 2008.

Camarinha-Matos, L., H. Afsarmanesh, N. Galeano, and A. Molina. "Collaborative Networked Organizations—Concepts and Practice in Manufacturing Enterprises." *Computers and Industrial Engineering* 57, no. 1: 46–60 (2009).

Chin, K, D. Gootzit, and J. Mann. "Key Issues for Portals, Content Management and Collaboration Best Practices Projects." Gartner Inc., ID Number: G00155820, April 24, 2008.

Chituc, C., A. Azevedo, and C. Toscano. "A Framework Proposal for Seamless Interoperability in a Collaborative Networked Environment." *Computers in Industry* 60, no. 5 (June 2009): 317–38.

Cross, R., J. Liedtka, and L. Weiss. "A Practical Guide to Social Networks." *Harvard Business Review* 83, no. 3 (March 2005).

Drakos, N., C. Rozwell, M. Cain, and J. Mann. "Key Issues for Social Software and Collaboration Initiatives, 2009." Gartner Inc., ID Number: G00164866, January 30, 2009.

Edmonston, A. "The Competitive Imperative of Learning." *Harvard Business Review* 86, nos. 7/8 (July–August 2008).

Evans, P., and B. Wolf. "Collaboration Rules." *Harvard Business Review* 83, nos. 7/8 (July–August 2005).

Fedorowicz, J., I. Laso-Ballesteros, and A. Padill-Melendez. "Creativity, Innovation and e-Collaboration." *International Journal of e-Collaboration* 4, no. 4 (2008): 1–10.

Fink, L. "Coordination, Learning and Innovation: The Organizational Roles of e-Collaboration and Their Impacts." *International Journal of e-Collaboration* 3, no. 3 (2007).

Fiore, S., R. McDaniel, and F. Jentsch. "Narrative-Based Collaboration Systems for Distributed Teams: Nine Research Questions for Information Managers." *Information Systems Management* 26, no. 1 (Winter 2009): 28.

Gordon, S., M. Tarafdar, R. Cook, R. Maksimoski, and B. Rogowitz. "Improving the Front End of Innovation with Information Technology." *Research-Technology Management* 51, no. 3 (May/June 2008): 50–58.

Iandoli, L. "JITCAR Special Issue—IT Collaboration in Organizations." *Journal of Information Technology Case and Application Research* 11, no. 1, (2009a).

———. "Leveraging the Power of Collective Intelligence Through IT-Enabled Global Collaboration." *Journal of Global Information Technology Management* 12, no. 3 (2009b).

Johansen, B. *Get There Early: Sensing the Future to Compete in the Present.* San Francisco: Berrett-Koehler, 2007.

Lynch, C. "Five Things Wikipedia's Founder Has Learned About Online Collaboration." *CIO Magazine,* June 28, 2007. www.cio.com/article/121711/Five_Things_Wikipedia_s_Founder_Has_Learned_About_Online_Collaboration (accessed March 9, 2011).

Kleinbaum, A., and M. Tushman. "Managing Corporate Social Networks." *Harvard Business Review* 86, nos. 7/8 (July–August 2008).

MacCormack, A., and T. Forbath. "Learning the Fine Art of Global Collaboration." *Harvard Business Review* 86, no. 1 (January 2008).

Majchrzak, A. "Social Networking and Collaboration." Presentation to the Society for Information Management's Advanced Practices Council, Atlanta, Georgia, January 21–22, 2009.

Majchrzak, A., A. Malhotra, J. Stamps, and J. Lipnack. "Can Absence Make a Team Grow Stronger?" *Harvard Business Review* 82, no. 5 (May 2004): 131–37.

Mann, J. "Q&A: Answers to Practical Questions About Collaboration Tools." Gartner Inc., ID Number: G00154888, February 1, 2008.

Mann, J., and B. Elliot. "The New Market for Unified Communications and Collaboration." Gartner Inc., ID Number: G00153236, November 23, 2007.

McAfee, A. "Enterprise 2.0: The Dawn of Emergent Collaboration." *MIT Sloan Management Review* 47, no. 3 (Spring 2006): 20–28.

Nohria, N., B. Groysberg, and L. Lee. "Employee Motivation: A Powerful New Model." *Harvard Business Review* 86, nos. 7/8 (July–August 2008).

Pisano, G., and R. Verganti. "Which Kind of Collaboration Is Right for You? *Harvard Business Review* 86, no. 12 (December 2008).

Reeves, B., T. Malone, and T. O'Driscoll. "Leadership's Online Labs." *Harvard Business Review* 86, no. 5 (May 2008).

Romano, N., J. Pick, and N. Roxtocki. "Editorial Introduction to the Special Issue on Collaboration Issues in Cross-Organizational and Cross-Border IS/IT." *Journal of Information Technology Theory and Application* 8, no. 4 (2007).

Sanders, N. "An Empirical Study of the Impact of e-Business Technologies on Organizational Collaboration and Performance." *Information Systems and Operations Management* 25, no. 6 (2007): 1332–347.

Schuh, G., A. Sauer, and S. Doering. "Managing Complexity in Industrial Collaborations." *International Journal of Production Research* 46, no. 9 (May 2008): 2485–498.

Smith, G., K. Watson, W. Baker, and J. Pokorski. "A Critical Balance: Collaboration and Security in the IT-Enabled Supply Chain." *International Journal of Production Research* 45, no. 11 (June 2007).

Smith, H. A., and McKeen, J. D. "Social Computing: How Should It Be Managed?" *Communications of the Association for Information Systems* 23, Article 23 (August 2008).

Tebbutt, D. "The Business Value of Collaboration Software." *CIO Magazine,* February 17, 2009. www.cio.com/article/481329/The_Business_Value_of_Collaboration_Software (accessed March 9, 2011).

Thomas, D., and R. Bostrom. "Building Trust and Cooperation Through Technology Adaptation in Virtual Teams: Empirical Field Evidence." *Information Systems Management* 25, no. 1 (2008): 45–56.

Thomas, D., R. Bostrom, and M. Gouge. "Making Knowledge Work in Virtual Teams." *Communications of the ACM* 50, no. 11 (November 2007).

Wikipedia. "Collaboration." en.wikipedia.org/wiki/Collaboration (accessed March 9, 2011).

Chapter 14

Social Computing: How Should It Be Managed?[1]

For the past several decades, large organizations have been in the forefront of deploying new technologies, but in recent years some IT managers have noticed that they are no longer on the leading edge of technology usage. With the mutual maturation of the personal computer and the Internet, the "bleeding edge" has been taken over by individuals who are persistently finding new and different ways to use technology for their personal benefit.

At first, it was just a few "geeks" sharing files with each other, but when Napster burst into public consciousness in the late 1990s, the music industry and others were shocked by the rapidity with which a simple innovation was able to undermine an established commercial business model. Although the industry fought back and Napster is no more, it is clear that peer-to-peer computing (P2P) is a force to be reckoned with (Smith and Konsynski 2004). Today, for example, all branches of the entertainment industry are trying to figure out how to deal with this major threat, which few of them saw coming. And most observers believe that this is just the tip of a huge change that is going to hit many different industries (Hinchcliffe 2006).

The power of P2P file sharing to disrupt the traditional business-to-customer relationship is just one of several changes we are now beginning to see in organizations. IT managers are recognizing that the interpersonal computing applications enabled by P2P and the Internet facilitate new ways of working, learning, and collaborating that are foreign to more conventional practices and that these have considerable strategic potential if they can be effectively managed. Evolving from the relatively anonymous sharing of music files, today's P2P applications have become richer and more interactive to enable sharing of photos, videos, bookmarks, opinions, and profiles and to connect friends. Collectively known as social computing, the early buzz has led to prognostications that this technology will fundamentally rewrite the rules of how many industries work (Mayfield 2008). Yet currently, organizations in general do not appreciate the value and strategic potential of social computing, possibly because they are dominated by a kind of tunnel vision that is fixated on technology and information (Brown and Duguid 2000). As a result, organizations often overlook the other resources available to them, especially those on the social periphery. In fact, many see social computing as an enormous time waster (Lombardi 2008).

---

[1]Smith, H. A., and J. D. McKeen. "Social Computing: How Should It Be Managed?" *Communications of the Association for Information Systems* 23, article 23 (October 2008): 409–18. Reproduced by permission of the Association for Information Systems.

Is social computing simply a social phenomenon trying to justify its existence? Or will it become the basis of future employee interfaces, new types of relationships with customers and suppliers, new ways of working and learning, and new sources of value and knowledge? To address these questions, this chapter examines our current understanding of social computing in organizations and attempts to describe this somewhat fuzzy concept and to provide a brief introduction to the different types of computing that can be referred to by this label. Next, it looks at some of the factors that are driving the considerable hype that is building around it. The next section describes a view of the future organization in which social computing plays a key role and contrasts it with the reality of how organizations are currently using it. Then it presents the challenges facing IT managers who need to balance two opposing views of how organizations should work, and finally it looks at some ways that IT organizations can prepare for a nebulous future in which social computing is at least part of IT functionality.

WHAT IS SOCIAL COMPUTING?

Social computing is the relatively new and broad term being used to denote the hardware, software, and applications that support any sort of social behavior. It is designed to create or re-create "social conventions and social contexts" (Wikipedia 2008) and enable people to use computing devices to interact with one another or communicate through them (as opposed to with the computer) (Bray and Konsynski 2007; Roush 2005). This definition covers a lot of ground, however. Current estimates are that 48 million different social computing sites are available, connecting millions of people in a wide variety of ways (Knights 2006).

Clearly, the rapidly evolving nature of social computing prohibits a comprehensive classification of its types and functionality. Nevertheless, given the sheer scope of this phenomenon, it is essential to attempt to understand this phenomenon and how it is affecting both individuals and organizations. Given that any description of social computing is therefore bound to be incomplete and out of date as soon as it is written, it is hoped that this discussion will elucidate the concepts associated with this new dimension of computing and highlight some ways in which it could affect organizations over the next two to five years.

Broadly speaking social computing is the result of the interaction of four elements:

Some Web 2.0 Applications
• Wikis
• Blogs
• Virtual worlds
• 3D user interface/visualization
• Presence awareness
• Instant messaging
• Social networking communities
• Reputation systems
• Collective intelligence systems
• Authoring
• RSS feeds
• Podcasts
• Massive Multiplayer Online Role-Playing Games
• Mash-ups

1. *Cheap connectivity devices.* The ability to connect to the Internet through a variety of relatively inexpensive and mobile devices (e.g., cellphones, Blackberries, game consoles, iPods, and laptops) has made anywhere/anytime connectivity a reality (Roush 2005; Wikipedia 2008).

2. *P2P communication.* Direct connectivity between two or more users, without the

mediation of an organizational "middleman," has led to an explosion of file and information sharing (e.g., music, porn, videos, VoIP) and created a layer of disinter-mediated communication that previously existed only through the telephone or by letter (Smith and Konsynski 2004).

3. *Web 2.0 Applications.* Not a technology per se, Web 2.0 is a trend in Web design and application development that is specifically focused on how to exploit the connectivity and communication that are available today to facilitate social relationships and sharing among users (Wikipedia 2008). In contrast to Web 1.0 design, which emphasizes trans-actions and access to information, Web 2.0 design stresses interaction and mass partici-pation (Raskino 2007). Using the Web as the foundation and modular design techniques (representing a subset of SOA), Web 2.0 applications are outward-facing platforms that provide the basis for collaboration, sharing, and conversation (Smith 2006). Thus for example, a wiki enables multiple people to co-author a document in a very easy-to-use fashion, but by itself it does nothing. Similarly, social networking sites, such as MySpace or Facebook, facilitate interpersonal connections but do not create them. A key charac-teristic of these applications is that they enable emergent structures and try not to impose preconceived ideas about how they should be used (McAfee 2005).

4. *Computing Behavior.* If there's one thing that everyone agrees on, it's that to take advantage of these new technical capabilities, our computing behavior will have to change. "I expect to see a big thematic change in the way people use technology," states Erik Brynjolfsson, director of the MIT Center for Digital Business (Brynjolfsson and McAfee 2007). Forrester Research Group concurs:

> "Web 2.0 is about specific technologies . . . that are relatively easy to adopt and master. Social computing is about the new relationships and power structures that will result. . . . Web 2.0 is the building of the interstate highway system in the 1950s; social computing is about everything that resulted next." (quoted in Hinchcliffe 2006)

Focus group members have already noticed differences in the behavior of the "mil-lennials" (i.e., those born after 1982) now beginning to arrive in the workplace. As one manager observed, "Millennials blend work and their personal lives more seamlessly." "They find it frustrating to be slowed down by a corporate working environment. They want to work wherever and whenever they want."

The promise of social computing is that technology will fit more naturally into our lives because it will adapt more readily to our locations, preferences, and schedules (Roush 2005). The challenge for organizations is to understand how to use social com-puting effectively—separating hype from reality and using it to deliver business value through opening up their traditional boundaries to the network and to new ways of working and sharing.

WHAT'S DRIVING SOCIAL COMPUTING IN ORGANIZATIONS?

It's easy for jaded IT managers to dismiss social computing as "just another technology fad." Most companies are approaching social computing very cautiously "because they have been fooled in the past by promises of collaboration tools" (Fontana 2007). As Harvard Business School's Andrew McAfee notes, "[T]here is a long history of deploying collaboration and having it gather dust" (Fontana 2007). One focus group member cynically called it "the second coming of knowledge management (KM)." Although social computing certainly shares some common themes with KM—collaboration, information sharing, social networking—some significant drivers of this new trend differentiate it and need to be understood by organizations making decisions about what to do with it.

A number of factors contribute to the buzz around social computing. Some are changes that are happening now; others are only hints of changes to come:

- *Today's reality.*   As noted above, three of the pieces that comprise social computing—cheap devices, anywhere/anytime connectivity, and Web 2.0 applications—are already here and spreading rapidly. Because of its viral nature and network effects (i.e., the more people who are connected, the more effective the result), social computing is leaking daily into organizations in a variety of forms and is already causing huge headaches for IT managers (Fontana 2007). "Managing social computing applications is like playing 'whack a mole,'" said an IT manager in the focus group, referring to the carnival game. "They just keep popping up; you can't kill them. It's a tidal wave."

    These three components have already had and are continuing to make significant impacts in many industries. For example, trends toward globalization and outsourcing are driving new demands for collaboration in global, virtual teams, more complex sourcing connections, and a deeper appreciation for the value of doing business through a network of relationships (Friedman 2005).

    Similarly, a mobile, customer-facing workforce supported by all the technology of a virtual office is increasingly a reality. This is leading to a need to redefine what work is and where it is done, and it is forcing organizations to make information and applications available wherever they are needed. A natural result is an overlap or blurring of our work and personal worlds. Increasingly, work is done where it is needed. E-mail on the golf course, order entry from a car, or a business document prepared at the cottage are all features of life in the new invisible "information field" in which many people now spend their lives (Roush 2005).

    Finally, there is mounting evidence that changes in computing behavior are having an impact on business. What started with the music industry through file sharing has fundamentally changed the entertainment industry and the ripple effects of this are spreading as companies find ways to appropriate new forms of value through the network (e.g., Anderson 2006) and consumers find new ways to subvert traditional business models. Wikis and blogs are rewriting the rules of corporate communication (Mayfield 2008). For example, 88 percent of the top 100 brands now have a Wikipedia entry, Wal-Mart now has paid bloggers, and online gaming is a $55 billion industry (Mayfield 2008; H. A Smith and McKeen 2007a; Weill 2007). And horror stories of the use of social networking tools making the world aware of product inadequacies haunt many companies (Knights 2006).
- *Tomorrow's potential.*   What is still unclear is how new computing behaviors and the capabilities enabled by new technology will affect the nature of work and shape consumer behavior. The demand for social computing tools is already here, thanks to their ease of use, flexibility, low cost, and portability. "In many cases, these tools are better than our expensive and elaborate work platforms," said one manager.

Another noted, "We just implemented a simple texting mechanism to schedule our teenaged employees for work. It was junk technically, but it was very successful because it functioned the way they want to interact and not how we wanted them to communicate" (i.e., through corporate e-mail).

However, companies with a youthful workforce and those with a retail presence may already see the possibilities of social computing, but most are still watching developments from the sidelines (Raskino 2007). "We see limited scope for social computing applications so far," said a focus group manager. "The business cases for these applications are extremely hard to make," another pointed out. Despite a growing recognition that social computing represents some sort of "next step" in computing (Brynjolfsson and McAfee 2007), there is no real understanding of what this might mean for the majority of organizations.

There is documented interest in using social computing as a way to engage employees, customers, and suppliers, which may lead to new ways of innovating. IBM is strongly promoting its collaboration tools as an effective way to generate ideas from a wide variety of sources (see www.collaborationjam.com). Eli Lilly uses it to solve problems by tapping into resource talent pools from around the world (see www.innocentive.com). Cambrian House uses social computing technologies to partially outsource both idea generation and product creation for new software products, while acting as middleman and coordinating activities (Brynjolfsson and McAfee 2007).

Finally, there is significant, though nascent, interest in the use of virtual worlds for business purposes. These worlds (e.g., Second Life), which are still miles from having practical business uses, are attracting interest from companies as varied as Adidas, Sun Microsystems, Reuters, and Toyota (Kharif 2006). Potential uses for this technology include to gain early experience of products and services, to create effective distance learning environments, and to make work more fun (O'Driscoll 2007; Smith 2006).

In short, although social computing is a reality—even in organizations today—we are still in the early stages of its evolution. As a result, it is a challenge for most companies to visualize social computing's potential, let alone recognize its potential impact on how they will be doing business in the future.

WHERE IS SOCIAL COMPUTING LEADING US?

Much more than in the past, we can see that today's technology innovations are engendering a set of complementary innovations in how we work and live (Brynjolffson and McAfee 2007). Convergence of technology so that data and applications can be seamlessly moved from device to device was the first step, and most managers have at least some understanding about how this is making work and technology more portable and accessible, enabling virtual work, virtual teams, work at home, and mobile working. What the next changes will be are less obvious. Predictions rely on the experiences of technology and media companies that are smaller and have been the early adopters of social computing for business, extrapolation from what is going on with social computing and individuals, and of course, the ever-present media and vendor "hype."

Bearing these caveats in mind, we can realistically expect to see several changes in organizations over the next two to five years. These will be more apparent in some firms than in others and will likely affect some aspects of work more than others (Young and Gomolski 2007):

- *More flexible organizational behavior.*   Most social computing applications share the following characteristics:
  - Participation through contribution and feedback
  - Openness in a variety of ways, such as voting, feedback, sharing information, and comments
  - Conversation
  - Community building by enabling those with a common interest to connect and communicate effectively (Mayfield 2008).

  As these behaviors become embedded in organizations, business cultures will increasingly adapt to the expectations of 360-degree feedback and sharing across hierarchical, business unit, and organizational boundaries (Austin et al. 2006).
- *New ways to manage digital content.*   There is no doubt that the amount of digital content available is growing geometrically in both sheer numbers and type (Smith and McKeen 2007). Social computing applications offer new ways of searching, managing, and effectively utilizing this deluge. For example, 3D visual interfaces enable users to comprehend up to 85 times more information than the 2D text base search systems (e.g., Google) in use at present (Smith and McKeen 2007). A variety of social computing applications are designed for improved information management. RSS feeds, improved search tools, tagging, blogs, personal home pages, and virtual worlds are just some of the tools that will give information context and make it easier to find and use in the future (Bray and Konsynski 2007; Hinchcliffe 2006; Trebutt 2006).
- *New styles of management.*   As noted above, this change is already apparent in many working lives. The focus group noted that, although in the past organizations have forbidden the personal use of such technologies as telephones and the Internet and, now, social computing, the trend is toward an environment where we are always available to both our work and personal lives. This will necessitate a change of management style and metrics. As one manager explained, "[W]e need to focus more on people's outputs. We don't live in a clocking-in environment anymore. We should care about what people deliver and their accountabilities." This suggests that employers will have to trust their staff in situations where they are unsupervised and that employees will have to inculcate organizational values and expectations and be expected to apply them appropriately wherever they are (Smith et al., 2004; Trebutt 2006). The focus group also felt that more attention will also be paid to improving work/life balance.
- *Adaptive organizational designs.*   The effect of the above changes will mean a shift in how organizations function. No one suggests that traditional command and control hierarchies will be completely eliminated, yet as organizations become more open and flexible, it will be natural that many traditional organizational boundaries will be broken down and that there will be less structure and greater agility in a variety of areas. These will include the roles people play, which will tend to be situational, rather than fixed; flatter structures with fewer layers of control and more reliance on other forms of control (e.g., deliverables, accountabilities,

ethics, and audits); and the breaking down of traditional internal boundaries between business units (Brynjolffson and McAfee 2007; Raskino 2007; Smith and McKeen 2007b). Similarly, participants pointed out a blurring of organizational boundaries as they do more collaborative projects with partners, suppliers, and clients. For some businesses, or some parts of businesses, this new openness will lead to new and continuously evolving business models and sources of value. Learning how to take advantage of the network for business value is still in its infancy, but for those who can adapt to "business in the wild," learn to use collective intelligence and bottom up innovation, and adopt new and less protective approaches to the management of intellectual property, social computing will be a great enabler (Young and Gomolski 2007).

It is likely that new organizational designs will combine the best of traditional approaches to management and value generation with new control, accountability, and decision-making mechanisms. For example, social computing tools will enable new and different types of decision-making trade-offs between local and centralized bodies. At Zara Clothes, local store managers now tell the company what items people want to wear, and the company makes them (Brynjolfsson and McAfee 2007). The U.S. military is using the same type of networked technology to ensure that relevant decisions are made by local personnel (Smith and Konsynski 2004). Finally, organizations that want to combine innovation with technology will need to develop a macro-level innovation process that balances formal and informal structures to facilitate learning and information exchange while also ensuring projects and companies are successful (Rizova 2006).

Most of the focus group companies currently have no policies governing the acceptable use of social computing and simply deny their employees access to these tools—a trend corroborated by a recent survey (Lombardi 2008). Also, policies are only the first step as organizations will have to develop social governance and etiquette around how such tools are used (e.g., around gossip, "flaming," what can and cannot be shared, etc.).

Forrester Research suggests that, as a result of social computing, we can expect to see three powerful changes taking place in organizations:

- Innovation will move from a top-down to a bottom-up model.
- Value will move from ownership to experiences.
- Power will shift from institutions to communities (cited in Hinchcliffe 2006).

The first shift is entirely likely given the ability of social computing to tap into collective intelligence (Brynjolfsson and McAfee 2007); the second two shifts will probably be much longer in coming, if at all. What is more likely in the near term is that organizations will develop hybrid designs that will take advantage of both the industrial strength processes and structures created in the past two decades and newer, more flexible forms of organizational action. The focus group agreed with many researchers that, although radical change will remain an option for some, it is much more likely that social computing will first be used in more targeted ways that complement, more than they disrupt, tried and true organizational designs (Young and Gomolski 2007; Brynjolfsson and McAfee 2007).

PULLING IN TWO DIFFERENT DIRECTIONS: THE CHALLENGE FOR IT MANAGERS

As is so often the case with new technologies, IT managers feel torn between their every-day reality and the glamorous and dynamic vision of the future as painted by the proponents of social computing. Participants were not so much skeptical of the capabilities of social computing technologies as concerned for how these would mesh with their every-day responsibilities of managing an efficient and effective IT organization. "Social computing is a challenge in our locked down environment," said one. Another noted, "Our information security principles conflict with social computing. There are some things we don't want hitting the six o'clock news." Table 14.1 summarizes the vision of social computing and contrasts it with the challenges it poses to IT management.

Social computing is often seen as "dangerous but seductive" (Trebutt 2006), and the focus group managers agreed. "We're being pulled in two directions. We need to change," said one, "but we also need to protect our corporate assets. We really need to be developing policies for how to do this." They saw their biggest challenge as security and protecting the reliability of the infrastructure they have built up. "If the security issue was addressed, we'd see social computing as much more acceptable," said another manager.

Some other challenges include the following:

* *Short business horizons.* As has often been the case in the past, business leaders have a much shorter time horizon in their thinking than IT and are often not prepared to anticipate or explore new technologies and their implications. Then, when the technology hits public awareness, they want it yesterday! "We have no active

TABLE 14.1 The Challenge of Social Computing from an IT Manager's Perspective.

The Vision	The IT Manager's Challenge
Blurred boundaries	Firewalls
Collaboration and sharing	Intellectual property and privacy protection
Situational applications	Maintaining transactional applications and operational integrity
Mass participation and accessibility	Authentication and authorization
Transient information	Creating a permanent record
Supports social behavior	Supports business behavior
Innovation and creativity	Efficient use of resources
Viral	Secure
Dynamic	Backup
Situational roles	Regulatory accountabilities
Social governance and etiquette	Organizational governance and policy
Collective intelligence; bottom-up innovation	Top-down business strategy
Emergent value	Defined business value based on a business case
Anywhere/anytime connectivity	Controlled communication
Ad hoc applications	Scalable applications

support for social computing," said one manager. "It's very hard for the business to see its value as yet." Yet, in some cases, business users see IT as holding them back because of security and regulatory considerations. "We need to work together with the business to identify the risks associated with social computing and protect our operational processes," said another. "And we need to make sure the decision makers understand what's involved in becoming more open."

- *Resources.* Social computing is touted as an effective collaboration and innovation tool, but using it for this purpose requires support and facilitation. "Our staff is maxed out at present," said a manager. "If we go down this road, we need to commit resources to doing it properly." Even in those companies that are actively promoting social computing applications, this is a challenge. "When we're stressed, we revert to our old behaviors," explained a participant.

- *Changing the culture.* IT managers recognize that organizational behavior must change if the value of social computing is to be realized. However, changing embedded cultural practices is often extremely difficult. Even where there is a strong emphasis on making information and people more accessible, social computing needs a champion to make sure "we don't slip back into our comfortable ways of behaving," agreed the focus group. Some organizations have tried wikis and blogs but have found that the adoption rate is initially high, but the drop off in participation is equally steep. This is consistent with the challenges KM managers faced, which effectively killed this function in most organizations. The question for many (and which remains unanswered) is whether new social computing tools (or "KM lite") will be able to drive the behavioral and cultural changes needed to make the technology effective (Spanbauer 2006).

PREPARING FOR THE FUTURE

Although most large organizations are not yet ready to embrace social computing, Gartner Group expects it will soon start to exploit the principles on which it is based by adapting them to a corporate context (Raskino 2007). And already key vendors have plans to offer corporate-grade social computing tools to the market (Raskino 2007). As a result, organizations can expect to see the hype growing, and IT functions can expect to see their role as protector of the corporate IT asset challenged (Trebutt 2006). Also, as might be anticipated, there will be a range of appropriate responses from "we should have nothing to do with this technology" to fully embracing it (Young and Gomolski 2007).

Literally no one is claiming to understand how social computing will change organizations. "The fallout is not yet clear," says Forrester Research (cited in Hinchcliffe 2006). "There are no best practices as yet," stated another researcher (Konsynski 2007). "The biggest challenge is to make [these] tools useful for business," explained a third researcher (Knights 2006). Nevertheless, the focus group agreed that this is a phenomenon that is not going away and with which companies must come to terms. Thus, most were taking one or more steps to prepare for what social computing might mean for their organizations, such as the following:

- *Experimentation.* Several companies in the focus group had small-scale social computing experiments ongoing in order to gain experience and better understand their implications. These experiments ranged from internal wikis and blogs to a corporate presence in Second Life to support for instant messaging. Probably the most widely known strategic experiments are IBM's Innovation Jams. The first, limited to its 50,000 employees over a 72-hour period, created a massive blogging environment and used a combination of software and facilitation to develop a new set of corporate values. "The results were very well received by staff," said a company executive, "because they are truly meaningful to them." This success led to two larger Jams, expanded to include IBM's partners, customers, and suppliers. Again, the results were impressive, according to the executive. "We were shocked at the innovative outcomes. There was a real sense of the power of collaboration" (Smith and McKeen 2007a).

- *Practice evolution.*   As noted above, very few companies have developed any policies around how and where social computing should be used, with the exception of forbidding it completely (Lombardi 2008). Many focus group managers felt that one goal of social computing experiments should be to help evolve practices and eventually corporate policies for its use. "We need to do this on a case by case basis," said a manager. "This is the only way we'll figure out how we need to manage it effectively. However, we have to build a box around these applications so that we can protect our other assets." Several firms had already established codes of conduct for Internet usage and felt that these could be adapted to social computing. Adherence to good privacy and security practices were also felt to be foundational components for successful social computing.

- *Vision.*   Most of all, it is important to work toward a common vision for social computing in a particular organization. Some of the factors that will affect this vision include the demographics of the workforce and the company's customers; geographic location and mobility of the workforce, company partners, suppliers, and customers; the degree to which the industry is regulated; the importance of creativity and innovation in the business; the organization's capability for change; and management's willingness to champion, source, and support new ways of working (Bradley 2007; Brynjolfsson and McAfee 2007; Knights 2006; Raskino 2007). "To understand how social computing will deliver value, we need to help people do what makes sense for them, without being prescriptive," said a participant. A key component of the vision for social computing will be the role IT will play. Will it simply provide a secure computing platform, tools, backups, and hardware and then get out of the way (Trebutt 2006)? Or will the organization expect social computing to be integrated into its current processes and applications in a more thoughtful way (Spanbauer 2006)? Or will social computing simply be just another set of tools in IT's kit (Brynjolfsson and McAfee 2007)? Each of these approaches will have "regenerative, innovative and destructive potential for today's IT" (Young and Gomolski 2007). A focus group manager pointed out that this is a normal position for IT to be in. "IT is constantly changing. Most IT jobs in our organizations didn't exist a decade ago," he stated. "Right now, we need to get a better handle on how social computing will change IT and what skills and capabilities we will need to support it, and this requires some thoughtful visioning."

The three key questions companies are asking about social computing are these: What is the value of these tools? How can we pick the right ones? What is the management playbook for using them effectively? (Fontana 2007) At present, there are no right answers, so organizations are going to have to find out for themselves through experimentation, practice, and visioning.

Conclusion

Social computing may be "inevitable" according to the focus group, but its use in organizations and its impact on how technology is used to deliver value is still far from clear. The predominant sentiment is probably one of "watchful confusion" as both business and IT managers try to grasp how to adopt and utilize technologies that continue to mutate rapidly and are integral to how a growing segment of our society wants to live and work. Social computing is definitely a powerful set of technologies, tools, and behaviors, but whether or not that power will eventually be perceived as a "good" thing is yet to be seen. What we do know is that, more than ever before, the impact of social computing will result from the deep and close connections that are created by the interaction of humans and technology. It would, therefore, behoove IT managers and other leaders to expand their horizons to include a greater understanding of social psychology. IT managers have been saying for some time that "I[I]t is people, not technology, that are our biggest challenge." Yet, somehow technology is always preeminent. Maybe the advent of social computing will be the catalyst of a more personcentric approach to technology, one in which technology use will eventually become "like wearing eyeglasses; the rims are always visible but the wearer forgets she has them on—even though they're the only things making the world clear" (Roush 2005).

References

Anderson, C. *The Long Tail.* New York: Hyperion, 2006.

Austin, T., D. Cearley, J. Mann, G. Phifer, D. Sholler, K. Harris, T. Bell, R. Knox, M. Cain, and M. Silver. "Predicts 2007: Big Changes Ahead in the High Performance Workplace." Gartner Inc., ID Number: G00144476, December 5, 2006.

Bradley, A. "Key Issues in the Enterprise Application of Web 2.0 Practices, Technologies, Products and Services 2007." Gartner Inc., ID Number: G00148544, June 14, 2007.

Bray, D., and B. Konsynski, "Virtual Worlds: Multi-Disciplinary Research Opportunities." Unpublished paper available from david_bray@bus.emory.edu, 2007.

Brown, J., and P. Duguid. *The Social Life of Information.* Boston: Harvard Business School Press, 2000.

Brynjolfsson, E., and A. McAfee. "Beyond Enterprise 2.0." *MIT Sloan Management Review* 48, no. 3 (Spring 2007): 50–64.

Fontana, J. "Social Networks Find Corp. Friends." *Network World* 24, no. 44 (November 12, 2007): 22.

Friedman, T. *The World Is Flat: A Brief History of the Twenty-First Century.* New York: Farrar, Straus and Giroux, 2005.

Hinchcliffe, D. "The Shift to Social Computing." Enterprise Web 2.0, March 12, 2006. blogs.zdnet.com/Hinchcliffe/wo-trackback.php?p=21 (accessed January 8, 2008).

Kharif, O. "Big Media Gets a Second Life." BusinessWeek.com, October 17, 2006. www.businessweek.com/technology/content/oct2006/tc20061017_127435.htm (accessed January 28, 2008).

Knights, M. "Harness the Power of Collaboration." *Computer Weekly,* August 15, 2006, 22–24.

Konsynski, B. "Business and Virtual Worlds." Unpublished presentation to the Society for Information Management's Advanced Practices Council, Chicago, September 2007.

Lombardi, R. "Web 2.0: Here and Now." *CIO Government Review* 10, no. 1 (January 2008): 12–16.

Mayfield, A. "A Bluffer's Guide to Social Media" (2008). www.spannerworks.com (accessed January 8, 2008).

McAfee, A. "Enterprise 2.0: The Dawn of Emergent Collaboration." *MIT Sloan Management Review* 47, no. 3 (Spring 2005): 21–28.

O'Driscoll, T. "Serious Gaming." Unpublished presentation to the Society for Information Management's Advanced Practices Council, Chicago, 2006.

Raskino, M. "In 2008, Enterprise Web 2.0 Goes Mainstream." Gartner Inc., ID Number: G00153218, December 17, 2007.

Rizova, P. "Are You Networked for Successful Innovation?" *MIT Sloan Management Review* 47, no. 3 (Spring 2006): 49–55.

Roush, W. "Social Machines: Computing Means Connecting." *MIT Technology Review* (August 2005).

Smith, D. "Advanced web Services Lead to the Next Generation of Enterprise-Class Computing." Gartner Inc., ID Number: G00144830, November 28, 2006.

Smith, H., and B. Konsynski. "Grid Computing." *MIT Sloan Management Review* 46, no. 1 (2004).

Smith, H., and J. McKeen. "Serious Gaming." *The CIO Brief* 13, no. 4 (2007a). Kingston, Ontario: Queen's University School of Business.

———. "Social Networks: KM's "Killer App?." *Communications of the Association for Information Systems* 19, article 27 (May 2007b): 611–21.

Smith, H., J. McKeen, and C. Street. "Linking IT to Business Metrics." *Journal of Information Science and Technology* 1, no. 1 (2004), 13–26.

Smith H. A., and J. D. McKeen. "Information Management: The Nexus of Business and IT." *Communications of the Association for Information Systems* 19, article 3 (January 2007), 34–46.

Spanbauer, S. "Knowledge Management 2.0." *CIO* 20, no. 5 (December 1, 2006).

Trebutt, D. "The IT Manager's Guide to Social Computing." *The Register,* July 21, 2006. www.theregister.co.uk/2006/07/21 (accessed January 8, 2008).

Weill, N. "How Wal-Mart Lost Its IT Mojo." *CIO* 21, no. 3 (November 1, 2007).

Wikipedia. "Social Computing." Wikipedia.com. en.wikipedia.org/wiki/social_computing (accessed January 8, 2008).

Young, C., and B. Gomolski. "Alternative Delivery Models: Implications for the IT Organization." Gartner Inc., ID Number: G00152131, October 3, 2007.

Chapter 15

Information Delivery: IT's Evolving Role[1]

It wasn't so long ago that IT was called "data processing" (DP) and information delivery consisted of printing out massive computer listings full of transaction data. If DP was particularly enlightened, business got summary reports, which might or might not contain useful information. The advent of online systems made data marginally easier to use, but it was still mostly data—that is, facts with very little context or analysis applied to them. "Usability" was talked about, but this aspect of information delivery was largely ignored. As a result, it was not unusual to find customer service representatives switching between ten or more different "screens" (each representing a different organizational data silo) to get the information they needed to do their job. But with the advent of Web technologies, organizations realized—despite the fact that they could force their employees to wend their way through an enterprise's Byzantine organizational structure and bits and bytes of data—customers were not going to go searching for the data they needed. Data had to be meaningful, provide an integrated picture of their interactions, and generally be significantly easier to interpret and understand. In other words, data had to become information, and it had to be delivered in ways customers could use.

While information delivery channels and practices were evolving, so too were organizations' needs for information. Many firms now realize that rather than simply processing transactions, they can "mine" what they collect to uncover new insights, often leading to substantial savings and/or revenue growth opportunities. Until recently, however, investments in information analysis and decision support languished as companies undertook higher-priority projects with more direct and immediate impact on their bottom lines. Today the success of how some companies use information for competitive advantage and operational effectiveness (e.g., Walmart, Dell) is causing business leaders to look more carefully at how well their firms are leveraging information.

Web technology has dramatically changed the ease with which information can be integrated and delivered on an ad hoc basis. Today it is both technically and financially feasible to deliver literally millions of pages of text to desktops as needed. As well, the technologies available to manage different types of information are improving rapidly and converging.

---

[1]Smith, H. A., and J. D. McKeen. "Information Delivery: IT's Evolving Role." *Communications of the Association for Information Systems* 15, article 11 (February 2005): 197–210. Reproduced by permission of the Association for Information Systems.

Traditionally, different software has been used to manage documents, records, and other information assets (Kaplan 2002). Now the lines of demarcation between them are blurring. Software, although still imperfect, is opening the door to a host of new possibilities for information management and delivery. All these factors are placing new pressures on IT to focus more thoughtfully on the *information* component of its function.

This chapter first surveys the expanding world of information and technology and why information delivery has become so important so rapidly. Then it discusses the value proposition of information in organizations. Next it describes the important components of an effective information delivery function in IT. Finally, it looks at how information delivery will likely evolve over the next five to ten years and what this will mean for IT and organizations.

INFORMATION AND IT: WHY NOW?

In the late 1990s, information management and delivery were barely on the radar screens of most IT managers (McKeen and Smith 2003). Today it is consuming a considerable amount of IT effort and has blossomed into a number of multifaceted, high-value IT activities. Of course, IT organizations have had some data management functions for many years, but these have been largely limited to database design and administration. As one participant claimed, "We've been talking around the subject of information for a long time, but it hasn't really been critically important until recently."

A number of reasons account for this new attention to information. First, there is no doubt that organizations are overwhelmed by all sorts of information. The number of documents, reports, Web pages, data items, and digital assets has literally grown exponentially in recent years. "Our ability to store and communicate information has far outpaced our ability to search, retrieve, and present it" (Varian and Lyman 2000). Research shows that the average knowledge worker now spends about a quarter of his or her day looking for information either internally or externally (Kontzer 2003).

Second, companies have begun to realize that information and how it is used has considerable value. Almost all organizations believe they could be doing more with the information they already have (Davenport et al. 2001). This is coupled with a new understanding of how value is derived from IT. Traditionally, organizations have expected to deliver value from their information systems alone (often through greater efficiencies in transaction processing), yet new research shows that improved information stemming from good information management practices, *in combination with excellent systems,* is a stronger driver of financial performance (Marchand et al. 2000). Participants noted that today information is being used in their organizations for much more than transactional decisions. "We are using all sorts of information in new ways," said one. "We are trying to understand the data drivers of our business and use it to manage our processes more effectively. We are also using data analysis to uncover strategic new business opportunities." Another noted, "In the past we sent reports to executives who would consider the information they contained and issue directives to their staff. Now we are sending information directly to frontline staff so they can take action immediately."

In addition to recognizing the value of transactional, operational, and strategic information, companies are also coming to realize that embedding information in their workflows can be extremely valuable. A firm's ability to extract and leverage explicit knowledge from its employees by formalizing it in systems and procedures directly contributes to its structural capital (Smith et al. 2006). Some companies (e.g., Skandia) have already realized significant benefits from standardizing their information as structural capital and distributing it appropriately (Kettinger et al. 2003).

Third, new laws governing what can and cannot be done with information are also leading to greater awareness in IT about what information is collected and how it is used and protected. Addressing privacy concerns, for example, requires development of more sophisticated methods of user identification and authorization, permission management, controls over information flows, and greater attention to accuracy and analysis of where and how individual items of information can be used (Smith and McKeen 2003). No longer can huge customer records be sent from system to system, for example, simply because some data elements are needed. Companies risk not only contravening the law but also embarrassment in the marketplace. Financial accountability legislation (e.g., Sarbanes-Oxley) is also driving greater attention to the integrity of information at every step in its collection. Requiring senior officers to *guarantee* the accuracy of the firm's financial statements is changing many previously *laissez-faire* attitudes toward information.

Finally, information possibilities are rapidly expanding. New technologies are creating different types of information, opening up innovative channels of information delivery, and providing new ways of organizing and accessing information. Just a few years ago, e-mail, instant messaging, and the Internet simply didn't exist. Today they are all major sources of new information *and* new delivery channels. Navigation tools, wireless technology, and vastly improved storage media (to name just a few) are driving new information applications that were not possible in the recent past. As the pace of new technology innovation ramps up, information delivery challenges and possibilities are, therefore, also escalating. In short, today IT personnel are finding that information delivery is a key element of almost every aspect of their work as well as a fundamental part of their ability to derive value from technology.

DELIVERING VALUE THROUGH INFORMATION

Information delivery is playing a critical role in several new areas in delivering value in organizations:

- *More effective business operations.*   Although information has long been used to run organizations, in the past it was largely paper and transaction based. Today executives have access to online "dashboards" that combine a wide variety of transaction, process, and supply-chain metrics to give them a much broader and more detailed picture of their operations. Typically, dashboards are designed differently for different needs (e.g., sales, logistics), functions (e.g., HR, accounting), and/or processes (e.g., inventory management) and for different spans of control. They usually include drill-down capabilities, highlight problem areas, and integrate information from several systems. Other types of operational information that are available to organizations include predictive analysis (e.g., trends, timelines), benchmarks (both internal and external), quality measures (e.g., defects, stockouts), and "scorecard" information (e.g., financial, internal business, customer, and learning and growth). What's also new is that these types of information are being given to frontline staff so they can better manage their own areas of responsibility, identify and avoid exceptions, and take action before problems arise. Operational information is often integrated with guidelines that direct courses of action so staff will better understand how to use it effectively.

- *E-business.*   This new channel is having considerable impact on how organizations present information about their products and services to customers. In the past, customers would often get conflicting information depending on which "door" they entered (i.e., which part of the business they contacted). E-business has forced organizations to confront their own internal inconsistencies, identify information gaps and inaccuracies, and deal with inadequacies in their offerings, which are much more apparent when presented in this medium. IT and senior executives often have to take a hard line with line-of-business leaders who tend to have a function-specific perspective on information. As one manager noted, "Taking the customer's point of view in e-business development cuts across our established lines of business and organizational distinctions. Often there are political issues about information ownership, organization, and presentation. These must be nipped in the bud and everyone forced to put the customer's needs first."

  The Web has also become a significant driver of interactions among companies, enabling them to transact business in new ways, manage their roles in different supply chains, and offer new services to business clients that didn't previously exist. In both the B2C and B2B spheres, e-business is largely about how information is integrated and presented to improve products and services. However, e-business is also changing the competitive landscape by making it considerably easier to comparison shop online. In the past, companies were able to be competitive by offering complex combinations of products and services, which discouraged one-to-one comparisons. Today whole new businesses have grown up to facilitate comparison shopping. These firms are placing themselves as intermediaries between a company and its customers (e.g., online travel, insurance quotes). Thus, companies that continue to use information to obfuscate their services, rather than inform their customers, could easily find themselves disintermediated and at a strategic disadvantage.

- *Internal self-service.*   New information channels are driving significant internal change as well. The Web is being used to simplify employee access to human resources materials and procedures, streamline procurement, manage approvals, provide information on benefits and entitlements, and maintain telephone numbers, to name just a few types of information that are now routinely accessible online. Microsoft makes more than 2.2 million documents available to its staff, and two-thirds of its employees visit its internal site at least twice a day (Gilchrist 2001; Williams 2001). U.S. Air Force staff can now access more than 18,000 types of forms online. As with e-business, however, internal self-service is driving a complete reanalysis of what information is collected and how it is presented, navigated, and used. "Portals and online self-service make administrative problem areas more visible. They also force managers to simplify policies and procedures," said one manager. Phase 2 of the U.S. Air Force self-service initiative, for example, will try to reduce the number of forms in the organization from 18,000 to 7,000 (Bednarz 2003).

- *Unstructured information delivery.*   Increasingly, organizations want to be able to access *all* their information online, including that which has traditionally been retained as paper documents. New software, navigation, and storage technologies are leading to the convergence of the records management, library management, and electronic document management functions in organizations (Kaplan 2002). In the past IT has had very little to do with unstructured information. Today IT is required to develop taxonomies, navigation, and access methods for unstructured information and even to integrate structured and unstructured information into work processes delivered to the desktop.

Another major area of unstructured information delivery in which IT is involved is e-mail and instant messaging. These technologies have captured the organizational imagination so rapidly that policies and best practices in this area are still catching up. Jurisprudence has recognized that these interchanges are corporate records. In response, organizations are developing procedures for managing these more effectively. The barrage of messages from outside corporate boundaries in combination with personal use of corporate e-mail and the vulnerability of corporate information to external hackers are giving IT managers severe migraines. Archiving e-mail, filtering spam, coping with viruses that tag along with messages, building sophisticated firewalls, and creating business cases for messaging technologies are all new IT activities that have sprung up to better manage these new forms of wanted and unwanted information.

IT is also investigating collaborative technologies that help capture and leverage the work of teams and groups. These technologies are being effectively used in such endeavors as providing the means whereby knowledge workers can share information about what they are doing, capturing best practices, brainstorming, tracking key decisions, and documenting a project's history. Often IT workers themselves are the first users of these technologies, bearing the brunt of the learning involved before they are rolled out to the rest of the organization.

• *Business intelligence.*   This is a function that is currently well developed in some organizations and not in others. However, the arena of business intelligence is growing rapidly in importance in organizations due to increased competition and the speed with which organizations must respond to competitive threats. Business intelligence includes both internal intelligence gathering (often known as data mining) and external intelligence gathering about trends, competitors, and industries. IT organizations are, at minimum, expected to design an effective internal information environment (aka a data warehouse) developed from their business information systems, within which users of a variety of skill levels can operate. Typically this requires an understanding of the context in which information will be used, modeling how data will be represented, and providing appropriate tools for different types of users. End-users can access this information in a variety of ways ranging from ad hoc queries to generating predesigned reports. More sophisticated organizations have full-time data analysts on staff whose jobs can range from answering questions for users to exploring the data in order to uncover new opportunities (Brohman and Boudreau 2004).

A key IT concern in the design and management of internal data warehouses is the speed with which inquiries can be answered. It is not unusual for a user to build an inquiry that will bring a modern computer system to its knees. Therefore, protecting operational systems and optimizing routine queries is of paramount importance. Many IT organizations design parallel universes in which data warehouses can operate without affecting the production environment.

External business intelligence gathering is a relatively new field. For some companies, this simply means providing access to news wires and online "clipping services." Other organizations, however, are designing sophisticated criteria that can be used to "crawl" the Web and organize information about competitors' products and services. In companies where product innovation is an important function, access to external research services is important. Many IT organizations now have librarians whose job is to assist users to find external information electronically. However, the future ideal will be to integrate external information more seamlessly into work processes and present it to users when needed.

- *Behavior change.*   Organizations already recognize that people pay more attention to what is measured. As a result, organizations have become increasingly more sophisticated about designing the metrics and scorecards they use to monitor both individual and corporate performance (see Kaplan and Norton 1996). It is less well recognized that information can both drive and inhibit certain behaviors in individuals. One participant explained, "More and more, our job is less about technology and more about behavior change. How we present information plays a big part in driving the behaviors the organization is looking for."

Promoting information-positive behavior means ensuring that the information that is available is trustworthy and of high quality and that information about the business is widely available to all levels of employees to help shape their behavior.

> People can sense information effectively only when they understand a company's business performance and how they personally can help to improve performance. . . . This common sense of purpose fosters an environment in which people begin to look beyond their own jobs and become concerned about the information needs of others. Sensing is enhanced and information valuation assessments become more precise. (Marchand et al. 2000)

Some companies have begun to use greater information transparency to modify and guide staff behavior with extremely positive results (Smith et al. 2004), but organizations have just scratched the surface of what is possible in leveraging the complex linkages between information and behavior. In general, information transparency highlights both strengths and weaknesses, successes and failures. Highlighting key information helps staff to focus their efforts in areas that are of concern to management. For example, publishing infection statistics by specialty unit in a hospital can change staff hand-washing habits. Similarly, stressing overall "file completion" information can help customer service staff solve holistic customer problems, rather than processing the individual transactions involved, and thus provide more effective customer service.

EFFECTIVE INFORMATION DELIVERY

The explosion of new information delivery opportunities in organizations has left IT departments scrambling to organize themselves appropriately and develop new skills, roles, practices, and strategies. Even more than with systems development, effective information delivery involves careful attention to the social and behavioral dimensions of how work is done. "Politics is a huge dimension of information delivery," said a participant. "Defining data means establishing one version of the truth and one owner. As we move to standardized definitions, single master files for corporate data items, and common presentation, we get into major battles. In the past we have had ten systems for ten nuances of information. Everyone built their own thing." Another said, "Information integration is very difficult to achieve on a large scale. This problem becomes even more difficult and important in global enterprises and with strategic alliances."

New Information Skills

Better information delivery means clarifying and making visible the knowledge frameworks and mental models that have been applied to create both data and information (Li and Kettinger 2004). Business and IT practitioners must recognize the existence of these frameworks and make appropriate judgments about how they affect the information that is delivered. Although IT staff have been doing this for years when designing reports and screen layouts, the organization's increasing reliance on structured information for decision making means that it is critical to consciously make appropriate decisions about how information is designed and presented. IT staff, therefore, not only need new skills in thinking about information, but they also need better training in analyzing how it will be accessed and used. Furthermore, with more integrated data, it is now essential that business rules be applied to who gets to see what information. "Our systems serve a number of different types of users," said an IT manager at a major pharmaceutical firm. "It is essential that we know who they are. Salespeople, doctors, pharmacists, hospitals, regulatory agencies, and patients all have different information needs and rights. We cannot afford to put the information into the wrong hands." Finally, as pointed out above, navigation and usability have long been afterthoughts of systems analysis and design. Today this must be an integral part of every IT deliverable.

New Information Skills Within IT

- Political judgment
- Information analysis
- Workflow analysis
- Information access
- Business rules for information use
- Usability
- Information navigation

New Information Roles

IT has a number of new or enhanced roles for managing the logistics of information delivery as well. IT's information responsibilities now include the following:

- Data custodianship
- Storage
- Integration
- Presentation
- Security
- Administration
- Personalization and multilingual presentations
- Document indexing and searching
- Unstructured content management and workflow
- Team and collaboration software
- Network and server infrastructure for information hosting/staging.

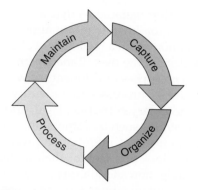

FIGURE 15.1 The Information Management Life Cycle

In addition, IT often hosts several key information management functions. Examples include library and information services, records and information management (e.g., archiving, regulatory compliance), information solutions delivery (including portal design), and data architecture and modeling.

Business responsibilities for information include ownership, quality, and currency. However, even here IT must sometimes establish and enforce the procedures and policies within which business will exercise these responsibilities. For example, some organizations have a formal system of information "expiry dates" for nonsystem-generated information, and reminders are sent to owners to ensure appropriate review and updating.

New Information Practices

Effective information delivery involves developing practices to manage different forms of information over their life cycles (see Figure 15.1). For each type of information, strategies, processes, and business rules must be established to address each of the four life cycle stages.

1. *Capture.* This includes all activities involved in identifying (i.e., analyzing and integrating) information for possible use. Typically, gaps appear at the borders between silos of information and when trying to connect structured and unstructured information. Capture may also involve digitizing information that is currently in paper format (e.g., documents). At present few organizations formally capture external business intelligence information such as economic, social, and political changes; competitive innovations; and potential problems with partners and suppliers. In the future, however, such information will be captured from an increasingly wide range of sources from both outside and inside the organization (Marchand et al. 2000). Furthermore, users will increasingly demand real-time or near-real-time information, and this will require further refinement of information-capture practices.

2. *Organize.* Organizing information involves indexing, classifying, and linking together sources. At the highest level, this involves creating a taxonomy—that is, a systematic categorization by keyword or term (Corcoran 2002). This provides an organizing framework for information that facilitates ease of access. A second layer of

organization involves creating metadata—that is, information about content and location. Metadata provide a roadmap to information, much as a card catalog points to the location and information about a book (Lee et al. 2001). Metadata are especially important for workflow design, the overall management of information, and information exchange among enterprises or different software applications. A third layer of organization is provided by processes that identify information ownership and ensure that it meets the necessary corporate, legal, and linguistic standards. These processes also manage activities such as authorship, versioning, and access. A final component of organization involves information presentation. Many organizations have developed a common look and feel for their materials, such as Web or portal pages, to enable ease of navigation and interoperability among platforms.

3. *Process.*   As noted above, organizations have only begun to leverage the value of their information. New information-delivery technologies and channels as well as the recognition of the business value of information are driving the development of new organizational capabilities based on information and technology. IT plays a significant role in the analysis of information and its capture in the form of structural capital. However, organizations also need businesspeople with deeper analytic skills who can combine their knowledge of business with knowledge of data. Statistical modeling and analytic skills will also be increasingly needed to identify opportunities and make sense of huge amounts of data.

4. *Maintain.*   Different types of information must be maintained differently. For unstructured content, such as documents and Web pages, maintenance involves keeping information up to date. All information needs to be regularly assessed as to how well it is meeting the business's needs. Finally, principles and standards must be established for information retention and preservation and for its disposal.

New Information Strategies

A final element of effective information delivery involves strategy. All organizations have a generic vision of delivering the right information to the right person at the right time. However, achieving this goal involves careful consideration of what an organization wants to accomplish with information and how it proposes to derive business value from it. Interestingly, many organizations are currently placing their highest priority on using information for internal management and administration. Employee self-service cuts out much administrative overhead in human resources management, procurement, and accounting. "There are huge savings to be gained by delivering better information on our operational processes and using information to better manage workflows and approvals," said a participant.

Some firms are also developing *microstrategies* for particular areas of the business or types of user. These small-scale initiatives often involve giving users subsets of data containing the specific information they need and appropriate analysis tools. One company has developed an information-access architecture that provides different types of tools to users depending on their abilities to use them to "mine" data. Basic users are given canned inquiries with drill-down capabilities and the ability to export information into an Excel spreadsheet. More skilled users are given basic analytic tools and access to metadata, and expert users are given professional analytic tools.

Information Delivery Best Practices

- Approach information delivery as an iterative development project. No one gets it right the first time.
- Separate data from function to create greater flexibility.
- Buy data models and enhance them. This will save many person-years of effort.
- Use middleware to translate data from one system to another. This is especially important for companies using several different packaged systems, each of which contains its own embedded data model.

- Evolve toward a real-time customer information file. These files are notoriously difficult to build all at once; however, having a single source of customer information makes managing customer privacy much easier and also makes it possible to offer new integrated products and services.
- Design information delivery from the end-user (whether external customer, employee, or supplier) backward. This substantially reduces internal in-fighting and focuses attention on what is really important.

At the other end of the strategy scale are companies such as CEMEX, Dell, and Walmart that have made information a strategic priority. Each of these companies has an enterprisewide strategy for using information. Walmart's sophisticated operational architecture collects information on all its transactions. It shares this information with its suppliers in near real time so they are better able to control production and distribution. It also uses a data warehouse to extract trend data, which are combined with real-time transaction information to develop a high degree of local awareness. Each manager is able to identify opportunities and take appropriate action (Cebrowski and Garstka 1998). CEMEX uses information to control every aspect of its cement production and delivery logistics worldwide. Dell shares production and product specification information with its partners to create a seamless supply chain that is owned by Dell, even though the company has limited contact with the actual products it sells (Kettinger and Marchand 2004).

THE FUTURE OF INFORMATION DELIVERY

Organizations have begun to discover the power of information, but they have barely scratched the surface of what will be possible over the next decade. Already new technologies are awaiting widespread implementation that will have as big an impact on information delivery as the Internet has had over the past decade. New technologies will not only change what is possible to do with information, but they will also change how we view the world of information delivery and how organizations and individuals behave with respect to information. Some of the most important future directions for information delivery include the following:

- *An Internet for physical information.* Wireless communications and radio frequency identification (RFID) product tags will soon enable organizations and industries to track individual physical objects (e.g., cans of beans, car parts) as they move through the supply chain. Already, Walmart is conducting large-scale trials of this technology with two hundred of its major suppliers. Within a few years, RFID will replace the Universal Product Code (Langton 2004). And this is just the beginning. As these technologies become more sophisticated, organizations will be able to track and remotely monitor the status of everything from the freshness of lettuce between the field and the store to the location of hospital supplies. Even though this technology is almost ready for prime time, most organizations are nowhere near ready to cope with making sense of such a large influx of information. This will be one of the biggest challenges of the coming decade (Smith and Konsynski 2003).

- *Networkcentric operations.* The growth of standardized communication protocols, network devices, and high-speed data access will soon make it possible to collect, create, distribute, and exploit information across an extremely heterogeneous global computing environment in the near future. Value will be derived from the content, quality, and timeliness of the information moving across the network. Three critical elements must be in place to achieve this goal:

  1. *Sensor grids.* These should be coupled with fast and powerful networks to move raw data. Small sensory devices and computers will be connected to other machines to evaluate and filter a wide variety of information, highlighting areas and anomalies to which the organization should pay attention.
  2. *High-quality information.* Along with sophisticated modeling and simulation capabilities and display technology, high-quality information will provide dramatically better awareness of the marketplace. This will enable more targeted strategies, support more focused logistics, and provide full-dimensional understanding of the business environment at a variety of locations and levels.
  3. *Value-added command and control processes.* Superior information will make the loop of control shorter, effectively taking decision rights away from competitors and providing rapid feedback to frontline workers.

  These new capabilities will be developed to achieve information advantage (i.e., to know more) and execution advantage (i.e., to produce less friction between parts) over competitors.

- *Self-synchronizing systems.* Traditionally, leaders have worked from the top down to achieve synchronization of effort. When decisions are made in this way, each iteration of the "observe-orient-decide-act" (OODA) loop takes time to complete with the front line passing information up the hierarchy until enough is accumulated to make a decision, which is then passed back down the organizational levels to the front line to take action. In contrast, we know that complex processes organize best from the bottom up (e.g., markets, the Internet, and evolutionary processes), and they are efficient and can allocate resources without high overheads. Such self-synchronization eliminates the lags in the OODA loop and accelerates responsiveness.

  In the future, information in organizations will be used to promote self-synchronization to enable a well-informed workforce to organize and coordinate complex activities from the bottom up without management involvement. Systems themselves will be designed to self-monitor and self-correct in a similar way. This will dramatically change the role of management and how organizations operate. Leaders will set the "rules of engagement" but be much less involved in the day-to-day running of their organizations (Smith and Konsynski 2003).

- *Feedback loops.*   A central feature of self-synchronization is the creation of closed feedback loops that enable individuals and groups to adjust their behavior dynamically. Researchers are already demonstrating the power of feedback to change behavior (Zoutman et al. 2004). Feedback mechanisms built into systems will require the creation of new metrics for monitoring such individual behavioral factors as transparency, information sharing, and trust. Similarly, organizations will incorporate feedback loops into their operations, continually scanning and evaluating and adapting strategies, tactics, and operations. With the right technology and infostructure (i.e., appropriately organized and managed information), different views can be brought to bear on a situation and adjustments made on an ongoing basis.

- *Informal information management.*   Finally, organizations have a significant unmined resource in the informal information kept by knowledge workers in their own personal files. Information-delivery mechanisms of the future will look for opportunities to organize and leverage this information in a variety of ways. For example, software exists today that "crawls" people's address books to find who in an organization knows people whom others in the organization want or need to contact. Other types of software analyze personal files to compile an expertise profile of individual employees. The field of informal information management is still in its infancy, but it is certainly one to which IT managers should pay attention because it represents a huge, untapped pool of information.

Conclusion

Information delivery in IT is an idea whose time has finally come. IT practitioners and experts have been talking about it for years, yet only recently has the business truly begun to understand the power and the potential of information. New technologies and channels now make it possible to access and deliver information easily and cheaply. As a result, information is now being used to drive many different types of value in organizations, from business intelligence to streamlined operations to lower administrative costs to new ways to reach customers. The challenges for IT are huge. Not only does effective information delivery require IT to implement new technologies, but it also means that IT must develop new internal nontechnical and analytic capabilities. Information delivery makes IT work much more visible in the organization. Developing standard data models, integrating information into work processes, and forcing (encouraging) business managers to put the customer/employee/supplier first in their decision making involve IT practitioners in organizational and political conflicts that most would likely prefer to avoid. Clearly, IT managers are front and center of an information revolution that will completely transform how organizations operate. The changes to date are just the tip of the information iceberg. In the not-so-distant future, new streams of information will be flooding into the organization, and IT managers will be expected to be ready with plans for its use. For the first time, senior business executives are ready to hear about the value of information. IT managers should take advantage of this new openness to develop the skills and capabilities they will need to prepare for the coming deluge.

References

Bednarz, A. "Air Force Streams Electronic Paperwork." *Network World* 20, no. 2 (January 13, 2003): 17–18.

Brohman, K., and M. Boudreau. "The Dance: Getting Managers and Miners on the Floor Together." Proceedings of Administrative Sciences Association of Canada, 2004.

Cebrowski, A., and J. Garstka. "Network-centric Warfare: Its Origin and Future." *Naval Institute Proceedings* 124, no. 1 (January 1998).

Corcoran, M. "Taxonomies: Hope or Hype?" *Online* 26, no. 5 (September/October 2002): 76–78.

Davenport, T., J. Harris, D. De Long, and A. Jacobson. "Data to Knowledge to Results: Building an Analytic Capability." *California Management Review* 43, no. 2 (Winter 2001): 117–38.

Gilchrist, A. "Corporate Taxonomies: Report on a Survey of Current Practice." *Online Information Review* 25, no. 2 (2001): 94–102.

Kaplan, R., and D. Norton. *The Balanced Scorecard.* Boston: Harvard Business School Press, 1996.

Kaplan, S. "Emerging Technology." *CIO Magazine,* January 15, 2002.

Kettinger, W., and D. Marchand. "Dell Inc.: Working an Informated Opportunity Zone." Unpublished case study prepared for the Society for Information Management's Advanced Practices Council, Chicago, May 2004.

Kettinger, W., K. Paddack, and D. Marchand. "The Case of Skandia: The Evolving Nature of I/T Value." Unpublished case study prepared for the Society for Information Management's Advanced Practices Council, Chicago, January 2003.

Kontzer, T. "Search On." *Information Week* 923 (January 20, 2003): 30–38.

Langton, J. "Wal-Mart Tests Alternative to Bar Code." *Globe and Mail,* June 3, 2004.

Lee, H., T. Kim, and J. Kim. "A Metadata Oriented Architecture for Building Datawarehouse." *Journal of Database Management* 12, no. 4 (October–December 2001): 15–25.

Li, Y., and W. Kettinger. "A Knowledge-Based Theory of Information: Clarifying the Relationship Between Data, Information, and Knowledge," Draft paper, Management Science Department, Moore School of Business, University of South Carolina, Columbia, 2004.

Marchand, D., W. Kettinger, and J. Rollins. "Information Orientation: People, Technology and the Bottom Line." *Sloan Management Review* Summer (2000).

McKeen, J., and H. Smith. *Making IT Happen.* Chichester, England: John Wiley & Sons, 2003.

Smith, H., and B. Konsynski. "Developments in Practice X: Radio Frequency Identification (RFID)—An Internet for Physical Objects." *Communications of the Association for Information Systems* 12, no. 19 (September 2003).

Smith, H., and J. McKeen. "The CIO Brief on Privacy." Kingston, Canada: The CIO Brief, School of Business, Queen's University, Kingston, Ontario, 2003.

Smith, H. A., J. D. McKeen, and T. A. Jenkin. "Exploring Strategies for Deploying Knowledge Management Tools and Technologies." *Journal of Information Science and Technology* 6, no. 3, 2009: 3–24.

Smith, H. A., J. D. McKeen, and C. Street. "Linking IT to Business Metrics." *Journal of Information Science and Technology* 1, no. 1 (2004): 13–26.

Varian, H., and P. Lyman. "How Much Information? 2000." Berkeley: University of California at Berkeley, School of Information Management and Systems, 2000. www2.sims.berkeley.edu/research/projects/how-much-info-2003 (accessed March 18, 2011).

Williams, S. "The Intranet Content Management Strategy Conference." *Management Services* 45, no. 9 (September 2001): 16–18.

Zoutman, D., D. Ford, A. Bassili, M. Lam, and K. Nakatsu. "Impacts of Feedback on Antibiotic Prescribing for Upper Respiratory Tract Infections." Presentation available from the authors (zoutman@cliff.path.queensu.ca), Queen's University, Kingston, Ontario, 2004.

Chapter 16

Master Data Management[1]

For at least three decades, IT planners have dreamed of creating an "intergalactic" data model that would provide their organizations with a set of fully integrated, high-quality data with which to work. From data dictionaries in the 1970s to data warehouses in the 1980s to Enterprise Application Integration (EAI) in the 1990s, the goal is laudable but has been practically impossible to achieve. There are simply huge challenges to surmount: poor data quality; synchronization issues; the politics of data ownership; the difficulties of agreeing on a single definition of every data item; legal and regulatory considerations, which appear to change constantly; getting the business to recognize the value of the work involved; and those old standbys—security, privacy and life cycle management.

The newest hot topic in IT is called master data management (MDM), and it is rapidly climbing the upward slope of the Gartner Hype Cycle (Thoo et al. 2008). One group defines MDM as follows:

> A set of disciplines, applications and technologies for harmonizing and managing the system of record and system of entry for the data and metadata associated with the key business entities of the organization. (White and Imhoff 2007)

MDM gets into the bits and bytes of data; it's not knowledge management or information management, which are of considerably more interest to business. Yet data management issues are the blocks with which effective information is built. We all know the saying "garbage in, garbage out." So is MDM an idea whose time has come? Or will it flounder because it's too big, too technical, and too expensive to get under control? And where does MDM fit with other current IT "hot" issues such as service-oriented architecture (SOA), business intelligence, content management, and data quality?

To address these questions, this chapter first outlines the business needs that MDM purports to address and defines what MDM is and is not. Next it looks at the "data ecosystem" and where MDM fits within it. Then, it outlines the value proposition for MDM and some of the challenges organizations face in defining a business case for it. The last two sections look first at some of the prerequisites that must be put in place before embarking on an MDM program and then describe "the data journey" of which MDM is only a part.

---

[1]Smith, H. A., and J. D. McKeen. "Master Data Management: Salvation or Snake Oil." *Communications of the Association for Information Systems* 23, article 4 (August 2008): 112–35. Reproduced by permission of the Association for Information Systems.

WHAT IS MDM?

MDM is either "the most overused IT buzzword," the exact meaning of which vendors have yet to agree on (Wailgum 2007), *or* it describes a discipline and technologies for developing a "consistent set of identifiers and extended attributes that describe the core entities of an organization"—that is, parties (e.g., customers, employees, and so on), places (e.g., locations, regions), or things (e.g., accounts, assets, products) (White et al. 2007), *or* possibly, something in between. MDM has been variously described as the following:

- "A wrapper concept for information management used by vendors" (one manager)
- "A means of centralizing key corporate data in order to provide consistent customer and product data across the business" (another manager)
- "Applications to create and maintain an integrated set of master data" (White and Imhoff 2007)
- Technologies that provide master data integration services (e.g., EAI, Extract Transform Load, Enterprise Information Integration) and master data stores and metadata repositories (White and Imhoff 2007)
- Not a technology but a modeling, mapping, and semantic reconciliation exercise that merges and resolves conflicting data sources and establishes a trusted, authoritative source of reference for commonly used information assets (White et al. 2007)
- A means of merging all disparate, conflicting records on customers or transactions into one authenticated master file (Yang 2005)
- A way to create a single unified view of the organization (Fisher 2007)
- Information management for core data (yet another manager)
- "A set of technologies to help enterprises better manage data flow, integrity and synchronization, plus a governance mechanism for enforcing data policies" (Wailgum 2007)

In short, as one manager noted, "MDM is a term that is overused and has multiple meanings. We must clarify what we mean by it." But, though the definition of MDM is vague, the problem it purports to solve certainly isn't. Here, there is general agreement that the data in most organizations is a mess, resulting from years of managing from a systemcentric perspective. "Most organizations have focused too narrowly on the systems side of the problem to the detriment of the data side" (Lee et al. 2006). One set of researchers described the situation facing organizations today as follows:

> The IT landscape is littered with legacy, packaged and developed applications, coupled with multiple data warehouses, and uncontrolled, unstructured data across the enterprise. This complex Web makes managing information as a strategic asset very difficult. (White and Genovese 2006)

As a result of several decades of developing data in silos, most organizations face a multitude of inconsistencies in data definitions, data formats, and data values, which make it next to impossible for an organization to understand and use its key data, such as information about its customers or products (Lee et al. 2006).

This problem has been exacerbated in recent years by a number of factors. First, technology's ability to store ever-increasing amounts of data has vastly outstripped the organization's ability to manage, analyze, and apply it (Davenport 2007). Second, by adding new "enterprise solutions" (e.g., ERP, CRM) to "manage data," organizations often unwittingly contribute to further data confusion. Many vendors have plugged some type of

> **Factors Increasing the Data Management Challenge**
> - Increasing storage capabilities
> - Layers of "enterprise" solutions
> - Multiple groups managing data
> - Ownership issues
> - Short term workarounds

MDM into their technology to create a "true view" of the enterprise, but this typically just adds new layers of complexity to the situation (Fisher 2007). Third, companies often try to solve the problem with makeshift structural solutions, which are ineffective at best and counterproductive at worst. One firm had fourteen different groups with some responsibility for generating master data (Flint 2004). Fourth, there are ownership issues. As one manager noted, "We've got tons of customer data spread around our organization, but the core teams are not willing to either govern it themselves or to give up ownership, so therefore this data is not managed." Another commented, "Our biggest obstacle is getting the line departments to pay attention. They hope IT can just make it happen and resist taking responsibility for data ownership." Finally, organizations are feeling pressures from the need to manage data globally, their desire to do trend analysis, increasing regulation demanding reconciled information, and more and more cross-functional systems development. Unfortunately, under pressure the easiest solution is often to develop "work-arounds"—that is, short-term solutions for each particular need, which do nothing to solve the long-term problem and drain resources away from addressing it (Lee et al. 2006).

In short, organizations want high-quality data, but they lack a roadmap to get there (Lee et al. 2006). MDM is being promoted as a means of developing such a roadmap—to focus companies on the job of creating a single view of their most important pieces of information in order to improve the accessibility of their most critical data (e.g., customers, products, employees). It is an initiative whose goal is to look at critical data in a cross-domain manner, achieve consistency, implement enterprisewide governance processes, and remove data silos (Friedman et al. 2006). Although technology may be needed to facilitate accessibility by unrelated applications, the focus group saw MDM as primarily a nontechnical data analysis and management activity focused on achieving consistency and quality so data can be used for multiple purposes. By emphasizing critical data, the hope is to make the task more manageable and ensure companies can at least understand who their customers, products, and suppliers are. Although MDM concepts are not new, they are a new twist on an old problem (White et al. 2006).

From the above discussion of what MDM is and is not, we can derive the following working definition:

> *Master data management (MDM) is an application-independent process that describes, owns, and manages core business data entities. It ensures the consistency and accuracy of these data by providing a single set of guidelines for their management and thereby creates a common view of key company data, which may or may not be held in a common data source.*

THE DATA ECOSYSTEM

The preceding definition represents a more focused approach to information management than typically has been used in the past, and hopefully, a more practical one. Rather than an "intergalactic" data model, the goal is to get companies to focus on the core data that really matter to them. Nevertheless, all too often, MDM is confused with a number of other important data and information management activities in the enterprise. Figure 16.1 clarifies where MDM fits into a "data ecosystem" by illustrating the other activities and technologies that are related to it. It is important to understand the relationships between the different entities in the ecosystem in order to recognize the work that must be done to make any MDM initiative successful and to integrate MDM into other concurrent information management activities within the organization.

IM Strategy and Principles

As we have noted elsewhere, information management is "the means to get above the fray and clarify how the enterprise will manage information as an integrated resource" (Smith and McKeen 2007). Unlike MDM, information management covers all forms of information needed and produced by the business, both structured and unstructured, and it addresses the complete information life cycle from acquisition or creation through organization, navigation, access, security, administration, storage, and retention. Because IM is not yet a separate organizational entity, many organizations are finding it essential to develop an enterprisewide framework that clarifies the policies, principles, roles, responsibilities, accountabilities, and practices for IM wherever it is done (Smith and McKeen 2007). Sometimes called enterprise information management, this function establishes the strategy for structuring, securing, and improving the accuracy, accessibility, and integrity of information assets (Friedman et al. 2006). Clearly, this

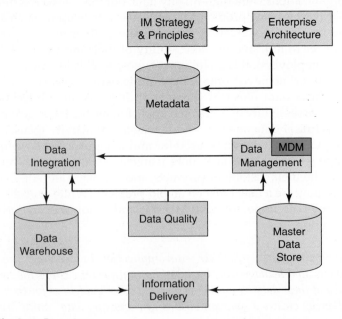

FIGURE 16.1 The Data Ecosystem

activity includes the core data addressed by MDM. However, while establishing essential and prerequisite guidelines for core data management, IM strategy and principles may be set at a higher level of the organization, on a broader scale, and by a different group of people. As such, it provides the context in which MDM is accomplished, but it does not do the work of master data management.

The outcome of the process will be the beginning of a metadata repository. It stores information definitions, standards for information use and change, and cross-references for all models, processes, and programs using a particular piece of information. The creation of a metadata repository for all data is a huge undertaking and, while highly valuable in the long run, it may not receive the necessary support from the business (Smith and McKeen 2007). Here again, MDM attempts to cut down the effort and increase the value of this work by focusing on core business data only.

Enterprise Architecture

Information management strategy and principles should be important contributors to an organization's enterprise architecture. Information and architecture should be as separate as possible, and information needs and qualities will clearly affect the processes of an organization. As they change, the organizational needs for (and uses of) data must be reflected in how data are managed and the information that is availabel about their uses (i.e., metadata). Again, establishing a dialogue and discipline for core corporate data first will have the highest value for the organization and biggest impact on process design (McKeen and Smith 2007).

Data Management

Data management is the process of applying information strategy and principles to individual data entities. It is the critical work of making decisions about data, often across organizational boundaries. It includes clarifying the roles and responsibilities for each piece of data and establishing proper protections and controls for change. Ideally, most organizations would like a "single version of the truth" for each data item. The reality today is that the typical legacy environment in many firms means that this is the long-term goal, and that in the short term there may be duplicate versions of the same or similar information used in different parts of the organization. These must be identified, managed, and synchronized where possible, and plans must be made to eliminate duplicates and variants over time (Smith and McKeen 2007).

Information stewards are responsible for data management. These businesspeople determine the meaning of information entities (e.g., customer) in addition to their business rules and contextual use. They should be responsible for the accuracy, timeliness, life cycle, and redundancy of the data about each entity. They also determine who may access data and provide guidance for the retention and deletion of information in accordance with regulatory and legal requirements. In addition, they make information about data availabel through the organization's metadata (Smith and McKeen 2007).

As a subset of the data management process, MDM focuses solely on a small number of core pieces of data, rather than all data. Focus group participants stressed that it is the management of core data that is at the heart of MDM. "MDM represents the processes and technologies used to create a single view of data," said one. Another noted that MDM is not an IT solution but a process and should not be seen as a quick fix like EAI. "Our vision is to create a single common data source that can be centrally managed to serve all business systems. To get there we need enterprise discipline." In short, "MDM is really only part of the overall data ecosystem," said a manager. "All parts of it must connect together in order for MDM to be effective."

Data Quality

Clearly, if an organization is going to create a single source for each of its core data entities, their quality is going to be of the utmost importance. Data quality has become increasingly important in recent years as organizations try to integrate and reconcile data from different parts of the enterprise for use in data warehouse, business intelligence, customer management, and compliance initiatives. "Our goal is clean, accurate data that will facilitate new business capabilities," said a manager. "You can't do any type of integration or data management without it." Without data quality, it is impossible to build trust or confidence in the data, and without this, user acceptance of any initiatives based on such data will be limited and benefits will not be achieved (Friedman et al. 2006). Improving data quality typically involves a number of exercises to reconcile differences in data definitions, data formats, data values, and data synchronization (Lee et al. 2006). A data quality effort therefore aims to ensure data are correct, complete, current, and consistent, while data management ensures it is in context and access to it is controlled (Davenport 2007). Although it is possible to have data quality without data management, it is not possible to have data management without data quality. MDM efforts therefore focus the costs and challenges of data quality on the most valuable data in the organization.

Data Integration

Similarly, data integration can occur without data management, but it is clearly highly desirable that the data management effort precede integration projects. At present many organizations use technologies such as EAI (McKeen and Smith 2003) to "translate" data from one function to another in order to achieve integration. Doing so adds extra steps to processing but can be effective in achieving an organization's short-term integration goals. However, as demands for integration increase and as more and more functions and applications use and modify the same pieces of data, the costs and complexity of such solutions mount, and the risk of creating and using poor-quality data on which to base business decisions increases. In the context of an MDM initiative, data integration serves two purposes, according to the focus group. First, it acts as an interim step toward achieving a single source of all key data, enabling data to be combined and collected in a data warehouse, which can then be used for a variety of information delivery and data analysis activities. "While a centrally managed single source of data is desirable," said a manager, "often hybrid models are more practical." Second, data integration is a necessary and practical step for those data that are not deemed to be core but which are created and updated by more than one application or business function.

The goal of data integration is to create a data warehouse that can be considered as a credible, trusted source of integrated information. "A data warehouse is not an authoritative source of data," explained one manager, "but it is moving in the right direction and can be used as a source for some types of work."

The goal of data management (or MDM) is to create the only authoritative source of information. Once MDM is in place, a master data store is created and all requests for these data are processed against it. Thus, a data warehouse is an after-the-fact reconciliation of data from a variety of sources, whereas a master data store is the source of information. Although both can be used for information delivery, the focus group stressed that decoupling data from applications through data management is the ideal. The costs and challenges of doing this explain why most companies have not made more progress with it.

THE MDM VALUE PROPOSITION

MDM is not an easy sell in organizations. "Eyes glaze over when you talk about it," said a manager. "We don't even use the term. Instead we talk about core data and the business capabilities that will result." Others agreed. "MDM is hard to sell on its own." "The vendors say 'Buy an MDM,' but it's not a technology; we need to put things in business terms." However, whatever it's called, there are clearly benefits to controlling the data mess that's present in most companies today. "If we can demonstrate these benefits," said a participant, "the business will sell itself on MDM."

But this has been tough to do in most organizations. "The business case for MDM is never compelling enough," complained one manager. Part of the reason may be the amount of effort required to yield benefits. Less complex and political initiatives, such as data cleansing and quality, can demonstrate payback within two years, but the lead time for making a difference with MDM is seen as five to ten years—much too long for most executives (Friedman et al. 2006).

Having a single source of a company's data provides obvious benefits:

- *Better information.*   Having "one version of the truth" and the ability to simply provide consolidated views of key corporate information is the holy grail of MDM (White and Genovese 2006). It addresses a central question of executives, shareholders and regulators that has regularly embarrassed IT: "What kind of company doesn't understand who its customers, products, and suppliers are?" (Fisher 2007). Having consistent information is seen as being important for improving compliance reporting, generating operational efficiencies, and achieving competitive differentiation. It also eliminates disagreements within the business about whose data is correct (Delbaere and Ferreira 2007; White et al. 2006). One manager noted, "Creating our common financial data took two and a half years and only happened because it was pushed through by the CFO, but now that we're down this road we can all see that there are tons of benefits." Among the focus group, regulatory compliance was seen as a big driver of MDM. "We're under incredible pressure to rationalize our data because of regulatory complexity. This is extremely hard to do without centralized data."

- *Cost savings.*   Although a variety of cost savings are attributable to MDM, most of the pain of poor data appears to be spread out across the organization, making the savings disparate and incremental, rather than large and obvious. Two main types of business cost can be avoided by improved data management (Lee et al. 2006). First are the costs caused by poor data quality (e.g., the need to verify data or poor decisions). Second are the costs caused by improving or assuring data quality (e.g., the effort to prevent, detect, or repair poor data). However, the focus group suggested that the cost savings argument was really a distraction and that the true value of MDM lay in improved business capabilities. What MDM does enable but does not create on its own is process simplification and the minimization of "handoffs" (Friedman 2006; White and Genovese 2006). Operational efficiencies are another indirect saving stemming from MDM since these are usually based on the availability of information (White et al. 2006). Thus, while cost savings will likely result from an MDM effort, they will not be large enough or clear enough to build a business case around.

- *Improved business capabilities.* Organizations are beginning to recognize that how they manage their key data is critical to their ability to improve agility and performance (Friedman 2006). Lack of trusted, quality information is widely seen as a strategic barrier inhibiting such capabilities as agility and competitive differentiation (White et al. 2006). Focus group members pointed out that data consistency is essential when dealing with partners and suppliers, particularly for global companies. "We want to move toward MDM because it will support flexibility," said one manager. "It facilitates globalization, acquisitions and divestitures, company reorganizations and product rebranding." Another noted how much easier it is to provide multilanguage support in an MDM environment with a single source of key corporate data. Participants also believed that it enables faster business transformation. "We can't predict the future, but we know it's going to change. Therefore, we have to make it easy to change," stated a participant. Finally, MDM makes it easier for companies to improve the customer experience. "Because there is only one source of data, we can develop stronger access controls, which ensure customer privacy. And because the data are more accurate, customers will be less frustrated when dealing with the company," explained another manager.

- *Improved technical capabilities.* There are also many benefits for IT in simplifying and streamlining data management and access. Eliminating data redundancy promotes the reuse and leveraging of corporate data and reduces the amount of work involved in providing business information (Friedman 2006; White and Genovese 2006). Locating key data in a single master data store helps avoid "spaghetti interfaces" and facilitates integration (White et al. 2006). MDM is also a prerequisite for the introduction of a services-oriented architecture (SOA) (Radcliffe et al. 2006). "The core capabilities of MDM are also significant advantages for SOA." said one manager. "The easiest services to provide are those which already have centralized data. For example, if you have to provide five different views of the customer, you could build five services, but this would destroy the value of SOA." Another added, "You can make a mess of SOA if you don't treat data properly." Other participants believe that MDM will help reduce IT costs through eliminating the need for unique applications and code and enabling a variety of sourcing options. "Once we have a single point of data, it doesn't matter where it is located; we can move databases around without the users even knowing," said one manager. They also suggested that there would be reduced IT work involved in preparing complex, and often conflicting, reports for auditors and regulatory bodies. In short, from the IT managers' point of view, MDM is an effort that will proactively address data quality and consistency and simplify integration and application development.

PREREQUISITES FOR MDM SUCCESS

There is broad agreement that the concept of MDM is an idea whose time has come, yet the fact remains that implementing it is "a brutal combination of bridging technological silos and brokering accords between corporate turfs" and has "daunting cultural, business process and technology components" (Wailgum 2007). Since the root of all data problems is in the processes and practices that create them, no software is going to magically solve data problems on its own (Fisher 2007). In fact, according to the focus group, technology often masks a myriad of problems by "papering over" significant issues. "We can provide the technologies, but unless the business has processes and workflow that will work with them, data management won't work," said one manager. "The real problem is the need to address the root cause of the data mess—that is, the functionality that creates it in the first place," said another.

Therefore, a successful MDM initiative must go back to the source: the core business processes and systems that create and update key company data. The focus group stressed that before any type of master data management can succeed, four prerequisites must be collaboratively addressed by the business and IT:

1. *Develop an enterprise information policy.* Because MDM will at some point become a highly political exercise, taking the time to articulate what the company policy is on core data and the key principles surrounding its management is essential (Friedman 2006; Wailgum 2007). Such a policy must delineate a number of principles around such issues as corporate data management objectives; data ownership and accountability; privacy, security, and risk management; the value of enterprise data; regulatory compliance; accommodating conflicting priorities; and policy effectiveness (Smith and McKeen 2005). As noted above, without such a context as a guideline, it is likely that the obstacles involved in any specific MDM project will prove to be insurmountable.

2. *Business ownership.* Although MDM is a collaborative effort and IT can provide considerable analytical skills for the work involved, determining what core data a company wants and what it will look like is fundamentally a business problem (Flint 2004). The focus group outlined several business roles and responsibilities that need to be undertaken in MDM work: executive sponsorship, business sponsorship, stakeholder involvement, data stewards (who work directly with the data definitions), and change management specialists. They stressed that all stakeholders must be involved in MDM or political problems will likely ensue. A key challenge is identifying a primary business owner for each piece of data. At the master entity level, it is likely that co-ownership or enterprise ownership will be needed with specific attributes owned by individual business units. Some firms have also established corporate data groups to "speak for the enterprise" and to predefine standards around data that "we eventually want to be in the core but are not yet built." Without a single business voice, extensive data governance is necessary to address the conflicting opinions that inevitably arise. One manager noted, "We

have fourteen hundred data managers, and they are each resistant to change; when you add in our suppliers' data, we can't get anything done."

3. *Governance.*   It is a challenge to get all stakeholders to agree on common definitions for the key data items they use daily (Wailgum 2007). Therefore, mechanisms must be created to resolve conflicts and make critical decisions at all levels. Changing core data often means changing business processes. Thus, MDM is ultimately a political and consensus-building effort (Fisher 2007). Nevertheless, because there are considerable technical impacts to data decisions, IT must be involved. Thus, a cross-functional and collaborative IT and business data governance process should be established (Davenport 2007; Delbaere and Ferreira 2007). Focus group members agreed wholeheartedly. "MDM can't be sustained without governance," said one. "We use a data roundtable to make decisions about data and understand their implications." However, they cautioned that the hard work of data management can't be offloaded to the governance group. "We still have a problem getting the business involved in this work," said one. "You almost need a catastrophe to get their attention." Research has found that companies need "extraordinary attention" to data management processes and governance in order for MDM to be successful (Davenport 2007). At Capital One, Davenport (2007) found that 25 percent of IT staff worked on data issues. This figure underscores the complexity and challenges involved in doing data management well, and the effort involved can be a major obstacle for both business and IT. Thus, there is still a temptation to "code around" data problems, said the focus group.

4. *The Role of IT.*   Although data management is first and foremost a nontechnical problem, technology and IT staff themselves have several important roles to play in MDM. First, IT analysts have the skills to develop a data strategy, model the data and undertake the work involved in defining its parameters and context (Fisher 2007). Second, effective technology is essential for maintaining data models and metadata repositories (Delbaere and Ferreira 2007). Third, IT staff will be needed to identify which applications use which data and where it comes from, tracking its flow from application to application. "Often the business doesn't know its data, and IT staff have to figure out how everything fits together," said one manager. Fourth, as the MDM initiative proceeds, IT will have to manage the synchronization of data and data cleansing projects as well as develop short-term tactical or hybrid solutions that help move the company toward its ultimate goal of a single source of master data. "Most organizations already have some form of master data in their legacy applications," explained a manager. "Therefore, any new MDM environment will have to coexist and synchronize with legacy components because you simply can't up and replace them overnight." Even though these are important responsibilities, the focus group stressed again that MDM work cannot be delegated to IT alone or it will fail.

THE DATA JOURNEY

When asked whether MDM was "salvation or snake oil," most of the focus group felt the question was moot as the realities of today's organizations make MDM almost impossible to deliver. MDM is certainly not a single project, they stressed, but it is instead a journey toward a single source of high-quality data. "MDM is a continuous effort," said one manager. "It's going to go through several cycles before we get it right." "MDM is a multiyear strategic initiative," said another. "There are different stages of capability to go through," said a third. A participant outlined the stages he sees in his organization:

- *Stage 1.* "I admit I've got data, so I'll inventory it."
- *Stage 2.* "Let's identify what data is used by which applications and processes. I'll discuss the role of information and ownership."
- *Stage 3.* "Let's limit how much data we move around and maybe design some information exchange requirements."

Clearly, more stages are involved, but the organization had only journeyed this far.

Best practice with MDM, it is generally agreed, is to start small and evolve toward a more holistic data strategy and roadmap (White et al. 2007). "This helps the organization understand where MDM fits into their current business strategies and priorities," said a manager. And repeated communication is essential. Many data management initiatives fail because of a lack of understanding of what can be expected on the journey, resulting in discouragement and lack of perseverance (Lee et al. 2006). In fact, executives are often unaware of the data problems that exist and/or believe that IT can handle them without additional time and resources. "Data problems tend to be masked by layers of subordinates. The CEO receives the data [he requested] and remains unaware of the cost of producing it" (Lee et al. 2007). Thus, it is extremely important to ensure that the challenges of effectively managing data are repeatedly presented to senior executives and supported by analysis.

The focus group discredited the current "solutions" offered by the vendor community for MDM. "Their different perspectives about MDM are conflicting and exasperating," said one manager. "Every vendor has its own approach, and they don't mesh," stated another. However, the managers grudgingly admitted that vendors can sometimes get funding for an MDM initiative when IT can't. "They're successful because they speak only about the business benefits," said a manager. "They present MDM as a 'silver bullet' while all IT talks about are the difficulties involved." Technology is not the place to start the MDM journey, they all agreed. "Sometimes manual processes can be simpler and cheaper than an IT solution in the beginning," one pointed out.

One vendor solution that some participants did find helpful was using an industry-based data model to kick-start their internal modeling initiative. "The problem we're having is limiting our scope," admitted one manager. "Every piece we set out to deal with leads to other problems. You need to have a holistic solution, but it's important not to 'boil the ocean'." Having a roadmap is therefore helpful, even if it changes over time (White et al. 2007). "If you know where you're going, you can watch for 'data pain points,'" said a participant, "and use these for opportunities to justify some data work."

One manager recommended doing information maturity assessments as a starting point. "We're still very applicationcentric and we need to become more information focused." In most organizations, information is still considered a byproduct of applications and processes, not as an asset in its own right. A manager summed up IT's dilemma stating, "We must raise the bar gradually on how we manage information; otherwise we will simply implode with the weight of so many layers of data and limited time and resources."

Conclusion

MDM is not a new idea. It is a wrapper for concepts and issues that have been plaguing IT for several decades. To this extent it is snake oil because there is no silver bullet when it comes to getting your data house in order. Right now, it appears that many vendors are jumping on the MDM bandwagon, and they are creating a lot of confusion as a result. Both the focus group and researchers agree that although MDM makes sense in theory, it is a discipline that many organizations may not be ready to adopt. Thus, before leaping blithely into an MDM initiative, it is wise to do your homework: identify some small, quick wins; focus your effort on one type of data; learn with the business how to manage the process; and develop and continually revisit an information roadmap and strategy. For companies willing to put in the effort, there is evidence that MDM delivers significant benefits, but each company will have to decide whether they're willing to pay the price to clean up their data detritus or wait until the next "big idea" comes along, complete with salesmen, and hope that it will be their salvation.

References

Davenport, T. Competing on Analytics: The New Science of Winning. Boston: Harvard Business School Press, 2007.

Delbaere, M., and R. Ferreira. "Addressing the Data Aspects of Compliance with Industry Models." *IBM Systems Journal* 46, 2 (2007): 319–35.

Fisher, T. "Demystifying Master Data Management." *CIO Magazine,* April 30, 2007.

Flint, D. "How Nestle Reduced Errors in Its Management of Master Data." Gartner Inc., ID Number: G00123052, November 16, 2004.

Friedman, T. "Key Issues for Data Management and Integration, 2006." Gartner Inc., ID Number: G00138812, March 30, 2006.

Friedman, T., D. Feinberg, M. Beyer, B. Gassman, A. Bitterer, D. Newman, et al. "Hype Cycle for Data Management, 2006." Gartner Inc., ID Number: G00140057, July 6, 2006.

Lee, Y., L. Pipino, J. Funk, and R. Wang. *Journey to Data Quality.* Cambridge, MA: The MIT Press, 2006.

McKeen, J. D., and H. A. Smith. *Making IT Happen: Critical Issues in Managing Information Technology.* New York: John Wiley & Sons, 2003.

———. "The Emerging Role of the Enterprise Business Architect." *Communications of the Association for Information Systems* 22, article 14 (February 2008): 261–74.

Radcliffe, J., A. White, and D. Newman. "How to Choose the Right Architectural Style for Master Data Management." Gartner Inc., ID Number: G00142610, September 8, 2006.

Smith, H. A., and McKeen, J. D. "Information Delivery: IT's Evolving Role." *Communications of the Association for Information Systems* 15, article 1 (February 2005): 197–209.

———. "Information Management: The Nexus of Business and IT." *Communications of the Association for Information Systems* 19, article 3 (January 2007), 34–46.

Thoo, E., T. Friedman, M. Beyer, D. Feinberg, A. Bitterer, T. Bell, et al. "Hype Cycle for Data Management, 2008." Gartner Inc., ID Number: G00158593, July 9, 2008.

Wailgum, T. "Master Data Management: Truth Behind the Hype." *CIO Magazine,* May 18, 2007.

White, A., and Y. Genovese. "Your Business Process Platform Needs and Enterprise Information Strategy." Gartner Inc., ID Number: G00139332, April 6, 2006.

White, A., D. Newman, D. Logan, and J. Radcliffe. "Mastering Data Management." Gartner Inc., ID Number: G00136958, January 25, 2006.

White, A., J. Radcliffe, and D. Newman. "The Important Characteristics of MDM Implementation Style." Gartner Inc., ID Number: G00146840, May 11, 2007.

White, C., and C. Imhoff. "Master Data Management: Creating a Single View of the Business." Master Data Management, June 21, 2007. archive.cnblogs.com/a/791414 (accessed March 18, 2011).

Yang, S. "Master Data Management." *Baseline, New York* 1, no. 45 (June 2005): Z.000.

MINI CASE
Information Management at Homestyle Hotels[2]

It had seemed like a good idea at the time, Ben Garrett thought glumly: just collect all information on the availability of each hotel room and provide it to management over the company's intranet. It would help each hotel manager adjust room rental rates according to whether or not they wanted to stimulate more reservations. Connect the information in that system to the online reservation system and voila!—a dynamic, real-time, sense-and-respond application able to automatically raise rates when demand was high and reduce them when demand declined. Now everyone was up in arms about it, and Ben, information services director for Homestyle Hotels, was uncomfortably deep in alligators.

Homestyle Hotels Inc. was formed as the result of a merger of Lifestyle Resorts and Home-Away Hotels and was now one of the larger chains in North America. When Ben joined the company five years ago, it was still in the dark ages, technologically speaking. Each individual hotel operated as its own little fiefdom with its own collection of hardware and software—some state of the art and some outrageously outdated. Each hotel manager was responsible for purchasing his or her own technology, and as a result almost every hotel had a different reservation system. Thus, it was impossible for the company to provide a consistent "look and feel" to its services, and this made branding and marketing extremely difficult. For example, some hotels knew if a customer had stayed with it before; others didn't. Furthermore, even basic information on such things as operating costs, occupancy, and profit and loss took at least a month to compile at each hotel. Then the central accountants took another six weeks to reconcile and adjust the numbers, so each quarterly report was almost a full quarter out of date before it arrived on the executives' desks.

"This is unacceptable," declared Fred Gains, the gruff COO who had hired him. "If we're going to compete as a national brand, we need better information to manage the chain as an enterprise."

That had been Ben's initial mandate—to rejuvenate and consolidate the firm's IT—so senior management would have better control over branding, marketing, and operations and, hence, make the chain more profitable. His top priority at the beginning had been common financial statements. "We can't move forward unless we know where we stand at present," he had told the IT steering committee members, who had agreed and had only just committed to spending money on an ERP system to replace the company's hodgepodge of financial applications. For the next three years, everybody had sweated. While Ben and his IT colleagues struggled to implement the ERP and get each hotel to adapt to common processes and financial information, the business was struggling to stay afloat after the most recent economic downturn. It had survived—barely—but the company had taken three years to turn a profit again. Everyone felt lucky to have lasted longer.

Last year the purse strings had finally loosened. Ben had begun to develop a true information strategy with his business partners in the resorts and hotels, and it wasn't too long before they bumped up against their first major problem. They had all been sitting in the conference room talking about the reservation system when it had dawned on Ben that everyone was talking about a different "client." The resorts worked largely with travel packagers. The bulk of their business came from tours and conferences; to them, a *client* was a tour company. The people actually occupying rooms were known as *customers*. The Home-Away people, on the other hand, dealt for the most part directly with the people who stayed in their rooms, whom they called *clients*. As a result, everyone had a different idea of what information should be gathered and how it should be used.

[2]Smith, H. A., and J. D. McKeen. "Information Management at Homestyle Hotels," #1-L05-1-010. Queen's School of Business, November 2005. Reproduced by permission of Queen's University, School of Business, Kingston, Ontario.

That problem had been resolved, but it had taken a lot of table thumping to get there. Defining the requirements was turning out to be a nightmare. Every piece of information—from customer name and address to room rates and descriptions—was in a different format or meant something slightly different to each hotel manager. Room rate, for instance, might reflect the "rack" rate, discount rate, seasonal rate, preferred rate, loyalty rate, corporate rate, or association/affiliate rate. Then there was the information that people were collecting in the so-called unused data fields. For example, certain hotel managers had adopted a series of codes to indicate whether a client was a problem or was suspected of stealing or destroying hotel property. They had put these codes in a field that had originally been designed to capture customer preferences. Other managers collected detailed information in online contact directories about customer preferences. Still others used an industry standard rating structure to denote common preferences (e.g., no-smoking rooms).

Now the project had deteriorated into a series of long, boring meetings about the meaning of each and every piece of information each hotel collected and attempts to define the collection in a data dictionary. Enthusiasm for the effort had declined with each meeting, and positions were hardening. The Lifestyles people said their information needs were *different* from those of the Home-Away people and that they should have a different system altogether. "How could these people have let their data get into such a mess?" Ben wondered for the ten-thousandth time. They were spinning their wheels on this one—*still* in the requirements definition phase—and everyone (Ben included) was unsure how they were going to pull this one off. "Maybe we should just *buy* a generic industry information application and force the hotels to comply with its data definitions," he mused aloud. Picking up the phone, he called the architecture team to set up a meeting to evaluate the availabel options.

The following week found Ben, his information architect, the technical architect, and Marie Bonheur, the recently promoted director of the Home-Away division (and the only businessperson who had seemed remotely in touch with the reality they were facing), sitting around a conference table sharing glossy brochures extolling the latest and greatest technology. Like most other large corporations, Homestyle Hotels was inundated with vendors flogging a great assortment of IT solutions. The ERP system had forced the company to adopt technical standards, and it was the technical architect's job to weed out any nonstandard hardware and software before it came to the attention of anyone else in the organization. Information standards were quite another matter, of course. As this project had shown, Homestyle was all over the map in that respect, with the single exception of the financials.

The choice soon came down to two software applications. Each provided a data dictionary, which users were allowed to tweak. Each provided a Web-enabled interface, which could be modified to show different views of the information. Each one would interface with Homestyle's ERP. There were some differences, however. Hotels Confidential (HC) appeared to provide exceptionally good information protection for customers. This was important when customers were connecting online, although Homestyle already had a firewall and virus scanners. Clear Reservations (CR) appeared to have better content management functions. "We absolutely need to get the business involved in this decision," said Bonheur. "We need their support if we're going to get their agreement to change their business processes."

"Let's set it up," said Ben. "But let's put a little effort into this first. Let's get the vendors to use some of our data. That will make it easier for the business to see what it's getting."

The two vendors, hungry for a huge national sale, had agreed to work with a select team to provide a live test involving a single hotel. The Home-Away Chicago had been chosen because it was the one that had adopted one of the industry standards that both HC and CR supported. After a few glitches, they were able to connect with the Chicago systems, and with a little "duct tape and a few toothpicks," they had managed to populate the prototypes on the salesmen's PCs. A room had been booked for the day. Each vendor had an hour to demo its wares; after that there would be a question-and-answer period, followed by discussion and, they hoped, a decision.

The HC team was already assembled when Ben, the architects, and Bonheur and her business colleagues, including Fred Gains, arrived. After brief introductions and the obligatory joke about how they hoped HC would find a "home" with

Homestyle, Ray Santos got down to work, bringing up a huge version of the HC software on the movie-size screen at the end of the room. Stressing each of its features in turn, Santos emphasized the points he had been told were his software's strengths. "With HC, complete privacy for your customers is built in. Our password protection has four levels so that different employees only see the information they *need* to do their job. Only system administrators can get at *all* the data. Security is built in. Hotel managers control and adjust room availabilities by monitoring their occupancy rates as often as they wish. They also have the ability to select and adjust key productivity metrics so they can better manage their individual costs. Individual staff members get specialized screens, depending on their role in the hotel. For example, housekeeping can see the unmade rooms and guest preferences, and reservations sees contact and credit card information. Once a week, the system collects a set of standard metrics that are made availabel to everyone in the executive suite."

The CR team arrived soon after Santos and his associates had been ushered out. After another stale joke about the company's name, Sandra Sawh began her presentation. She, too, focused on the CR software's strengths. "With our product lines, we can offer you cradle-to-grave information management," she stated. She then went on to demonstrate the functions it provided for data mining and for drilling down into data. "For example, every executive can see the status of every hotel on this color-coded chart every day. If the chart shows a hotel is red, he or she can click on the hotel and see its metrics, and if they still want more, they can look at the hotel's occupancy rates and compare them with previous years and months. Naturally, we offer a full Web-based interface for customers, but we believe your existing information security should be enough to protect it. As for privacy, we also offer role-based screens."

After seeing CR's team out, Ben opened the floor to discussion. Gains started, "Well, there's no question in *my* mind that we have to go with CR.

That's the only way our head office will get some control over the individual hotels. Right now none of us knows *what* they're doing until it's too late! I'm going to call the manager in Chicago as soon as this presentation's over; I want to know why his availability rate is so high!"

Bonheur spoke up. "Well, I must say I have to disagree with you, Fred. HC is definitely the better product for the way we work. Let's look at the facts. We have two different *types* of hotels that work in two different ways, *and* they're spread out all over North America. The hotel managers are in the best position to know their customers and to know what the information *means*. They can't have head office down their throats every time they turn around!"

Ben looked around. Half of the people in the room were nodding in agreement with Bonheur. The other half had their arms crossed and hostile expressions on their faces. No guesses which ones were going with Gains and which with Bonheur. This had *seemed* like a good idea at the time, Ben thought, but it was now clear that the controversy lay not just in *what* information was collected, but also in *who* got it and *when*. World War III was about to begin. Just then a temporary reprieve arrived in the form of the waiter with their lunch trolley. "Ladies and gentlemen, I suggest we all take a lunch break and come back at this issue in an hour. While you're doing that, I'll see if I can pull together some recommendations that will make sense for our organization."

Discussion Questions

1. Does it make good business sense to integrate across the different lines of business represented by Lifestyle Resorts and Home-Away Hotels? What exactly would you integrate (beyond financial information) and why?
2. Outline a process for Homestyle to follow in order to decide between the two software options (i.e., HC and CR)? What selection criteria would you use? Who should make the decision?

MINI CASE
Innovation at International Foods[3]

Josh Novak gazed up at the gleaming glass-and-chrome skyscraper as he stepped out of the cab. "Wow!" he thought to himself. "I've hit the big time now." The International Foods Group (IFG) Tower was a Chicago landmark as well as part of the company's logo, which appeared on the packages of almost every type of food one could imagine—breakfast cereals, soft drinks, frozen pizza, cheese, and snack foods, to name just a few. Walking into the tower's marble lobby, Josh could see displays of the company's packaging from its earliest days, when its dairy products were delivered by horse and wagon, right up to the modern global entity it had become.

After signing in with security, Josh was whisked away to the 37th floor by an efficient attendant who walked him down a long hall of cubicles to a corner office overlooking Lake Michigan. On the way, Josh passed display photos of the company's founder, old Jonas Wilton looking patriarchal, and several of the family scions, who had grown the company into a major national brand before the IPO in the 1980s had made IFG a public company. Josh, having "Googled" the company's history last night in response to this summons, knew that IFG was now the largest purveyor of food products the world had ever known. While many decried the globalization of the food business, IFG kept right on growing, gobbling up dozens of companies each year—some because IFG wanted to stomp on its competition and others because it wanted their good ideas.

Josh's own small company, Glow-Foods, a relative newcomer in the business, was fortunately one of the latter, but Josh was a little puzzled about this command performance. After all, he himself wasn't anyone important. The owners of the company all received multiple millions and were sticking around—as per contract—during the transition. The next level, including Josh's boss, had mostly jumped ship as soon as the "merger" was announced. "This isn't my thing," drawled Nate Greenly over beer one night at the local pub. "Corporate America isn't going to let us stay as we are, no matter what they say. Get out while you can," he advised. But Josh, with a freshly minted MBA in his pocket, thought differently. And so here he was, walking into the CIO's office hundreds of miles away from the cramped loft in Toronto where Glow-Foods was headquartered.

As the office door swung open, two people dressed in "power suits" turned to meet him. "Uh oh, I'm not in Kansas anymore," thought Josh as he mentally reviewed his outfit of neatly pressed khakis and golf shirt, which was a big step up from his usual attire of jeans and a T-shirt. A tall man with silver hair stepped forward with his hand held out. "You must be Josh," he boomed. "Welcome. I'm John Ahern, and this is my associate, Tonya James, manager of IT marketing. Thanks for coming today. Please, have a seat." Josh complied, slinging his backpack over the corner of the leather chair while taking in the rich furnishings of the office and the panoramic view. After a bit of chitchat about the weather and the prospects of their respective baseball teams, John pulled out a black leather folder.

"Well, we won't keep you in suspense anymore, Josh. As you know, when we took over Glow-Foods we decided to completely align our processes, including IT. It doesn't make any economic sense to run separate data centers and applications, so we already have a team in place to transfer all your hardware and software to our centralized corporate systems over the next month. We'll be replacing your Macs with PCs, and everyone will get training on our ERP system. We're going to keep a small team to deal with the specifically Canadian issues, but other than that we see no need for an IT function in Toronto any

[3]Smith, H. A., and J. D. McKeen. "Innovation at International Foods," #1-L09-1-002. Queen's School of Business, December 2009. Reproduced by permission of Queen's University, School of Business, Kingston, Ontario.

more. Josh nodded glumly, thinking about his friends who would be losing their jobs and all the fun they'd had during those all-nighters brainstorming new ways to help Glow-Foods products go "viral." *Nate was right,*he thought glumly. *They don't really get us at all.*

"That said," John continued. "We are very impressed with the work you and your team have done in using social networking, mashups, and multimedia to support your marketing strategy. Your ability to reach the under-thirty demographic with technology is impressive." He turned to Tonya, who added. "Here at IFG, we have traditionally marketed our products to women with children. We have a functional Web site—a place where customers can find out about our products and where to buy them. More recently, we've added their nutritional content, some recipes, and a place where customers can contact us directly with questions, but it's really unidirectional and pretty dry."

Josh nodded in agreement with this assessment. The difference in the two companies' approaches was night and day. Although not everything they had tried at Glow-Foods had worked, enough of it had succeeded that demand for the company's products had skyrocketed. Young adults and teens had responded en masse to the opportunity to post pictures of themselves drinking their Green Tea Shakes in unusual places on the Glow-Foods Web site and to send a coupon for their favorite Glow-Foods product to a friend. Serialized company mini-dramas popped up on YouTube and viewers were asked to go online to help shape what happened to the characters—all of them using Glow-Foods products extensively. Contests, mass collaboration in package design, and a huge network of young part-time sales reps linked through Facebook all contributed to making the brand hip and exciting—and drove sales through the roof.

John adjusted his French cuffs. "We want to tap into the youth and young adult market with IT, and we think you're the one who can help us do this. We're going to give you a team and whatever resources you need right here in Chicago. With our global reach and much larger budgets, you could do great things for our company." John went on to outline a job offer to Josh that sent tingles down his spine. "I really have hit the big time," he thought as he signed the documents making him a team

manager at IFG at a salary that was almost double what he was earning now. "I can't wait to get started."

Six weeks later he was being walked down the same hall by Tonya, now his immediate boss, and into her office, a smaller version of his with a window looking onto another high-rise. "What's next?" he asked. "I've booked a meeting room for you to meet your new team at ten-thirty," Tonya explained. "But before that, I want to go over a few things with you first. As the manager of IT Marketing, I am personally thrilled that we're going to be experimenting with new technologies and, as your coach and mentor at IFG, I'm going to make it my job to see that you have the resources and support that you need. However, you may find that not everyone else at this company will be as encouraging. We're going to have some serious obstacles to overcome, both within IT and with the larger company. It will be my responsibility to help you deal with them over the next few months as you put your ideas together. But you need to know that IFG may have different expectations of you than Glow-Foods. And you may find you will get a better reception to your ideas if you look a bit more professional." Josh winced and nodded. He'd already ramped up the wardrobe for his first day with a sports jacket, but clearly he needed to do more. "Finally, I'd like you to come up here every Friday afternoon at four o'clock to go over your progress and your plans. My schedule is usually fully booked, but if you have any questions you can always send me an e-mail. I'm pretty good at getting back to people within twenty-four hours. Now let's go meet your new team. I think you'll be happy with them."

An hour later Josh and his new team were busy taking notes as Tonya outlined their mandate. "You have a dual role here," she explained. "First, I want you to work with Ben here to develop some exciting new ideas for online marketing. We're looking for whatever creative ideas you have." Ben Nokony was the team's marketing liaison. Any ideas would be vetted through him, and all proposals to the individual product teams would be arranged by him. "Second, I need you to keep your eyes open and your ears to the ground for any innovative technologies you think might work here at IFG. These are our future, and you're our vanguard." Josh glanced around at his team, an eclectic group. They seemed eager and enthusiastic, and he knew they were talented, having had a say in choosing them. With the exception of Ben, all were new to IFG, experienced in using a variety of new media, and under thirty years old. They were going to do great things together, he could see.

The next couple of weeks were taken up with orientation. Ben introduced each of the major product divisions to the team, and everybody had come back from each meeting full of new possibilities. Tonya had also arranged for the team to meet with the chief technology officer, Rick Visser, who was in charge of architecture, privacy and security, risk management, and the technology roadmap. Rick had been pleasant but cool. "Please remember that we have a process for incorporating new technology into our architecture," he explained as he handed over a thick manual of procedures. "In a company our size we can't operate without formal processes. Anything else would be chaos." The team had returned from that meeting full of gloom that their ideas would all be shot down before they were even tried. Finally, they had met with the IT finance officer. "I'm your liaison with corporate finance," Sheema Singh stated. "You need to work with me to develop your business cases. Nothing gets funded unless it has a business case and is approved through our office."

Finally, having dragged some chairs into Josh's eighteenth-floor and marginally larger cubicle and desk, the team got down to work. "This is ridiculous," fumed Mandy Sawh, shuffling her papers on her lap. "I can't believe you need to book a conference room two weeks in advance around here. Who knows when you need to get together?" "Okay, team, let's settle down and take a look at what you've got," said Josh. One by one, they outlined their preliminary ideas—some workable and some not—and together they identified three strong possibilities for their first initiatives and two new technologies they wanted to explore. "Great work, team," said Josh. "We're on our way."

The problems began to surface slowly. First, it was a polite e-mail from Rick Visser reminding them that access to instant messaging and Facebook required prior approval from his group. "They want to know why we need it," groused Veejay Mitra. "They don't seem to understand that this is how people work these days." Then Ben got a bit snippy about talking directly to the product teams. "You're supposed to go through me," he told Josh's team. "I'm the contact person, and I am

supposed to be present at all meetings." "But these weren't 'meetings,'" Candis Chung objected. "We just wanted to bounce some ideas around with them." Next, it was a request from Sheema to outline their proposed work, with costs and benefits, for the next fiscal year—beginning six months from now. "Can't we just make up a bunch of numbers?" asked Tom Webster. "We don't know how this stuff is going to play out. It could be great and we'll need lots of resources to scale up, or it could bomb and we won't need anything." Everywhere the team went, they seemed to run into issues with the larger corporate environment. Tonya was helpful when Josh complained about it at their Friday afternoon meetings, smoothing things over with Rick, helping Josh to navigate corporate procedures, and even dropping by to tell the team they were doing a great job.

Nevertheless, Josh could sense his own and everyone else's frustration as they prepared for their first big project review presentation. "They want us to be innovative, but they keep putting us in a straight-jacket with their 'procedures' and their 'proper way to go about things,'" he sighed to himself. Thank goodness, the presentation was coming together nicely. Although it was only to the more junior executives and, of course, John and Rick, he had high hopes for the vision his team was developing to get IFG out and interacting with its customers.

"And in conclusion, we believe that we can use technology to help IFG reach its customers in three new ways," Josh summarized after all of his team members had presented their ideas. "First, we want the company to connect directly with customers about new product development ideas through an interactive Web site with real-time response from internal staff. Second, we want to reach out to different communities and gain insights into their needs and interests, which in turn will guide our future marketing plans. And third, we want to implement these and other ideas on the 'cloud,' which will enable us to scale up or down rapidly as we need to while linking with company databases. Any questions?"

There was a moment of stunned silence, and then the barrage began. "What's the business value of these initiatives?" asked Sheema. "I can't take them upstairs to our finance committee meeting without a clear commitment on what the benefits are going to be." Ben looked nonplussed. "We don't really know," he said. "We've never really done this before, but we like the ideas." "I'm concerned that we don't bite off more than we can chew," said John thoughtfully. "What if these customers don't like the company or its products and say bad things about us? Do we have any procedures for handling these types of situations?" "There's definitely a serious risk to our reputation here," said Rick, "but I'm more concerned about this 'cloud' thing. We haven't even got cloud in our architecture yet, and this plan could make company intellectual property availabel to everyone in cyberspace!" Sheema spoke again. "I hate to mention this, but didn't we do something like this community project about ten years ago? We called it knowledge management, and it flopped. No one knew what to do with it or how to handle the information it generated." On and on they went, picking holes in every part of every idea as the team slumped lower in their seats.

Finally, Tonya stood up. "I'd like to thank you all for raising some legitimate and important concerns," she said. "And I'd like to thank Josh and his team for some fine work and some excellent ideas. Marketing was looking for creativity, and we have delivered on that part of our mandate. But now we have a more important job. And that is innovation. Innovation is about more than good ideas; it's about delivering the best ones to the marketplace. We're in a new world of technology, and IT can't be the ones to be saying 'no' all the time to the business. Yes, we need to protect ourselves, and we don't want to throw money at every half-baked idea, but we've got to find a way to be open to new ideas at the same time. We know there's value in these new ideas—we saw it work at Glow-Foods. That's why Josh is here. He has a proven track record. We just have to find a way to identify it without taking too much risk."

The room sat in stunned silence as Tonya looked from one to the other. At last, John cleared his throat. "You're right, Tonya. We want creativity and innovation, and we need a better way to get it than we have now. I think what we need is a process for creativity and innovation that will help us overcome some of the roadblocks we put in place." As Josh mentally rolled his eyes at the thought of yet another process, Tonya replied. "I think you're partially right, John. Processes do have their place, but we also need some space to play with new ideas before we cast them in concrete. What I'd like to do over the next two weeks is speak with Josh and his team and each of you and then develop a plan as to how we can, as an IT department, better support innovation at IFG."

Discussion Questions

1. In discussion with Josh, Tonya foreshadows "some serious obstacles to overcome." Describe these obstacles in detail.
2. How can Josh win support for his team's three-point plan to use technology to help IFG reach its customers?

MINI CASE
CRM at Minitrex[4]

Georges Degas, Director of Sales at Minitrex, looked at his salesman with concern and sympathy as the man described another sales call where he had been made to look unprofessional! It was bad enough that he didn't know that the company he'd just phoned was already a Minitrex customer, but being told that he was the third caller this week from Minitrex was horrible. "I'd be better off with a Rolodex and handwritten notes than this system," he grumbled.

To keep track of customer information, salespeople use the Customer Contacts system, the brainchild of Degas's boss, Jon Bettman, VP of marketing. Bettman's position was created eighteen months ago in an effort to centralize sales and marketing activities at Minitrex. The sales and marketing team is responsible for promoting and selling an array of products to its customers. There are two distinct product lines, each developed by a separate division (insurance and financing) that also provides after-sale customer service. The idea behind having a department dedicated to sales and marketing was to create opportunities for cross-selling and up-selling that didn't exist when salespeople were tied to just one of the company's product categories.

The insurance division, led by Harold Blumfen, VP of insurance, is a major profit maker for Minitrex. Blumfen's group is divided into industry-specific teams whose goals are to develop deep industry knowledge and design short-term insurance products to meet clients' needs. Irascible and brilliant, Blumfen believes that computers are good for billing and other accounting functions but cannot replace people for customer knowledge and support. His division uses a credit administration system (developed more than twenty years ago) to track customer billings and payments and a general management system to keep track of which products a customer has bought and what services the customer is entitled to. Both are fundamentally back-end systems. The industry teams keep front-end customer knowledge in their own documentation and in their heads.

The mission of the financing division is to provide business sectors with financing services that are competitive with those of the big banks. As with the insurance division, its products and customer service are designed and delivered through its own industry-specific teams. However, unlike Blumfen, the VP of financing, Mariella Hopkins, is an IT enthusiast. Hopkins joined Minitrex about four years ago after a successful banking career. Her mandate, which she has undertaken with alacrity, was to "combine big banking services with small company flexibility." To do this, her division funded the development of a management business center application, which acts as an online customer self-service system. Customers can obtain statements and financing online and often can get credit approved instantly. Customer-service representatives use the same basic system, with additional functionality, to track customer transactions and to provide customer support as needed.

"The company is always promising better systems, "thought Degas," but when it comes down to it, no one can agree on what to do. Being customercentric seems to depend on whose view of the customer is being used. Meanwhile, salespeople can't do their jobs properly. Just imagine what our customers think!"

Bettman has been trying to get the company to see the importance of having timely, accurate, and integrated customer information without much success. To give his sales force a better way to keep track of sales prospects, he developed his Customer Contacts system, which schedules sales calls on a periodic basis and provides mechanisms for generating and tracking new leads; it also forms the basis on which the marketing department pays the salespeople's commissions. Real-time information on sales by product, salesperson, and region gives Bettman and his team excellent feedback on how

[4]Smith, H. A., and J. D. McKeen. "CRM at Minitrex," #9-L05-1-002. Queen's School of Business, January 2005. Reproduced by permission of Queen's University, School of Business, Kingston, Ontario.

well their centralized marketing strategies are performing. For purposes of invoicing and servicing the accounts, the Customer Contacts system also feeds data into the insurance and financing divisions' systems after sales are made.

"I'll see what I can do about this," Degas had promised his frustrated salesman, knowing that it would take a miracle to improve the situation. "I'll speak with the director of IT today and get back to you."

Degas put in a call to Denny Khan, Minitrex's long-suffering director of IT. Khan, who reported to the CFO, was outranked by Bettman, Blumfen, and Hopkins. To his surprise, Khan answered the phone right away. "I was just leaving for lunch," he explained. "What can I do for you?"

As soon as Degas began to explain what had happened that morning, Khan cut him off. "I know, I know. But the VPs would say, 'Our systems work fine for our needs, so why change them? We have a lot more urgent IT needs to spend our money on.' Blumfen doesn't want to spend a nickel on IT and doesn't want to have to work with Hopkins. Hopkins is open to collaboration, but she doesn't want to compromise her existing system, which is working well. And Bettman can't do anything without their cooperation. Furthermore, none of them will assign dedicated business staff to help us put together a business case and requirements. Their line is 'We don't have the budgets for this. Of course, we'll answer IT's questions, but it's their job to give us the systems we need.'"

"I see the same attitude in our business activities," agreed Degas. "Our sales force often doesn't know what services the business teams are providing to the customers. I don't see how management can expect to make informed decisions when they're not sharing basic information. Isn't there some way we could at least get common customer data—even if we use the data in different ways? And surely, with each unit identifying, prioritizing, and paying for IT opportunities, the duplication of support services must cost an arm and a leg."

"Sure," Khan agreed, "but each unit developed its own terminology and specialized data items over time, so these only work for *their* systems. Sharing is impossible unless everyone agrees on what information everyone needs about our customers. I'd like to see something done about this, but when I take it to the IT prioritization committee, it always seems to get bumped off the list. To the best of my knowledge, there has never been an effective business case to improve CRM. And anyway, I don't own this issue!"

"You're probably right, but I'm not sure how to go about this," said Degas. "Let me think about it and get back to you."

Discussion Questions

1. Explain how it is possible for someone at Minitrex to call a customer and not know (a) that this is a customer and (b) that this is the third time this week that they had been called.
2. Outline the steps that Bettman must take in order to implement CRM at Minitrex. In your plan be sure to include people, processes, and technology.

Chapter 17

Developing IT Capabilities[1]

IT professionals are usually the best in the organization when it comes to business process re-engineering. Why is it, then, that the IT group often has some of the most "under-engineered" processes in the company? It's true. IT is great at looking at business processes in other parts of the organization but not as comfortable looking at how its own work gets done. (Gomolski 2004)

This observation has not been lost on senior IT executives. They are the first to admit that they may not have standard, verifiable, and high-performing capabilities across the IT department. Furthermore, today's competitive environment is driving these same executives to provide guaranteed levels of service at reduced costs. This can be achieved only by enhancing the way in which IT work is done. As a result, IT executives are investigating revamping their internal IT capabilities as a vehicle to reduce IT costs, gain efficiencies, and improve the quality of their service in order to reap enhanced benefits from the IT investment.

This chapter explores how companies are managing and developing their internal IT capabilities and looks at how IT capabilities are identified, how people's skills are mapped onto these capabilities, and what outcomes can be expected from a focus on capabilities. The first section offers some definitions to clarify the discussion and describes the perceived value of focusing on IT capabilities within organizations. Then it presents a five-step framework for developing and managing IT capabilities.

WHY FOCUS ON IT CAPABILITIES?

In IT, terms such as *competencies, capabilities, skills, resources, services, experiences, processes, attitudes, procedures,* and even *methods* are often used interchangeably. Therefore, it is important to clarify the terminology surrounding capability management:

- *Capability.* This is the ability to marshal resources to affect a predetermined outcome. Portfolio management, for instance, is the capability to manage a set of IT applications as a logical whole.

---

[1]McKeen J. D., H. A. Smith, and S. Singh, "A Framework for Enhancing IT Capabilities." *Communications of the Association for Information Systems* 15, article 36 (May 2005): 661–73. Reproduced by permission of the Association for Information Systems.

- *Competency.* This is the degree of proficiency in marshalling resources to affect a predetermined outcome. Thus, a capability indicates your ability to do something, whereas competency reflects how good you are at doing it.
- *Processes.* These are well-defined activities within capabilities. Portfolio management, for instance, includes the following processes: business case development, project prioritization, resource allocation, performance benchmarking, and portfolio analysis.
- *Procedures and methods.* These are "how to" or step-by-step instructions for implementing a process.

Why focus on IT capabilities? Rockart et al. (1996) argue that there is a direct linkage between IT capabilities and organizational value and identify eight imperatives that IT organizations must fulfill to support the organization's strategic thrusts. Ross et al. (1996) also see a direct relationship between IT capabilities and organizational value in specific IT assets that collectively guarantee long-term competitiveness for organizations. Combining these findings with their own work on IT leadership and outsourcing, Feeny and Willcocks (1998) suggest that the development of nine core IT capabilities is necessary for IT organizations to meet the three enduring challenges of uniting business and IT vision, delivering IT services, and designing an IT architecture. These IT capabilities are as follows:

1. *Leadership.* Integrating IT effort with business purpose and activities.
2. *Business systems thinking.* Envisioning the business process that technology makes possible.
3. *Relationship building.* Getting the business constructively engaged in IT issues.
4. *Architecture planning.* Creating a coherent blueprint for a technical platform that responds to current and future business needs.
5. *Making technology work.* Rapidly achieving technical progress by one means or another.
6. *Informed buying.* Developing and managing an IT sourcing strategy that meets the interests of the business.
7. *Contract facilitation.* Ensuring the success of existing contracts for IT services.
8. *Contract monitoring.* Protecting the business's contractual position, current and future.
9. *Vendor development.* Identifying the potential added value of IT service suppliers.

Other important IT capabilities include governance, business management, and skills management. Although it is difficult to prove that the existence of any or all of these IT capabilities result in organizational value, there is a strong sense that enhanced IT capabilities improve the chances of successfully converting IT investments into measurable outcomes for the organization. According to Weill (1989), successful IT investments are the result of "conversion effectiveness." Hence, these core IT capabilities could collectively be considered to constitute conversion effectiveness.

A FRAMEWORK FOR DEVELOPING KEY IT CAPABILITIES

If the existence of key capabilities enables IT investments to be successfully converted to organizational value, then it logically follows that we need strategies for building these IT capabilities. Based on their experience, participants suggested that organizations

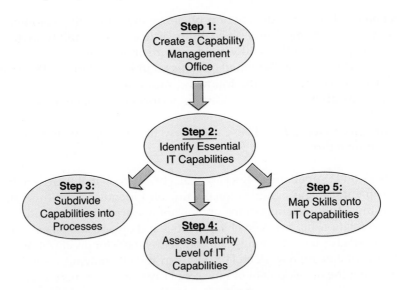

FIGURE 17.1   A Framework for Developing Key IT Capabilities

should have a framework to identify, develop, and manage key IT capabilities. The framework that emerged is depicted in Figure 17.1. Each step in this framework is described in the remainder of this chapter.

Step 1: Create a Capability Management Office

The first step for organizations is the creation of a set of activities, structures, policies, and governance principles to advance the development of their IT capabilities. To accomplish this task, many firms create a "capability management office." Not only is this office the focal point for capability development and management (i.e., steps 2 through 5), but its creation signals the importance IT senior management attaches to this activity. Although most managers agreed that this was an important activity if IT capabilities were to improve, there was significant variation among organizations in the group as to how they actually carried out this step.

One company created an entity called the "capability support group," which had the overall responsibility for the enhancement of IT capabilities. Another company formed an internal group called the "capabilities council" to investigate current practice within IT as part of a companywide ISO initiative. However, the capabilities management office is configured, at a minimum it was agreed that it should administer the following activities:

- Define and assign responsibility for all capabilities.
- Develop strategies for the development of these capabilities.
- Ensure that adequate resources and funding are provided to develop them.
- Secure software support for these activities.
- Adopt a continuous capability improvement approach.
- Develop organizational training plans.
- Report the status of organizational capability performance.

It was also strongly recommended that this office, while assuming overall responsibility for the development of a capabilities management program, assign individual responsibilities to individual capabilities. According to one manager, "Making a capability someone's 'day job' is more effective at generating improvement than addressing it as a sideline or trying to grow it by committee."

Step 2: Identify Essential Capabilities Aligned with Business Goals

Each IT organization should go through the exercise of identifying its essential capabilities and linking them with business goals. However, these capabilities shouldn't be aligned too closely with current business practices. According to one manager, "Capabilities should be less functional and focus more on the outcomes that the organization needs to be able to create." This argues against simply adopting an existing list of core capabilities such as those suggested by Feeny and Willcocks (1998). Group participants felt that there was significant value in deriving one's own list . . . or at least in tailoring an existing list to suit one's particular goals. Identifying capabilities is an introspective analysis of the key activities that IT must execute effectively. It forces management to examine key business directives, not just IT challenges, and to establish priorities. This is a trip well worth taking. In some cases this exercise can bring IT much closer to the business and actually enhance alignment.

Despite the obvious linkage with the business, in practice identifying essential capabilities is largely an internal IT exercise. As a result, there is a tendency for the identification of key capabilities to result in a list that is much more *IT-speak* than *business-speak.* For instance, capabilities might be couched in terms of level of service, fail-soft mechanisms, solution delivery, and help desk provisioning. Such a list would be easily recognized by IT professionals while being somewhat obscure to their business counterparts. Participants argued that measures should be taken to ensure that the resulting essential capabilities be tied as closely as possible to the business—starting with the language.

Following are two lists of capabilities. Firm B has adopted a set of capabilities that is remarkably devoid of IT terminology and, as a result, could apply to a line of business as easily as it applies to IT.

Firm A

1. Skills Regeneration
2. Enterprise Architecture
3. Shared Services Governance & Development
4. Development Methodology
5. Project Initiation and Investment Management
6. Business Process Definition & Change Management
7. Infrastructure Alignment & Crisis Control
8. Partner Management & Outsourcing

Firm B

1. People Management
2. Strategy and Planning
3. Portfolio Management

4. Resource Management
5. Solution Delivery
6. Service Management
7. Asset Management

Another company (Firm C), after identifying a set of capabilities, realized that it was not tied closely enough to the business. It feared the situation where IT could demonstrate high competence on specific capabilities while the business faltered. As a result, it revisited its capabilities, earmarking those that explicitly tied it to the business. This exercise resulted in the identification of twelve capabilities, of which five were classified as "business enablement"; the other seven were classified under the headings of "IT utility" and "business operations." The company decided to depict these capabilities as a wheel (see Figure 17.2) to reinforce their dynamic nature as well as their mutual interdependence.

It is interesting to note that Firm C identified "IT Competencies & Culture" as a capability. This is an explicit recognition that the definition and management of IT capabilities are themselves capabilities! Another obvious difference with Firm C is the level of detail. This begs the question of how many capabilities there should be. Within the

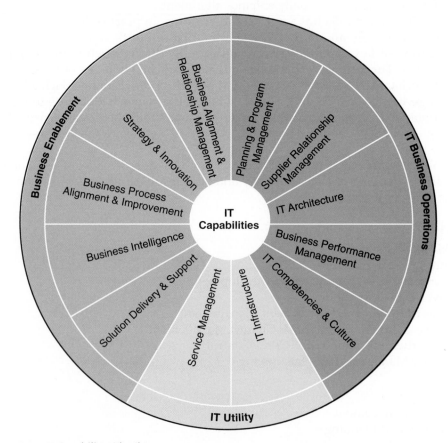

FIGURE 17.2 IT Capability Wheel

focus group, the number of capabilities ranged from seven to twelve, which is probably a good working range. More than twelve would become too granular, and fewer would be overly generic and would risk losing focus and definition.

Step 3: Subdivide IT Capabilities into Key Processes

Once key capabilities have been identified, the next step is to subdivide them into processes. The result of this step should be a set of well-defined activities that can be measured and managed. A set of well-articulated processes enables organizations to evaluate their overall performance with respect to key capabilities. "Portfolio management," for instance, is a capability that is difficult to measure. "Business case development," however, is a well-defined component process of portfolio management, and performance on this process can be measured. Using the seven capabilities identified by Firm B above, Table 17.1 shows how these were subdivided into forty clear processes.

In the absence of accepted methodologies for subdividing capabilities into processes, managers offered some advice based on their experience. One suggested starting with such basics as configuration/capacity management, IT asset management, procurement, or vendor management. Another suggested starting with service delivery, where there are well-identified activities such as service-level agreements, application life cycles, and quality assurance. Gomolski (2004) suggests a different approach: to focus on the "pain points" within the organization. For instance,

> if your staff is still responding to end-user requests in an ad hoc fashion, you'll want to look at your request management processes. Or if you find that basic information about IT capabilities isn't getting out to your internal customers, you'll want to focus on your communications processes. Maybe IT planning is weak, or budget estimates fail to hit the mark.

The approaches in Table 17.1 are inside-out approaches—that is, they focus on internal capabilities to distill component processes. There is also the outside-in approach, which takes advantage of the fact that there are external sources of well-defined IT processes already in existence. Perhaps the best-known source is the Software Engineering Institute (SEI) at Carnegie Mellon University with its capability maturity model (CMM) for software development. Other popular IT process frameworks used by some participants are the IT Infrastructure Library (ITIL) and CobiT (Control Objectives for Information and Related Technology). Other available frameworks less directly tied to IT are these:

- *Six Sigma.*   A methodology in which processes are continuously refined until their outcomes fall within an acceptable level of defects.
- *ISO.*   A set of standards focused on achieving uniform business processes.

Most focus group members felt that a combination of both the inside-out and the outside-in approaches is best. They recommended starting with an external source of processes to ensure that your list is comprehensive, then linking this list to your organization's key capabilities. It was suggested that adopting externally defined processes runs the risk of appearing foreign to IT staff, making it more difficult for them to develop an understanding and to foster feelings of ownership.

TABLE 17.1   Competencies and Processes

Capabilities	Processes
1 People Management	1. Recruiting and hiring 2. Coaching and motivating 3. Performance management and career planning 4. Identifying and developing talent
2 Strategy and Planning	5. Account management 6. External benchmarking 7. Strategy development 8. Architecture development 9. Business process influence/enabling 10. IT marketing
3 Portfolio Management	11. Business case development 12. Project/service prioritization 13. Portfolio investment determination 14. Resource investment/allocation 15. Performance benchmarking 16. Portfolio analysis
4 Resource Management	17. Staffing strategy development 18. Resource capacity management 19. Staff sourcing 20. Resource assignment 21. Budget management
5 Solution Delivery	22. Project management 23. Solution configuration 24. Solution development and integration 25. Architecture implementation 26. Solution verification and validation
6 Service Management	27. Solution release 28. Service-level management 29. Asset availability management 30. Asset capacity management 31. Incident management 32. Problem management 33. Change management
7 Asset Management	34. Asset inventory management 35. Asset affiliation management 36. Asset life cycle management 37. Security/permeability enforcement 38. Supplier relationship management 39. Lease/contract management 40. Knowledge management

Step 4: Assess the Maturity Level of IT Capabilities

The reputation for developing software plagued with deficiencies has put pressure on the IT industry over the years to convert software development from an art into a science. Arguably the most successful development to date beyond the systems development life cycle and structured design has been the CMM framework. Not only is this the most widely accepted standard in North America for software development, but many companies insist on dealing with only those IT shops that can demonstrate a level of quality management prescribed by it.

Today the CMM approach has been applied to many tasks in addition to software development. The five CMM levels for software development are as follows (CMMI Product Team 2002):

Level 1 (initial). Software development follows few rules. The project may go from one crisis to the next. The success of the project depends on the skills of individual developers. They may need to finish the project in a heroic effort.

Level 2 (repeatable). Software development successes are repeatable. The organization may use some basic project management to track cost and schedule. The precise implementation differs from project to project within the organization.

Level 3 (defined). Software development across the organization uses the same rules and events for project management. Crucially, the organization follows the same process even under schedule pressures, ideally because management recognizes that it is the fastest way to finish.

Level 4 (managed). Using precise measurements, management can effectively control the software development effort. In particular, management can identify ways to adjust and adapt the process to particular projects without measurable losses of quality or deviations from specifications.

Level 5 (optimizing). Quantitative feedback from previous projects is used to improve project management, using the measurement skills shown in level 4.

Some organizations have adopted these CMM maturity levels, and others have created their own levels. Obviously, the definition of each maturity level must be tailored to a specific IT capability as the preceding definitions pertain to only software development. One company uses the following six levels:

1. *No capability.* No observable value added.
2. *Aware.* Clear understanding of need.
3. *Developing.* Defined action plan and actively engaged.
4. *Practicing.* Demonstrating and achieving value.
5. *Optimizing.* Measuring results and investing in continual improvement.
6. *Leading.* Recognized proficiency and consistent value contribution.

As long as a capability's maturity levels are well defined, the group felt that the framework is immaterial. They agreed it is more important that the maturity levels used be effective in assessing capabilities and driving continuous improvement. It was widely recognized that not all processes within a capability would be at the same maturity level at any given point in time. What does it mean for a capability if some of its component processes are at a maturity level 2 while others are at a maturity level 3? Again, participants felt it is more important to have measurable improvement than uniformity across and within capabilities (i.e., all component processes at the same maturity level).

It is crucial that the capability management office has a snapshot of the overall maturity of each capability in order to focus attention correctly. At one company a team of senior managers reviews each capability's maturity to identify high-priority process improvement areas. They then develop a plan for the advancement of these highlighted processes, establish a timeline, and hold individuals accountable against delivery of these improvements. At another organization each capability is assigned an executive owner who is tasked to meet measurable objectives regarding the maturity of his or her capability. A quarterly report outlines the capability's current state and desired future state, timelines for deliverables, a description of overall progress and performance, and a gap assessment (HR, budget, information/tools/technology, schedule, quality, sustainability, and measurement). An interesting aspect of this report (reproduced in Table 17.2) is its use of verbal descriptions in combination with quantitative indicators. Furthermore, each capability owner must articulate what will be different about the organization's performance as a result of having this future state capability. This unique requirement forces each capability owner to link his or her capability directly to a distinct organizational outcome. This exercise has proven invaluable for ensuring that any improvements in the maturity of IT capabilities have associated business impact.

A key question for IT executives is this: What level of maturity should we target for our capabilities? There was general consensus that IT vendors are likely forced to "aim high," whereas other companies might be satisfied with midrange maturity. One manager suggested his company felt that the gain in moving from level 2 to level 3 on the maturity index was significant but the gain in moving higher was substantially reduced, suggesting that capability maturity levels could be subject to the "law of diminishing returns."

Step 5: Link IT Skills to IT Capabilities

The final part of the framework for IT capability development is the link between skills and capabilities. Failure to do this results in a significant disconnect between individuals and capabilities and a belief that individuals have little to do with capability maturity beyond that of following the dictates of established procedures. This is surprising in light of the fact that even a cursory glance at the processes within Table 17.1 reveals that many are very closely related to individual skills. Interestingly, only one company in the group had explicitly addressed this issue. Others, despite being well advanced in terms of identifying key processes and mapping them onto capabilities, chose indirect methods for tying individual skills to key capabilities.

Feeny and Willcocks (1998) identify three types of IT skills: (1) business, (2) technical, and (3) interpersonal. For each of their nine key capabilities, they then ranked the need for each type of skill as being high, medium, or low. An IT leadership capability, for example, requires a high level of business skills, a medium level of technical skills, and a high level of interpersonal skills. How these skills are to be developed, assessed, and linked to individuals and/or career development was not discussed.

TABLE 17.2   IT Capability Progress and Performance Chart

IT Capability	Portfolio management (for example)		
Operational Definition	Written description of this particular capability		
Owner	Name of the individual		
Future End-State Vision	Describes what will be different about IT	POD[1]	POA[2]
	performance as a result of having this future state	5	8
	capability	Impact	P&P[3]
	Process 1: Description	Medium	S
End-of-Year Deliverables	Process 2: Description	High	N
	Process n: Description	Low	S
Overall Progress and Performance	What did you plan to get done this quarter, and what did get done? If there is variance, what was the source of the error?		

Gap Assessment[4]	Process 1	Process 2	Process n	Explanation[5]
Human Resources	G	Y	G	***
Budget	Y	Y	G	***
Information/Tools/Technology	G	G	G	
Schedule	G	G	G	
Quality	G	R	Y	***
Sustainability	G	G	Y	***
Measurement	G	G	G	

[1]POD is "point of departure" (i.e., your current state) on a scale of 1 to 10.

[2]POA is "point of arrival" (i.e., your end state) on a scale of 1 to 10.

[3]P&P is "pace and performance," where "S" is satisfactory and "N" is not satisfactory.

[4]G = green, Y = yellow, and R = red.

[5]Detailed explanation required for any row that isn't "green."

The sole company that had addressed this issue created matrices to map individual skills (such as "conceptual thinking") against roles (such as "application architect" or "business analyst"). Different levels of these skills would be needed for particular roles; for instance, a level 3 business analyst would require greater mastery of each requisite skill than a level 2 business analyst. When roles are mapped to processes and processes are mapped to capabilities, it is possible to connect individuals to the capabilities that have been identified as being critical for the IT organization. Furthermore, these matrices make the progression between levels within roles explicit and, therefore, the focus of annual performance reviews and career advancement discussions. In this company a number of communities of practice had been established to further disseminate key skills throughout the organization (e.g., a business analyst community).

In those companies without direct links between individual skills and key IT capabilities, indirect links exist. In one firm, process improvement was made everyone's job. Anyone in the organization was encouraged to "raise a process improvement." These initiatives were maintained within a process improvement database and reviewed on a quarterly basis by a senior management team. This initiative successfully engaged individuals in terms of their awareness of the need for continuous process improvement. Another organization included organizational process skills within its internal training programs for job roles. This ensured awareness and knowledge of key processes across the IT department. The key point is that individuals must be connected (either directly or indirectly) to the process of developing IT capabilities.

Conclusion

The improvement of IT capabilities and processes within organizations will undoubtedly result in enhanced benefits from IT investments. Improving performance on such activities as solution delivery and asset management alone promises substantial results. When IT departments take the next step and identify those capabilities and processes that are vital to the business and develop those capabilities and processes to advanced maturity levels, the rewards promise to be dramatic. This chapter sets out a step-by-step framework that should assist IT organizations in reaching this goal.

References

CMMI (Capability Maturity Model Integration) Product Team. "CMMI for Systems Engineering/Software Engineering/Integrated Product and Process Development/Supplier Sourcing, Version 1.1, Continuous Representation (CMMI-SE/SW/IPPD/SS, V1.1, Continuous)." Carnegie Mellon University, Software Engineering Institute, Pittsburgh, PA, March 2002. www.sei.cmu.edu/pub/documents/02.reports/pdf/02tr011.pdf (retrieved March 20, 2011).

Feeney, D. F., and L. Willcocks. "Core IS Capabilities for Exploiting Information Technology." *Sloan Management Review* 39, no. 3 (1998): 9–21.

Gomolski, B. "It's Time to Re-engineer IT." *Computerworld* 38, no. 16 (April 19, 2004): 30.

Rockart, J. F., M. J. Earl, and J. W. Ross. "Eight Imperatives for the New IT Organization." *Sloan Management Review* 38 (Fall 1996): 43–55.

Ross, J. W., C. M. Beath, and D. L. Goodhue. "Develop Long-term Competitiveness Through IT Assets." *Sloan Management Review* 38 (Fall 1996): 31–42.

Weill, P. "The Relationship Between Investment in Information Technology and Firm Performance in the Manufacturing Sector." Unpublished Ph.D. thesis, Stern School, New York University, 1989.

Building Better IT Leaders
from the Bottom Up[1]

> For IT to assume full partnership with the business, it will have to take a leadership role on many vital organizational issues. . . . This leadership role is not the exclusive prerogative of senior executives—it is the duty of all IT employees. Effective leadership has enormous benefits. To realize these benefits, leadership qualities should be explicitly recognized, reinforced, and rewarded at all levels of the IT organization. This only happens when a concerted effort is made to introduce leadership activities into the very fabric of the IT organization. Leadership is everyone's job. (McKeen and Smith 2003)

This quote, taken from a book we published several years ago, remains as true today as it was then. But a lot has happened in the interim. Chiefly, in the chaotic business conditions of late, IT leadership development got sidetracked. The dot-com boom and bust soured many companies on the top-line potential of IT and refocused most CIOs on developing strong processes to ensure that IT's bottom line was kept under control (Roberts and Mingay 2004). But the wheel has turned yet again, and there is now renewed emphasis on how IT can help the organization achieve competitive differentiation and top-line growth (IBM 2004).

The many new challenges facing IT organizations today—achieving business growth goals, enterprise transformation, coping with technical and relationship complexity, facilitating innovation and knowledge development, and managing an increasingly mobile and virtual workforce—calls for strong IT leadership. Unfortunately, few IT leadership teams are well equipped for the job (Mingay et al. 2004). Traditional hierarchical structures with command-and-control leadership are not only ineffective, but they also can actually become a barrier to the development of a high-performance IT department (Avolio and Kahai 2003). New communications technologies are enabling new ways of leading and empowering even the most junior staff in new ways. These factors are all bringing senior IT managers around to a new appreciation for the need to build strong IT leaders at all levels of their organization.

This chapter looks first at the increasing importance of leadership in IT and how leadership is changing over time. Next, it examines the qualities that make a good IT leader. Then it looks at how companies are trying to develop better IT leaders at all levels in their organizations. Finally, it outlines the value proposition for investing in IT leadership development.

---

[1]Smith, H. A., and J. D. McKeen. "Building Better IT Leaders: From the Bottom Up." *Communications of the Association for Information Systems* 16, article 38 (December 2005): 785–96. Reproduced by permission of the Association for Information Systems.

THE CHANGING ROLE OF THE IT LEADER

The death of the traditional hierarchical organizational structure and top-down command-and-control leader has been predicted for at least two decades (Bennis and Nanus 1985), but it's dying a slow and painful death. Although much lip service is paid to the need for everyone in IT to be a leader, the fact remains that the traditional style of leadership is still very much in evidence, especially in large IT organizations.

There appear to be at least three reasons this is the case. First, until now, there has been very little pressure to change. As one manager pointed out, "We've been focusing on centralizing our IT organization in the last few years, and centralized decision making is inconsistent with the philosophy of 'Everybody leads.'" Those IT managers struggling with the complexities engendered by nonstandard equipment, nonintegrated systems, and multiple databases full of overlapping but inconsistent data can be forgiven if this philosophy suggests the "Wild West" days of IT, when everyone did their own thing.

Second, the organizations within which IT operates are largely hierarchical as well. Their managers have grown up with traditional structures and chains of command. They are comfortable with them and are uncomfortable when they see parts of their organization (e.g., IT) behaving and being treated differently by their CIO (Feld and Stoddard 2004). Senior management may, therefore, pressure IT to conform to the ways of the rest of the firm. This situation has recently become exacerbated by new compliance regulations (e.g., Sarbanes-Oxley, privacy legislation) that require hierarchical accountability and severely limit flexibility. Third, many senior executives—even within IT—find it difficult to relinquish control to more junior staff because they know they still have accountability for their results. Keeping a hands-on approach to leadership, they believe, is the only way to ensure work gets done right.

However, in spite of the remarkable tenacity of the hierarchical organization, there are signs that traditional leadership modes in IT are now in retreat, and there is a growing recognition that IT organizations must do a better job of inculcating leadership behaviors in all their staff (Bell and Gerrard 2004). There are some very practical reasons all IT staff are now expected to act as leaders, regardless of their official job titles:

- *Top-line focus.* CEOs are looking for top-line growth from their organizations (IBM 2004). New technologies and applications largely drive the enterprise differentiation and transformation efforts that will deliver this growth. Strong IT leadership teams are needed to take on this role in different parts of the organization and at different levels. They can do this effectively only by sharing clear goals and direction, understanding business strategy, and having the requisite "soft" skills to influence business leaders (Roberts and Mingay 2004).

- *Credibility.* No IT leadership initiatives within business will be accepted unless IT is consistently able to deliver results. This aspect of leadership is often called "management" and considered somewhat less important than transformational aspects of leadership, but IT's credentials in the latter rest solidly on the former (McKeen and Smith 1996; Mingay et al. 2004). No business organization will accept IT leadership in other areas unless it has demonstrated the skills and competencies to consistently deliver on what it says it will do. Furthermore, distinguishing between leadership and management leads to a dysfunctional IT organization. "Managers who don't lead are boring [and] dispiriting, [whereas] leaders who don't manage are distant [and] disconnected" (Mintzberg 2004). We have too often forgotten that top-level leaders are developed over time from among the rank and file, and that is where they learn how to lead.

- *Impact.*   There is no question that individuals within IT have more opportunities to affect an organization, both positively and negatively, than others at similar levels in the business. The focus group felt that this fact alone makes it extremely important that IT staff have much stronger organizational perspectives, decision-making skills, entrepreneurialism, and risk-assessment capabilities at lower levels. Today, because even small decisions in IT can have a major impact on an organization, it is essential that a CIO be confident that his or her most junior staff have the judgment and skills to take appropriate actions.

- *Flexibility.*   Increasingly, IT staff and organizations are expected to be responsive to rapidly changing business needs and help the enterprise compete in a highly competitive environment. This situation requires IT staff to have not only the technical skills required to address a variety of needs, but the ability to act in the best interests of the organization wherever opportunities arise. "We are no longer order takers in IT," stated one manager. "All our staff are expected to do the right things for our firm, even when it means saying 'no' to senior business management." Similarly, doing the right things involves being proactive. These actions take significant amounts of organizational know-how to pull off—leadership skills that rank-and-file IT staff are not noted for at present.

- *Complexity.*   The responsibilities of IT have grown increasingly complex over the past two decades (Smith and McKeen 2006). Not only is IT expected to be a high-performance organization, but it is also expected to offer change and innovation leadership, interact with other organizations to deliver low-cost services, chart a path through ever-growing new technology offerings, and offer content leadership (Mingay et al. 2004). The complexity of the tasks, relationships, knowledge, and integration of these now needed in IT means that leadership cannot rest in the hands of one person or even a team. Instead, new ways of instilling the needed skills and competencies into all IT staff must be found.

- *New technology.*   E-mail, groupware, instant messaging, and the Internet are all changing how leaders work—especially in IT. Increasingly, staff are virtual or mobile and their interactions with their managers are mediated by technology. At the same time, IT staff have much greater access more quickly to the same information as their managers. New technologies change how information is acquired and disseminated, how communication takes place, and how people are influenced and decisions made. Traditional forms of control are, thus, increasingly ineffective (Avolio and Kahai 2003).

All of these factors are driving the need to push leadership skills and competencies further down in the IT organization. Traditional hierarchies will likely remain in place to define authority and accountability, and *leadership* is likely to become increasingly situational—to be exercised as required by tasks and conditions (Bell and Gerrard 2004). With the demands on IT projected to be ever greater in the next decade, the need for more professional and sophisticated IT leadership is also greater than ever before (Feld and Stoddard 2004). In fact, many believe that IT leadership will determine "which [IT] organizations disappear into the back office of utility services and which ones build companywide credibility and drive business growth and ability" (Mingay et al. 2004).

WHAT MAKES A GOOD IT LEADER?

In many ways the qualities that make a good IT leader resemble those that make any other good leader. These can be divided into two general categories:

1. *Personal mastery.* These qualities embody the collection of behaviors that determine how an individual approaches different work and personal situations. They include a variety of "soft" skills, such as self-knowledge, awareness of individual approaches to work, and other personality traits. Most IT organizations include some form of personal mastery assessment and development as part of their management training programs. Understanding how one relates to others, how they respond to you, and how to adapt personal behaviors appropriately to different situations is a fundamental part of good leadership. One company's internal leadership document states, "Leaders must exercise self-awareness, monitor their impact on others, be receptive to feedback, and adjust to that feedback." "The higher up you get in IT, the greater the need for soft skills," claimed one member. Another noted the positive impact of this type of skills development: "It's quite evident who has been on our management development program by their behaviors." An increasingly important component of this quality for IT staff is personal integrity—that is, the willingness to do what you say you are going to do—both within IT and with external parties such as users and vendors.

2. *Leadership skill mastery.* These qualities include the general leadership skills expected of all leaders in organizations today, such as motivation, team building, collaboration, communication, risk assessment, problem solving, coaching, and mentoring. These are skills that can be both taught and modeled by current leaders and are a necessary, but not sufficient, component of good IT leadership (McKeen and Smith 2003).

However, good IT leaders are required to have a further set of skills that could be collectively called "strategic vision" if they are going to provide the direction and deliver the impact that organizations are expecting from IT. Because this is a "soft skill," there is no firm definition of this quality, but several components that help to develop this quality at all levels in IT can be identified, including the following:

- *Business understanding.* It should go without saying that for an IT leader to have strategic vision, he or she should have a solid understanding of the organization's current operations and future direction. This is well accepted in IT today, although few IT organizations have formal programs to develop this understanding. Most IT staff are expected to pick it up as they go along, mostly at the functional business process level. This may be adequate at junior levels, but being able to apply strategic vision to a task also involves a much broader understanding of the larger competitive environment, financial management, and marketing. "Our customers are now our end users. With our systems now reaching customers and reaching out horizontally in the organization and beyond, IT staff *all* need a broader and deeper appreciation of business than ever before," said one manager.

- *Organizational understanding.*   A key expectation of strategic vision in IT is enterprise transformation (Mingay et al. 2004). This involves more than just generating insights into how technology and processes can be utilized to create new products and services or help the organization work more effectively; it also involves the effective execution of the changes involved. IT professionals have long known that technology must work in combination with people and processes to be effective. This is why they are now expected to be experts in change management (Markus and Benjamin 1997; McKeen and Smith 2003; Orlikowski and Hofman 1997). But being able to drive transformation forward involves a number of additional skills, such as political savvy (to overcome resistance and negative influences), organizational problem solving (to address conflicting stakeholder interests), effective use of governance structures (to ensure proper support for change), and governance design (to work with partners and service providers) (Bell and Gerrard 2004; Kim and Maugorgne 2003). Because IT people come from a technical background and their thinking is more analytical, they typically do not have strong skills in this area and need to acquire them.

- *Creating a supportive working environment.*   Most IT work is done in teams. Increasingly, these teams are virtual and include businesspeople, staff from vendor companies, and members from different cultures. Motivating and inspiring one's colleagues to do their best, dealing with relationship problems and conflicts, and making decisions that are consistent with the overall goals of the organization and a particular initiative are the job of every IT staff member. Since much leadership in a matrixed organization such as IT is situational, an IT professional could be a leader one day and a follower the next. Thus, that person must know how to create a work environment that is characterized by trust, empowerment, and accountability. This involves clear communication of objectives, setting the rules of engagement, developing strong relationships (sometimes virtually), and providing support to manage risks and resolve issues (Anonymous 2004; Avolio and Kahai 2003; Bell and Gerrard 2004).

- *Effective use of resources.*   A good IT leader knows how to concentrate scarce resources in places where they will have the biggest payoff for the organization. This means not only making use of processes and tools to stretch out limited staff but also understanding where resources should *not* be used (i.e., saying "no"). In the longer term, using resources wisely may mean using job assignments and budgets to enhance people's capabilities, identifying and developing emergent leaders, and using reward and recognition programs to motivate and encourage staff (Anonymous 2004). Unfortunately, IT staff have often been spread too thinly, underappreciated, and not given time for training. Good IT leaders value their people, run interference for them when necessary, and work to build "bench strength" in their teams and organizations.

Leadership Styles Vary According to the Degree of Involvement of Team Members

- **Commanding.** "Do what I tell you."
- **Pacesetting.** "Do as I do now."
- **Visionary.** "Come with me."
- **Affiliate.** "People come first."
- **Coaching.** "Try this."
- **Democratic.** "What do you think?"

(after Roberts and Mingay 2004)

- *Flexibility of approach.* A good IT leader knows where and how to exercise leadership. "Skill mastery must be complemented with the ability to know when and where particular behaviors/skills are required and . . . how they should be deployed" (McKeen and Smith 2003). Even though this is true in all parts of the organization, leadership in IT can be a rapidly shifting target for two reasons. First, IT staff are well-educated, well-informed professionals whose opinions are valuable. "Good IT leaders know when to encourage debate and also when to close it down," said a manager. Second, the business's rapid shifts of priority, the changing competitive and technical environment, and the highly politicized nature of much IT work mean that leaders must constantly adjust their style to suit a dynamic topography of issues and priorities. "There is a well-documented continuum of leadership styles. . . . The most appropriate style depends on the enterprise style and the business and strategic contexts" (Roberts and Mingay 2004).

- *Ability to gain business attention.* A large component of IT leadership is focused not on the internal IT organization but outward toward all parts of the business. One of the biggest challenges for today's IT leaders is the fact that the focus of their work is more on business value than on technology (Mahoney 2004). The ability to motivate business executives, often in more senior positions, to lead business transformation and to gain and maintain executive attention is central to establishing and maintaining IT credibility in an organization (McDonald and Bace 2004). A good IT leader knows how to position his or her contribution in tangible, business terms; how to interact with business leaders; and how to guide and educate them about the realities of IT use. "Bringing value to the business is a very important trend in IT leadership," stated one participant.

IT leaders will need more or fewer of these qualities, depending on the scope and type of their work. Obviously, IT staff responsible for sourcing will need a different mix of these skills than will those with an internal IT focus or those with a business focus. They will also be more important the higher one moves in the management hierarchy. Nevertheless, these are skills that IT organizations should endeavor to grow in all their staff from the most junior levels. Since these skills take time and practice to develop and are in increasing demand, senior IT managers should put concrete plans in place to ensure that they will be present when needed.

HOW TO BUILD BETTER IT LEADERS

Everyone agrees that fostering leadership skills throughout all levels of IT is important to IT's future effectiveness (Bell and Gerrard 2004; McKeen and Smith 2003; Mingay et al. 2004; Mintzberg 2004). However, the reality is that leadership development is very hit and miss in most IT organizations. Over the past five years, many formal leadership courses have been cut or scaled back substantially because of cost-control initiatives. When offered, most IT leadership programs limit attendance to managers. Few organizations have articulated a comprehensive program of leadership development that includes other initiatives besides training.

Leadership development in IT is not as simple as sending a few handpicked individuals on a training course. In fact, formal training may be one of the *least* effective

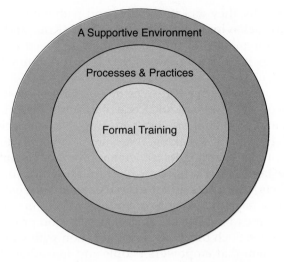

FIGURE 18.1 Effective Leadership Development Involves More Than Training

(and most expensive) aspects of building better IT leaders (Kesner 2003). Any comprehensive leadership development program has three layers (see Figure 18.1). The first, most important, and probably most difficult one is an environment within which leaders at all levels can flourish. It is often suggested that leaders, like cream, will naturally rise to the top regardless of the conditions in which they work. The reality is that more and better leaders are created when organizations have a supportive process for developing them that is widely understood. What's needed is "a culture that nurtures talented managers, rather than one that leaves them to struggle through a Darwinian survival game" (Griffin 2003). There is general agreement on what constitutes this type of culture:

- *Well-articulated and instantiated values.* Values guide how staff should behave even when their managers aren't around. They provide a basis for sound decision making (Stewart 2004). "If you're going to push leadership down in the organization, you have to push values down as well," stated one manager. Others noted that senior IT leadership should primarily be about forming and modeling values, not managing tasks. Values are especially important now that staff are more mobile and virtual (Cascio and Shurygailo 2003). A strong value system is crucial to bringing together and motivating a large, diverse workforce and helping staff act in ways that support the company's brand and values. Unfortunately, although many organizations have values, they are often out of date or not modeled by management (Stewart 2004).
- *A climate of trust.* Trust that management means what it says about values and leadership development must be established early in any program. Trust is established by setting expectations and delivering results that meet or exceed those expectations. By sending clear messages to staff and exhibiting positive attitudes about staff behavior, senior IT managers will help people feel they can begin to take some risks and initiatives in their work (Cascio and Shurygailo 2003). If people feel their culture is based on fair processes and that they can draw lessons from both

good and bad results, they will start to respond with the type of high performance and leadership behaviors that are expected (Kim and Maugorgne 2003). Conversely, senior managers must take steps to weed out counterproductive behaviors, such as poor collaboration, that will undermine this climate (Roberts and Mingay 2004).

- *Empowerment.*   Empowerment thrives in a climate of trust, but leaders need to deliberately encourage it as well. In IT one of the most important ways to do this is to create mechanisms to support staff's making difficult decisions. One company recognized this by explicitly making "We'll support you in doing the right things" a central element in revamping its leadership promise. To make it real and visible, the company established a clear process through which junior staff can resolve potential conflicts with users about disagreements on what is "the right thing." Furthermore, they have established committees to help manage the risks involved in IT work, get at the root cause of recurring issues, and protect the promises made to business partners. Such processes, in conjunction with values and trust, create a management system that empowers people and frees them to make appropriate decisions (Stewart 2004). By staying connected with staff as teachers, coaches, champions, and mentors, more senior leaders help more junior staff to take "intelligent risks" and sponsor initiative (Taurel 2000).

- *Clear and frequent communication.*   As with other types of change, one cannot communicate too much about the need to create an environment to foster leadership. "In spite of all we know about communication, it's still one of our biggest leadership gaps," said a participant. Open, two-way communication is the hallmark of modern leadership. Leaders and followers are gradually learning how to effectively use the electronic nervous system that now runs through all organizations (Avolio and Kahai 2003). Use of information technology and multiple channels is now the norm, and redundancy is advisable because of the increased opportunities for miscommunication in the virtual world. Senior executives are now using IT to communicate interactively with their most junior staff (Stewart 2004). One company has established an "Ask Phil" e-mail whereby any member of IT can direct questions to the CIO. Leadership is about developing relationships with people. It engages them and helps direct them to a particular goal. Learning to leverage all conduits of communication to build and sustain an array of relationships is, therefore, central to becoming an effective IT leader (Avolio and Kahai 2003).

- *Accountability.*   Acceptance of accountability is a key component of leadership. A climate where accountabilities are clear is an important aspect of a leadership development culture (Bell and Gerrard 2004). Natural leaders often first come to senior management's attention because they consistently deliver on what they promise. More recently, the concept of accountability is being extended to include expectations that IT staff will assist the business in achieving its growth goals and that IT will not create technical impediments to implementing business strategies (Mingay et al. 2004). Unfortunately, IT accountability is frequently absent, and this has negatively affected the perceptions of IT leadership in the rest of the organization (Feld and Stoddard 2004). No member of IT should be allowed to abdicate responsibility for delivering results. However, focus group members stressed that in order to create a culture of accountability, IT leaders must also provide the processes, tools, and support to produce successful results.

The second layer of a leadership development program involves building leadership activities into IT's processes and daily work. Well-designed and documented processes for such activities as planning, budgeting, conflict resolution, service delivery, and financial reviews and approvals clearly articulate the individual elements that contribute to leadership in particular situations. They make it easier for more junior staff to carry out these activities and to learn what is expected of them (Bell and Gerrard 2004). They also establish boundaries within which staff can exercise judgment and take risks.

Human resources management practices are a key component of fostering leadership at this level as well. Many companies have begun to document the competencies that they expect staff to exhibit in each job category and level. These typically include leadership as well as technical skills. "It gets harder to do this the higher up the management hierarchy one goes," stated one manager. "At the more senior levels, leadership skills are much more individualized and are more difficult to capture, but we're working on it." Specific training and development strategies work well for each job stream at more junior levels. With more senior positions, development plans should be created for each individual.

Job assignments are one of the most important ways to develop leadership expertise. In fact, some experts suggest that 80 percent of the levers management has at its disposal in this area are related to how a company uses assignments and job postings to influence an individual's experience (Kesner 2003). Job rotations, stretch assignments, and on-the-job coaching and mentoring are all effective ways to build leadership skills. Occasionally, this may entail taking risks and not always appointing the most qualified person for a particular job (Roberts and Mingay 2004). Sometimes, this should involve moving a person out of IT into the business for an assignment. All organizations should have processes in place to identify emergent leaders and take proactive steps to design individualized strategies of coaching and assignments that will fit their unique personalities (Griffin 2003). Succession planning should be a significant part of this process as well. Recruiting leaders from outside is sometimes necessary, but this is a far more risky and expensive way to address succession than growing leaders from within (Roberts and Mingay 2004).

Finally, at the core of any leadership development program is formal training. Commitment to formal leadership training in organizations has been patchy at best. Training can be internally developed or externally purchased. The fastest-growing segment of executive education is customized programs for a particular organization that are specifically tied to business drivers and values (Kesner 2003). In-house programs are best for instilling vision, purpose, values, and priorities. External training is best used for introducing new knowledge, practices, and thinking to leadership.

Because of the time and expense involved, leadership training should be used strategically rather than comprehensively. Often IT resources can be so stretched that finding time for development is the biggest challenge. One company reasserted the importance of training by promising its staff that it would spend its entire annual training budget for the first time! This organization sees training as one tool for helping individuals make their best contributions and achieving success; interestingly, it has found that making it easier to find appropriate courses through the creation of a formal curriculum and streamlining the registration and payment processes has led to a significant uptake in employees' taking advantage of development opportunities.

INVESTING IN LEADERSHIP DEVELOPMENT: ARTICULATING THE VALUE PROPOSITION

Although leadership development is widely espoused, many organizations have reduced their budgets in recent years, and that has hit formal training programs hard. One manager remarked that his staff knew senior management was serious about development when it maintained training budgets while trimming in other areas. However, as mentioned above, training is only one facet of a good leadership development program, and doing it right will take executive time and consistent attention, in addition to the costs involved in establishing and following through on necessary communications, procedures, and planning. It is essential to articulate the value proposition for this initiative.

Experts suggest that several elements of value can be achieved by implementing a leadership development program. Using a rubric established by Smith and McKeen (2003), these elements include the following:

- *What is the value?*   Because different companies and managers have different perceptions of value, it is critical that the value that is to be achieved by a leadership development program be clearly described and agreed on. Some of the value elements that organizations could achieve with leadership development include improved current and future leadership capabilities and bench strength (preventing expensive and risky hires from outside), improved innovation and alignment with business strategy, improved teamwork (both internally and cross-functionally), improved collaboration and knowledge sharing, greater clarity of purpose and appropriate decision making, reduced risk, and a higher-performing IT organization. When these value objectives are understood, it is possible to develop metrics to determine whether or not the program is successful. Having a focus and metrics for a leadership program will ensure that management pays attention to it and that it doesn't get shunted into a corner with the "soft and fuzzy stuff" (Kesner 2003).
- *Who will deliver the value?*   Because leadership development is partially HR's responsibility and partially IT's, clarifying which parts of the program should be delivered by which group is important. Similarly, much of the coaching, mentoring, and experiential components will be fulfilled by different managers within IT. It is, therefore, important for senior management to clarify roles and responsibilities for leadership development and to ensure that they are implemented consistently across the organization. Ideally, senior IT management will retain responsibility for the outer layer of the leadership program—that is, creating a supportive working environment. At one company the senior IT team created several packaged presentations for middle managers to help them articulate their "leadership promises."
- *When will value be realized?*   Leadership development should have both long- and short-term benefits. Effective training programs should result in visible behavior changes, as noted above. The initial impacts of a comprehensive leadership initiative should be visible in-house within a year and to business units and vendors within eighteen to twenty-four months (McDonald and Bace 2004). Again, metrics are an essential part of leadership programs because they demonstrate their success and effectiveness. Although there is no causal link between

leadership development and improved business results, there should be clear and desirable results achieved (Kesner 2003). Using a "balanced scorecard" approach to track the different types of impacts over time is recommended. This methodology can be used to demonstrate value to IT managers, who may be skeptical, and to HR and senior management. It can also be used to make modifications to the program in areas where it is not working well.

- *How will value be delivered?* This is the question that everyone wants to ask first and that should only be addressed *after* the other questions have been answered (Smith and McKeen 2003). Once it is clear *what* IT wants to accomplish with leadership development, it will be much easier to design an effective program to deliver it.

Conclusion

Leadership development in IT is something that everyone agrees is increasingly important to helping companies achieve their business goals. However, all too often it is a hit-and-miss exercise, depending on management whim and budget availability. It is now clear that senior IT leaders must make leadership development a priority if IT is going to contribute to business strategy and help deliver services in an increasingly competitive environment. To do this, leadership development in IT must start with the most junior IT staff. An effective program involves more than just training. It must include the creation of a supportive work environment and the development of processes that deliver on management's promises. However, no leadership program should be implemented in a vacuum. There should be a clearly articulated proposition outlining its value to the organization and a set of metrics to monitor its effectiveness. Like technology itself, leadership development will be effective only if management takes a comprehensive approach that integrates culture, behavior, processes, *and* training to deliver real business value.

References

Anonymous. "A Guide for Leaders." Presentation to the IT Management Forum, November 2004.

Avolio, B., and S. Kahai. "Adding the 'E' to Leadership: How It May Impact Your Leadership." *Organizational Dynamics* 31, no. 4 (January 2003): 325–38.

Bell, M., and M. Gerrard. "Organizational Chart Is Falling into Irrelevance." Gartner Inc., ID Number: QA-22-2873, July 6, 2004.

Bennis, W. G., and B. Nanus. *Leaders: The Strategies for Taking Charge.* New York: Harper and Row, 1985.

Cascio, W., and S. Shurygailo. "E-leadership and Virtual Teams." *Organizational Dynamics* 31, no. 4 (January 2003): 362–76.

Feld, C., and D. Stoddard. "Getting IT Right." *Harvard Business Review* 82, no. 2 (2004): 72–79.

Griffin, N. "Personalize Your Management Development." *Harvard Business Review* 81, no. 3 (March 2003).

IBM. "CEO Survey 2004: Executive Summary." IBM Consulting Services. w3-2.ibm.com/ services/bcs/news_pubs/features/2004/0224_ survey.html (accessed January 2005).

Kesner, I. "Leadership Development: Perk or Priority?" *Harvard Business Review* 81, no. 3 (May 2003).

Kim, W., and R. Maugorgne. "Tipping Point Leadership." *Harvard Business Review* 81, no. 4 (April 2003).

Mahoney, J. "Demands for Business Growth Make CIOs Reallocate Their Time." Gartner Inc., ID Number: PA-22-6613, June 29, 2004.

Markus, L., and R. I. Benjamin. "The Magic Bullet Theory in IT-Enabled Transformation." *Sloan Management Review* Winter (1997): 55–68.

McDonald, M., and J. Bace. "Keys to IT Leadership: Credibility, Respect, and Consistency." Gartner Inc., ID Number: TU-22-8013, June 28, 2004.

McKeen, J., and H. Smith. *Management Challenges in IS: Successful Strategies and Appropriate Action.* Chichester, England: John Wiley & Sons, 1996.

———. *Making IT Happen: Critical Issues in IT Management.* Chichester, England: John Wiley & Sons, 2003.

Mingay, S., J. Mahoney, M. P. McDonald, and M. Bell. "Redefining the Rules of IT Leadership." Gartner Inc., ID Number: AV-22-9013, July 1, 2004.

Mintzberg, H. "Enough Leadership." *Harvard Business Review* 82, no. 11 (November 2004).

Orlikowski, W. J., and J. D. Hofman. "An Improvisational Model for Change Management: The Case of Groupware Technologies." *Sloan Management Review* Winter (1997): 11–21.

Roberts, J., and S. Mingay. "Building a More Effective IT Leadership Team." Gartner Inc., ID Number: TU-22-5915, June 28, 2004.

Smith, H. A., and J. D. McKeen. "Developing and Delivering on the IT Value Proposition." *Communications of the Association for Information Systems* 11, article 25 (April 2003): 438–50.

———. "IT in 2010: The New Frontier." *MIS Quarterly Executive* 5, no. 3 (September 2006): 125–36.

Stewart, T. "Leading Change When Business Is Good: An Interview with Samuel J. Palmisano." *Harvard Business Review* 82, no. 12 (December 2004): 8.

Taurel, S. "On Leadership." Corporate document, Eli Lilly and Co., 2000.

Chapter 19

Managing IT-Based Risk[1]

I t's another one of those dramatic "paradigm shifts" for which it is famous. Not so long ago, IT-based risk was a fairly low-key activity focused on whether it could deliver its projects successfully and keep its applications up and running (McKeen and Smith 2003). But with the opening up of the organization's boundaries to external partners and service providers, external electronic communications, and online services, managing IT-based risk has morphed into a "bet the company" proposition. Not only is the scope of the job bigger, but also the stakes are much higher. As companies have become more dependent on IT for everything they do, the costs of service disruption have escalated exponentially. Now, when a system goes down, the company effectively stops working and customers cannot be served. And criminals routinely seek ways to wreak havoc with company data, applications, and Web sites. New regulations to protect privacy and increase accountability have also made executives much more sensitive to the consequences of inadequate IT security practices—either internally or from service providers. In addition, the risk of losing or compromising company information has risen steeply. No longer are a company's files locked down and accessible only by company staff. Today, company information can be exposed to the public in literally hundreds of ways. Our increasing mobility, the portability of storage devices, and the growing sophistication of cyber-threats are just a few of the more noteworthy means.

Therefore, the job of managing IT-based risk has become much broader and more complex, and it is now widely recognized as an integral part of any technology-based work—no matter how minor. As a result, many IT organizations have been given the responsibility of not only managing risk in their own activities (i.e., project development, operations, and delivering business strategy) but also of managing IT-based risk in all company activities (e.g., mobile computing, file sharing, and online access to information and software). Whereas in the past companies have sought to achieve security through physical or technological means (e.g., locked rooms, virus scanners), understanding is now growing that managing IT-based risk must be a strategic and holistic activity that is not just the responsibility of a small group of IT specialists but, rather, part of a mind-set that extends from partners and suppliers to employees and customers.

[1]Smith, H. A., and J. D. McKeen. "A Holistic Approach to Managing IT-Based Risk." *Communications of the Association for Information Systems* 25, article 41 (December 2009): 519–30. Reproduced by permission of the Association for Information Systems.

This chapter explores how organizations are addressing and coping with increasing IT-based risk. It first looks at the challenges facing IT managers in the arena of risk management and proposes a holistic view of risk. Next it examines some of the characteristics and components needed to develop an effective risk management framework and presents a generic framework for integrating the growing number of elements involved in it. Finally, it describes some successful practices organizations could use for improving their risk management capabilities.

A HOLISTIC VIEW OF IT-BASED RISK

With the explosion in the past decade of new IT-based risks organizations face, it is increasingly recognized that risk means more than simply "the possibility of a loss or exposure to loss" (Mogul 2004) or even a hazard, uncertainty, or opportunity (McKeen and Smith 2003). Today, *risk* is a multilayered concept that implies much more is at stake.

> "IT risk has changed. IT risk incidents harm constituencies within and outside companies. They damage corporate reputations and expose weaknesses in companies' management teams. Most importantly, IT risk dampens an organization's ability to compete." (Hunter and Westerman 2007).

As a result, companies are beginning to talk about "enterprise risk management" as a more comprehensive and integrated approach to dealing with risk (Slywotzky and Drzik 2005). Although, as the focus group agreed, not every risk affecting an enterprise will be an IT-based risk, the fact remains that a large number of the risks affecting the enterprise have an IT-based component. For example, one firm's IT risk management policy notes that the goal of risk management is to ensure that technology failures or data integrity do not compromise the company's strategic objectives, the company's reputation and stakeholders, or its success and reputation.

This heightened sensitivity to IT-based risk has even reached many boards of directors:

> "Ever since the Y2K scare, boards have grown increasingly nervous about corporate dependence on information technology. . . . [However,] "few understand the full degree of their operational dependence . . . [and] lack the fundamental knowledge needed to ask intelligent questions about . . . IT risk. . . . This leaves CIOs . . . pretty much on their own." (Nolan and McFarlan 2005)

Thus, in spite of the increasing number and complexity of IT-based threats facing organizations, it is still very difficult to get senior business leaders to give the attention (and the resources) needed to effectively manage them. A recent global survey noted, "while the security community recognizes that information security is part of effective business management, managing information security risk is still overwhelmingly seen as an IT responsibility worldwide" (Berinato 2007). Another study of several organizations found that none had a good view of all key risks and 75 percent had major gaps in their approach to IT-based risk management (Coles and Moulton 2003). In short, while IT has become increasingly central to business success, many enterprises have not yet adjusted their processes to incorporate IT-based risk management (Hunter and Westerman 2007).

Knowing what's at stake, risk management is perennially in the top ten priorities for CIOs (Hunter et al. 2005) and efforts are being made to put effective capabilities and processes in place in IT organizations. However, only 5 percent of firms are at a high level of maturity in this area, and most (80 percent) are still in the initial stages of this work (Proctor 2007). Addressing risk in a more professional, accountable, and transparent fashion is an evolution from traditional IT security work. At a recent Gartner symposium the following was pointed out:

> "[T]raditionally, [IT] security has been reactive, ad hoc, and technically-focused. . . . The shift to risk management requires an acceptance that you can't protect yourself from everything, so you need to measure risk and make good decisions about how far you go in protecting the organization." (Proctor 2007)

Companies in the group largely reflected this transitional state. "Information security is a primary focus of our risk management strategy," said one manager. "It's very, very visible but our business has yet to commit to addressing risk issues." Another stated, "We have a risk management group focused on IT risk, but lots of other groups focus on it too. . . . As a result, there are many different and overlapping views, and we are missing integration of these views." "We are constantly trying to identify gaps in our risk management practices and to close them," said a third.

There is, however, no hesitation about identifying the sources of risk. Every company in the group had its own checklist of risk items, and the experts have developed several different frameworks and categorizations that aim to be comprehensive (see Appendix A for some of these). What everyone agrees on is that any approach to dealing with IT-based risk must be holistic—even though it is an "onerous" job to package it as a whole. "Every category of risk has a different vocabulary," explained one focus group manager. "Financial, pandemic, software, information security, disaster recovery planning, governance and legal—each view makes sense, but pulling them together is very hard." Risk is often managed in silos in organizations, resulting in uncoordinated approaches to its management and to decision-making incorporating risk (Mogul 2004). This is why many organizations, including several in the focus group, are attempting to integrate the wide variety of issues involved into one holistic enterprise risk management strategy that uses a common language to communicate (Mogul 2004; Nolan and McFarlan 2005; Slywotzky and Drzik 2005).

The connection among all of the different risk perspectives is the enterprise. Any IT problem that occurs—whether with an application, a network, a new system, a vendor, or a hacker (to name just a few)—has the increasing potential to put the enterprise at risk. Thus, a holistic view of IT-based risk must put the enterprise front and center in any framework or policy. A risk to the enterprise includes anything (either internal or external) that affects its:

- Brand
- Reputation
- Competitiveness
- Financial value
- End state (i.e., its overall effectiveness, efficiency, and success)

Figure 19.1 offers an integrated, holistic view of risk from an enterprise perspective.

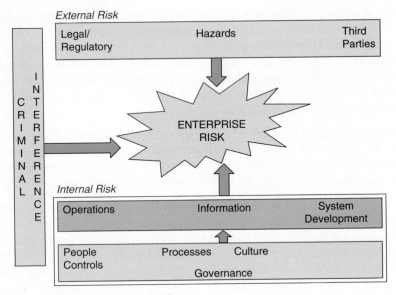

FIGURE 19.1   A Holistic View of IT-Based Risk

A wide variety of both internal and external IT-based risks can affect the enterprise. Externally, risks can come from the following:

- Third parties, such as partners, software vendors, service providers, suppliers or customers
- Hazards, such as disasters, pandemics, geopolitical upheavals, or environmental considerations
- Legal and regulatory issues, such as failure to adhere to the laws and regulations affecting the company, including privacy, financial reporting, environmental reporting, e-discovery, and so on

Internally, some risks are well known, such as those traditionally associated with IT operations (availability, accessibility) and systems development (not meeting schedules or budgets or delivering value). Others are newer and, although they must be managed from within the organization, they may include both internal and external components. These include the following:

- Information risks, such as those affecting privacy, quality, accuracy, and protection
- People risks, such as those caused by mistakes or lack of adherence to security protocols
- Process risks, such as problems caused by poorly designed business processes or by failure to adapt business processes to IT-based changes
- Cultural risks, such as risk aversion and lack of risk awareness
- Controls, such as ineffective or inadequate controls to prevent or mitigate risk incidents
- Governance, such as ineffective or inadequate structure, roles, or accountabilities to make appropriate risk-based decisions

Finally, there is the risk of criminal interference, either from inside or outside the organization. Unlike other types of risk, which are typically inadvertent, criminal actions are deliberate attacks on the enterprise, its information, or sometimes its employees or customers. Such threats are certainly not new. Everyone is familiar with viruses and hackers. What is new, however, is that many more groups and individuals are targeting organizations and people. These include other national governments, organized crime, industrial spies, and terrorists. "These people are not trying to bring systems down, like in the past," explained a group member. "They are trying to get information."

HOLISTIC RISK MANAGEMENT: A PORTRAIT

Tackling risk in a holistic fashion is challenging, and building an effective framework for its management will not occur overnight. It is therefore important to keep the big picture in mind, or the process could degenerate into overwhelming bureaucracy. It is interesting to note that there is much more agreement from the focus group and other researchers about what effective risk management *looks like* than *how* to do it. This section therefore presents an impressionist portrait of what constitutes holistic risk management in order to show what this big picture should portray. A closer look at the detailed elements composing this picture will also be needed, but first it is essential that all people and functions involved in risk management agree on what image is being created. Otherwise, if one person is trying to create a Picasso while another is painting "Whistler's Mother," it is unlikely that the resulting portrait will be pleasing to anyone!

With this in mind, we sketch some of the characteristics and components of a portrait of effective, holistic risk management:

1. *Focus on what's important.*   "Risks are inevitable," admitted a manager. "The first question we must ask is 'What are we trying to protect?'" said another. "There's no perfect package, and some residual risk must always be taken." A third added "Risks are inevitable, but it's how they're managed—our response, contingency plans, team readiness, and adaptability—that make the difference." In short, risk is uncertainty that matters, something that can hurt or delay an enterprise from reaching its objectives (Hillson 2008). Although many managers recognize that it's time to take a more strategic view of risk, "[W]e still don't have our hands around what's important and what we should be monitoring and protecting" (Berinato 2007). Risk management is therefore not about anticipating all risks but about attempting to reduce significant risks to a manageable level (Austin and Darby 2003) and knowing how to assess and respond to it (Slywotzky and Drzik 2005). Yet, more than protecting the enterprise, risk management should also enable IT to take more risk in the safest possible way (Caldwell and Mogul 2006). Thus, the focus of effective risk management should not be about saying 'no' to a risk, but how to say 'yes,' thereby building a more agile enterprise (Caldwell and Mogul 2006).

2. *Expect the image to change over time.*   Few companies have a good grasp of risk management because IT is a discipline that is evolving rapidly (Proctor 2007). As a result, it would be a mistake to codify risk practices and standards too rapidly,

according to the focus group. Efforts to do this have typically resulted in "paperwork without context," said one manager. Within a particular risk category, risk management actions should be "continuous, iterative, and structured," group members agreed. In recognition of this reality, most participant organizations have a mandatory risk assessment at key stages in the system development process to capture the risk picture involved with a particular project at several points in time and many have regular, ongoing reviews of required operational controls on an annual or biannual basis to do the same thing. In addition, when incidents occur, there should always be a process for evaluating what happened, assessing its impact, and determining if controls or other management processes need to be adapted (Coles and Moulton 2003). Finally, organizations should also be continually attempting to simplify and streamline controls wherever possible to minimize their burden. This is a process that is often missed, admitted one manager.

However, despite the fact that each of these steps is useful in keeping one aspect of the risk picture in mind, it is also essential to stand back from these initiatives and see how the whole image is developing. It is this more strategic and holistic view that is often missing in organizations and that firms often fail to communicate to their staff. One of the greatest risks to organizations comes from employees themselves, not necessarily through their intentional actions, but because they don't recognize the risks involved in their actions (Berinato 2007). Therefore, many believe it is time to recognize that risk cannot be managed solely through controls, procedures, and technology but that all employees must understand the concepts and goals of risk management because the enterprise will always need to rely on their judgment to some extent (Symantec Corporation 2007). In the same vein, many managers also need to better understand this risk picture because they frequently do not comprehend the size and nature of the risks involved and thus resource their management inappropriately (Coles and Moulton 2003). As a result they tend also to delegate many aspects of risk management to lower levels in the organization, thus preventing the development of any longer-term, overall vision (Proctor 2008; Witty 2008).

3. *View risk from multiple levels and perspectives.*   Instead of dealing with security "incidents" in a one-at-a-time manner, the group's managers are trying to do a better job of root cause analysis and understanding risks in a more multifaceted way. To date, risk management has tended to focus largely on the operational and tactical levels, but the managers suggest that risk management should also be viewed in a strategic way. One manager explained, "We need to assess risk trends and develop strategies for dealing with them. Tactics for dealing with future threats will then be more effective and easier to put in place." Another noted, "We must aim for redundancy of protection—that is, multiple layers, to ensure that if one layer fails, others will catch any problems."

Furthermore, risk, security, and compliance are often intermixed in people's minds. Each of these is a valid and unique lens through which to view risk, with the challenge arising when all three are seen as being the same. For example, one expert noted that 70 percent of a typical "security" budget is spent on compliance matters, not on protecting and defending the organization (Society for Information

Management 2008), and this imbalance means that overall spending in many firms is skewed. One firm uses the "prudent man" rule to deal with risk, which recommends a diversity of approaches—being proactive, prevention, due diligence, credibility, and promoting awareness—to ensure that it is adequately covered and that all stakeholders are properly protected. Monitoring and adapting to new international standards and laws, completing overall health checks, and analysis of potential risks are other new dimensions of risk that should be incorporated into a firm's overall approach to risk management.

DEVELOPING A RISK MANAGEMENT FRAMEWORK

With the big picture in mind, organizations can begin to develop a framework for filling in the details. The objective of a risk management framework (RMF) is to create a common understanding around risk, to ensure the right risks are being addressed at the right levels, and to involve the right people in making risk decisions. An RMF also serves to guide the development of risk policies and integrate appropriate risk standards and processes into existing practices (e.g., the SDLC). No company in the focus group had yet developed a comprehensive framework for addressing IT-based risk, although many had significant pieces in place or in development. In this section, we attempt to piece these together to sketch out what an RMF might contain.

An RMF should serve as a high-level overview of how risk is to be managed in an enterprise and can also act as a structure for reporting on risk at various levels of detail. Currently, many companies have created risk management policies to guide staff as to how IT risk and security are to be treated and require all staff to read and sign them. Unfortunately, such policies are typically so long and complex as to be overwhelming and ineffective. "Our security policy alone is two hundred pages. How enforceable is it?" complained a manger. Another noted that the language in his company's policy was highly technical. As a result, user noncompliance in following the recommended best practices was considerable. Furthermore, a plethora of committees, review boards, councils, and control centers are often designed to deal with one or more aspects of risk management, but they actually contribute to the general complexity of managing IT-based risk in an organization.

It should not be surprising that this situation exists, given the rapidity with which technologies, interfaces, external relationships, and dependencies have developed within the past decade. Organizations have struggled to simply keep up with the waves of legislation, regulation, globalization, standards, and transformation that seem to continually threaten to engulf them. An RMF is thus a starting point for providing an integrated, top-down view of risk, defining it, identifying those responsible for making key decisions about it, and mapping which policies and standards apply to each area. Fortunately, current technology makes it easy to offer multiple views and multiple levels of this information, enabling different groups or individuals to understand their responsibilities and specific policies in detail and see links to specific tools, practices and templates, while facilitating different types of reporting to different stakeholders at different levels. By mapping existing groups, policies, and guidelines into an RMF, it is easier to see where gaps exist and where complexities in processes should be streamlined.

A basic RMF includes the following:

- *Risk category.*   The general area of enterprise risk involved (e.g., criminal, operations, third party, etc.).
- *Policies and standards.*   These state, at a high level, the general principles for guiding risk decisions, and they identify any formal corporate, industry, national, or international standards that should apply to each risk category.[2] For example, one company's policy regarding people states the following, in part:

  > *Protecting the integrity and security of client and corporate information is the responsibility of every employee. Timely and effective reporting of actual and suspected privacy incidents is a key component of meeting this responsibility. Management relies on the collective experience and judgment of its employees.*

  Another company policy regarding culture states, "We need to embed a risk management focus and awareness into all processes, functions, jobs, and individuals."
- *Risk type.*   Each type of risk associated with each category (e.g., loss of information, failure to comply with specific laws, inability to work due to system outages) needs to be identified. Each type should have a generic name and definition, ideally linked to a business impact. Identifying all risk types will take time and probably require much iteration as "there are an incredible variety of specific risks" (Mogul 2004). However, developing lists and definitions is a good first step (Baccarini et al. 2004; Hillson 2008; McKeen and Smith 2003) and is already a common practice among the focus group companies, at least for certain categories of risk.
- *Risk ownership.*   Each type of risk should have an owner, either in IT or in the business. As well, there will likely be several stakeholders who will be affected by risk-based decisions. For example, the principal business sponsor could be the owner of risk decisions associated with the development or purchase of a new IT system, but IT operations and architecture as well as the project manager will clearly be key stakeholders. In addition to specialized IT functions, such as IT security, audit and privacy functions in the business will likely be involved in many IT risk-based decisions. Owners and stakeholders should have clear responsibilities and accountabilities. In the focus group, some major risk types were owned by committees, such as an enterprise risk committee, or the internal audit, social responsibility and risk governance committee, or the project risk review council on which stakeholder groups were represented.
- *Risk mitigation.*   As an RMF is developed, each type of risk should be associated with controls, practices, and tools for addressing it effectively. These fall into one of two categories: compulsory and optional. Group members stressed that overemphasis on mitigation can lead to organizational paralysis or hyper-risk sensitivity. Instead participants stressed the role of judgment in right sizing mitigation activities wherever possible. "Our technology development framework does not tell you what you have to do, but it does give you things to consider in each phase," said one manager. "We look first at the overall enterprise risk presented by a project,"

---

[2]Some international standards include Committee of Sponsoring Organizations (COSO) of the Treadway Commission, www.coso.org; SAI Global, www.saiglobal.com; and the Office of Government Commerce's Management of Risk (M_o_r) (www.ogc.gov.uk/guidance_management_of_risk.asp).

said another, "and develop controls based on our evaluation of the level and types of risk involved." The goal, everyone agreed, is to provide a means by which risks can be managed consistently, effectively, and appropriately.[3]

- *Risk reporting and monitoring.* This was a rather controversial topic in the focus group. Although everyone agreed it is important to make risk and its management more visible in the organization, tracking and reporting on risk have a tendency to make management highly risk averse. One manager said:

> *"We spent a year trying to quantify risks and developing a roll-up report, but we threw it away because audit didn't understand it and saw only one big risk. This led to endless discussion and no confidence that IT was handling risk well. Now we use a very simple reporting framework presenting risk as high, medium, or low. This is language we all understand."*

There are definitely pressures to improve risk measurement (Proctor 2007), but clearly care must be taken in how these metrics are reported. For example, one company uses a variety of self-assessments to ensure that risks have been properly identified and appropriate controls put in place. However, as risk management procedures become better understood and more codified, risk reporting can also become more formalized. This is particularly the case at present with operational process controls and fundamental IT security, such as virus or intrusion detection.

However, risk monitoring is an ongoing process because levels and types of risk are changing continually. Thus, an RMF should be a dynamic document as new types of risk are identified, business impacts are better understood, and mitigation practices evolve. "We need to continually monitor all categories of risk and ask our executives if the levels of risk are still the same," said a focus group member. It is clear that failure to understand how risks are changing is a significant risk in itself (Proctor 2007). It is therefore especially important to have a process in place to analyze what happened when an unforeseen risk does occur. Unless efforts are made to understand the root causes of a problem, it is unlikely that effective mitigation practices can be put in place (Austin and Darby 2003).

IMPROVING RISK MANAGEMENT CAPABILITIES

Risk management in most areas does not yet have well-documented best practices or standards in place. However, the focus group identified several actions that could lead to the development of effective risk management capabilities:

- *Look beyond technical risk.* One of the biggest inhibitors of effective risk management is too tight a focus on technical risk, rather than on business risk (Coles and Moulton 2003). A traditional security approach tends to exclude this, often focusing only on technical threats or specific systems or platforms.

---

[3]"Risk Management Guide for Information Technology Systems" (csrc.nist.gov/publications/nistpubs/800-30/sp800-30.pdf), the National Institute of Standards and Technology's Special Publication 800-30, provides guidance on specific risk mitigation strategies.

- *Develop a common language of risk.* A clearer understanding of business risk requires all stakeholders—IT, audit, privacy, legal, business managers—to speak the same language and use comparable metrics—at least at the highest levels of analysis where the different types of risk need to be integrated.
- *Simplify the presentation.* Having a common approach to discussing or describing risk is very effective, said several focus group members. While the work that is behind a simple presentation may be complex, presenting too much complexity can be counterproductive. The most effective approaches are simple: a narrative, a dashboard, a "stoplight" report, or another graphic style of report.
- *Right size.* Risk management should be appropriate for the level of risk involved. More effective practices allow for the adaptation of controls while ensuring that the decisions made are visible and the rationale is communicated.
- *Standardize the technology base.* This is one of the most effective ways to reduce risk, according to the research, but it is also one of the most expensive (Hunter et al. 2005).
- *Rehearse.* Many firms now have an emergency response team in place to rapidly deal with key hazards. However, it is less common that this team actually rehearses its disaster recovery, business continuity, or other types of risk mitigation plans. One manager noted that live rehearsals are essential to reveal gaps in plans and unexpected risk factors.
- *Clarify roles and responsibilities.* With so many groups in the organization now involved in managing risk in some way, it is critical that roles and responsibilities be documented and communicated. Ideally, this should be in the context of an RMF. However, even if an RMF is not in place, efforts should be made to document which groups in the organization are responsible for which types of enterprise risk.
- *Automate where appropriate.* As risk management practices become standardized and streamlined, automated controls begin to make sense. Some tools can be very effective, noted the focus group, provided they are applied in ways that facilitate risk management, rather than becoming an obstacle to productivity.
- *Educate and communicate.* Each organization has its own culture, and most need to work with staff, business managers, and executives to make them more aware of risk and the need to invest in appropriate management. However, some organizations, like one insurance company in the focus group, are so risk-phobic that they need education to enable them to take on more risk. Such companies could benefit from better understanding their "risk portfolio" of projects (Day 2007). Such an approach can often help encourage companies to undertake more risky innovation initiatives with more confidence.

Conclusion

Organizations are more sensitized to risk than ever before. The economy, regulatory, and legal environment; business complexity; the increasing openness of business relationships; and rapidly changing technology have all combined to drive managers to seek a more comprehensive understanding of risk and its management (Rasmussen 2007). Whereas in the past, risk was managed in isolated pockets by such functions as IT security, internal audit, and legal, today recognition is growing that these arenas intersect and affect each other. And IT risk is clearly involved in many types of business risk these days. Criminal activity, legal responsibilities, privacy, innovation, and operational productivity, to name just a few, all have IT risk implications. As a result, organizations need a new approach to risk—one that is more holistic in nature and that provides an integrative framework for understanding risk and making decisions associated with it. Accomplishing this is no simple task, so developing such a framework will likely be an ongoing activity, as experts in IT and others begin to grapple with how to approach such a complex and multidimensional activity. This chapter has therefore not tried to present a definitive approach to risk management. There is general agreement that organizations are not ready for this. Instead, it has tried to sketch an impression of how to approach risk management and what an effective risk management program might look like. IT managers and others have been left to fill in the details and complete the portrait in their own organizations.

References

Austin, R., and C. Darby. "The Myth of Secure Computing." *Harvard Business Review* June 2003.

Baccarini, D., G. Salm, and P. Love. "Management of Risks in Information Technology Projects. *Industrial Management + Data Systems* 104, no. 3–4 (2004).

Berinato, S. "The Fifth Annual Global State of Information Security." *CIO Magazine,* August 28, 2007.

Caldwell, F., and R. Mogul. "Risk Management and Business Performance Are Compatible." Gartner Inc., ID Number: G00140802, October 18, 2006.

Coles, R., and R. Moulton. "Operationalizing IT Risk Management." *Computers and Security* 22, no. 6, 2003.

Day, G. "Is It Real? Can We Win? Is It Worth Doing? Managing Risk and Reward in an Innovation Portfolio. *Harvard Business Review* December 2007.

Hillson, D. "Danger Ahead." *PM Network* March 2008.

Hunter, R., and G. Westerman. *IT Risk: Turning Business Threats into Competitive Advantage.* Boston: Harvard Business School Press, 2007.

Hunter, R., G. Westerman, and D. Aron. "IT Risk Management: A Little Bit More Is a Whole Lot Better. *Gartner EXPCIO Signature Report,* February 2005.

McKeen, J., and H. Smith. *Making IT Happen: Critical Issues in IT Management.* Chichester, England: John Wiley & Sons, 2003.

Mogul, R. Gartner's Simple Enterprise Risk Management Framework. Gartner Inc., ID Number: G00125380, December 10, 2004.

Nolan, R., and W. McFarlan. "Information Technology and the Board of Directors." *Harvard Business Review* October 2005.

Proctor, P. IT "Risk Management for the Inexperienced: A CIO's Travel Guide to IT 'Securistan.'" Presentation to Gartner Symposium ITxpo 2007 Emerging Trends, San Francisco, CA, April 22–26, 2007.

———. "Key Issues for the Risk and Security Roles, 2008." Gartner Inc., ID Number: G00155764, March 27, 2008.

Rasmussen, M. "Identifying and Selecting the Right Risk Consultant." Forrester Research Teleconference, July 12, 2007.

Slywotzky, A., and J. Drzik. "Countering the Biggest Risk of All." *Harvard Business Review,* April 2005.

Society for Information Management. "Executive IT security." Private presentation to the SIM Advanced Practices Council, May 2008.

Symantec Corporation. "Trends for July–December 2006." *Symantec Internet Security Threat Report* XI (March 2007).

Witty, R. "Findings: IT Disaster Recovery Can Upsell Business Continuity Management." Gartner Inc., ID Number: G00155402, February 19, 2008.

A Selection of Risk Classification Schemes

McKeen and Smith (2003)

- Financial risk
- Technology risk
- Security
- Information and people
- Business process
- Management
- External
- Risk of success

Baccarini, Salm, and Love (2004)

- Commercial risk
- Economic circumstances
- Human behavior
- Political circumstances
- Technology and technical issues
- Management activities and controls
- Individual activities.

Jordan and Silcocks (2005)

- Project risk
- IT services
- Information assets
- IT service providers and vendors
- Applications
- Infrastructure
- Strategic
- Emergent

Rasmussen (2007)

- Information security risk
- Policy and compliance
- Information asset management
- Business continuity and disaster recovery
- Incident and threat management
- Physical and environment
- Systems development and operations management

Combined Focus Group Categories

- Project
- Operations
- Strategic
- Enterprise
- Disaster recovery
- Information
- External
- Reputation
- Competitive
- Compliance and regulatory
- Forensic
- Opportunity
- Ethical
- Physical
- Business continuity
- Business process

Chapter 20

The Identity Management Challenge[1]

As organizations increasingly extend the online delivery of their services and data across departmental, organizational, and even jurisdictional boundaries, they must trust that they can identify and authenticate the customers, businesses, employees, and third parties using them. Traditional approaches to identity management, such as documents, clearly don't work in the online world, yet to date there is no online equivalent of the passport or photo ID. Instead, each organization and sometimes individual programs within organizations, have established a variety of identity management practices, such as passwords or "shared secret" questions.

However, as the integration of data and services progresses, IT managers are trying to grapple with more holistic and standardized approaches to identity and authentication that could simplify access to multiple services and enable organizations to collaborate and cooperate across global organizational boundaries to deliver services. As well, since all organizations must be concerned with identity theft and fraud, managers are continually challenged to implement practices that keep identity information secure and private.

Identity management (IDM) typically includes controls to prevent, detect, or correct harmful events and steps to identify a user, authenticate or prove the user is who he says he is, authorize what types of information can be accessed, and account for what a user does. Effective identity management is therefore widely seen as being an essential component for the safe and secure delivery of online information and services. Furthermore, as work extends to mobile and virtual activities, more and more identity management frameworks and standards must be integrated with a variety of devices, platforms, and protocols.

This chapter explores the challenges of IDM that organizations are currently facing and how they are approaching this issue, both internally and collaboratively with other organizations. It discusses the key management components of IDM, as opposed to its technical components. It looks first at the basic concepts of IDM, its essential elements, and its organizational stakeholders. Next, it looks more deeply into why IDM is increasingly a business concern, in addition to an IT concern. Third, it describes the key challenges facing IT managers as they try to address the rapidly evolving needs for IDM in their organizations. Fourth, it distills some

---

[1]Smith, H. A., and J. D. McKeen. "The Identity Management Challenge." *Communications of the Association for Information Systems* 28, no. 1, article 11 (March 2011): 169–80. Reproduced by permission of the Association for Information Systems.

key principles of effective IDM. Finally, it makes several recommendations for IT managers about how they can improve on their current IDM efforts.

IDENTITY MANAGEMENT (IDM) BASICS

Almost all of us recognize and are familiar with some of the basic concepts of identity management, even if we are not aware of it. Most IDM frameworks recognize three main components (Aitoro 2008; Allan and Perkins 2009; Smith 2007):

1. *Registration or identification.* These are processes that answer the question "Who are you?" Whether we are employees, customers, or citizens, we are constantly being asked who we are by the systems we use. Typically, we are given a unique username for each system we use, often leading to confusion when we forget who we are in a particular situation!
2. *Authentication.* These processes answer the question "How do I know it's you?" At minimum, we are required to provide a password, which may be as simple as our phone number but may also be a complex combination of letters and numbers that we are required to change on a regular basis. Other, less commonly used, methods of authentication include shared secrets (i.e., questions about yourself), biometrics (i.e., fingerprint or iris scans), or a file or swipe card that works in combination with a password.
3. *Authorization.* These processes answer the question "What are you allowed to do or see?" and validate that the user has the right to access a specific resource. As more and more detailed information is being made available online (e.g., banking, medical records, intellectual property), this is becoming a crucial question for both individuals and organizations. Companies and governments are now bound by legislation (varying in different parts of the world) to protect the information they collect, while individuals need to know that their personal information is protected and will not be used for purposes they did not authorize. Both want to ensure that criminals, profilers, hackers, and other unapproved users do not gain access to their information.

What is often less well understood is the foundation of people, process, and technology on which identification, authentication, and authorization are built. This provides the basis for trust in the IDM process itself and assurance that the proper protections are in place (Doctorow 2007). Without trust that the IDM process provides effective identification, authentication, and authorization, companies and individuals will not want to conduct business online. Until quite recently, this organizational infrastructure has been buried deep within most IT organizations and their applications. IT has been responsible for creating the processes, implementing the technology, and providing the staff to undertake the following:

• *IDM Administration.* A large part of IDM work has traditionally involved registering and deregistering users of IT systems and managing their passwords (Allan and Perkins 2009). For example, it has been estimated that one-half of all help desk calls are for password resets (Waters 2007). Administration also includes determining what systems and information an individual is entitled to access and monitoring usage to ensure that no unauthorized transactions take place.

- *Information privacy.* Protecting personal privacy is closely linked to access control. Organizations need practices in place to assure individuals that their information will be protected and ensure that it will only be used when and where needed by persons authorized to do so.
- *Security.* Organizations must also protect their data from being lost or fraudulently accessed (Suess and Morooney 2009). A strong identification, authentication, and authorization process can prevent most unauthorized access not only to personal data but also to corporate intellectual property by persons or companies not known to the organization and to the applications that actually run the company. However, it cannot prevent access by persons who are authorized to see this information and who use it inappropriately or by unauthorized persons who get physical access to it (e.g., by walking into an office or hijacking an identity). Thus, physical and virtual security goes beyond basic IDM practices.
- *Risk.* All IDM practices should be based on an assessment of the risk involved to both individuals and organizations. The more electronic access an organization provides, the greater the risk of theft, fraud, and disruption (Small 2006). Group members pointed out that the biggest risks are from insiders and that problems often arise through error rather than deliberate action. "This is why we need to have very specific access controls," said one. "There should be no generic internal IDs for anyone." Clearly, there are levels of risk based on a combination of the type of information involved, who is accessing it, and under what circumstances. There is little risk associated with a competitor accessing a company's cafeteria menu and high risk in the same individual accessing its employee or client list. Thus, appropriate IDM needs to be linked to the level of risk involved to provide the assurance that the right information protection is in place without causing undue irritation or frustration with the controls being used.
- *Regulatory compliance.* Finally, all organizations have legal responsibilities to properly identify and authenticate users of their data and applications as well as those accessing their services (Smedlinghoff 2008). Compliance becomes increasingly challenging when companies hire external third parties to do work for them. One manager noted that his company has to have legal oversight for all external access provided to vendors and partners because his company is legally responsible for what happens to its data. Other managers noted that they are legally required to review key transactions done by their employees, to have all staff review acceptable use practices, and to separate roles and responsibilities with respect to key transactions.

Organizations still typically undertake their own identification, authentication, and authorization services, as well as the underlying administration and other assessments, but there is much discussion about how IDM could be done differently and more effectively. Federated IDM is an approach that suggests that companies could agree to trust their partners' IDM services and vouch for each other's users (Fest 2008; Smedlinghoff 2008; Waters 2007). Many of the companies in the focus group were exploring doing this on a case-by-case basis because managing identities internally is becoming increasingly complex and challenging. "It's becoming unfeasible to own the identity repository for every individual accessing our data," said one manager. "We need identity federation because we don't want identity management to be our primary focus." Other companies are exploring turning identity services over to a trusted third party that would be able to develop a standardized approach to federation on behalf of a number of companies. Unfortunately, serious legal concerns to federation have inhibited its use.

The legal and compliance issues associated with federated IDM underscore one of the biggest challenges involved in implementing any effective IDM: the complexities arising from the multiple interests of the stakeholders it serves. Within a single organization, IT, legal, HR, and individual business units are all involved in its governance in the focus group companies. Stakeholder considerations multiply exponentially when an organization opens itself up to external access of any type. As one researcher notes, "[IDM] is an intricate mix where. . . . Parties might be influenced by privacy desires and regulations, legal liability, security vulnerabilities . . . , enjoyment or productivity, profit motives, application flexibility and more. Some goals sit in uneasy tension with others" (Maler 2009).

IDM AS A BUSINESS ENABLER

In the past IDM has been largely a technical matter and considered an internal IT function of limited interest to the business. Today however, IDM has become an essential business enabler, and with this transition has come not only greater visibility for IDM but also a host of new issues for business and IT managers to collectively address. Unfortunately, most business leaders are unaware of how much the IDM environment has changed recently (Kalin 2005; Neuenschwander 2006; Small 2006). "For many years, identity management was exclusively an enterprise proposition with an emphasis on security, authorization for resource access and institutional control of all aspects of identity provisioning and usage" (Maler 2009). As a result, IDM has largely been seen by business as a technical issue rather than as a business one (Wagner and Allan 2009). This perception is now slowly changing as businesses run up against their internal IDM limitations and IDM practices have been unable to respond effectively to new business needs (Kho 2009).

The focus group was unanimous about the need to see IDM as a business enabler. "The business climate is changing rapidly with competition from different sources, globalization, and a mobile workforce. We need to be more flexible about how we work with people and we need to work in ways we haven't before. So IDM is really a foundation piece to enable business transformation," said one manager. Another explained, "The ROI for IDM is not great, but we just need to do it; it's 'table stakes' for us." A third noted, "Our failure to address the limitations of our legacy IDM processes has become a real barrier to business transformation."

Unfortunately, the strong technical focus of many IDM specialists has obscured business's understanding of this issue. As with other infrastructure projects, the need for funding has too often focused on nitty-gritty details without explaining in business terms why IDM is so important (Kalin 2005). Focus group managers recognized this problem. "We need an alternative approach to IDM based on business value," said one manager. "IDM is a 'huge dilemma' for us. Business is not taking ownership for it, and IT is having to fund it on its own. But traditional approaches simply don't work today," said another.

What IT managers, and increasingly business leaders, are coming to understand, is that effective IDM, in collaboration with security, is the means whereby organizations can balance their risk and flexibility needs and make appropriate business decisions as they become more mobile, global, digital, and interconnected with customers and other companies (Shuey and West 2005; Small 2009; Wagner and Allan 2009). In the risk:flexibility equation, the risks of poor identity management are much better known and described than the flexibility component. IDM risks include fraud or identity theft, privacy and regulatory noncompliance, reputational loss resulting from information loss or theft, and financial loss if customers and partners lose trust in an organization's ability to protect their information (Allan et al. 2009; Britt 2008; Perkins 2009; Shuey and West 2005). The risk component of IDM was also more widely incorporated in the practices of the focus group organizations as well. For example, one large organization now has a chief information security officer who is responsible for IDM at the enterprise level. Another has implemented processes to manage identity risks across several initiatives. Legal departments of their organizations are also active in providing oversight for external partnering arrangements because companies are concerned about who is using their data and who has access to their intellectual property. In short, as one manager stated, an important organizational priority is to "develop IDM capabilities that will enable us to work together without sacrificing security or productivity."

Beyond risk management however, business enablement/flexibility is an equally important component of the IDM value proposition. One manager stated, "We need to be more flexible about how we work with people and to work in ways we haven't worked before." A composite list of business needs that require strong IDM compiled from the focus group includes the following:

- Support for a more mobile and global workforce
- Speedier mergers and acquisitions
- Increased linkages with partners and suppliers
- The ability to deal with increasing volumes of information and present a consolidated view of data from across many different systems
- Protection for massive amounts of data moving around the world and between companies
- Improved online customer service and customer access to information
- Increased collaboration
- More rapid access to external capabilities (i.e., outsourcing)
- Addressing complex external relationships (i.e., a partner one day and a competitor the next; a partner in one area and a competitor in another).

Table 20.1 illustrates how one manager views the IDM flexibility:risk equation with respect to enabling collaboration. Note that there is not a one:one correspondence between the services enabled and the risks involved, further complicating the equation.

Other business IDM needs relate to cost containment and productivity. In many cases, users are frustrated with multiple sign-ons and complex and time-consuming security access processes that do not appear to add value (Kho 2009; Maler 2009; Perkins 2009). Finally, many organizations want to provide improved customer experiences, build customer and partner ecosystems, and facilitate new ways of working and remote access (Allan et al. 2009; Kho 2009; Small 2009).

TABLE 20.1   Effective IDM Balances Business Flexibility and Risk Management

Enabling Collaboration	Managing Risk
• Give users access to the resources they need to be productive. • Link business processes across security boundaries. • Quickly roll out new services to customers and partners.	• Ensure individuals are efficiently granted appropriate rights to resources and services. • Ensure *only* authorized individuals are granted access rights. • Monitor what authorized users are doing with their access to identify insider threats. • Be able to monitor, audit, and report on the implementation and effectiveness of controls for compliance and regulatory purposes.

IDM CHALLENGES FOR IT MANAGERS

Each of these business needs—to improve customer experiences, build customer and partner ecosystems, and facilitate new ways of working and remote access—represents a series of IDM challenges for IT managers. Whereas in the past, IT has been able to limit access to data and applications through building a secure firewall around an organization prohibiting external access, today's organizations are increasingly becoming more porous and are heading toward complete deperimeterization (Maler 2009). "As we increase the number of our strategic partnerships IT becomes a barrier without effective IDM," said one manager. "We don't want to become identity managers for everyone who accesses our data," said another. "Therefore, we need to do IDM differently than we have been."

Managing IDM in a deperimeterized world means moving away from an IDM approach that is data- and applicationcentric. In the legacy environment that most IT managers have inherited, IDM is managed on a system-by-system basis (Waters 2007). As a result, users often have many usernames and passwords. One study found that 37 percent of enterprises have between seven and twelve passwords per employee, and 12 percent have twelve or more (Kho 2009). Thus, it is no surprise that, even internally, managing user identities and entitlements has become increasingly complex and that IDM in many organizations has become siloed and fragmented (Allan et al. 2009). Furthermore, legacy systems often have numerous vulnerabilities and flaws, given that they were designed for a firewalled world (Aitoro 2008). One manager described her company's current state of IDM as follows:

> *"We have no consolidated view of which employees have access to which assets. We cannot validate access rights and privileges. Access is not revoked in a timely fashion when an employee changes jobs or leaves. Our user administration is complex and overlapping, and pre-employment checks cannot be confirmed prior to granting information access to workers."*

Many organizations are struggling with elevating IDM from being done by individual systems to being managed at an enterprise level. As a starting point, focus group members were trying to develop enterprise policies and procedures for both internal staff and external access. Developing the right processes and governance is critical, they stressed, because of the flexibility:risk trade-offs involved. "Our goal is to develop a single, enterprise ID," said one manager, "and to have one integrated, automated IDM life cycle."

Unfortunately, such an integrated, enterprise process is still more of a goal than a reality. Organizations are hampered in developing it by a number of factors. First, as noted above, there is limited business understanding of the business benefits of effective IDM and, thus, limited funding available for building the infrastructure and staffing the process (Kho 2009). Second, governance is typically fragmented between IT, the business, HR, and legal departments (Maler 2009; Wagner 2009). Third, current IDM practices and processes are often manual (Small 2006). Fourth, the security risks are increasing rapidly (Kho 2009; Nash 2009), and fifth, the number and type of devices not provisioned by an organization (i.e., cellphones, laptops, etc.) and the number and type of remote or external users needing access are increasing exponentially (Waters 2007).

While IT managers are working on these internal challenges, they are poorly supported by the available technologies, standards, and legal frameworks. Although IDM is about more than technology, tools can be useful in many aspects of the life cycle, including administration, audit and analytics, authentication, and authorization. Unfortunately, the available tools do not map well to these IDM functions, and there is considerable confusion about their capabilities (Kreizman et al. 2009). Many tools are proprietary, making it difficult to easily deploy IDM across enterprise boundaries (Kho 2009; Saran 2007). These problems are exacerbated by a lack of common language, standards, and accepted best practices in IDM (Kho 2009; Neuenschwander 2006). As one manager explained, "Without common standards and a common understanding of IDM principles, it is very difficult for organizations to move forward and engage in federated IDM, though that is what we would all like to do."

Most countries' legal frameworks are also woefully lacking in numerous ways. One study found that there are no universally accepted standards of identity proofing or common standards of what attributes should be used to identify an individual or a business (Smith 2007). This means that every organization, and their legal department, is left to determine what attributes they should collect for appropriate access control. Thus, in most focus group companies, every external relationship must be manually configured and legal approval sought. "We are held to be legally accountable for who is using our data," said one manager. Another noted, "We must assess each vendor individually regarding their standards and practices." In some cases, organizations' legal obligations are unclear, and in others companies appear to be overregulated, resulting in considerable confusion (Neuenschwander 2006; Saran 2007; Smith 2008). Finally, for global companies, the challenge is even greater as they must factor different countries' privacy laws into their access equations. "In many cases, we must control what data leave a country, preventing global service providers from accessing certain kinds of data," explained a manager. The overall result is that legal concerns have meant that federated IDM has been much slower to take off than initially expected, and external access to company data and processes is still limited and largely manual.

Overall, managing access across an enterprise of any size at any deeper level than coarse access control is "a Herculean effort" (Neuenschwander 2006). What's needed, according to the focus group, is a different approach to IDM. "At present, we have point products, point problems, fragmented policies, and processes that simply don't work for our business environment," stated a manager. Others agree: "The increased scale of network access today exceeds the original models of IDM" (Small 2006). "[The current] fragmented, siloed approach cannot meet the needs for business agility in enterprises with ever-increasing numbers of internal and external users across hetero-geneous legacy, client/server, web and service-oriented architecture environments" (Allan et al. 2009).

PRINCIPLES OF EFFECTIVE IDM IN THE FUTURE

Newer approaches to IDM are by no means well established, and there are still many gaps in our understanding about how these might work. However, several principles to guide this development are quite widely accepted. These include the following:

- *Approach IDM holistically.* Focus group managers agree that IDM should be an integrated part of an organization's overall security framework that consists of several layers, each of which works with the others to create an environment of trust and protection (see Figure 20.1). A layered approach provides multiple forms of backup protection in case vulnerabilities are detected, while integration ensures that practices are as efficient as possible from both a user and a cost point of view. A comprehensive framework should support both internal and external access, address governance and process as well as technical concerns, and integrate IDM into policy setting (Suess and Morooney 2009; Wagner and Allan 2009).
- *Focus on business value.* As noted above, the business-enabling elements of IDM can often get lost in the technological jargon that too often characterizes IDM plans and discussions (Smith 2008). Several elements of business value should be consid-

Compliance: Demonstrate policy enforcement aligned to regulations, standards, laws, and agreements.

Identity and Access: Provide controlled and secure access to information, applications, and assets for both internal and external users.

Information Security: Protect and secure data and information assets.

Application Security: Continuously manage, monitor, and audit access to applications.

Infrastructure Security: Comprehensively manage threats and vulnerabilities across networks, servers, and end points.

Physical Security: Monitor and control access to buildings and secure areas.

FIGURE 20.1 IDM Is Part of a Holistic Security Framework

ered in developing an IDM framework. First, IDM should be designed to help make effective business decisions and manage the flexibility:risk trade-offs that are involved (Allan et al. 2009; Small 2006). Second, it should reduce the cost of providing effective IDM (Perkins 2009; Small 2009). Third, it should increase trust both internally and externally in an organization's IDM practices (Smith 2007). Fourth, it should support the development of electronic services, virtual and remote work, and global sourcing (Wagner and Allan 2009). Finally, by streamlining IDM practices, it should enhance productivity and adherence to acceptable-use policies (Kalin 2005; Maler 2009; Small 2006).

- *Adopt standards wherever possible.* It was widely recognized in the focus group and elsewhere that enterprise IDM should adhere to open standards in order to facilitate provisioning of cross-enterprise services (Smith 2008). However, these standards are just beginning to be developed and are still far from being broadly accepted (Kho 2009; Saran 2007). Thus, at present, companies must largely create their own—either on their own or within their industry. Several members of the focus group are participating in standards-creating bodies that are designed to create small federated IDM environments in order to be able to trust identities created within them. Similarly, other third-party IDM services are beginning to emerge (Fest 2008; Neuenschwander 2006). It is therefore important for IT managers to monitor these developments and to adopt standardized approaches as they become available.

- *Develop a roadmap.* IDM is a rapidly evolving field (Allan et al. 2009). Moving from traditional approaches to newer and more effective ones will take time and require vision and the development of a roadmap (Allan et al. 2009; Smedlinghof 2008). Such a roadmap would not only create the framework, policies, and standards for IDM, but it would also develop the processes and infrastructure required to achieve it. Streamlining processes to structure IDM activities more effectively and eliminate duplication of effort is a good first step (Allan et al. 2009). Improved integration of business and IT IDM processes is another (Shuey and West 2005). Finally, efforts need to be made to simplify security technology such as developing a single sign-on for systems that links to user roles, segmenting data to enable more granular access, and improving monitoring and reporting (Kreizman et al. 2009; Small 2006). Focus group members were at different stages of developing such roadmaps, but all were actively working on them.

- *Decouple IDM from applications, environments, and companies.* The goal of newer approaches to IDM is to abstract it from specific entities. Clearly, it must be decoupled from individual applications so that it can be managed holistically. However, it must also make identities portable across systems, technical environments and devices (Small 2006; Smedlinghoff 2008). And it must be designed to rapidly connect (and disconnect) users and partners as required (Perkins 2009; Wagner and Allan 2009). Some newer approaches to IDM are usercentric, putting customers at the center of IDM by making them owners of their own data rather than many different companies. These use identity management services that act as identity containers and provide proof of identity to companies as permitted by a customer, who can choose what information to release to a company (Maler 2009). Even though there is agreement that such IDM services are not yet practical for most companies, decoupling IDM as much as possible from proprietary practices is good preparation for the direction that most observers (and the focus group) believe that IDM is headed (Djordjevic and Dimitrakos 2005; Kho 2009; Maler 2009).

MOVING FORWARD WITH IDM: ADVICE FOR IT MANAGERS

No IT manager or business leader should ever underestimate the challenges involved in IDM as the field struggles to keep up with our increasingly networked, global, and mobile world. Members of the focus group had several recommendations for other IT managers about how to begin moving toward the next level of IDM. These include the following:

- *Identify IDM needs and set policy.*   An important step in evolving IDM is to better understand the organization's needs for IDM both internally and externally. As noted above, there is no standard list of identity attributes or an external identity management body, so organizations are forced to fend for themselves in determining acceptable internal and external authentication; layers of authentication, such as situational or corporate access; IDM triggers, such as changing jobs or adding a new vendor; and the level of granularity of access that is desirable. Understanding IDM needs is fundamental to establishing access policies and to developing effective IDM processes, stated the group.
- *Address IDM process and governance.*   It is widely accepted that many organizations have inadequate and immature IDM processes (Allan et al. 2009; Kho 2009; Suess and Morooney 2009). Many focus group members were in the process of assessing the current state of their IDM and determining their strategy and vision for adapting it to meet their needs. One manager explained her organization's IDM goals as "We want to have one enterprise ID; one integrated, automated full life cycle process; one (or a very few) sign-ons; one book of record; and improved compliance, service, and productivity." Other managers were concentrating on improving the process for external access. "We need a process for assessing vendor IDM practices," said one. Another was looking at how to recognize external identities from trusted third parties. All these processes need governance, and business ownership of IDM was viewed as essential to making the right decisions about how the flexibility:risk trade-offs are handled. "The trouble in our organization is that we have no overall owner," said a manager. "Ownership is split between IT, operations, and our lines of business." A single leader and clarity about roles and responsibilities were deemed essential to improving. Another manager added, "We need to make process changes to get the sequence of events right, and we need to reengineer our workforce management process to better integrate with our IDM process." Viewing IDM as a life cycle can be useful in helping to develop and manage an improved process (see Figure 20.2).
- *Integrate IDM with architecture.*   IDM technology is an important component of any organization's approach to IDM, stated the focus group, but only if it is combined with effective processes and behavioral changes. Most of the technical challenges involved stem from poor systems integration and a lack of standards. These can best be addressed by an organization's architecture group as it plans and designs how applications and infrastructure will evolve. Clearly, IDM

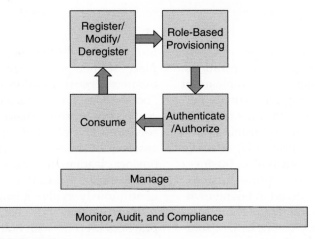

FIGURE 20.2   The IDM Life Cycle

should also be integrated with the organization's security framework, and many enterprises are working to extract IDM from their applications and develop a single enterprise sign-on that is linked to access and other controls. In the longer term, most focus group organizations were hoping that IDM will eventually become a service that is provided by a third party or is jointly owned by a federation of related organizations. Although this has not been widely implemented at present, architects and security specialists should be aware of standards developments and any initiatives in their industry to share identity information.

- *Incorporate traceability and auditability.*   What is often overlooked in considering IDM is the back end of the life cycle process, including monitoring accounts, user activity, and compliance reporting. Increasingly, these activities are becoming part of legal and regulatory best practices. Focus group managers explained that a significant amount of their time is now devoted to this work and that new tools and policies are needed in this area. "The top three threats to enterprise security are insider related," stated one manager. These include employee error, data theft, and insider sabotage. Overall, insider fraud costs U.S. companies over $600 billion annually (Small 2009). To address these risks, many managers have been given new oversight roles and responsibilities but inadequate processes and tools to help them. "IDM has created work for me that I never expected," said a manager. "I now receive several messages a day to revalidate transactions that are being done by my staff. Every executive has a responsibility to review what is being done." Some of the monitoring that is now considered important includes monitoring the volume of user activity, the types and locations of activities, and ensuring activities are properly segregated to prevent fraud. Finally, reports must also demonstrate compliance with all regulations and laws. Ideally, as much of this work as possible should be automated, while governance and processes also need to be designed to effectively incorporate these new requirements for IDM.

Conclusion

Identity management is a huge and constantly changing challenge for organizations. IT managers must balance the substantial risks involved in becoming increasingly networked and opening their firewalls to clients and partners with the resulting business value delivered. Like so much else in IT, effective IDM must be viewed from both a business and a technical lens and requires business leaders to be actively involved in taking ownership of the decisions involved. There is no straightforward and easy-to-implement solution for IDM. As a result, IT managers are all too often caught between a rock and a hard place—either being seen as the obstacle to business transformation or having to take "bet the company" risks with inadequate data and access controls. However, they do themselves no favor by failing to articulate IDM issues in business terms when speaking with business leaders. It is therefore incumbent on all organizational leaders to work together to continuously evolve a practical and holistic framework that will ensure that their IDM practices keep up with both the opportunities and the risks of a transforming world.

References

Aitoro, J. "Identity Management." *Government Executive* 40, no. 7 (June 15, 2008): 30–33.

Allan, A., and E. Perkins. "Key Issues for Identity and Access Management, 2009." Gartner Inc., ID Number: G00165392, March 6, 2009.

Allan, A., E. Perkins, and T. Scholtz. "Gartner Identity and Access Management Program Maturity Model." Gartner Inc., ID Number: G00170668, October 8, 2009.

Britt, P. "Taking the Byte Out of Cybercrime." *Information Today* 25, no. 11 (December 2008).

Djordjevic, I., and T. Dimitrakos. "A Note on the Anatomy of Federation." *BT Technology Journal* 23, no. 4 (October 2005): 89–106.

Doctorow, C. "A Conversation with Cory Doctorow and Hal Stern." *ACM Queue* 5, no. 3 (April 2007): 16–23.

Fest, G. "Identity Management: The Lure and Peril of OpenID." *Bank Technology News* 21, no. 4 (April 2008): 10–11.

Kalin, S. "How to Tackle Identity and Access Management." *CIO Magazine,* December 1, 2005, www.cio.com.

Kho, N. D. "The Changing Face of Identity Management." *EContent* 32, no. 3 (April 2009): 21–25.

Kreizman, G., A. Allan, P. Carpenter, E. Perkins, and R. Wagner. "Gartner Identity and Access Management Capability Models, 2009." Gartner Inc., ID Number: G00166023, March 10, 2009.

Maler, E. "The Design of Everyday Identity." *Online Information Review* 33, no. 3 (2009): 443–57.

Nash, K. "Tough Work Ahead to Defend Digital Infrastructure; Review of Security Needs Provides a Long List of Issues to Address." *CIO Magazine* 22, no. 15 (July 1, 2009). www.cio.org.

Neuenschwander, M. "Identity Management Market Shifts—Who's Out There?" *Network Security* 2006, no. 12 (December 2006): 7–10.

Perkins, E. "Cost Cutting in Enterprises and Six Ways Identity and Access Management Programs Can Help, 2009 Update." Gartner Inc., ID Number: G00167403, April 20, 2009.

Saran, C. "Lack of Interoperability and Liability Hold Back Identity Management IT." *Computer Weekly*, November 13, 2007, 16.

Shuey, R., and A. West. "Building a Balanced Identity Management Infrastructure." *EDUCAUSE Review* 41, no. 5 (September/October 2005): 138–39.

Small, M. "Unify and Simplify: Re-thinking Identity Management." *Network Security* 2006, no. 7: 11–14.

———. "Keeping the bad guys out: keeping the customers happy." The British Journal of Administrative Management." Summer 2009, 32–33.

Smedlinghoff, T. "Legal Obstacles Delaying Federated Identity Management." *CIO Magazine,* January 30, 2008, www.cio.com.

Smith, D. "The Challenge of Federated Identity Management." *Network Security* 2008, no. 4, 7–9.

Smith, H. A. "Identity Management and Authentication: A Fundamental of Improved Service Delivery." Report of the IDMA&A Task Force to the XI Lac Carling Conference, Niagara Falls, Ontario, 2007.

Suess, J., and K. Morooney. "Identity Management and Trust Services: Foundations for Cloud Computing." *EDUCAUSE Review* 44, no. 5 (2009): 25–42.

Wagner, R. "Roundup of identity and access management research 3Q09: core IAM and IAM governance." Gartner Inc., ID Number: G00170862, September 24, 2009.

Wagner, R., and A. Allan. "Highlights from the Gartner European Identity and Access Summit, 2009." Gartner Inc., ID Number: G00167237, April 17, 2009.

Waters, J. "ID Management Definition and Solutions." *CIO Magazine*, May 2, 2007.

Linking IT to Business Metrics[1]

From the first time IT started making a significant dent in corporate balance sheets, the holy grail of academics, consultants, and business and IT managers has been to show that what a company spends on IT has a direct impact on its performance. Early efforts to do this, such as those trying to link various measures of IT input (e.g., budget dollars, number of PCs, number of projects) with various measures of business performance (e.g., profit, productivity, stock value) all failed to show any relationship at all (Marchand et al. 2000). Since then, everyone has properly concluded that the relationship between what is done in IT and what happens in the business is considerably more complex than these studies first supposed. In fact, many researchers would suggest that the relationship is so filtered through a variety of "conversion effects" (Cronk and Fitzgerald 1999) as to be practically impossible to demonstrate. Most IT managers would agree. They have long argued that technology is not the major stumbling block to achieving business performance; it is the business itself—the processes, the managers, the culture, and the skills—that makes the difference. Therefore, it is simply not realistic to expect to see a clear correlation between IT and business performance at any level. When technology is successful, it is a *team* effort, and the contributions of the IT and business components of an initiative cannot and should not be separated.

Nevertheless, IT expenditures must be justified. Thus, most companies have concentrated on determining the "business value" that specific IT projects deliver. By focusing on a goal that matters to business (e.g., better information, faster transaction processing, reduced staff), then breaking this goal down into smaller projects that IT can affect directly, they have tried to "peel the onion" and show specifically how IT delivers value in a piecemeal fashion. Thus, a series of surrogate measures are usually used to demonstrate IT's impact in an organization. (See Smith and McKeen 2003 for more details.)

More recently, companies are taking another look at business performance metrics and IT. They believe it is time to "put the onion back together" and focus on what really matters to the enterprise. This perspective argues that employees who truly understand what their business is trying to achieve can sense the right ways to personally improve performance that will show up at a business unit and organizational level. "People who understand the

[1]Smith, H. A., J. D. McKeen, and C. Street, "Linking IT to Business Metrics." *Journal of Information Science and Technology* 1, no. 1 (2004): 13–26. Reproduced by permission of the Information Institute.

business and are informed will be proactive and . . . have a disposition to create business value every day in many small and not-so-small ways" (Marchand et al. 2000). Although the connection may not be obvious, they say, it is there nevertheless and can be demonstrated in tangible ways. The key to linking what IT does to business performance is, therefore, to create an environment within which everyone thoroughly understands what measures are important to the business and is held accountable for them. This point of view does not suggest that all the work done to date to learn how IT delivers value to an organization (e.g., business cases, productivity measures) has been unnecessary, only that it is incomplete. Without close attention to business metrics *in addition,* it is easy for IT initiatives and staff to lose their focus and become less effective.

This chapter looks at how these controversial yet compelling ideas are being pursued in organizations to better understand how companies are attempting to link IT work and firm performance through business metrics. The first section describes how business metrics themselves are evolving and looks at how new management philosophies are changing how these measures are communicated and applied. Next it discusses the types of metrics that are important for a well-rounded program of business measurement and how IT can influence them. Then it presents three different ways companies are specifically linking their IT departments with business metrics and the benefits and challenges they have experienced in doing this. This section concludes with some general principles for establishing a business measurement program in IT. Finally, it offers some advice to managers about how to succeed with such a program in IT.

BUSINESS MEASUREMENT: AN OVERVIEW

Almost everyone agrees that *the* primary goal of the business is to make money for its shareholders (Goldratt and Cox 1984; Haspeslagh et al. 2001; Kaplan and Norton 1996). Unfortunately, in large businesses this objective frequently gets lost in the midst of people's day-to-day activities because profit cannot be measured directly at the level at which most employees in a company work (Haspeslagh et al. 2001). This "missing link" between work and business performance leads companies to look for ways to bridge this gap. They believe that if a firm's strategies for achieving its goal can be tied much more closely to everyday processes and decision making, frontline employees will be better able to create business value. Proponents of this value-based management (VBM) approach have demonstrated that an explicit, firmwide commitment to shareholder value, clear communication about how value is created or destroyed, and incentive systems that are linked to key business measures will increase the odds of a positive increase in share price (Haspeslagh et al. 2001).

> Measurement counts. What a company measures and the way it measures influence both the mindsets of managers and the way people behave. The best measures are tied to business performance and are linked to the strategies and business capabilities of the company. (Marchand et al. 2000)

Although companies ascribe to this notion in theory, they do not always act in ways that are consistent with this belief. All too often, therefore, because they lack clarity about the links between business performance and their own work, individuals and even business units have to take leaps of faith in what they do (Marchand et al. 2000).

Nowhere has this been more of a problem than in IT. As has been noted so often in the past, IT investments have not always delivered the benefits expected (Bensaou and Earl 1998; Holland and Sharke 2001). "Efforts to measure the link between IT investment and business performance from an economics perspective have . . . failed to establish a consistent causal linkage with sustained business profitability" (Marchand et al. 2000). Value-based management suggests that if IT staff do not understand the business, they cannot sense how and where to change it effectively with technology. Many IT and business managers have implicitly known this for some time. VBM simply gives them a better framework for implementing their beliefs more systematically.

One of the most significant efforts to integrate an organization's mission and strategy with a measurement system has been Kaplan and Norton's (1996) balanced scorecard. They explain that competing in the information age is much less about managing physical, tangible assets and much more about the ability of a company to mobilize its intangible assets, such as customer relationships, innovation, employee skills, and information technology. Thus, they suggest that not only should business measures look at how well a company has done *in the past* (i.e., financial performance), but they also need to look at metrics related to customers, internal business processes, and learning and growth that position the firm to achieve *future* performance. Although it is difficult putting a reliable monetary value on these items, Kaplan and Norton suggest that such nonfinancial measures are critical success factors for superior financial performance in the future. Research is showing that this is, in fact, the case. Companies that use a balanced scorecard tend to have a better return on investment (ROI) than those that rely on traditional financial measures alone (Alexander 2000).

Today many companies use some sort of scorecard or "dashboard" to track a variety of different metrics of organizational health. However, IT traditionally has not paid much attention to business results, focusing instead on its own internal measures of performance (e.g., IT operations efficiency, projects delivered on time, etc.). This has perpetuated the serious disconnect between the business and IT that often manifests itself in perceptions of poor alignment between the two groups, inadequate payoffs from IT investments, poor relationships, and finger-pointing (Bensaou and Earl 1998; Holland and Sharke 2001). All too often IT initiatives are conceived with little reference to major business results, relying instead on lower-level business value surrogates that are not always related to these measures. IT organizations are getting much better at this bottom-up approach to IT investment (Smith and McKeen 2003), but undelivered IT value remains a serious concern in many organizations. One survey of CFOs found that only 49 percent felt that their ROI expectations for technology had been met (Holland and Sharke 2001). "Despite considerable effort, no practical model has been developed to measure whether a company's IT investments will definitely contribute to sustainable competitive advantage" (Marchand et al. 2000). Clearly, in spite of significant efforts over many years, traditional IT measurement programs have been inadequate at assessing business value. Many IT organizations believe, therefore, that it is time for a different approach to delivering IT value, one that holds IT accountable to the same measures and goals as the rest of the business.

KEY BUSINESS METRICS FOR IT

No one seriously argues that IT has no impact on an organization's overall financial performance anymore. There may be disagreement about whether it has a positive or a negative impact, but technology is too pervasive and significant an expense in most firms for it not to have some influence on the corporate bottom line. However, as has been argued above, we now recognize that neither technology nor business alone is responsible for IT's financial impact. It is instead a joint responsibility of IT *and* the business. This suggests that they need to be held accountable *together* for its impact. Some companies have accepted this principle for individual IT projects (i.e., holding business and IT managers jointly responsible for achieving their anticipated benefits), yet few have extended it to an enterprise level. VBM suggests that this lack of attention to enterprise performance by IT is one reason it has been so hard to fully deliver business value for technology investments. Holding IT accountable for a firm's performance according to key financial metrics is, therefore, an important step toward improving its contribution to the corporate bottom line.

However, although financial results are clearly an important part of any measurement of a business's success today, they are not enough. Effective business metrics programs should also include nonfinancial measures, such as customer and employee satisfaction. As noted above, because such nonfinancial measures are predictive of future performance, they offer an organization the opportunity to make changes that will ultimately affect their financial success.

Kaplan and Norton (1996) state "the importance of customer satisfaction probably cannot be overemphasized." Companies that do not understand their customers' needs will likely lose customers and profitability. Research shows that merely adequate satisfaction is insufficient to lead to customer loyalty and ultimately profit. Only firms where customers are completely or extremely satisfied can achieve this result (Heskett et al. 1994). As a result, many companies now undertake systematic customer satisfaction surveys. However, in IT it is rare to find external customer satisfaction as one of the metrics on which IT is evaluated. While IT's "customers" are usually considered to be internal, these days technology can make a significant difference in how external customers perceive a firm and whether or not they want to do business with it. Systems that are not reliable or available when needed, cannot provide customers with the information they need, or cannot give customers the flexibility they require are all too common. And with the advent of e-business, self-service systems are being designed to interface directly with external customers. It is, therefore, appropriate to include external customer satisfaction as a business metric for IT.

Another important nonfinancial business measure is employee satisfaction. This is a "leading indicator" of customer satisfaction. That is, employee satisfaction in one year is strongly linked to customer satisfaction and profitability in the next (Koys 2001). Employees' positive attitudes toward their company and their jobs lead to positive behaviors toward customers and, therefore, to improved financial performance (Rucci et al. 1998; Ulrich et al. 1991). IT managers have always watched their own employee satisfaction rate intently because of its close links to employee turnover. However, they often miss the link between IT employee satisfaction and customer satisfaction—both internal customer satisfaction, which leads to improved general employee satisfaction, and external customer satisfaction. Thus, only a few companies hold IT managers accountable for general employee satisfaction.

Both customer and employee satisfaction should be part of a business metrics program for IT. With its ever-growing influence in organizations, technology is just as likely to affect external customer and general employee satisfaction as many other areas of a business. This suggests that IT has three different levels of measurement and accountability:

1. *Enterprise measures.*   These tie the work of IT directly to the performance of the organization (e.g., external customer satisfaction, corporate financial performance).
2. *Functional measures.*   These assess the internal work of the IT organization as a whole (e.g., IT employee satisfaction, internal customer satisfaction, operational performance, development productivity).
3. *Project measures.*   These assess the performance of a particular project team in delivering specific value to the organization (e.g., business case benefits, delivery on time).

Functional and project measures are usually well addressed by IT measurement programs today. It is the enterprise level that is usually missing.

DESIGNING BUSINESS METRICS FOR IT

The firms that hold IT accountable for enterprise business metrics believe this approach fosters a common sense of purpose, enables everyone to make better decisions, and helps IT staff understand the implications of their work for the success of the organization (Haspeslagh et al. 2001; Marchand et al. 2000). The implementation of business metrics programs varies widely among companies, but three approaches taken to linking IT with business metrics are distinguishable.

1. *Balanced scorecard.*   This approach uses a classic balanced scorecard with measures in all four scorecard dimensions (see the "Sample Balanced Scorecard Business Metrics" feature). Each metric is selected to measure progress against the entire enterprise's business plan. These are then broken down into business unit plans and appropriate submetrics identified. Individual scorecards are then developed with metrics that will link into their business unit scorecards. With this approach, IT is treated as a separate business unit and has its own scorecard linked to the business plan. "Our management finally realized that we need to have everyone thinking in the same way," explained one manager. "With enterprise systems, we can't have people working in silos anymore." The scorecards are very visible in the organization with company and business unit scorecards and those of senior executives posted on the company's intranet. "People are extremely interested in seeing how we're doing. Scorecards have provided a common framework for our entire company." They also provide clarity for employees about their roles in how they affect key business metrics.

Sample Balanced Scorecard Business Metrics

- Shareholder value (financial)
- Expense management (financial)
- Customer/client focus (customer)
- Loyalty (customer)
- Customercentric organization (customer)

- Effectiveness and efficiency of business operations (operations)
- Risk management (operations)
- Contribution to firmwide priorities and business initiatives (growth)

Although scorecards have meant that there is better understanding of the business's drivers and plans at senior management levels, considerable resistance to them is still found at the lower levels in IT. "While developers see how they can affect our customers, they don't see how they can affect shareholder value, profit, or revenue, and they don't want to be held accountable for these things," stated the same manager. She noted that implementing an effective scorecard program relies on three things: good data to provide better metrics, simplicity of metrics, and enforcement. "Now if someone's scorecard is not complete, they cannot get a bonus. This is a huge incentive to follow the program."

2. *Modified scorecard.*   A somewhat different approach to a scorecard is taken by one company in the focus group. This firm has selected five key measures (see the "Modified Scorecard Business Metrics" feature) that are closely linked to the company's overall vision statement. Results are communicated to all staff on a quarterly basis in a short performance report. This includes a clear explanation of each measure, quarterly progress, a comparison with the previous year's quarterly results, and a "stretch" goal for the organization to achieve. The benefit of this approach is that it orients all employees in the company to the same mission and values. With everyone using the same metrics, alignment is much clearer all the way through the firm, according to the focus group manager.

Modified Scorecard Business Metrics

- ***Customer loyalty index.*** The percent of customers who said they were very satisfied with the company and would recommend it to others.
- ***Associate loyalty index.*** Employees' perception of the company as a great place to work.
- ***Revenue growth.*** The percentage of this year's total revenues with last year's total revenues.

- ***Operating margin.*** The operating income earned before interest and taxes for every dollar of revenue.
- ***Return on capital employed.*** Earnings before interest and tax divided by the capital used to generate the earnings.

In IT these key enterprise metrics are complemented by an additional set of business measures established by the business units. Each line of business identifies one or two key business unit metrics on which they and their IT team will be measured. Functional groups within IT are evaluated according to the same metrics as their business partners as well as on company and internal IT team performance. For example, the credit group in IT might be evaluated on the number of new credit accounts the company acquires. Shared IT services (e.g., infrastructure) are evaluated according to an average of all of the IT functional groups' metrics.

The importance the company places on these metrics is reflected in the firm's generous bonus program (i.e., bonuses can reach up to 230 percent of an individual's salary) in which all IT staff participate. Bonuses are separate from an individual's salary, which is linked to personal performance. The percentage influence of each set of business measures (i.e., enterprise, business unit, and individual/team) varies according to the level of the individual in the firm. However, all staff have at least 25 percent of their bonus linked to enterprise performance metrics. No bonuses are paid to anyone if the firm does not reach its earnings-per-share target (which is driven by the five enterprise measures outlined in the "Modified Scorecard Business Metrics" feature). This incentive system makes it clear that everyone's job is connected to business results and helps ensure that attention is focused on the things that are important to the company. As a result, interest is much stronger among IT staff about how the business is doing. "Everyone now speaks the same language," said the manager. "Project alignment is much easier."

3. *Strategic imperatives.*   A somewhat different approach is taken by a third focus group company. Here the executive team annually evaluates the key environmental factors affecting the company, then identifies a number of strategic imperatives for the firm (e.g., achieve industry-leading e-business capability, achieve 10–15 percent growth in earnings per share). These can vary according to the needs of the firm in any particular year. Each area of the business is then asked to identify initiatives that will affect these imperatives and to determine how they will be measured (e.g., retaining customers of a recent acquisition, increased net sales, a new product). In the same way, IT is asked to identify the key projects and measures that will help the business to achieve these imperatives. Each part of the company, including IT, then integrates these measures into its variable pay program (VPP).

The company's VPP links a percentage of an individual's pay to business results and overall business unit performance. This percentage could vary from a small portion of one's salary for a new employee to a considerable proportion for senior management. Within IT, the weight that different measures are accorded in the VPP portion of their pay is determined by a measurement team and approved by the CIO and the president. Figure 21.1 illustrates the different percentages allocated to IT's variable pay component for a typical year. Metrics can change from year to year depending on where management wants to focus everyone's attention. "Performance tends to improve if you measure it," explained the manager. "Over the years, we have ratcheted up our targets in different areas. Once a certain level of performance is achieved, we may change the measure or change the emphasis on this measure."

An important difference from the scorecard approach is the identification of key IT projects. "These are not all IT projects, but a small number that are closely aligned with the strategic business imperatives," stated the manager. "Having the success of these projects associated with their variable pay drives everyone's behavior. People tend to jump in and help if there's a problem with one of them." The goal in this process is for everyone to understand the VPP measures and to

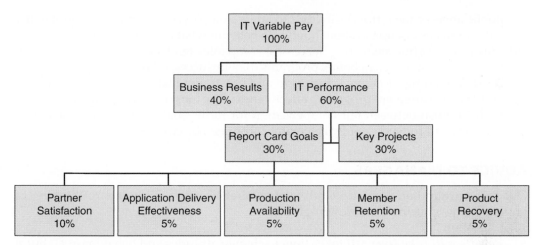

FIGURE 21.1   Percentage Weightings Assigned to IT Variable Pay Components for a Particular Year

make them visible within IT. Targets and results are posted quarterly, and small groups of employees meet to discuss ideas about how they can influence business and IT goals. "Some amazing ideas have come out of these meetings," said the manager. "Everyone knows what's important, and these measures get attention. People use these metrics to make choices all the time in their work."

Each of these business measurement programs has been implemented somewhat differently, but they all share several key features that could be considered principles of a good business metrics program for IT:

1. *Focus on overall business performance.*   These programs all focus employees on both financial and nonfinancial enterprise performance and have an explicit expectation that everyone in the organization can influence these results in some way.
2. *Understanding is a critical success factor.*   If people are going to be held accountable for certain business results, it is important that they understand them. Similarly, if the organization is worried about certain results, this must be communicated as well. Holding regular staff meetings where people can ask questions and discuss results is effective, as is providing results on a quarterly basis. Understanding is the goal. "If you can ask . . . a person programming code and they can tell you three to four of their objectives and how those tie into the company's performance and what the measures of achieving those objectives are, you've got it" (Alexander 2000).
3. *Simplicity.*   Successful companies tend to keep their measures very simple and easy to use (Haspeslagh et al. 2001). In each approach outlined above, a limited number of measures are used. This makes it very easy for employees to calculate their bonuses (or variable pay) based on the metrics provided, which further strengthens the linkage between company performance and individual effort.
4. *Visibility.*   In each of the programs discussed above, metrics were made widely available to all staff on a quarterly basis. In one case they are posted on the company's intranet; in another they are distributed in a printed report; in a third they are posted in

public areas of the office. Visibility encourages employee buy-in and accountability and stimulates discussion about how to do better or what is working well.

5. *Links to incentive systems.*   Successful companies tend to include a much larger number of employees in bonus programs than unsuccessful ones (Haspeslagh et al. 2001). Extending incentive schemes to all IT staff, not just management, is important to a measurement program's effectiveness. The most effective programs appear to distinguish between fair compensation for individual work and competencies and a reward for successfully achieving corporate objectives.

ADVICE TO MANAGERS

Our focus group had some final advice for other IT managers who are thinking of implementing a business metrics program:

- *Results will take time.*   It takes time to change attitudes and behavior in IT, but it is worth making the effort. Positive results may take from six months to a year to appear. "We had some initial pushback from our staff at the beginning," said one manager, "but now the metrics program has become ingrained in our attitudes and behaviors." Another manager noted, "We had a few bumps during our first year, but everyone, especially our executives, is getting better at the program now [that] we're in our third year. It really gets our staff engaged with the business." If there has been no dramatic difference within three years, management should recognize that it is either using the wrong measures or hasn't got employee buy-in to the program (Alexander 2000).

- *Have common goals.*   Having everyone measured on the same business goals helps to build a strong team at all levels in the organization. It makes it easier to set priorities as a group and to collaborate and share resources, as needed.

- *Follow up on problem areas.*   Companies must be prepared to take action about poor results and to involve staff in their plans. In particular, if companies are going to ask customers and employees what they think, they must be prepared to act on the results. All metrics must be taken seriously and acted on if they are to be used to drive behavior and lead to continuous improvement.

- *Be careful what you measure.*   Measuring something makes people pay attention to it, particularly if it is linked to compensation. Metrics must, therefore, be selected with care because they will be a major driver of behavior. For example, if incentives are solely based on financial results, it is probable that some people may be so driven that they will trample on the needs and interests of others. Similarly, if only costs are measured, the needs of customers could be ignored. Conversely, if a metric indicates a problem area, organizations can expect to see a lot of ingenuity and support devoted to addressing it.

- *Don't use measurement as a method of control.*   A business metrics program should be designed to foster an environment in which people look beyond their own jobs and become proactive about the needs of the organization (Marchand et al. 2000). It should aim to communicate strategy and help align individual and organizational initiatives (Kaplan and Norton 1996). All managers should clearly understand that a program of this type should not be used for controlling behavior, but rather as a motivational tool.

Conclusion

Getting the most value out of IT has been a serious concern of the business for many years. In spite of considerable effort, measurement initiatives in IT that use surrogates of business value or that focus on improving internal IT behavior have not been fully successful in delivering results. What has not been tried until very recently is expecting IT to participate in achieving specific enterprise objectives—the same goals as the rest of the organization. This chapter has shown that there are significant benefits to holding IT accountable for key business metrics. Not only are there demonstrable financial returns, but there is also considerable long-term value in aligning everyone's behavior with the same goals; people become more supportive of each other and more sensitive to the greater corporate good, and decisions are easier to make. A good business metrics program, therefore, appears to be a powerful component of effective measurement in IT. IT employees may initially resist accountability for business results, but the experiences of the focus group demonstrate that their objections are usually short lived. If a business measurement program is carefully designed, properly linked to an incentive program, widely implemented, and effectively monitored by management, it is highly likely that business performance will become an integral part of the mind-set of all IT staff and ultimately pay off in a wide variety of ways.

References

Alexander, S. "Business Metrics." *Computerworld* 34, no. 24 (2000): 64.

Bensaou, M., and M. Earl. "The Right Mind-set for Managing Information Technology." *Harvard Business Review* 76, no. 5 (September–October 1998): 110–28.

Cronk, M., and E. Fitzgerald. "Understanding 'IS Business Value': Derivation of Dimensions." *Logistics Information Management* 12, no. 1–2 (1999): 40–49.

Goldratt, E., and J. Cox. *The Goal: Excellence in Manufacturing.* Croton-on-Hudson, NY: North River Press, 1984.

Haspeslagh, P., T. Noda, and F. Boulos. "Managing for Value: It's Not Just About the Numbers." *Harvard Business Review* July–August (2001): 65–73.

Heskett, J., T. Jones, G. Loveman, E. Sasser, and L. Schlesinger. "Putting the Service Profit Chain to Work." *Harvard Business Review* March–April (1994): 164–74.

Holland, W., and G. Sharke. "Is Your IT System VESTed?" *Strategic Finance* 83, no. 6 (December 2001): 34–37.

Kaplan, R., and D. Norton. *The Balanced Scorecard.* Boston: Harvard Business School Press, 1996.

Koys, D. "The Effects of Employee Satisfaction, Organizational Citizenship Behavior, and Turnover on Organizational Effectiveness: A Unit-Level, Longitudinal Study." *Personnel Psychology* 54, no. 1 (Spring 2001): 101–14.

Marchand, D., W. Kettinger, and J. Rollins. "Information Orientation: People, Technology and the Bottom Line." *Sloan Management Review* (Summer 2000): 69–89.

Rucci, A., S. Kirn, and R. Quinn. "The Employee-Customer-Profit Chain at Sears." *Harvard Business Review* 76 (January/February 1998): 82–97.

Smith, H. A., and J. D. McKeen. "Developing and Delivering on the IT Value Proposition." *Communications of the Association for Information Systems* 11, article 25 (April 2003): 438–50.

Ulrich, D., R. Halbrook, D. Meder, M. Stuchlik, and S. Thorpe. "Employee and Customer Attachment: Synergies for Competitive Advantage." *Human Resource Planning* 14 (1991): 89–103.

MINI CASE
Leveraging IT Vendors at SleepSmart[2]

The numbers were in, and Greg Danson breathed a sigh of relief. They looked good. In-stock levels had increased yet again, inventory value per square foot had declined, and sales and general administration costs had come down for the third quarter in a row. "Maybe *now* they'll see we mean business," he said with satisfaction. "They" were the analysts who worked for the leading financial institutions and investment firms. His company, SleepSmart—a leading bed and bedding retailer— had taken a public beating in the past few years. Chief among the criticisms had been the company's outdated technology. "If SleepSmart hopes to compete with retail giants like Sears, Target, and Walmart, it will have to move its technology into the current century . . . and fast," they noted. The result had been a steady decline in the price of SleepSmart's stock.

As SleepSmart's CIO, Greg had always privately agreed with the analysts. Over the years, he had looked longingly at some of the technology other retailers had installed. Although the exact details were secret, he knew that they had databases that gave them up-to-the-minute sales figures, and their systems were integrated with their suppliers and with each other. All of these efforts enabled other retailers to do more (i.e., provide more merchandise and better customer service) with less (i.e., at lower cost). It had been a happy time for him when the other executives had finally been forced to recognize that technology had to be an integral part of SleepSmart's business strategy. This was the first time in his thirty years with the firm that IT had enjoyed serious executive support and investment. Until recently, IT had always been relegated to a supporting role. "We're retailers, not technology gurus," the other executives had explained. "We know what our customers want. We don't need to be leading edge. Just keep our cash registers working."

The company had been in business for almost a hundred years, growing from a small, family-owned mattress manufacturer to a large, national chain store with more than five hundred locations. Growth was essential in the present competitive environment, so in recent years SleepSmart had diversified into all kinds of bedroom furniture, bedding, curtains, and even closet design. Its fledgling BathSmart division was seeking to extend its market reach even further. And its Web site even sold pajamas and nightgowns. But in the rush to diversify, little attention had been paid to streamlining and integrating the firm's technology. Systems did not "talk" to other systems; it took weeks to pull sales figures together from the different divisions; customers were confused. "Why is my SleepSmart Bonus Club statement still coming to my old address when I've already given you my new one, but my charge card bill manages to come to the right address every month?" was a common complaint. Customers didn't realize how many separate systems needed name and address updates. In short, the company's systems had been embarrassingly old-fashioned, and the nudge from the analysts had been a welcome wake-up call, as far as Greg was concerned.

With the company's purse strings finally pried open, Greg had been given the mandate to rebuild the mishmash of systems the company had accumulated into a state-of-the-art technology platform within three years. The first step was relatively simple: draw up a comprehensive "technology blueprint" identifying the desired state of the company's IT platform. After consultation with the business about its current and future needs, followed by an assessment of the current state of the firm's technology (dismal), all of the major technology vendors were consulted for their ideas. Naturally, they all knew how to solve SleepSmart's problem: install their own proprietary

---

[2]Smith, H. A., and J. D. McKeen. "Leveraging IT Vendors at SleepSmart," #1-L06-1-001. Queen's School of Business, May 2006. Reproduced by permission of Queen's University, School of Business, Kingston, Ontario.

software and hire them to implement it! Brushing aside all the hype, Greg had been impressed with the quality of the vendors' presentations and the depth of their retail knowledge. Many had invested substantial amounts in their industry-specific products and brought a breadth of experience to the planning process that his staff didn't have.

This was the fun part. It was a chance to wipe the slate clean of all of the mixed-up, disparate, and overlapping systems and data and really dream big about the future. The new integrated technology blueprint solved all these problems. It called for one financial system, one HR system, and one customer-facing program. There would be one data warehouse and one integrated view of the customer. From this, a three-year plan was developed to help make SleepSmart more cost efficient and to give staff better information for doing their jobs.

But as usual, the devil was in the details. "The *only* way we can do all this work at the same time is by using our suppliers' competencies," he told his chief architect, Stan Bailey, and his other IT directors. "We simply don't have enough staff or skills in-house."

Like most other companies, SleepSmart had worked with a number of different vendors over the years to address their needs and had developed strong competencies in contract development and management. Typically, the IT guys would scour the marketplace to find the product or service they wanted, and they would negotiate with each vendor for the best price. They would then monitor the contract to ensure SleepSmart got value for its money. In the meantime, the vendors were always looking for ways to sell more product because that's how they were compensated. "Doing the deal" was the focus of both groups.

The problem, as Greg explained patiently to his staff, was that this process took time and generated negative energy between the company and the vendor. "We simply don't have the time to do business this way anymore," he stated. "We need another approach to working with our vendors if we're going to get all this work done in time."

And there was another problem. Stan put his finger on it: The business executives didn't want to have anything to do with their internal "tech guys"—let alone the vendors—even though they were going to be spending tens of millions (or more) with vendor firms. "We're busy enough as it is. Just take the money and fix the technology," was their mantra. "But if we're really going to achieve the kind of transformational change that's going to affect 'the Street's' view of us, our business executives are going to have to be onside one-hundred-and-fifty percent," Stan said. Greg's team considered outsourcing large chunks of the work involved in implementing their plan, but he rejected this idea. "We're betting the company here. We need more control and involvement in these projects."

Stan and the others agreed. "This can't be a normal outsourcing deal," Stan noted. "We want access to their best minds. We want innovation, but we want to ensure we're getting business value."

A number of large vendors were interested in helping get the SleepSmart strategic IT plan off the ground. Microsoft, IBM, SAP, Oracle, Cisco, and others *all* wanted to help. Each had something to offer the company. What Greg and Stan *didn't want or need* was to have to run interference among them. "It's bad enough when we have to deal with two vendors on a single project," groused Stan. "Whenever anything goes wrong, they end up pointing fingers at each other. Sorting out the problems *always* ends up being our job!"

"*That's* the solution to this whole problem," exclaimed Greg. "We need to create a different environment where we can work more collaboratively with our vendors . . . *and* where they can work collaboratively with each other!" Thus was born the SleepSmart Strategic Technology Alliance (SSTA), although the delivery wasn't easy. No one had ever attempted to get so many different competitors to cooperate. "You'll never get IBM and Microsoft working together," scoffed Stan. "Their product and service offerings overlap. How are you going to draw the line between them?"

But Greg was adamant that the *only* way SleepSmart could achieve transformational change was if everyone (business and vendors included) worked together on the same plan to achieve a real win–win–win. The SSTA framework he drew up was both innovative and challenging. Its objectives were designed to create a unique relationship that would deliver *mutual* business value. Its key principles were as follows:

- A commitment to mutual success
- A commitment to favorable price and maximum value

- A commitment to introducing best practices into SleepSmart's technology transformation
- Speed of execution
- A shared governance framework that involved business, IT, and the vendors

Greg's directors had challenged him at the meeting where he had first presented his idea. "How is *this* strategic alliance different from all the others we've had?" they asked. "Why would any vendor want to do this?"

This had forced him to think more deeply about what he wanted to achieve. "The *key* is that we want to work together to deliver optimal business results for *all* the organizations involved," he said as he paced his office. "It's got to be good for everyone."

Greg's next move was to consult with SleepSmart's potential vendor partners. These had already been identified through the blueprint exercise, but would they be willing to work with other companies (and sometimes rivals) in a more collaborative and less competitive way? Finding out the key leverage points for each one helped him to design relationships that would deliver sustainable benefits to each that were beyond price. For example, he promised each partner a larger part of SleepSmart's spend on technology if it would agree to prenegotiated prices and discounts. Covering these in advance with each vendor's executives meant that basic terms, discounts, and volumes of business wouldn't have to be discussed by the lower levels of the business every time they bought new technology. Not only would this save everyone time and effort, but it also meant lower cost of sales for the suppliers, who wouldn't have to invest in any presales activities.

The revised framework won reserved praise from Greg's IT staff. "*If* we can make this work, it will be better for everyone," agreed Stan. "But there are going to have to be *big* changes in how we work. Getting all these guys in the same room to share information about their products and services is unprecedented. Are you sure you can pull this off?"

Greg went back to the vendors for more talks. As the details were worked out, the process had to move higher and higher in each organization as the individual account executives realized that they couldn't commit to what Greg wanted without higher-level approvals. Greg wanted

openness and sharing between SleepSmart and all its vendors. *Everyone* else wanted confidentiality.

As he got further into the details, he also had to go up the ladder within SleepSmart. Just as the vendors needed to be fully committed to collaboration and sharing, so too did the business. Greg made presentations to the firm's CFO, CEO, and finally even the board of directors. "We can't pull this off without full business participation," he said to the executive team. "You're investing millions on these projects. You need to put your best people on these teams to make sure they deliver the kinds of value you want." The businesspeople wanted to know how the SSTA would increase the company's share price. He explained that the idea of the SSTA was to leverage suppliers' competencies to make SleepSmart a retail showcase. SleepSmart would win by getting state-of-the-art technology at lower-than-average prices. Each of the vendors would win by improving their retail offerings, which they could, in turn, sell to others. All members would develop enhanced organizational competencies in the rapid implementation of technology to achieve business value.

The SSTA was announced to "the Street" and in the national press by SleepSmart's CEO and the heads of its five vendor partners. Then the teams got to work. Guided by a technology footprint that clearly delineated which vendor products would be used where and by regular, detailed strategy updates from SleepSmart business executives, Greg and the SSTA began delivering on their promises. Two years later their innovative uses of technology were beginning to win awards for "most influential technology retailer," for "best in show for innovative retail technology," and for "enterprise architecture excellence."

But it was the numbers that told the real story. Greg had watched them slowly turn around, improving slightly at first, then significantly every quarter. They were what everyone wanted to see. This last set was the best yet. He allowed himself a moment of satisfaction. He and the SSTA had worked night and day to fundamentally redesign and build the company's entire retailing infrastructure. Cycle time had improved, costs had declined, and technical service quality was at an all-time high. Results were visible. But would the financial community finally notice?

Greg got his answer the next week. After acknowledging SleepSmart's efforts to lower its costs, the analysts noted that the company's overall revenues had declined slightly—a bad sign. Now that SleepSmart had all its technical fundamentals right, the analysts suddenly wanted to see top-line growth! So the stock price was still in the dumpster. Greg sighed with frustration. There was only so much a CIO could do for the company. Just how much could IT really be used to generate more revenue? How much was up to the business? How could he get the business to understand enough about technology to see its top-line potential? There wasn't enough time or money to allow the business to really experiment with it in a hands-on fashion. Was it really his job anyway? *I can lead them to water, but I can't make them drink,* he said to himself. *It's their business; I can only offer them effective options.*

This was going to be an even bigger challenge than the one the company had come through. At the start, at least there had been some clear technical problems that had to be fixed. Integration, single view of the customer, faster information—all these helped reduce costs and increase flexibility. Now all these were in place, and the company was ready to grow sales, but that wasn't happening. What could be done to bring in the customers or to increase the amount spent when customers shopped at SleepSmart?

Furthermore, now that the business was three years down the road, the SSTA was wearing thin and needed renewing. Most of the players had changed, some more than once. Many partners had come out with new offerings and were lobbying to get them included in the technology blueprint, thus disrupting the carefully negotiated balance among them. Competition was rearing its ugly head among the partners. Other suppliers, offering completely new technology, were pressuring Greg to give them favored SSTA status, but managing the relationships in the alliance was incredibly complicated as it was. Between working with the business partners and working with the different vendors and their staff, Stan and his small team were going flat out already.

"We've done well, but we can't make money by just winning awards," said Greg to no one in particular. "I'm going to have to refocus and reinvigorate this alliance *and* figure out how to help the business grow revenue." He picked up the phone and called Stan. "Let's grab a coffee. I need to pick your brain."

Discussion Questions

1. Identify the advantages and disadvantages of the SSTA. Do you think that this sort of vendor partnership can prosper in the long run? Why or why not?
2. Focusing IT on the top line (i.e., growing revenues) is very different from focusing IT on the bottom line (i.e., reducing costs). Explain.
3. Brainstorm some ideas of how SleepSmart could generate additional revenues using IT.

MINI CASE
Project Management at MM[3]

"We've got a real 'warm puppy' here," Brian Smith told Werner McCann. "Make sure you make the most of it. We could use a winner."

Smith was MM's CIO, and McCann was his top project manager. The puppy in question was MM's new venture into direct-to-customer marketing of its *green meters,* a product designed to help better manage electrical consumption, and the term referred to the project's wide appeal. The strategy had been a hit with analysts ever since it had been revealed to the financial community, and the company's stock was doing extremely well as a result. "At last," one had written in his popular newsletter, "we have a company that is willing to put power literally and figuratively in consumers' hands. If MM can deliver on its promises, we fully expect this company to reap the rewards."

Needless to say, the Green project was popular internally, too. "I'm giving it to you because you have the most project-management experience we've got," Smith had said. "There's a lot riding on this one." As he walked away from Smith's office, McCann wasn't sure whether to feel complimented or terrified. He had certainly managed some successful projects for the company (previously known as ModMeters) over the past five years but never anything like this one. *That's the problem with project management,* he thought. *In IT almost every project is completely different. Experience only takes you part of the way.*

And Green was different. It was the first truly enterprisewide project the company had ever done, and McCann was having conniptions as he thought about telling Fred Tompkins, the powerful head of manufacturing, that he might not be able to have everything his own way. McCann knew that, to be successful, this project had to take an outside-in approach—that is, to take the end customers' point of view on the company. That meant integrating marketing, ordering, manufacturing, shipping, and

service into one seamless process that wouldn't bounce the customer from one department to another in the company. MM had always had separate systems for each of its "silos," and this project would work against the company's traditional culture and processes. The Green project was also going to have to integrate with IT's information management renewal (IMR) project. Separate silos had always meant separate databases, and the IMR project was supposed to resolve inconsistencies among them and provide accurate and integrated information to different parts of the company. This was a huge political challenge, but, unless it worked, McCann couldn't deliver on his mandate.

Then there was the issue of resources. McCann groaned at the thought. MM had some good people but not enough to get through all of the projects in the IT plan within the promised timelines. Because of the importance of the Green project, he knew he'd get good cooperation on staffing, but the fact remained that he would have to go outside for some of the technical skills he needed to get the job done. Finally, there was the schedule that had to be met. Somehow, during the preliminary assessment phase, it had become clear that September 5 was to be the "hard launch" date. There were good reasons for this—the fall was when consumers usually became concerned with their energy consumption—but McCann worried that a date barely twelve months from now would put too much pressure on his team. "We've got to get in there first, before the competition," Smith had said to him. "The board expects us to deliver. You've got my backing and the support of the full executive team, but you *have* to deliver this one."

Six Weeks Later

It was full steam ahead on the Green project. It's *amazing* what a board mandate and executive

---

[3]Smith, H. A., and J. D. McKeen. "Project Management at MM," #1-L05-1-009. Queen's School of Business, November 2005. Reproduced by permission of Queen's University, School of Business, Kingston, Ontario.

sponsorship can do for a project, thought McCann, who knew how hard it usually was to get business attention to IT initiatives. He now had a full-time business counterpart, Raj Sambamurthy. Samba, as he was known to his colleagues, had come out of Tompkins's division and was doing a fantastic job of getting the right people in the room to make the decisions they needed to move ahead. The Green steering committee was no Mickey Mouse group either. Smith, Tompkins, and every VP affected by the project were meeting biweekly with him and Samba to review every aspect of the project's progress.

McCann had pulled no punches when communicating with the committee. "You've given me the mandate and the budget to get this project off the ground," he had told them. "But we have to be clear about what we're trying to accomplish." Together, they had hammered out a value proposition that emphasized the strategic value of the project and some of the measures they would use to monitor its ultimate success. The requirements and design phase had also gone smoothly because everyone was so motivated to ensure the project's success. "Linking success to *all* our annual bonuses sure helped *that!*" McCann had remarked wryly to Samba.

Now McCann was beginning to pull together his dream team of implementers. The team had chosen a package known as Web-4-U as the front end of the project, but it would take a lot of work to customize it to suit their unique product and, even more, to integrate it with MM's outmoded back-end systems. The Web-4-U company was based in Ireland but had promised to provide 24/7 consulting on an as-needed basis. In addition, Samba had now assembled a small team of business analysts to work on the business processes they would need. They were working out of the firm's Cloverdale office, a thirty-minute drive from IT's downtown location. (It was a shame they couldn't all be together, but space was at a premium at headquarters. McCann made a mental note to look into some new collaboration software he'd heard about.) Now that these two pieces were in place, McCann felt free to focus on the technical "guts" of the system. "Maybe this will work out after all," he said.

Three Months to Launch Date

By June, however, McCann was tearing out what little hair was left on his head. He was seriously considering moving to a remote Peruvian hamlet and breeding llamas. "*Anything* would be better than this mess," he observed to Yung Lee, the senior IT architect, over coffee. They were poring over the project's critical path. "The way I see it," Lee stated matter-of-factly, "we have two choices: We can continue with this inferior technology and meet our deadline but not deliver on our functionality, *or* we can redo the plan and go back to the steering committee with a revised delivery date and budget."

McCann sighed. Techies *always* saw things in black and white, but his world contained much more gray. And so much was riding on this—credibility (his, IT's, the company's), competitiveness, stock price. He dreaded being the bearer of this bad news, so he said, "Let's go over this *one* more time."

"It's not going to get any better, but here goes." Lee took a deep breath. "Web-4-U is based on outmoded technology. It was the best available last year, but *this* year the industry has agreed on a new standard, and if we persist in using Web-4-U, we are going to be out of date before Green even hits the street. We need to go back and completely rethink our technical approach based on the new standard and then redesign our Web interface. I know it's a setback and expensive, but it has to be done."

"How come we didn't know about this earlier?" McCann demanded.

Lee replied, "When the standard was announced, we didn't realize what the implications were at first. It was only in our quarterly architecture meeting that the subject came up. That's why I'm here now." The architects were a breed apart, thought McCann. All tech and *no* business sense. They'd lost almost three months because of this. "By the way," Lee concluded, "Web-4-U knew about this, too. They're scrambling to rewrite their code. I guess they figured if you didn't know right away, there would be more chance of you sticking with them."

The chances of *that* are slim to none, thought McCann. His *next* software provider, whoever that was, was going to be sitting right here under his steely gaze. Seeing an agitated Wendy Chan at his door, he brought the meeting to a hasty close. "I'm going to have to discuss this with Brian," he told Lee. "We can't surprise him with this at the steering committee meeting.

Hang tight for a couple of days, and I'll get back to you."

"OK," said Lee, "but remember that we're wasting time."

Easy for *you* to say, thought McCann as he gestured Chan into his office. She was his counterpart at the IMR project, and they had always had a good working relationship. "I just wanted to give you a heads-up that we've got a serious problem at IMR that will affect you," she began. Llamas began prancing into his mind's eye. "Tompkins is refusing to switch to our new data dictionary. We've spent months hammering this out with the team, but he says he wasn't kept informed about the implications of the changes, and now he's refusing to play ball. I don't know *how* he could say that. He's had a rep on the team from the beginning, and we've been sending him regular progress reports."

McCann was copied on those reports. Their pages of techno-jargon would put *anyone* to sleep! He was sure that Tompkins had never got past the first page of any of those reports. His rep was a dweeb, too, someone Tompkins thought he could live without in his daily operations.

"Damn! This is something I *don't* need." Like all IT guys, McCann *hated* corporate politics with a passion. He didn't understand them and wasn't good at them. Why hadn't Samba and his team picked up on this? They were plugged into the business. Now he was going to have to deal with Chan's problem as well as his own if he wanted to get the Green project going. Their back-end processes wouldn't work at all unless everyone was using the same information in the same format. Why couldn't Tompkins see that? Did he *want* the Green project to fail?

"The best way to deal with this one," advised Chan, "is to *force* him to accept these changes. Go to John Johnson and tell him that you need Tompkins to change his business processes to fit our data dictionary. It's for the good of the company, after all." Chan's strong suit wasn't her political savvy.

"You're right that we need Tompkins on our side," said McCann, "but there may be a better way. Let me talk to Samba. He's got his ear to the ground in the business. I'll speak with him and get back to you."

After a bit of chitchat, Wendy Chan left McCann to his PERT chart, trying again to determine the extra cost in time if they went with the new technology. Just then the phone rang. It was Linda Perkins, McCann's newly hired work-at-home usability designer. She was one of the best in the business, and he was lucky to have snagged her just coming off maternity leave. His promise of flexible working hours and full benefits had lured her back to work two months before her year-long leave ended. "You've *got* to do something about your HR department!" Perkins announced. "They've just told me that I'm not eligible for health and dental benefits because I don't work on the premises! Furthermore, they want to classify me as contingent staff, not managerial, because I don't fit in one of their petty little categories for employees. You promised me that you had covered all this before I took the job! I gave up a good job at LifeCo so I could work from home."

McCann had indeed covered this issue in principle with Rick Morrow, IT's HR representative, but that had been almost eight months ago. Morrow had since left the firm. McCann wondered if he had left any paperwork on this matter. The HR IT spot had not yet been filled, and all of the IT managers were upset about HR's unreceptive attitude when it came to adapting its policies to the realities of today's IT world. "OK, Linda, just hang in there for a day or two and I'll get this all sorted out," he promised. "How's the usability testing coming along?"

"That's *another* thing I wanted to talk with you about. The team's making changes to the look and feel of the product without consulting me," she fumed. "I can't do my job without being in the loop. You *have* to make them tell me when they're doing things like this."

McCann sighed. Getting Perkins on the project had been such a coup that he hadn't given much thought to how the lines of communication would work within such a large team. "I hear you, Linda, and we'll work this out. Can you just give me a few days to figure out how we can improve things?"

Hanging up, he grabbed his jacket and slunk out of the office as quickly as he could before any other problems could present themselves. If he just kept walking south, he'd make it to the Andes in three, maybe four, months. He could teach himself Spanish along the way. At least the llamas would appreciate his efforts! MM could take its project and give it to some other poor schmuck. *No way* was he going back! He walked furiously down the street, mentally ticking off the reasons he had been a fool to fall for Smith's sweet talk. Then, unbidden, a plan of attack formed in his head. Walking always did the trick. Getting out of the office cleared his head and focused his priorities. He turned back the way he had come, now eager to get back in the fray. He had some things to do right away, and others he had to put in place ASAP.

Discussion Questions

1. Some organizational factors increase a project's likelihood of success. Identify these "facilitators" for the Green project.
2. Other organizational factors decrease a project's likelihood of success. Identify these "barriers" for the Green project.
3. Outline the things that McCann needs to do right away.

MINI CASE
Managing Technology at Genex Fuels[4]

"You have got yourselves into a terrible predicament," said V. R. "Sandy" Sandhuramen, his soft Indian accent belying the gravity of his words. "You are incredibly lucky you have managed to do business as well as you have, but this situation cannot be allowed to carry on." Sandy, a high-priced technology consultant, had been hired by Genex Fuel's new CIO, Nick Devlin, to review the company's technology portfolio and help him and his newly appointed IT architect, Chuck Yee, get a handle on the firm's technology needs.

Genex, a major producer of crude oil and natural gas, is the largest marketer of petroleum and petroleum products in the region. It is structured into three distinct business divisions, each comprising a number of functional segments. Until recently, IT had been decentralized into the three divisions, each with its own director of IT who reported to the divisional executive vice presidents (EVPs). Devlin, formerly the director of the corporate division, had been appointed CIO and given the specific mandate to bring in SAP as the primary technology platform for all the divisions.

"We have to start behaving like we're one business," said the CEO when he appointed Devlin. "I want a much more agile and responsive IT organization than we've had in the past. It seems to me that every time I ask IT to look into something I've heard or read about, they always come up with a thousand and one reasons why it *won't* work. We need to be able to use technology competitively, and that won't happen unless you can get ahead of the curve."

Devlin's excitement about his new mandate had lasted just about a week, until the true scope of the challenge became clear. He had asked each divisional IT director for an inventory of hardware and software currently in place and to briefly outline the work that was in their plans for the coming year. "We must have one of every piece of hardware and

software ever produced," Devlin marveled as he scanned their reports. On the one hand, there was a new customer management system called COMC, which had been implemented to improve real-time information exchange between the company's 135 bulk fuel sites and Genex headquarters. On the other hand, IT was still running an archaic DOS-based marketing system called MAAS to provide customer service and reports. "And they want to bring in SAP!" he groaned. "We need a plan, and we need it soon."

That was when Devlin had engaged Sandy to work with Yee. "First, I want a no-holds-barred assessment of our current situation," he had said, and now they were in his office, outlining the "terrible predicament."

"The biggest problem you face at present," said Sandy, "is the fact that you have absolutely no standards and no integration, as you discovered for yourself, Nick." There was a lot of technology out there—both old and new—and it was a political hot potato. Almost every system had its group of advocates, some very senior in the company. All the EVPs had invested their individual technology budgets in the hardware and software that they felt could best support their work. The problem was that maintaining this mishmash was now costing an arm and a leg. And it was highly doubtful that the company was getting true value for its technology investment.

"We should be able to leverage our existing investments so we can invest in new technology," said Yee. "Instead, almost all our budget is taken up with holding these systems together with toothpicks and tape."

"One of the most challenging situations," Sandy went on, "is Price One."

Obsolete but absolutely essential, Price One is the fuel-pricing system that stores the pricing algorithms for all fuels marketing functions, including

---

[4]Smith, H. A., and J. D. McKeen. "Managing Technology at Genex Fuels," #9-L05-1-004. Queen's School of Business, February 2005. Reproduced by permission of Queen's University, School of Business, Kingston, Ontario.

aviation, marine, retail, branded associates, and industrial and wholesale. Although pricing is an integral part of marketing, Price One cannot communicate with COMC and is not easily adaptable to changes in the business environment. Price One perfectly reflected the business and technology that existed ten years ago, but this has now become a real drawback. To get around these limitations while continuing to use Price One, staff manually feed information from pricing requests in COMC to Price One to get approval because both systems use different terminology in coding products for different pricing methods.

Price One also lacks the ability to link information from different systems to ensure data integrity. As a result, Price One has accumulated some irrelevant data groups under pricing for products, and such corrupted data can be detected only by an experienced individual who has been dealing with that product group for decades and who would know at a glance the validity of the data. One of Price One's critical flaws is its inability to link with other systems, such as COMC, and to pick up competitive market information in order to approve price. Previous plans to rewrite this system have been resisted strenuously by management because of the expense. Now the system is on its last legs.

"And like most oil and gas companies," Sandy observed, "you have automated very few of your information assets as other types of organizations have done." Typically for the industry, Genex had grown by acquiring other, smaller firms and had inherited an enormous amount of physical data. It now has more than two million items of paper and microfilm. It has one hundred twenty thousand tapes of data. Some items date back to the 1940s and came from numerous sources. The company's seismic assets, on which it bases many of its decisions and which has a replacement cost estimated at more than two billion dollars, are stored on a wide variety of media from analog tapes, magnetic reels, and cartridges to optical discs to paper, film, and microfilm. They are spread out across five conventional physical warehouses.

This system of data management is problematic for two main reasons. First, with land sales occurring every two weeks, it is extremely difficult to make timely decisions based on all known information about a property. Clearly, the more seismic information a company can bring to bear on its decisions, the better it can decide where it wants to do further work. Second, the company's data assets, on which its future depends, are extremely vulnerable. There is no backup. When needed, the only copy of the information requested is physically transported to Genex's offices. The tapes on which the data reside deteriorate further with each reading. Furthermore, much information resides on obsolete forms of media and is getting increasingly difficult to access.

"Finally, IT is getting a lot of pressure from the executive office," reported Sandy. "These guys have seen what's going on in other companies, and they want to see Genex move into the twenty-first century. Staff at Genex cover vast territory and must work from home, from local facilities, or on the road. Not only does Genex need to provide a virtual working environment for these workers, but it also needs to consider how they can work together as a team without having physical colocation for communication."

"Well, I guess we have it all," said Devlin. "Integration problems, outdated hardware and software, inconsistent data, expensive workarounds, pressure to modernize, and substantial budget limitations." Turning to Yee and Sandy, he smiled. "Now what are we going to do about it? Where do we start?"

Discussion Questions

1. What evidence is the CEO using to suggest that Genex is not using technology competitively?
2. Did Devlin need to hire Sandy, a "high-priced technology consultant," to tell him that technology at Genex was a mess?
3. Devise a strategy to successfully implement enterprisewide systems (such as SAP) at Genex.

INDEX